Inequality in America

Inequality in America

Causes and Consequences

Robert S. Rycroft and Kimberley L. Kinsley, Editors

BLOOMSBURY ACADEMIC
NEW YORK • LONDON • OXFORD • NEW DELHI • SYDNEY

BLOOMSBURY ACADEMIC
Bloomsbury Publishing Inc
1385 Broadway, New York, NY 10018, USA
50 Bedford Square, London, WC1B 3DP, UK
29 Earlsfort Terrace, Dublin 2, Ireland

BLOOMSBURY, BLOOMSBURY ACADEMIC and the Diana logo are trademarks
of Bloomsbury Publishing Plc

First published in the United States of America by ABC-CLIO 2021
Paperback edition published by Bloomsbury Academic 2025

Library of Congress Cataloging-in-Publication Data

Names: Kinsley, Kimberley L., author. | Rycroft, Robert S., author.
Title: Inequality in America : causes and consequences / Kimberley L. Kinsley
and Robert S. Rycroft, editors.
Description: First Edition. | Santa Barbara, California : ABC-CLIO, 2021. |
Includes bibliographical references and index.
Identifiers: LCCN 2020052214 (print) | LCCN 2020052215 (ebook) | ISBN
9781440865145 (hardcover) | ISBN 9781440865152 (ebook)
Subjects: LCSH: Equality—United States. | Wealth—United States. |
Minorities—United States. | United States—Economic conditions—21st
century. | United States—Social conditions—21st century.
Classification: LCC HM821 .I5343 2021 (print) | LCC HM821 (ebook) | DDC
305—dc23
LC record available at https://lccn.loc.gov/2020052214
LC ebook record available at https://lccn.loc.gov/2020052215

ISBN: HB: 978-1-4408-6514-5
PB: 979-8-7651-3885-4
ePDF: 978-1-4408-6515-2
eBook: 979-8-2161-0241-0

To find out more about our authors and books visit www.bloomsbury.com
and sign up for our newsletters.

*In loving memory of my wife, Sally, who was my partner
through thick and thin for nearly a half century.*
Robert S. Rycroft

*To my daughters, Emily and Katie, for teaching me more
than I could ever learn in a classroom about life.*
Kimberley L. Kinsley

Contents

Section VIII: Consumer Issues

Section IX: Public Policy

Section X: The Future of Inequality

Preface

From the end of World War II in 1945 until the early 1970s, the general trend in American life was toward a more equal society. Public discussion of inequality issues was relatively limited, however. To be sure, the 1950s and 1960s saw the rise of the civil rights movement and the emergence of the so-called War on Poverty, but the main goals of these campaigns were to allow the most disadvantaged members of society to enjoy the benefits of a rapidly growing, affluent society and to combat discrimination at both personal and institutional levels. The position and stability of the United States' vast middle class was never in question.

Since the early 1970s, however, the trend in inequality has reversed itself. We have returned to levels of economic inequality (in terms of both income and wealth) unseen since the run-up to the Great Depression. A potential leavening factor, the vaunted social mobility of the American dream, does not appear to be that exceptional in the American case now that long-time series of economic data from many countries allow us to replace anecdotes with actual evidence. We better recognize now the two-way causation between economic inequality and inequality in what some might consider "noneconomic" areas of life, such as education, health, housing, environment, and access to justice. Of course, no area of life is truly noneconomic. As an example, economic inequality can have implications for individual health. The poor may have inadequate knowledge of healthy lifestyles and be unable to afford health insurance and high-quality medical treatment, leading to deteriorating health. At the same time, poor health can limit the ability to work, save, invest, and thus achieve a comfortable standard of living. Similar linkages can be seen with other noneconomic factors. The middle class, meanwhile, finds itself shrinking in size, its ranks steadily depleting in response to a host of complex economic, political, and cultural factors. As a result, obtaining and maintaining a middle-class standard of living seems more difficult than ever before. And many in the middle class may wonder whether that lifestyle is all that it is cracked up to be.

Public discussion of inequality issues has risen apace with the rise in inequality concerns. As of this writing during the current presidential election cycle (2019–2020), inequality issues have risen to the fore of political debate, with arguments raging about the benefits and drawbacks of proposals—a federal $15 minimum wage, Medicare-for-All, a wealth tax, a 70-percent marginal tax rate on labor income, subsidies to renters, college debt forgiveness, and many more—to reduce the gap between the haves and the have-nots in American society. Even the government's rollout of emergency measures to minimize the public health and economic costs of the COVID-19 crisis, as well as the global warming debate, shares significant inequality dimensions.

The chapters in this book are an attempt to bring students and other readers up to speed on the current state of the inequality debate in the United States. Written by experts in the field, each chapter is intended to be accessible to those with limited background on the issues. The structure of the book is purposeful.

Troy Paino, currently president of the University of Mary Washington, in Fredericksburg, Virginia, and formerly president of Truman State University, in Missouri, provides an introduction to the subject matter by reflecting on his experience with students as the president of two different types of institutions located in two different parts of the country, each buffeted in different ways by the winds of globalization and technological and political change.

Stacey Jones and Cameron Hub provide us with vital background material in "The History of Inequality in America" to assess where we have come from and where we are.

The next section "The Causes and Consequences of Inequality" is broken into several parts addressing many of the dimensions of inequality. One dimension, economic inequality (in terms of income and wealth), consists of chapters by Robert J. Gitter on "Immigration," Robert Perrucci and Carolyn Cummings Perrucci on "Intergenerational Mobility," Lauren DiRago-Duncan and Robert S. Rycroft on "Labor Markets," Devin Wiggs and Beth Redbird on "Monopolization and Rent Seeking," Thomas E. Lehman and Bradley W. Conn on "Technological Change," Kimberley L. Kinsley and Robert S. Rycroft on "Wealth Inequality," and Jared A. Knowles and Erin E. George on "Workplace Discrimination."

A second dimension is inequality in access to educational services. Patricia Crain de Galarce and Anna Maria Jones discuss "Early Childhood Education." Josipa Roksa and Blake R. Silver examine "Higher Education." A third dimension is inequality with respect to health and health care. "Access to Health Care" is examined by Joel B. Teitelbaum and Laura G. Hoffman. "Economic Status and Health" is the subject of Gesine K. Hearn's chapter. "Substance Abuse" is the topic of Thomas S. Weinberg's chapter.

The topic of housing and communities is the fourth dimension addressed. Renee E. Walker and Tamicah Gelting examine the phenomenon of "Food Deserts." Haydar Kurban reviews the academic literature on "Housing and Neighborhoods."

A fifth dimension is family life and inequality. Shannon N. Davis and Myriam Halimi look at the impact on inequality of "Parenting Styles." Chris Wienke writes about how inequality influences "Marriage, Cohabitation, and Divorce." A sixth dimension is the environment. Angela G. Mertig looks at "Environmental Justice."

The seventh dimension is the justice system. Kimberley L. Kinsley examines "Civil Justice" while Dana Hubbard looks at "Criminal Justice." An eighth dimension is consumer issues. Katie Fitzpatrick assesses "Consumer Credit and Payday

Loans." Ivan C. Roten, Madeline Hamiter, and Jarrod Johnston consider "Financial Education."

The next section of the book covers policy issues. What policies to combat inequality has the United States employed, and what might be some new policy directions for the future? The "welfare" system broadly defined is the subject of Justin Jarvis and Garrett Lee Fiegenbaum in "Cash Assistance to the Poor." Elizabeth M. Legerski examines "Children and Family Policy." "Community Development Programs" are the subject of Rhonda Phillips's chapter. Christy Irish and Allison Ward Parsons tackle the important area of "Education Reform Policies." Analisa Packham looks at "Food and Nutrition Programs." Alice Louise Kassens considers "Health Insurance." "Housing Inequality" is addressed by Lei Zhang. John D. Abell and Elizabeth Perry-Sizemore examine "Regulation of Labor Markets." Henry Ordower looks at "Taxes."

The book concludes with two assessments of the future of inequality in the United States and its possible consequences as we move deeper into the twenty-first century. Oren M. Levin-Waldman asks the question, "Is Inequality a Threat to Democracy?" while Kristen Tzoc and Heather Beth Johnson speculate about "The Future of Inequality in America."

What could be a more important topic as we enter the third decade of the twenty-first century?

Kimberley L. Kinsley and Robert S. Rycroft

Introduction

Growing inequality in the United States is threatening our nation's future. Recent political discourse focuses on segments of the American population left behind by the global and technologically driven economies of the twenty-first century. In this era of haves and have-nots, groups are pitted against each other in a way that reflects the growing polarization of our politics: rural versus urban; coastal versus middle states; baby boomers versus millennials and Generation Z; white and Asian versus Black and Hispanic; college-educated, white-collar professionals versus the blue-collar working class; the 1 percent versus everyone else.

Much of this analysis focuses on global trends that always have a tinge of inevitability to the decline of opportunity for certain portions of our population. Globalization and technology undercut the demand for the working-class jobs of a manufacturing economy. The emergence of the high-tech industries powering the economy do not have much need for the cheap labor that contributed to the United States' industrial past. The basic premises of how the economy works have shifted under our feet, and there's a demand for a response to the growing hopelessness of large segments of the population. But what is that response?

There is no shortage of proposed solutions from across the political spectrum. Conservatives continue to look to private industry. Since the Reagan years, supply-side adherents who found a home in the Republican Party have fought for lower taxes in the belief that a freer market would ultimately generate more wealth, spurring a reinvestment in production, employment, and workers' wages. Unfortunately, four decades of subscribing to this economic philosophy has further exacerbated the problem. Wealth has steadily and rapidly concentrated at the top since the 1980s. By 2015, the richest 1 percent of American taxpayers drew more than 20 percent of the nation's income. Since the Trump administration's 2017 tax cuts, this concentration of wealth at the top has only accelerated. Since the 1970s, the share of income accruing to the top 1 percent has nearly doubled, while the share of income going to all other workers has fallen by nearly 10 percent. Tax cuts on capital gains, retreat from antitrust, and financial deregulation have done little to restore the middle class and our country's equilibrium.

Liberals and progressives want to redistribute wealth, open borders for a freer flow of immigration, and adopt "green" policies, as well as promote new social norms to empower populations left behind by the global tech economy. Although this side has not witnessed as many political victories as their colleagues on the

xvi   Introduction

Right, the Affordable Care Act (ACA) as well as policy proposals such as the Green New Deal, reparations for descendants of slaves, free college education, single-payer government health care, and student loan forgiveness all exemplify this approach. While the ACA expanded health coverage to millions, it did little to slow the growing social and economic inequality in this country. The other proposals have been routinely dismissed by critics as either too expensive or impractical in their application.

Some of the people most negatively affected by the move away from the twentieth-century manufacturing economy even see some of these proposals as worsening their plight. The free flow of unskilled immigrants, for example, offers a safety valve for employers to keep wages low in the same way that moving manufacturing plants overseas did. A focus on renewable energy, while a reasonable response to climate change and the country's dependence on fossil fuel, does little to address the economic suffering of those dependent on the coal industry for survival.

From the populism of the Tea Party to the new Social Democrats, our current politics reflect an intense reaction to the economic forces driving this inequality. The Republican Party under President Donald Trump is trying to restore an old economic order by promising the return ("Make America Great Again") to those halcyon days of low-skilled, high-wage manufacturing jobs. Seal the borders, impose tariffs, promote fossil fuel over clean energy, and watch twentieth-century jobs in manufacturing and mining return. Politicians such as Bernie Sanders, Elizabeth Warren, and Alexandria Ocasio-Cortez, on the other side of the political spectrum, argue that after four decades of stagnating middle-class wages, tax cuts for the wealthy, and bailouts for bankers and billionaires in the wake of the 2008 financial crisis, a governmental redistribution of wealth, power, and opportunity is the only cure. Inequality is driving U.S. politics toward rage and polarization and toward warring populisms.

The current challenges facing workers, communities, and the economy in an age of rapid change driven by technology, globalization, and global warming require new and creative solutions to the threat inequality poses. However, the old binary choices—big government versus little government, regulation versus free market, free trade and immigration versus protectionism and isolation—appear insufficient and inadequate. Unfortunately, extreme partisanship has paralyzed governmental institutions to a point where it is hard to imagine an effective, more nuanced approach to the problem.

I have served as president of two public universities since the Great Recession. One, Truman State University, Missouri's public liberal arts and sciences university, is situated in the middle of what some would call Trump Country (a completely inadequate descriptor). Located in Kirksville, Missouri, just thirty miles south of the Iowa border, this region has been on the wrong side of America's economic transformation since 1980. During my years at Truman State University, I witnessed firsthand the effect of globalization on a community whose manufacturing base all but vanished at the end of the twentieth century.

In 2016, I left Truman to become the president of the University of Mary Washington (UMW) in Fredericksburg, Virginia, an institution of higher learning that touts a similar public liberal arts mission to Truman but in a very different place. Just fifty miles south of Washington, DC, UMW is in the middle of a region that is much more reflective of the changes driving the economy of the twenty-first century. But Fredericksburg also struggles with the tensions that rapid change in demographics and technological innovation invariably create. The pace of that change promises to only accelerate with the arrival of Amazon HQ2 just fifty miles up I-95.

Both places have their problems—one because the new economy driven by globalization and technology has left it behind, and the other because it is in the middle of those changes and struggles to keep pace and make sense of it all.

At both Truman and UMW, I have dealt with the growing consensus that the vast inequities in our society are gumming up the cogs of economic and social mobility. Institutions of higher education are expected to grease the skids of such mobility, but are they effectively doing this? If our next generation loses hope that its members can achieve fulfilling, productive lives that will adequately support them and their families, faith in those institutions that sustain our democracy will continue to erode, creating even more social, political, and economic instability.

By all measures, those under age forty have particular reason to be concerned about their futures. During their life, they have observed a country that has showered much of its bounty on the already affluent at the expense of most Americans and their futures. In 2017, people between the ages of twenty-five and thirty-four were earning less than people in that same age group were in 2000. Since the turn of the century, median net worth has declined for every age group under fifty-five. Federal and state policy has done much to feed this growing generational gap in income and wealth. While social programs such as Medicare and Social Security that go to support older Americans have been spared cuts, programs that benefit younger Americans have not.

Take higher education as an example. Over the past decade, states have cut college funding by an average of 16 percent per student. In response, tuition has risen, and students have taken on more debt. In 2018, national student debt surpassed $1.5 trillion. Three years after the start of repayment, the student loan default rate is around 10 percent, but that default rate continues to climb to 16 percent after another two years. Those borrowers defaulting on their loans are disproportionately low-income students. In other words, the very institutions that are supposed to foster economic opportunity and mobility are becoming engines of inequality—accessible to students with means but financially debilitating to those with need.

After almost a decade as a university president and a quarter century in higher education, my overwhelming feeling is that we have let this generation down. I witness it in their diminished expectations for their futures. They have lost faith in the very institutions—government, banks, police, health care, and education, among others—that are supposed to provide security, opportunity, and fairness.

And why not? It is hard to identify an institution that is actually working to the benefit of all citizens. This includes the institution to which I have devoted my life's work.

Obsessed with rankings, higher education's proxy for status, colleges and universities have consistently allocated their precious resources in ways that have contributed to economic inequality. At Truman, I inherited a school with an excellent academic reputation. With faculty devoted to undergraduate education and a talented student body, Truman year in and year out proudly markets itself as the number-one public university in *U.S. News & World Report*'s ranking of Carnegie master's schools in the Midwest. But that ranking has come at a cost. Truman, the beneficiary of state policies in the 1980s and 1990s, received relatively generous per-pupil funding to solidify its position as a "highly selective" institution. Knowing that the infamous *U.S. News* rankings were driven by inputs, the school started to spend that public money to "buy students" with strong academic credentials measured by ACT scores and high school grades. It worked. Public dollars were directed at expensive merit scholarships, and Truman's reputation soared. Unfortunately, very few of these students stayed behind to work on the problems facing Kirksville and the surrounding Northeast Missouri region at a time when the area needed them the most. The school became an institution that educated smart kids but had a diminishing impact on the region it was originally called to serve.

Similarly, Virginia is a state obsessed with status. Interested in leading a school that could be anchored in the needs of its community, I came to Mary Washington knowing that the Commonwealth's system of public higher education had a sterling reputation. With schools such as the University of Virginia, the College of William & Mary, and Virginia Tech University, to name but a few, some would argue that it is the very best network of public institutions in the country. Virginians certainly do. The state benefits from a historical commitment to a liberally educated citizenry (thanks, Thomas Jefferson), but the state is bound by a caste system that perpetuates policies that direct a disproportionate share of public resources to the so-called talented tenth. In Virginia, the privileged do well, but too many from disadvantaged backgrounds are left behind.

Based on my experiences at both places, I could relate to Brian Rosenberg, president of Macalester College, when he sarcastically wrote that without the *U.S. News & World Report* rankings, students and their parents "might not have known that extremely selective colleges, with more affluent and privileged students, have higher graduation rates than those that served fewer affluent and privileged students—and that those selective colleges and universities deserved to be rewarded for performing so invaluable a service to society" (*Chronicle of Higher Education*, August 21, 2018). In the pursuit of rankings and reputation, two things academic leaders often crave for their own sense of self-worth, private and public money continues to flow to the advantaged at a cost to those who are most in need of the transformative power of education.

It does not have to be this way. As I tell my colleagues, faculty, and students, inequality in our society is a direct result of policy choices, which are themselves the outcome of politics. We are not subject to uncontrollable forces that have predetermined our social and economic structures; they have come about by choice. This is why I am committed to a civic conception of education rooted in community. Education must prepare our students for democratic engagement, because political choices shape distributive outcomes. It is my belief that this volume will enrich our understanding of those forces that have produced social and economic inequities. What we do with that understanding is up to us.

Troy Paino

The History of Inequality in America

Economic inequality raises fundamental issues of justice and fairness. Inequality is not new, but the vigor of the contemporary debate on the issue has rarely been matched in American history. A 2020 poll found that more than 60 percent of Americans believe that there is too much economic inequality in the United States (Horowitz, Igielnic, and Kochhar 2020). The perception of wide and growing inequality intensifies debates over issues as diverse as education ("tuition-free college"), health care ("Medicare-for-All"), immigration ("build the wall"), and race ("Black Lives Matter"). Understanding inequality in the United States today requires understanding how the country arrived at this point. In the words of French economist Thomas Piketty, "each country has its own intimate history with inequality" (Piketty 2015, 69).

For the United States, that history begins in the late 1700s. From an economic standpoint, the young United States started out as a remarkably egalitarian nation, without the entrenched class, income, and wealth disparities of older European nations. Following that period, the United States experienced a steep rise in economic inequality in the 1800s as the nation became more industrial and urban and the economy more global. The country then experienced a sharp fall in inequality from about 1910 to the 1970s due to growth in education, a retreat from globalization, and a political climate favorable to working Americans. Since the 1970s, the United States has experienced a steady rise in inequality once again, because of a stall in educational growth, an acceleration of globalization, and a rightward shift in the political climate.

Today's racial and gender inequalities also have a distinctively American history, rooted in slavery and in the separate economic spheres for men and women that characterized the beginnings of the nation's history. While progress has been made toward racial and gender equality, significant economic disparities remain. A close examination of the history of inequality in the United States yields rich insights as to how demographic, economic, political, and social forces have shaped—and continue to shape—the evolution and nature of inequality.

DEFINING AND MEASURING INEQUALITY

Although *inequality* is an almost ever-present word in news and politics today, its exact meaning is hard to pin down. Most people have an intuitive understanding of it but if asked to explicitly define it would likely give a wide range of answers. This hazy use reflects the fluidity of the concept of inequality. In fact, the status of "inequality" as a buzzword perhaps comes from the fact that inequality can be understood in so many ways. Inequality is a multidimensional phenomenon, making it impossible to choose a single, "correct" metric of inequality. Understanding economic inequality therefore requires not simply knowledge of facts and statistics regarding inequality but also an inquiry into the methodologies that produce those statistics. What do we really mean when we say our society is "economically unequal"?

The first question that the historian of economic inequality must confront is *inequality among whom*: inequality among everyone in the world, among countries, among individuals, among racial/ethnic groups? Economists such as Branko Milanovic boldly aim to address inequality across all individuals in the world—global inequality—which is a combination of inequality across nations and inequality within them (Milanovic 2016). Within a single nation, some economists focus on inequality across geographical areas, such as between regions (e.g., North versus South), between cities and rural areas, or across political units such as states or provinces. Others focus on inequality between demographic groups, such as racial or gender inequality. Classical economists such as Adam Smith and David Ricardo were concerned about the distribution of income between labor, land, and capital (known as the "functional distribution of income") because they viewed the economy as made up of classes of workers, landowners, and capitalists.

Much of the contemporary discussion of inequality is centered on the distribution of economic resources across the entire population. An important decision here is whether the appropriate unit of analysis is the household (or family) or the individual. Arguably, economic resources are shared within households, making the household the appropriate unit of analysis. That said, the assumption that resources are shared equally within households has been challenged by microeconomic studies of the household (Lundberg and Pollak 2007). Further muddying the water are changes in household demographics, such as the long-run increase in the share of single-person households, which complicate comparisons of household inequality over the long run.

A second question to be considered is *inequality of what?* The economic well-being of a group or an individual is multidimensional. The measurement of inequality forces us to choose a metric for comparison while recognizing that no single metric will provide the full picture. An important distinction in the measurement of inequality has to do with *wealth* versus *income*. In the United States, there is broad agreement that wealth inequality is significantly greater than income inequality. Put another way, income is more equally distributed than wealth.

The *wealth* of a household (or individual) is the total value of material or financial assets owned (home, saving accounts, investments, etc.) minus the value of any debt (mortgage, credit card balances, student loans, etc.). Wealth is a significant determinant of economic well-being. In today's economy, wealth protects households from interruptions in income due to job loss or illness; enables households to access quality housing, good public schools, and higher education; and provides some households with a source of income in retirement. Much earlier in American history, wealth in the form of land was the primary source of income for a predominantly agricultural economy.

The *income* of a household (or individual) is defined as resources received over a fixed time, such as a month or a year. For most people today, income consists mainly of a wage or salary but could also include interest, rent, profits, government payments, royalties, gifts, and so on. Like wealth, income is a significant determinant of well-being: income provides households with the means of purchasing food, housing, and other goods. If there is income left over, it also enables households to accumulate wealth.

Multiple complexities arise in the measurement of income (Stone et al. 2020). One question that arises is whether before-tax or after-tax income is the more relevant measure for the discussion of inequality. A second question is whether to include payments from government sources, such as Social Security benefits or unemployment insurance, in the measurement of a household's income. A significant number of inequality studies avoid the complexities of measuring income by focusing only on *earnings*—the share of income coming from work in the labor market.

A further question in the measurement of income is whether to make adjustments to income in order to more accurately measure economic well-being. One may, for example, adjust income to account for local differences in price levels, given that the purchasing power of a given income varies significantly by location (Donovan 2015). Adjustments may also be made for household size: an income of $50,000 for a single-person household is not equivalent to $50,000 for a family of four. The choice of a time period also matters in measuring inequality. Arguably, the relevant measure should consider an individual's income over an entire lifetime rather than just in a single year. Even in a society where all persons had the same income at each stage of their lifetimes, age differences could produce significant inequality at a single point in time. Finally, it could be argued that *consumption* is a better indicator of economic well-being than income is, making consumption (expenditures on goods and services) the more relevant metric of inequality.

Another possible answer to the question of *inequality of what* is inequality of *opportunity*. If everyone in society has the same opportunity for economic success, does it matter that some achieve better economic outcomes than others? An equitable process does not guarantee equitable results. Consider, for example, a lottery in which a million entrants each have the same chance to win a million-dollar prize. Each participant in the lottery has an equal opportunity to win, but the end result is nonetheless extremely unequal. Ethical debates around inequality require a clear distinction between opportunities and outcomes.

Economic inequality is arguably more tolerable in the presence of *economic mobility*—the opportunity to change one's initial economic circumstances. The "rags to riches" story figures prominently in American mythology, but to what extent is it possible or likely for an American to be born poor and end up rich or even middle class? And is that rise more or less likely today than it was in earlier eras of American life? Studies of economic mobility aim to determine the extent to which individuals or families can change their economic situation, either over the course of a lifetime or over generations. Those studies find that in the early days of the nation, the United States was exceptional in its level of economic mobility, rightfully earning its reputation as the "best poor man's nation" (Long and Ferrie 2018). Over time, however, mobility decreased. Economists today find that adjusting for inflation, adults in the 2010s were much less likely to earn more than their parents could than adults in the 1960s were able to earn (Chetty et al. 2017). By the twenty-first century, U.S. economic mobility was no longer exceptionally high and was, in fact, lower than that of nations such as Canada, France, and Germany (Corak 2004).

A third question that arises in the inequality literature is precisely *how* to go about measuring inequality. How does one effectively capture inequality graphically or numerically? Economists and statisticians use several different methods for measuring inequality; some are more easily interpreted than others. Measurement tools such as the *Lorenz curve* and the *Gini coefficient* summarize the entire distribution of income or wealth. These measures have the advantage of distilling the entire distribution into a single picture or number but the disadvantage of being somewhat opaque—that is, few outside of the economics profession immediately grasp the meaning of a Gini coefficient of 0.45, for example. More transparent metrics focus on particular points of the distribution and the ratios between them. The *90-50 ratio*, for example, tells us how much someone at the 90th percentile of the income distribution earns relative to someone at the 50th percentile, while the *50-10 ratio* tells us how much someone at the 50th percentile earns relative to someone at the 10th percentile.

Another relatively straightforward measure of inequality is the *wealth or income share*. The wealth or income share tells us the percentage of wealth or income of a given slice of households, such as the share of those falling in the top 10 percent of the distribution. Table 1, for example, shows the share of wealth held by those in the top 10 and top 1 percent of the wealth distribution from 1774 to 2012; table 2 gives income shares over the entire distribution from 1774 to 2018. Finally, *earnings ratios* are useful in measuring economic differences between groups. For example, recent estimates put the median income of women at 65 percent of the median income of men and put Black per capita income at 65 percent of white per capita income (see tables 3 and 4).

Table 1   The Distribution of Wealth: 1774–2012

Year	Wealth-Holding Population	Percent of Wealth Held by:	
		Top 10%	Top 1%
1774	All households	59.0	16.5
1774	Free households	53.2	14.3
1774	All adult males	58.4	16.5
1774	Free adult males	52.5	14.2
1860	All adult males	76.8	32.7
1860	Free adult males	73.0	29.0
1870	All adult males	70.0	27.0
1890	Families	72.2	25.8
1913	All households	(NA)	44.0
1922	All households	78.6	36.4
1929	All households	84.0	49.7
1930	All households	84.0	49.2
1940	All households	77.6	38.0
1945	All households	74.6	33.2
1950	All households	71.4	29.8
1955	All households	71.0	29.0
1960	All households	72.7	29.3
1965	All households	72.1	28.4
1970	All households	70.0	27.5
1975	All households	68.1	24.4
1980	All households	66.8	24.5
1985	All households	64.2	25.2
1990	All households	65.8	28.1
1995	All households	67.8	29.9
2000	All households	69.4	33.0
2005	All households	70.3	34.1
2010	All households	75.7	39.4
2012	All households	77.1	41.8

Sources: 1774–1890: Carter et al. 2006, Series Be39-Be42. 1913–2012: Saez and Zucman 2016.

For the computation of percentile shares of wealth, households are ranked according to their wealth. In all years other than 1860 and 1870, wealth is defined as net worth: total assets minus liabilities. In 1860 and 1870, wealth is defined as total assets.

Table 2   The Distribution of Income: 1774–2018

	Shares of Aggregate Income:							
Year	Lowest Fifth	Second Fifth	Third Fifth	Fourth Fifth	Highest Fifth	Top 10 Percent	Top 5 Percent	Top 1 Percent
1774	12.6			39.6	47.8	32.2	23.1	8.5
1850	11.7			35.6	52.7	36.5	24.9	10.4
1860	10.7			34.4	54.9	38.0	25.6	10.0
1870	11.1			33.7	55.1	39.3	27.2	9.8
1913	(NA)			(NA)	(NA)	42.3	(NA)	18.8
1920	(NA)			(NA)	(NA)	43.4	27.5	18.4
1929	(NA)			(NA)	(NA)	46.7	33.1	21.2
1930	(NA)			(NA)	(NA)	45.3	31.2	18.1
1940	(NA)			(NA)	(NA)	47.7	31.3	19.3
1950	3.1	10.5	16.7	23.6	45.6	39.0	23.9	15.9
1960	3.2	10.6	17.6	24.7	44.0	35.6	20.5	12.6
1970	4.1	10.8	17.4	24.5	43.3	33.8	16.6	10.8
1980	4.2	10.2	16.8	24.7	44.1	34.2	16.5	10.7
1990	3.8	9.6	15.9	24.0	46.6	38.7	18.5	14.5
2000	3.6	8.9	14.8	23.0	49.8	43.9	22.1	18.3
2010	3.3	8.5	14.6	23.4	50.3	43.9	21.3	18.3
2018	3.1	8.3	14.1	22.6	52.0	(NA)	23.1	(NA)

Sources: 1774, 1850, 1860, 1970: Lindert and Williamson 2016, 38, 115, 116, 154–55.
1910, 1920, 1929: Lindert and Williamson 2016, 173, citing Piketty and Saez 2003.
1920–1970: "5% Share," Carter et al. 2006, Series Be28. 1950, 1960: "Income Shares by
Quintile," Carter et al. 2006, Series Be2 to Be6. Distribution of money income among
households, 1947–1998, 1970–2018: "Table H-2. Share of Aggregate Income Received
by Each Fifth and Top 5 Percent of Households, All Races: 1967 to 2018," Census.gov.
1913–2014, top 10 percent and 1 percent: World Inequality Database.

Finally, regardless of how they would ideally choose to measure inequality, researchers must base their measurements and conclusions on data that exist. Looking back into the statistical "dark ages" of the colonial era and the eighteenth and nineteenth centuries, historians of inequality must mine a hodgepodge of surviving documents to construct estimates of wealth and income inequality. To build a picture of the wealth distribution in the early United States, researchers draw on archival sources such as bills of sale, wills, tax surveys, and probate records (Jones 1980; Williamson and Lindert 1980). To reconstruct the income distribution, researchers draw information from sources such as local censuses, tax lists, occupational city directories, and account books (Milanovic, Lindert, and Williamson 2011; Lindert and Williamson 2016). Initiated in 1790 and taken every ten years since, the U.S. Census provides an organizing framework of data on household demographics that enables researchers to weave fragmentary pieces of information together into a tentative picture of the whole.

Described as "the first measured century," the twentieth century saw the introduction of tax systems, surveys, and statistical methods that allowed much greater precision in the measurement of economic inequality. The permanent introduction of the federal income tax in 1913 (after a few short-lived prior episodes) generated tax records that provided insight into the evolution of top income shares over the long run in the United States (Kuznets and Jenks 1953; Piketty and Saez 2003). Income tax records also provide indirect information regarding the distribution of wealth: scholars use income tax records to infer the amount of wealth that would be necessary to generate a given capital income (Saez and Zucman 2016). Since the 1960s, ongoing surveys such as the Current Population Survey and the Survey of Consumer Finances have provided regular, detailed insight into the distribution of income and wealth. Recently, economists have brought together data sources from multiple countries to construct a long-run, comparative picture of the international evolution of inequality, with the resulting data available to researchers on the World Inequality Database. The most well-known product of this research program is Piketty's 2014 book *Capital in the Twenty-First Century*, which sparked extensive international discussion of inequality. Other recent breakthroughs in the study of inequality have come from Raj Chetty's Opportunity Insights team, which applies cutting-edge empirical methods to big data in order to unravel the forces behind today's dismal levels of economic mobility in the United States (OpportunityInsights.org).

Ultimately, there is no single method or statistic that gives a full picture of economic inequality. Instead, scholars are faced with something more like an incomplete jigsaw puzzle. They must look at an individual piece, figure out what it is and how it fits with other pieces they have, and rely on the pieces available to make an educated judgment as to what the complete picture really is.

HISTORICAL INEQUALITY TRENDS ACROSS AMERICAN HOUSEHOLDS

American history has seen long periods in which economic inequality among households has increased and other lengthy periods in which economic inequality has decreased. Of course, this bird's-eye view of inequality misses many important twists and turns in the United States' inequality story. In addition, as we go back further in time, the concepts we use to measure and describe inequality—income, wealth, mobility—change shape relative to their modern-day equivalents. We run the risk of misrepresenting the past as a lower-income version of the present. The very nature of the economy and of economic institutions has changed over time, not merely the distribution of wealth and income among households and individuals.

Nonetheless, there is value in forcing some consistency of measurement onto the past in order to trace a rough sketch of what general trends in economic inequality have looked like over the course of American history. Without this continuity, we create distinct economic periods that have no common grounds for comparison. Doing so risks alienating us from our own history and impairing our ability to understand how history has shaped our own economic reality.

Different metrics of inequality—income, wealth, earnings—tell a consistent story about inequality in the United States. Drawn with a broad brush, the picture is this: (1) unprecedented levels of economic equality during the colonial period, from the 1600s to about 1790; (2) rising inequality during the antebellum era from roughly 1790 to the outbreak of the Civil War in 1861; (3) continued high levels of inequality from the Civil War through the postbellum era to about 1910; (4) a so-called great leveling of inequality over much of the twentieth century, from the 1910s to the 1970s; and (5) a resurgence of inequality beginning in the 1970s and continuing to the present day.

The reader might rightly object at this point, How can any discussion of inequality claim that there were high levels of equality during the colonial period, given the presence of slavery? While the colonial era was quite egalitarian in a narrowly economic sense, this chapter does not claim that it was egalitarian in other dimensions. A society with slavery cannot be called "equal" in any broad sense of the term. Framing this introduction around long-run trends in the inequality of income and wealth admittedly shifts the conversation away from more reprehensible forms of inequality, such as slavery. This introduction does, however, later discuss the economic history of slavery and racial inequality.

The Colonial Period: 1607 to 1790

The distribution of both wealth and income in colonial America among free colonists (slaves not included) was quite egalitarian, both in comparison with peer countries such as England and Holland and by historical standards. Our understanding of the distribution of wealth among the colonists comes from scholarship that draws on historical documents such as wills and probate records (Main 1965, 1977; Jones 1980). As shown in table 1, in 1774, at the close of the colonial era, wealth was much less concentrated at the top of the distribution than at any other point in American history. The top 1 percent of households held only 16.5 percent of total wealth, and the top 10 ten percent, 59.0 percent. At the lower end of the distribution, scholars agree that the poorest of the free colonists were much better off than their European counterparts. This fact was largely due to the abundant supply of land for settlement. From the colonists' perspective, land was available in "virtually limitless supply" at the cost of seizing, clearing, and defending it from Native Americans, the French, and wild animals.

The nature and distribution of colonial wealth varied significantly between the North and the South. Land and buildings were the primary form of wealth held by colonists in the northern regions of New England and the Middle Atlantic. Over the course of the colonial era, the westward movement of northern colonists into new land served to maintain the equality of the wealth distribution. In the South, the value of slaves accounted for about one-third of wealth, with the remaining two-thirds consisting of land and other property. Given that the slave population held no wealth, the southern wealth distribution was more unequal than that of the North. The share of slaves in the South grew from 7.3 percent of the population in 1680 to 39.0 percent by 1770 (Lindert 2006). This growth increased the economic significance of slavery and widened the economic and political gap between the North and the South.

Turning from wealth to income, historians surmise that the American colonists had incomes that were more equal than those of American incomes today and those of their Western European contemporaries. Sources used to reconstruct the colonial income distribution include documents such as historical accounts of pay rates, local censuses, urban directories, probates, and tax lists. Such a reconstruction requires a number of heroic assumptions, and the resulting estimates should be seen as educated conjectures (see Curtis and Lindert n.d.). As shown in table 2, when the total colonial income in 1774 is summed up and allotted to households along the income distribution, it is estimated that the richest 1 percent of households received only an estimated 8.5 percent of total income. In comparison, in England, Wales, Holland, and the Netherlands, the share going to the richest 1 percent at this time was closer to 15 percent (Lindert and Williamson 2016, 39). In the United States of 2018, income inequality was even greater, with the richest 1 percent of U.S. households receiving almost 20 percent of income (see table 2).

While the specific numbers are open to debate, what emerges clearly from the historical record is that colonists at the lower end of the income ladder had substantially greater economic opportunity than their European contemporaries did. By 1770, for example, the wages of workers in cities such as Philadelphia and Boston appear to have been equal to or even higher than wages in London (Rosenbloom 2019). For the free, America was indeed the "best poor man's country." The American Revolution likely reduced inequality further—although not by raising the incomes of the poorest. Rather, the Revolutionary War reduced the incomes of the rich, especially in the South, destruction, dislocation, and the disruption of trade.

Why were the incomes of free colonists so equal? The main equalizing force was the availabilty and abundance of land. The colonial economy was overwhelmingly agricultural and local, with agriculture occupying 85 percent of the workforce (Atack and Passell 1994). Land was not only the main component of colonial wealth, but it was also the primary source of colonial income. A relatively equal distribution of farmland meant a relatively equal distribution of income. Further, the possibility of clearing farmland placed a floor beneath the wages of the lowest-paid workers.

Abundant land may also partially explain the tragic persistence of slavery in America. Economist Evsey Domar argues that Americans refused to abolish slavery in part because it was not possible for landowners to hire sufficient low-wage workers when those workers could instead clear farmland of their own. According to the Domar hypothesis, only two of the following can coexist: free land, free labor, and large-scale agriculture (Domar 1970). Land abundance may have prolonged slavery even as it equalized the wealth and incomes of free colonists. It must also be recognized that the land seemed free for the taking to European colonists, but it was not empty: it was the home of Native Americans, who were displaced, often violently, by colonization.

At the close of the colonial period, Thomas Jefferson, a slave owner himself, expressed hope that the United States would develop into an equal society in which "aristocracy will finally shrink into insignificance" (Ellis 2018, 82). His remark and its context capture the tension between egalitarian ideals and unequal realities that has been an enduring theme of America's history.

The Antebellum Era: 1790 to 1860

In discussing the nation's future with Thomas Jefferson, John Adams, the country's second president, was less optimistic about economic equality. Adams predicted that "as long as Property exists it will accumulate in Individuals and Families . . . the Snow ball will grow as it rolls" (Ellis 2018, 82). The decades leading up to the Civil War, known as the antebellum era, saw a level of growth of inequality in America that was more in line with Adam's fears than with Jefferson's hopes.

Wealth inequality increased in the early decades of the nation's history. Historians estimate that the share of wealth held by the wealthiest 1 percent of adult men roughly doubled from 1774 to 1860, growing from 16.5 percent to 32.7 percent (see table 1). The share held by the wealthiest 10 percent also grew, rising from about one-half to nearly three-quarters of all wealth. In the North, the trend toward greater wealth inequality was driven mainly by the forces of industrialization and urbanization (Steckel and Moehling 2001). The newly wealthy included early industrialists such as textile manufacturer Francis Lowell and firearm maker Samuel Colt. The wealthy also included those fortunate or foresighted enough to own increasingly valuable land in cities that were growing due to high birth rates, immigration, and new manufacturing jobs that drew in workers from rural areas. A comment made by business and real estate mogul John Jacob Astor shortly before his death in 1848 reflects this evolving reality: "Could I begin life again, knowing what I now know, and had money to invest, I would buy every foot of land on the island of Manhattan" (Steckel and Moehling 2001, 181). Alongside real estate, new investment opportunities on solidifying capital markets enabled "the wealthy to pull ahead of the rest of society, especially in the cities of the Northeast, on the strength of their savings, access to credit, and capital gains" (Lindert and Williamson 2016, 139). The nation, especially the North, was seeing the birth of forms of economic inequity that are still with us today.

The southern wealth story is inextricably intertwined with the institution of slavery. By 1860, the United States contained two economies under one flag: the free-labor, family farm economy of the North and the slave economy of the South (Wright 2016). As one scholar put it, the antebellum South was "the wealthiest region in the nation when slave values are included, but the poorest when they are not" (Wright 2006, 60). The ending of the African slave trade in 1807 cut off the supply of new slaves to America, increasing the monetary value of existing slaveholdings. By 1860, slaves made up nearly half of all southern wealth (Wright 2016). Abraham Lincoln wrote in 1860 that the immense value of slaveholdings "has a vast influence on the minds of those who own [slaves and] . . . who battle any policy which depreciated their slaves as property" (Huston 2003, 55).

Within the South, wealth was very unevenly distributed. Slave owners, among them rich plantation owners, had about four times the wealth of the average northerner. At the same time, white southerners who did not own slaves were barely half as wealthy as the average northerner. The numerous laws passed in the South during this era to deal with "paupers and vagrants" suggest a growing southern poverty problem (Wright 2016). By 1860, although wealthier than other regions when counting slaveholdings, the South had fallen behind the North in important aspects of economic development such as education and industrialization. When the Civil War put an end to the abomination of slavery, the South found itself lagging significantly behind the North in nonslave wealth and in economic development.

The forces that increased wealth inequality during the antebellum era—urbanization and industrialization—also increased income inequality. Research by economic historians Peter Lindert and Jeffrey Williamson describes a pronounced rise in inequality from 1774 to 1860 (Lindert and Williamson 2016). According to their reconstruction of the income distribution, the share of income going to those in the top 10 percent of the income distribution rose from 32 percent in 1774 to 38 percent in 1860; the share going to the top 1 percent rose from 8.5 to 10 percent over the same period (see table 2). Further breakdowns of the income distribution reveal growing gaps between urban and rural wages, between northern and southern wages, and between white-collar and unskilled wages. Explanations for increased income dispersion include rapid population growth that increased the supply of labor and reduced wages, technological progress that disproportionately favored industry and cities, and the development of a financial system that increased investment returns for the wealthy (Lindert and Williamson 2016).

Overall, the antebellum record with regard to both income and wealth supports a hypothesis advanced by Nobel Prize–winning economist Simon Kuznets nearly a century later: in its early phase, economic growth leads to increased inequality. Why? There are at least three reasons: a growing gap between the wages of urban and rural low-skilled workers, growing inequality *within* cities between low and high-skilled workers, and population shifts from the more egalitarian rural areas to the increasingly unequal cities (Lindert and Williamson 2016). All three forces, along with the increasing economic divide between North and South, worked in the direction of increasing inequality during the antebellum era. Arguably, the roots of today's inequality can be traced to the early nineteenth century.

The Civil War and the Postbellum Era: 1860 to 1910

The Civil War brought the greatest wartime loss of life in the nation's history but led to the emancipation from slavery of almost four million people, nearly one American in eight. In terms of economic inequality, the effects of the war differed greatly between the victorious North and the defeated South. In the North, the war did nothing to slow the trend toward greater inequality. In fact, forces driving inequality between whites both within the North and nationwide were even stronger in the Civil War decade than over the six decades between 1800 and 1860 (Lindert and Williamson 2016, 159). These forces included continued urbanization, growth in the urban-rural wage gap, and a continued rise in the wage premiums of skilled and white-collar workers. The imposition of taxes, mainly on the rich, to fund the war was not sufficient to curtail the forces increasing inequality.

In the South, the economic effects of the Civil War and emancipation were dramatic. Not only did they "convert the nation's wealthiest region into its poorest," as one analysis described it, they "produced America's greatest redistribution of wealth and income" (Lindert and Williamson 2016, 165). Northern victory and the emancipation of slaves converted the "property" that wealthy southerners had accumulated in the form of slaves into free men, women, and children. On the balance sheet, this meant an enormous reduction of the wealth and income of slaveholders. Whereas in 1860 nearly 59 percent of America's wealthiest 1 percent were southerners, by 1870 the share of southerners in the "top one percent" had dropped to 18 percent (Soltow 1975, quoted in Lindert and Williamson 2016).

After emancipation, Black incomes rose relative to their "incomes" under slavery, narrowing the income distribution in the South. The most frequent path out of slavery led to sharecropping, a system under which sharecroppers agreed to farm someone else's land in return for 50 percent of the total output. The sharecropping system was enormously disadvantageous to sharecroppers. Nonetheless, economic historians estimate that even with some reduction in time spent working, freedom increased the incomes of southern Blacks by about 30 percent over the meager sustenance they had received as slaves (Lindert and Williamson 2016, 63). The more significant gain was immeasurable: freedom itself.

During the decades that followed the Civil War, the level of economic inequality remained high as the United States' industrialization and urbanization continued. Whereas prior to the Civil War, America's economic activity had been a balanced mix of agriculture, manufacturing, and services, after the war America transformed itself into an "urban-industrial powerhouse" (Atack and Passell 1994, 489). By 1890, manufacturing surpassed agriculture as the most productive sector of the economy. The postbellum era witnessed the creation of many large companies whose names became recognized far and wide: retailers such as Neiman-Marcus, Woolworth's, and Marshall Field's, and manufacturers such as Pillsbury, International Harvester, and Standard Oil. Manufacturing became national, sometimes even international, in scale, as the telegraph and the expansion of railroads allowed firms to coordinate production and distribution across geographically dispersed markets. A wave of mergers in the late nineteenth century further increased the scale of American corporations (Chandler 1977; Lamoreaux 1985). By 1894, American companies produced more manufactured goods than any other country in the world. By 1900, with per capita income equivalent to about $6,000 today, the United States held the title of "world's largest economy."

Not surprisingly, the rise of large industry brought a rise in wealth inequality. The share of wealth held by the richest 1 percent of families grew from 25.8 percent in 1890 to 36.4 percent in 1922 and even further, to 49.7 percent by 1929, on the eve of the Great Depression (table 1). By the early twentieth century, the concentration of wealth in the United States was comparable to that of European nations (Williamson and Lindert 1980, 33). The late nineteenth century would later come to be known as the "Gilded Age," a phrase that had been introduced by Mark Twain and Charles Dudley Warner in their 1873 novel *The Gilded Age: A Tale of Today*. The Gilded Age saw the rise of millionaires (billionaires in today's dollars) such as steel magnates John D. Rockefeller, Henry Clay Frick, and Andrew Carnegie, who topped *Forbes* magazine's list of the wealthiest Americans when it was first published in 1918. Alongside the explosion in wealth, the turn of the twentieth century also brought growing awareness of urban poverty and social problems and a rise in the popularity of the Socialist Party. A central concern of the Socialist Party was that the increased concentration of wealth was a threat to democracy, a fear echoed by Teddy Roosevelt's 1914 warning that "there can be no real political democracy unless there is something approaching economic democracy" (Wheeler 2018, 9).

Although the wealth distribution became much more unequal in the late nineteenth century, the distribution of income remained quite unequal but relatively unchanged, at least in the aggregate. At the very top of the distribution, income inequality did increase somewhat. Table 2 shows that the share of income received by those in the top 1 percent of the distribution rose from 9.8 percent in 1870 to 17.8 percent in 1910. However, inequality remained fairly stable over the rest of the distribution. The share going to the top 10 percent only rose slightly, from 39.3 to 40.6 percent. The stability of the national income distribution is somewhat deceiving, however, in that it masks a great deal of economic change that seems to have more or less balanced out across the income distribution taken as a whole.

Several forces pushed in the direction of increasing inequality during the postbellum era. Urbanization continued, with the population shifting from rural areas to the more economically unequal cities. The share of Americans living in cities rose from under a fifth in 1860 to nearly half by 1920. The growth of large corporations increased the demand for educated white-collar managers. Progress in education did not keep up with the increased demand, and as a result, wage premiums for the well-educated minority grew. Within large companies, machinery and repetitive, assembly-line processes replaced skilled blue-collar workers, hollowing out the center of the wage distribution. Massive flows of immigration from Europe increased the supply of less-skilled workers, putting downward pressure at the lower end of the wage distribution.

Other forces reinforcing inequality included unionization and a persistent racial wage gap. Craft unions and their federation—the American Federation of Labor (AFL)—were created to promote the interests of their skilled members, increasing the wage gap between skilled craft workers and less-skilled workers. The stubbornness of the wage gap between Black and white workers also contributed to overall wage inequality. Whereas one might have expected a reduction in racial income inequality in the decades following emancipation, the severe and violent repression of Black people during the Jim Crow era kept the wages of Black workers low, maintaining inequality.

Other currents of American economic development flowed in the direction of equalizing the distribution of income. As in the colonial era, the westward expansion of the frontier tended to equalize incomes. Even as immigrants poured in from Europe, there was a countervailing internal migration of Americans to states west of the Mississippi. Also in the West, the end of the the "gold rush" meant an end to extraordinarily high incomes due to newly discovered mineral wealth. In addition, income gaps between regions shrank as the spread of industrialization brought income levels in the Midwest and South closer to those of the more heavily populated Northeast.

Overall, the relative stability of the income distribution at the national level in the postbellum era gives a misleading impression. Breaking down changes in inequality by skill, race, region, and industry reveals a much more complex and informative inequality story.

The Great Leveling: 1910 to 1970

The decades from roughly 1910 to 1970 saw a reversal of the trend toward growing inequality. Economic historians widely agree that during this period, almost every industrial country, including the United States, experienced a marked decline in the share of income and wealth captured by those at the top of the distribution (Atkinson, Piketty, and Saez 2011). These decades, especially the ones following World War II, also saw remarkable economic growth, challenging the idea of an inevitable trade-off between growth and equality (Okun 1975). Given the many significant political and economic events of this period, there is no lack of potential explanations for the "great leveling" of inequality: the introduction of progressive income taxation, two world wars, the Great Depression, the New Deal, the expansion of education, advances in technology, civil rights legislation, and other factors. Economists and historians are still engaged in active debate as to the exact role of these events in reducing inequality. The vigor of the debate stems from the fact that the great leveling of the twentieth century may hold lessons for reducing today's increasing levels of inequality.

Looking first at wealth, the concentration of wealth in the United States reached historically high levels in the late 1920s before beginning a long decline. On the eve of World War I, the wealth distribution was already quite unequal by historical standards. By 1913, the share of wealth held by the top 1 percent was an incredible 44 percent of total wealth (table 1). The introduction of progressive income taxation in 1913 and estate taxation in 1916 reduced the share of wealth held by the top 1 percent in 1922 to 36.4 percent—still a very high percentage when compared with most other periods in U.S. history. In the Roaring Twenties, wealth concentration roared back, thanks to a booming stock market and a dramatic fall in the tax rates on high incomes. The share of wealth held by the top 1 percent of households peaked at nearly 50 percent before the stock market crash of 1929 and the subsequent Great Depression sent the wealth distribution roller coaster rapidly downward. Wealth concentration dropped sharply in the 1930s and 1940s and then more slowly in the 1950s and 1960s. Tax policy and financial markets fluctuations were the main factors that shaped the evolution of the wealth distribution.

Broadly, the income distribution of this era followed the same pattern as the wealth distribution, with a peak in inequality in the 1920s followed by a long decline. The twentieth-century experience put the study of the income distribution on the map (or more accurately, put it *back* on the map, as it was of deep interest to early political economists such as Adam Smith, David Ricardo, and Karl Marx). The developments of the twentieth century inspired economists such as Nobel Prize winner Simon Kuznets to return to questions of income distribution. In his 1955 address to the American Economic Association, Kuznets postulated an inverted U-shaped pattern to inequality: growing income inequality during the early stage of economic growth followed by a period of falling inequality once greater prosperity enabled broadly shared participation in education and democracy (Kuznets 1955). The events of the period seemed to confirm his hypothesis.

Since Kuznets's groundbreaking work, scholars have followed his lead in constructing a detailed picture of the evolution of income distribution in the twentieth century. Their work partially confirms Kuznets's prediction of an inverted U-shaped pattern. After a period of rising inequality in the nineteenth century, there was a turning point in the 1920s, followed by a reversal in the trend. The share of income going to the top 1 percent of households rose from 9.8 percent in 1870 to a peak of 21.2 percent in 1929 (table 2). Then, over the next four decades, income concentration fell, with the share of income going to the top 1 percent falling back down to 10.8 percent by 1970. The share of income going to the top 5 percent also fell by about half from 1910 to 1970. As of 1970, incomes were at least as equally distributed as they had been in the remarkably income-egalitarian colonial period.

To explain the decline in inequality, economic historians point to a complex interaction of demographic, economic, and political forces. A progressive federal income tax was introduced in 1913, and unlike previous attempts, it stuck. This new tax code did a great deal to level posttax incomes. World War I, which one scholar described as a "watershed in the evolution of labor-market institutions in the United States" (Wright 2006), was another major factor. The war cut off the flows of immigration to American shores that had kept the wages of low-skilled workers relatively low. This reduction in immigration was sustained after war's end by restrictive immigration quotas passed in 1921 and 1924. Between 1915 and 1970, the foreign-born share of the labor force in the United States dropped from over 21 percent to 5.4 percent (Goldin and Katz 2008, 38).

Declining birth rates also contributed to the reduction in the supply of labor, giving workers more leverage to demand higher pay. Wages at the lower end of the distribution also rose as a result of the Great Migration of African Americans from the nation's lowest-paid jobs in the South to better-paying employment in the North (Collins and Wanamaker 2015). Dramatic advances in educational attainment also served to lower inequality. High school enrollment and graduation rates "increased spectacularly" between 1910 and 1940, increasing the supply of highly skilled and white-collar workers and reducing their ability to command high wages (Goldin 1998).

The Great Depression and its aftermath served to further reduce inequality. The financial crash of 1929 led to tighter regulation of the financial sector, curbing high incomes on Wall Street. Franklin Roosevelt's New Deal responded to the crisis by introducing income-equalizing policies such as the minimum wage, unemployment insurance, and protections for unions. A rapid wave of unionization followed in the 1930s, increasing the share of workers belonging to unions to nearly one in four by 1940 (Freeman 1998). Together, New Deal policies and increased unionization replaced the unfettered competition of nineteenth-century labor markets with a more federally regulated, centralized bargaining system (Rosenbloom and Sundstrom 2011, 277).

Events during and after World War II reinforced the centralization and federal control of labor markets, keeping the trend in inequality headed downward. Wartime production brought strong demand for industrial workers, increasing blue-collar wages. The war also brought wage and price regulations that tended to equalize earnings (Goldin and Margo 1992).

The postwar decades of the 1950s and 1960s are sometimes referred to as a "golden age" of widely shared economic growth. Growth was fueled by government spending on infrastructure and defense as well as private spending on housing, automobiles, and new gadgets such as television sets. The economic boom increased the demand for educated workers. Rising demand for college graduates was matched by an extraordinary increase in the supply, as the educational frontier moved to college education. Postwar measures such as the GI Bill, a federal law that provided a range of educational and other benefits to World War II veterans returning from the war, reinforced the expansion of education. It should be noted that it did not do so uniformly, however, as this seemingly race-neutral policy was in practice applied with substantial racial bias (Wright 2013).

Blue-collar workers also benefited from the strong economic growth of the 1950s and 1960s. The cooperation between the government, businesses, and workers that was established during the war continued to function in the postwar decades. Businesses and workers arrived at mutually beneficial agreements under the terms of an informal compact historians refer to as the "Treaty of Detroit" (Levy and Temin 2011). Unionized workers earned middle-class wages, while corporations enjoyed protection from foreign competition due to both trade restrictions and the fact that Europe and Japan were still recovering from the devastation of World War II. However, it should not be forgotten that Black and other minority groups were largely left out of these wage gains (Katznelson 2005).

The postwar decades did see some progress in racial economic equality. The civil rights movement of the 1950s and 1960s culminated in the passage of the Civil Rights Act of 1964, providing at least some federal leverage toward the objective of greater economic equality along race and gender lines (Wright 2013). Across regional lines, the North-South economic divide was narrowed by the awarding of contracts to southern manufacturers during WWII, setting in motion a rising tide of southern business growth. The civil rights movement loosened race-based restrictions on economic activity that were not only unjust but also inefficient, and this loosening benefited both Black and white workers in the South (Wright 2013). By the 1970s, the United States had a "second chance to start with great equality" (Lindert and Williamson 2017, 11).

Overall, it may appear that there are too many answers to the question of why economic inequality declined in the mid-twentieth century. Was the cause trade policy? Rising education levels? Civil rights measures? In 2016 economic historians Peter Lindert and Jeffrey Williamson outlined six basic forces that shape the trajectory of inequality: unpredictable political or natural shocks (e.g., wars, pandemics), demographic shifts, education and skill levels, trade policy, technological change, and financial market events (Lindert and Williamson 2016, 250). To ask which *one* of these forces resulted in the great leveling of the twentieth century is to ask the wrong question. The explanation for the great leveling lies in the interplay of these complementary forces within the context of an imperfect political and social consensus around shared prosperity.

The Return of Inequality: 1970 to the Present

While the United States may have had a second chance at equality in the 1970s, it was a chance not taken. In the midseventies, the trend toward greater equality reversed. Economic and political crises abruptly ended the golden age of shared prosperity. Politically, the 1970s began with the United States mired in a controversial war in Vietnam. President Richard Nixon took office in January 1969 after waging a presidential campaign based on inflaming racial tensions. In 1971, Nixon replaced the so-called War on Poverty that had been a centerpiece of the administration of his predecessor, Lyndon B. Johnson, with a "War on Drugs" that sparked unprecedented levels of incarceration, especially in poorer communities of color. In 1973, the Organization of the Petroleum Exporting Countries (OPEC) quadrupled the price of oil, prompting a global recession and extreme inflation.

The 1980s brought the election of Ronald Reagan as president and a policy shift toward *supply-side economics*—the theory that economic growth is best achieved by lowering taxes and decreasing government regulation of business. The newly elected president significantly lowered the tax rates on income from investments such as stocks, bonds, and real estate (capital gains). The Reagan administration loosened rules on the banking industry, a decision that led to a wave of bank failures in what is known as the "savings and loans crisis" of the late 1980s. Reagan also signaled a more antiunion stance on the part of the federal government when in October 1981, he fired more than eleven thousand unionized air traffic controllers because they refused to return to work as part of a labor dispute. The 1990s saw the election of William "Bill" Clinton, whose centrist policies softened but did not reverse the movement toward deregulation. The 1990s also brought strong economic growth and low unemployment, fed in part by an information technology revolution that saw the rise of the internet and the dot-com boom. This economic expansion continued unevenly into the 2000s. As the 2000s began, economic inequality was on an upward march, although the depth of this trend was not yet widely recognized.

The Great Recession of 2008 brought an economic reckoning. The dramatic failures of financial institutions, the controversial federal bailouts of others, and the subsequent wave of mortgage foreclosures on millions of homes across the

United States led to a questioning of American economic performance and to increased scrutiny of persistent, entrenched socioeconomic factors driving steadily rising inequality in American society. Why, argued many, should the government be bailing out Wall Street when less fortunate Americans are losing their homes? Growing awareness of inequality brought a resurgence of discussion, debate, and even protest.

In September 2011, the Occupy Wall Street movement took over New York's Zuccotti Park and was rapidly emulated by demonstrations across the nation, featuring protesters declaring, "We are the ninety-nine percent." The Occupy movement claimed that large corporations and the extremely wealthy controlled politics for the benefit of rich Americans—the "1 percent"—to the detriment of the other 99 percent. By 2012, bookstore shelves were filled with commentaries on inequality—notable among them, Timothy Noah's *The Great Divergence*, on the causes of inequality, and Nobel Prize winner Joseph Stiglitz's *The Price of Inequality*, on the consequences of inequality. The surprise success of Piketty's seven-hundred-plus-page *Capital in the 21st Century* followed in 2014, spurring extensive conversation about the causes of inequality as well as debate over Piketty's policy recommendation of a tax on wealth.

These protests, books, and countless articles sprang up in direct response to the fact that the decades leading up to the Great Recession had seen "the most sustained rise in inequality since the nineteenth century" in the United States (Yellen 2016, 44). Between 1970 and 2016, wealth inequality increased sharply, eventually reaching levels not previously seen since the end of the Gilded Age. As shown in table 1, in 1976, the wealthiest 1 percent of American households had 22 percent of all wealth. Their share rose to 33 percent by 2001 and 40 percent by 2016. The Great Recession of 2008 briefly interrupted this trend, but it did not stop the upward progression in wealth inequality. By contrast, at the lower end of the wealth distribution, households saw their already minimal wealth shrink even further. By 2016, the average net worth of a household in the top 10 percent of the wealth distribution was $5.3 million, more than three hundred times greater than the average net worth of $16,300 for households in the lower 50 percent of the distribution (Bricker et al. 2017). The rising cost of education and a dramatic rise in student loan debt help to explain the worsening balance sheets of families at the lower end of the wealth distribution.

Rising income inequality mirrored the increase in wealth inequality. In the United States as a whole, GDP per capita roughly doubled from 1970 to 2010, growing from $25,000 to nearly $53,000, measured in 2015 dollars. However, the income gains associated with the economy's increased production were heavily concentrated at the top of the distribution. The share of income received by the top 10 percent of households rose from 33.8 percent in 1970 to 43.9 percent in 2010 (see table 2). Even within the top percent of earners, inequality rose, as "the bulk of the increase went to the top 1 percent of income recipients and much of that to those in the top 0.1 percent" (Arrow 2011). Divergence in incomes occurred along the entire income distribution, with inequality also increasing among the "other 99 percent" (Autor 2014). By 2016, the top 10 percent of families earned an average of $487,500 annually, compared to average annual earnings of $25,650 for families in the bottom 40 percent (Bricker et al. 2017). In the words of former Federal Reserve Board chair Janet Yellen, "It is no secret that the past few decades of widening inequality can be summed up as significant income and wealth gains for those at the very top and stagnant living standards for the majority" (Yellen 2016, 44).

To explain the steady rise in inequality over the past several decades, scholars point to an interrelated set of economic and political forces. As one might expect, the standard economic explanations of growing inequality emphasize the forces of supply and demand. The *skill-biased technological change* explanation for grow- ing inequality contends that technological advances increased the demand for highly skilled workers relative to that of less-skilled workers. In contrast with the 1910 to 1970 period, when rapidly expanding education levels helped to build a prosperous middle class, after 1970, growth in education did not keep up. Without counterbalancing growth in supply, the wages of college-educated workers grew relative to those with less education, increasing inequality. At the same time, by automating straightforward white-collar work, such as bookkeeping, technology replaced workers at the middle of the distribution, hollowing out the middle class.

Increased business globalization served to intensify the effects of technological change. Not only did globalization expand the market for goods and services, increasing the rewards to those at the top, but it also placed less-skilled American workers in direct competition with their counterparts in other countries. Many of these countries were "developing nations," in which employers could pay wages that were a fraction of those historically commanded by American workers, espe- cially those who worked in unions. Increased flows of immigration to the United States also eroded wages on the low end.

While this supply-and-demand explanation goes a certain distance in explain- ing recent growth in income inequality, it also raises new questions. Globalization and technological advancement took place across the globe, but not all countries experienced the same increase in inequality as a result. Why was the rise in inequality particular steep in the United States? It is because the political and social context in which these developments took place matters. Market forces operate within a political and social context that affects the distribution of eco- nomic rewards.

Economic historians Frank Levy and Peter Temin argue that the economic crisis of the 1970s precipitated a policy shift in the United States (Levy and Temin, 2011). The political commitment to shared prosperity that had characterized much of the twentieth century was replaced by a political environment they label the "Wash- ington Consensus." The Washington Consensus involved policies such as deregu- lation, the erosion of the minimum wage, weakened private-sector unionism, increased low-skilled immigration, and increased international trade. It also involved greater societal acceptance of inequality, justified by the view that "a ris- ing tide will lift all boats." According to their argument, the recent rise in inequal- ity is not the inevitable result of economic and demographic forces. Instead, it resulted from the way these economic and demographic forces played out in a political context that favored the profits of the few over the prosperity of the many.

If today's inequality results from past political choices, it follows that future inequality can be reduced by today's policy choices. Scholars of inequality have offered a number of suggestions for slowing or reversing the rise in inequality. Piketty, who argues that inequality is driven fundamentally by the accumulation of wealth, proposes a wealth tax to reduce inequality. Economists Claudia Goldin and Lawrence Katz emphasize improvements in education as the path to reduced inequality. In particular, they advocate greater access to quality preschool education, better K-12 education, and more generous and transparent financial aid for college education. In his 2015 book *Inequality: What Can Be Done*, the late inequality scholar Anthony Atkinson elaborates fifteen proposals for reducing inequality, some highly original. Prominent inequality historians Peter Lindert and Jeffrey Williamson list their three top recommendations for leveling inequality as "improving education, taxing large inheritances, and taming financial instability with regulatory vigilance" (Lindert and Williamson 2016, 262). It is interesting, perhaps intentional, that the policies proposed by Lindert and Williamson echo policies advocated more than two centuries earlier by Thomas Jefferson to keep inequality in check in the young republic. The history of inequality is already written; it is today's policy choices that will shape the future.

RACIAL INEQUALITY

> America is not another word for Opportunity to all her sons.
>   W. E. B. Du Bois, *The Souls of Black Folk*

It is impossible to adequately discuss racial inequality in America in a few pages, even when limiting the discussion to economic dimensions of inequality. That said, this section aims to provide an overview of economic inequality based on race, highlighting particular historical landmarks and turning points.

The very concept of *race* is itself a historical artifact loaded with the prejudices of a previous era. Here, while acknowledging myriad complexities, among them the problematic notion of the concept of race and the growing share of multiracial individuals, the discussion will focus on the deep economic inequality between Black and white people that has been a through-line of America's history. This is not done in an attempt to erase inequality faced by people of other racial or ethnic identities. Rather, the aim is to provide an inroad to further exploration of economic inequality along racial and ethnic lines.

The history of Black-white racial inequality in America begins with slavery, initially present throughout all of America's colonies. It is difficult, and perhaps misguided, to attempt to measure the cost of slavery in monetary terms, although demand for reparation—monetary or other compensation to currently living African Americans to make up for the harm done by slavery—may eventually require this reckoning. Economically, slavery was exploitation in the neoclassical sense—slaves "received 'income' (primarily food, clothing, and shelter) less than the value of their marginal product at any point in time and over the life cycle" (Margo 2016, 305). The economic gains from this forced theft spilled over from slave owners to others in the free economy, implicating all as beneficiaries of slavery. Compounding its harms, slavery left a legacy of racist attitudes and ideology. Defending slavery required the development of false and "intensified perceptions, ideologies, and rhetoric of racial inferiority" (Wright 2006). Emancipation ended the stark legal dichotomy between enslaved and free but by no means ended discrimination, segregation, and violence on the basis of race, which continue to the present day.

In studying racial economic inequality since emancipation, economists have generally taken a quantitative approach, looking at change over time in measures such as income or wealth. While these measurements capture only one aspect of a multidimensional issue, quantitative measurements of Black-white inequality can help trace the trajectory of racial inequality over time. An example of this exercise can be found in table 3, which shows Black per capita income (the total income of all Black households divided by the number of Black people) as a percentage of the per capita income of white people. Were white and Black households to make up separate nations, the comparison presented here would be equivalent to comparing the per capita GDPs of the two nations. Such a comparison has recognizable limitations, offering a limited viewpoint on the overall racial inequality picture. Yet it does speak to major trends in the history of inequality between Blacks and whites in America.

Table 3   Black Per Capita Income as Shares of Per Capita Income

Year	Black-White Income Ratio (%)
1870	28
1900	32
1940	38
1950	42
1955	43
1960	47
1965	50
1970	56
1975	59
1980	58
1985	59
1990	59
1995	60
2000	63
2005	64
2010	64
2015	67
2018	65

Sources: 1870–1940: Margo 2006. 1950–1965: Calculated by the author from U.S. Census table P-3: "Race and Hispanic Origin of People by Mean Income and Sex: 1947 to 2018," following methodology in Margo 2006. 1970–2018: Calculated by the author from U.S. Census table P-1: "CPS Population and Per Capita Money Income."

Despite initial progress during Reconstruction, the era that followed the Civil War, many obstacles toward Black economic progress remained and became more entrenched as time went on. In 1870, five years after slavery ended nationwide, the per capita income of Black individuals stood at only 28 percent of that of whites (see table 3). In the seventy years that followed, from 1870 to 1940, Black per capita income relative to white incomes grew only ten percentage points—from 28 to 38 percent.

What explains this glacial pace of improvement? One can cite a long list of ways in which the United States failed to live up to ideals of racial equality. One historian, for example, described "deep barriers to black advancement in this era . . . [in the form of] denial of access to education and restricted job opportunities outside of the agricultural sector" (Wright 2013, 37). Educational opportunities were segregated by racial lines, explicitly so in the South, with a large discrepancy in educational spending on Black and white students (Margo 1990). Labor markets in both the North and the South were also highly segregated by race. Politically, Blacks were disempowered by laws and practices that impeded their right to vote. Between 1890 and 1903, every southern state adopted laws to disenfranchise Black voters (Wright 2013, 42). Moreover, the regime of segregation and white supremacy was maintained not only by laws and social norms but by violence—including murder by lynching. Lynching, while more frequent in the South, was not limited to the South nor to the nineteenth century; it extended as far north as Duluth, Minnesota, where a white mob lynched three Black men on June 15, 1920. The initial hopes of Reconstruction faded into the darkness of the Jim Crow era.

The new century and the rise of progressivism did little to improve matters in this realm. A generous characterization might be that race was a "blind spot" of the progressive movement of the early 1900s. To the extent that the economic situation of Blacks improved at all in the early 1900s, it was due to employment opportunities created by World War I combined with the willingness of Black families to migrate as economic refugees out of the South. World War I had the dual effect of increasing demand for labor and cutting off the flows of European immigration. Black people migrated from the South in response to these employment opportunities. However, their arrival was often met by racial violence or "white flight"—a phenomenon in which neighborhoods emptied of white families when Black people became neighbors (Boustan 2017). Black people were largely left behind by the New Deal programs of the 1930s. Social Security, for example, was not extended to Blacks for the first quarter century of its existence (Temin 2017, 52).

Convergence of Black and white incomes picked up after 1940. World War II compressed incomes across the country and lessened overall inequality. Black migration and employment levels increased during wartime. The narrowing of Black-white educational gaps also played a significant role in income convergence. Between 1940 and 1980, 40 percent of the Black-white education gap disappeared (Smith and Welch 1989). These gains were due in large measure to the civil rights movement of the 1950s and 1960s, which produced significant changes in federal laws and policies. In 1954, the Supreme Court's *Brown v. the Board of Education* decision ended legal segregation in education. A decade later, the 1964 Civil Rights Act and the 1965 Voting Rights Act addressed racial disparities in employment and political participation. Black women in particular experienced a surge of income growth during this period. From 1940 to 1975, Black per capita income as a percentage of white income increased from 38 to 59 percent, making the postwar period the period of greatest income convergence between Blacks and whites in U.S. history (see table 3). The rate of income gains, however, would not be sustained past the 1970s.

In the 1970s, income convergence between Blacks and whites began to slow. One contributing factor was the fact that the Black-white education gap was not narrowing as quickly as it had been in previous decades. Political changes also slowed Black progress. In 1971, Richard Nixon replaced the War on Poverty with the War on Drugs, a shift of emphasis that paved the way for increased racial inequality. Harsh criminal sentencing for drug-related offenses, disproportionate enforcement in poorer communities, and racial discrimination in the criminal justice system led to an era of mass incarceration of people of color. Instead of improving communities' standard of living, these punitive policies maintained economic inequality and had devastating consequences for Black people, particularly young men.

Several economic headwinds have continued to slow Black economic progress since the 1970s. In the labor market, the manufacturing industry's decline that began in the 1970s hit Black workers particularly hard. Racial discrimination continued to slow progress as well, as evidenced by a field experiment showing that those with names perceived as white were 50 percent more likely to be called back for job interviews than those with Black-sounding names (Bertrand and Mullainathan 2004). Well into the twenty-first century, large racial disparities in the environments in which Black and white children grow up continued to translate into much lower rates of upward intergenerational mobility for Black children, especially boys (Chetty et al. 2020). Overall, both qualitative and quantitative evidence demonstrate that the hopes of the civil rights movement were not fulfilled in the half century that followed.

The wealth gap between Black and white households proved even more resistant to change than the income gap did. That fact is perhaps unsurprising, given that for the population overall, wealth inequality dwarfs income inequality. The racial wealth gap resulted from historical inequities as well as the ongoing racial income gap. After the Civil War, initial plans to distribute land to emancipated slaves were abandoned, meaning that Black families began their economic journeys with literally no financial resources or assets. The vast majority were thus forced to support themselves as sharecroppers rather than landowners.

Nearly a century later, Black households were still being denied crucial wealth-building opportunities. In the postwar decades, segregation and redlining prevented Black families from building wealth through homeownership at the same time that inexpensive mortgages and aid to veterans helped build the wealth of white families. The passage of the Fair Housing Act in 1968 did little to improve the racial wealth gap, perhaps because it arrived at the same time that that slowing income growth kept the purchase of a home out of reach for many Black households (Margo and Collins 2011). The ongoing income gap between Black and white households continued to contribute significantly to the wealth gap, as lower incomes made it more difficult to build wealth by saving (Aliprantis and Carroll 2019). In 2016, the average wealth of Black-headed households was $140,000, compared to an average more than six times greater of $901,000 for white-headed households. The 2016 racial wealth gap was as wide as it had been in 1962, two years before the passage of the Civil Rights Act of 1964.

The nation thus saw the election of Barack Obama, its first African American president, with racial gaps in wealth and income that had changed little since the 1970s. Black income relative to white income had increased only six percentage points over a thirty-year period, with Black income still averaging less than two-thirds of white income. Black households still held less than one-sixth the wealth of white households, on average. These income and wealth statistics shine a light on the economic reality of racism in American society.

A close look at the numbers reveals an even more alarming trend in recent history. As table 3 shows, the convergence between Black and white incomes reversed from 2015 to 2018, when the Black income share decreased from 67 to 65 percent. The slow path toward equality of incomes appears to have doubled back. While this is a slight decrease, it is a troubling one, as it casts doubt on the assumption that it is only a matter of time until racial inequality is eliminated. Perhaps it also serves as a call to action, as it is a reminder that our choices as a society determine whether convergence will resume.

The short lesson with regard to economic inequality along racial lines is that history matters. Abundant evidence that there is no biological link between skin color and economic productivity is insufficient to emancipate the economic outcomes of today's Black Americans from the nation's tragic history. Perhaps no aspect of economic inequality is more crucial than its relationship to racism and discrimination, and no aspect calls more urgently for a critical revision of long-standing narratives of American history and economics. Further, inequality between Black and white Americans is only one dimension of racial and ethnic inequality. The evolving mix of identities present in the United States and the unfortunate ability of racism to mutate into new, more virulent forms means there is much more work to be done to understand and respond to racial and ethnic inequality.

GENDER INEQUALITY

Economic inequality between men and women has decreased significantly over the course of U.S. history. Economic inequality based on gender is a distinct issue from economic inequality across households or individuals. A nation could, for instance, have a great deal of inequality across households but very little inequality between men and women (or the opposite). Gender inequality is also a distinct question from racial inequality. While there is no biological basis for racial inequality, there are biological differences between men and women that have led to differences in their economic roles, especially in the past, when the workplace placed greater value on brawn relative to brain. Yet gender, like race, is ultimately a historical artifact, one currently under interrogation by scholars. With those caveats in mind, the trajectory of gender inequality over the course of American history may be summarized as a bumpy road from separate economic spheres for men and women toward incomplete convergence in their economic roles.

During the colonial era, with the economy overwhelmingly agricultural, the work of free men and women took place mainly in the context of the family farm. Farmwork included not only growing crops and raising animals but also producing goods such as food, clothing, soap, candles, and medicines. As described by one historian, "agriculture was in the hands of the men, and [home] manufacturing, for the most part, in the hands of the women" (Degler 1980, 364). Along with domestic chores, women's work also included substantial time devoted to childcare, given that women of that era gave birth to an average of seven children. In the political realm, free women could not vote and, if married, could not own property. Those limitations were severe, even as they pale in comparison to the bondage and forced labor experienced by women in slavery across all of colonial America.

The antebellum era from 1790 to 1860 saw the beginning of America's transition to an industrial economy. The economy remained largely agricultural, and the overwhelming majority of women still worked only within the scope of the home, farm, or plantation as "unpaid workers in family enterprises, mostly farm wives and daughters and slaves" (Ruggles 2015, 1804). However, manufacturing was growing and required cheap labor. To entice young, single women to take jobs, manufacturers, most well known among them the Lowell textile mills in Massachusetts, invented new institutional arrangements such as supervised boarding homes. The wage ratios presented in table 4 show that the wages of women who were manufacturing workers are estimated to have been less than half those of paid to men. Although manufacturing brought new opportunities, the majority of women working outside the home in the antebellum era were employed as domestic servants. As of 1850, there were "more women in domestic service than in teaching and manufacturing combined" (Degler 1980, 372). Work outside the home may have prompted a desire for further economic independence. The right to control one's own wages was one of the demands of the first women's rights convention, held in 1848 in Seneca Falls, New York.

Table 4   Labor Force Participation by Gender and Women's Relative Earnings: 1815–2018

| Year | Labor Force Participation Rate (%) | | | | Female Earnings as Percent of Male Earnings | |
| | Male | | Female | | | |
	White	Nonwhite	White	Nonwhite	Weekly	Annual
1815	(NA)	(NA)	(NA)	(NA)	28.8	(NA)
1820	(NA)	(NA)	(NA)	(NA)	33.7	(NA)
1850	89.9	79.5	(NA)	(NA)	48.5	(NA)
1860	88.1	82.8	13.1	35.7	(NA)	(NA)
1870	91.1	94.7	12.4	39.7	(NA)	(NA)
1880	91.7	95.4	13.4	42.0	(NA)	(NA)
1890	(NA)	(NA)	(NA)	(NA)	53.9	46.3
1900	91.5	93.7	19.4	43.7	55.4	(NA)
1910	91.7	96.0	22.1	58.1	(NA)	(NA)
1920	90.1	93.0	21.9	42.9	55.9	(NA)
1930	(NA)	(NA)	(NA)	(NA)	57.8	55.6
1940	84.5	86.6	25.7	39.8	(NA)	57.9
1950	83.3	82.5	29.3	38.6	(NA)	(NA)
1955	(NA)	(NA)	(NA)	(NA)	(NA)	63.9
1960	81.7	78.1	35.1	44.0	(NA)	60.7
1970	77.7	71.4	41.2	47.7	(NA)	59.4
1980	76.7	69.3	50.0	53.8	64.2	60.2
1990	76.0	70.6	57.1	59.7	72.0	71.6
2000	75.5	71.2	59.5	61.7	76.9	73.7
2010	72.0	67.6	58.5	59.0	81.2	76.9
2018	69.5	67.6	56.4	59.4	81.1	81.6

Sources: Labor force participation rates: 1850–1990: Sobek 2006. 2000–2010: Calculated by the author from U.S. Census Bureau 2012; 2018: Calculated by the author from U.S. Bureau of Labor Statistics, n.d.

Earnings ratios: 1815–1930: Margo 2006. 1940: O'Neill and Polachek 1993. 1955–2018: Institute for Women's Policy Research 2019.

Notes: The labor force participation rate is the percent of noninstitutionalized civilians aged sixteen and higher employed or looking for work. For 1910, the unusually high labor force participation rates are likely the result of the wording of the 1910 census question. For 1815, the earnings ratio is that of female domestic workers to male agricultural workers. For 1820–1930, the earnings ratio is that of female manufacturing workers to male manufacturing workers. For 1955–2018, the weekly female-to-male earnings ratio is estimated only for those working full-time, and for 1940–2018, the annual female-to-male earnings ratio is estimated for full-time, year-round workers.

The Civil War brought significant change in women's economic position. As husbands left for the war, the majority of states passed legislation expanding the rights of married women to control property (Hoff 1991). Slavery had effects on women's labor force history that lasted beyond the Civil War and emancipation. Under slavery, it is estimated that 90 to 95 percent of adult Black women worked in the fields (Degler 1980, 388). The legacy of slavery, along with the low earnings of most Black men, meant that even after emancipation, Black women worked outside of the home at wage-earning jobs at much higher rates than white women did. In 1880, 42 percent of nonwhite women were in the labor force as compared to only 13.4 percent of white women (see table 4).

In the decades following the Civil War, accelerating urbanization and industrialization created new employment opportunities for women outside the home while at the same time increasing the distance between the spheres of home and work. As shown in table 4, the labor force participation of white women grew from 13.1 percent in 1860 to 22.1 percent in 1910, driven largely by the movement of single women into the workforce, especially in urban areas. The labor force participation of nonwhite women remained significantly higher, at more than 40 percent. The gap between the labor force participation rate of single women and that of married women widened and appears to have been widest sometime just after World War I (Goldin 1991, 12).

In terms of pay, the surveys available show that the earnings of female manufacturing workers were about half those of male manufacturing workers at the end of the nineteenth century (see table 4). The workplace was highly segregated by gender. A study of some 150,000 employees made by the Bureau of Labor in the mid-1890s found only 800 cases where men and women were employed at roughly the same jobs; in 600 of the 800 cases, women's wages were lower than men's, usually by a third (Degler 1980, 382). The typical working woman of the nineteenth century was young and single, and she left work when she married, limiting women's motivation and ability to organize for higher pay.

The decades of the great leveling, from 1910 to about 1970, saw married women join single women in the workforce. By 1970, the labor force participation of white women stood at 41.2 percent and that of nonwhite women at 47.7 percent. In terms of earnings, in 1970, a woman working full time earned about fifty-nine cents for every dollar earned by a full-time-working man. Somewhat paradoxically, the postwar decades of the fifties and sixties brought a reassertion of the value of homemaking even as married women were entering the workforce in numbers never before seen. As late as 1964, the Women's Bureau, the federal agency governing "women's work," stated that it was not its policy to encourage married women and mothers of young children to seek employment outside the home. This stance reflected long-standing notions that taking care of the family home and the children within was married women's most important responsibility (Degler 1980). Said economic historian Julie Matthaei, "By 1970 it was no longer clear what womanhood was: the nineteenth-century ideal—the full-time homemaker—had been joined by the wage-earning homemaker and the second-career women" (Matthaei 1982, 322).

The tensions between the increased employment rates of women and the idealization of their role as homemakers came to the surface and broke in the late 1960s and 1970s. The battle between work and home was won by work, at least numerically. Between 1970 and 2010, the share of white women working outside the home rose from 41.2 to 58.5 percent. The share of nonwhite women working outside the home increased from 47.7 to 59 percent over the same forty-year period (table 4). Perhaps more significantly, women organized and leveraged the Civil Rights Act of 1964 in order to challenge the wage gap between men and women and to push down barriers separating "men's work" from "women's work." After the 1970s, the proportion of women in traditionally male professions such as law and medicine shot up dramatically: the share of women among law school graduates, for example, rose from 5 percent in 1970 to more than 40 percent by 1990 (Jones 2009).

As the length and depth of women's participation in the workforce intensified, women's wages rose accordingly. Relative to men's, women's wages increased significantly between 1980 and 2010, at which time the weekly earnings of women had risen to a little more than 80 percent of those of men. Economic historian Claudia Goldin predicts that economic progress should eventually eliminate earnings differences between men and women (Goldin 1990, 59). It remains to be seen whether economic progress will do so. For American women, significant challenges remain in reconciling family and career within a policy environment that is not fully supportive of women's employment and a cultural environment where outdated and misogynistic beliefs about women and work are still very much alive.

CONCLUSION

A consideration of the history of inequality demonstrates that while some level of inequality has always been a reality of American society, the degree of inequality has changed over time, as a result of economic, social, demographic, political, and other forces. In every stage of American history, from the Declaration of Independence to the nation's emergence as an economic superpower, inequality has had powerful effects on the lives of families and individuals. Studying and understanding inequality is therefore fundamental to understanding life in the United States. Limitations of space have meant that some significant dimensions of inequality are not addressed here, even in passing—among them, inequality based on disability, gender identity, religion, immigration status, and more. The hope is, nonetheless, that this discussion provides a framework and set of concepts that may fruitfully be applied to understanding and responding to other dimensions of inequality.

History offers multiple insights for our understanding of inequality. The first is that simplistic explanations—"factor x causes inequality"—should be dismissed in favor of a recognition that inequality has feedback effects with other aspects of society. For example, simplistically, one might argue that unequal educational opportunity leads to inequality. But peeling this back a layer, it is likely also the case that economic inequality results in unequal educational opportunities. The careful examination of history suggests that inequality results from a complex web of forces that interact differently at different points in history. History provides us insight into the nature of these forces and their interactions—insight that can help us understand the consequences of today's actions for inequality in the future.

A second lesson to be drawn from this history is that inequality is not inevitable. The United States has seen eras of rising inequality and eras of falling inequality. Nor is increasing inequality an inevitable result of the eras being affected by choices and action. The waxing and waning of inequality over the course of history suggest that were we to desire less inequality in the future, there are measures that could be taken. Lindert and Williamson end their path-breaking study of the history of income inequality, for example, by recommending that, in order to reduce future inequality, we improve education, tax large inheritances, and tame financial instability with effective regulation. The message of history is that economic forces alone do not dictate the course of inequality. The economy is in a dynamic relationship with political, social, and even biological forces, as the pandemic of 2020 has powerfully demonstrated. The political environment shapes the economy, but increasingly, economic power shapes the course of politics.

Finally, the attempt to understand the forces that have shaped inequality in the past can help us form and question our own values. Perhaps the fact that inequality has always been present means it is unavoidable or that it is beneficial because it provides incentives for hard work and innovation. On the other hand, perhaps growing inequality indicates a flawed system that needs to be reformed. The primary lesson one can draw from this past history is that we are part and parcel of a still-unfolding history of inequality in America. Our choices matter.

Stacey Jones and Cameron Hub

Further Reading

Aliprantis, Dionissi, and Daniel Carroll. 2019. "What Is behind the Persistence of the Racial Wealth Gap?" *Economic Commentary*, February 28.

Arrow, Kenneth. 2011. "Economics and Inequality." *Boston Review*, November 30.

Atack, Jeremy, and Peter Passell. 1994. *A New Economic View of American History from Colonial Times to 1940*. 2nd edition. New York: W. W. Norton and Company.

Atkinson, Anthony B., and Francois Bourguignon. 2015. "Introduction: Income Distribution Today." In *Handbook of Income Distribution*, edited by Anthony B Atkinson and Francois Bourguignon, xvii–xiv. Oxford: Elsevier.

Atkinson, Anthony B., Thomas Piketty, and Emmanuel Saez. 2011. "Top Incomes in the Long Run of History." *Journal of Economic Literature* 49 (1): 3–71.

Autor, David H. 2014. "Skills, Education, and the Rise of Earnings Inequality among the 'Other 99 Percent.'" *Science* (May 23): 843–51.

Bertrand, Marianne, and Senhil Mullainathan. 2004. "Are Emily and Greg More Employable than Lakisha and Jamal? A Field Experiment on Labor Market Discrimination." *American Economic Review* 94 (4): 991–1013.

Boustan, Leah Platt. 2017. *Competition in the Promised Land: Black Migrants in Northern Cities and Labor Markets*. Princeton, NJ: Princeton University Press.

Boustan, Leah Platt, and William J. Collins. 2014. "The Origin and Persistence of Black–White Differences in Women's Labor Force Participation." In *Human Capital in History: The American Record*, edited by Leah Platt Boustan, Carol Frydman, and Robert A. Margo, 205–40. Chicago: University of Chicago Press.

Bricker, Jesse, Lisa J. Dettling, Alice Henriques, Joanne W. Hsu, Lindway Jacobs, Kevin B. Moore, Sarah Pack, John Sabelhaus, Jeffrey Thompson, and Richard A. Windle. 2017. "Changes in U.S. Family Finances from 2013 to 2016: Evidence from the Survey of Consumer Finances." *Federal Reserve Bulletin* 103 (3): 1–40.

Carter, Susan B. 2006. "Labor Force." In *Historical Statistics of the United States, Millenial Edition On Line*, edited by Susan B. Carter, Scott Sigmund Gartner, Michael R. Haines, Alan L. Olmstead, Richard Sutch, and Gavin Wright, 2.13–2.35. Cambridge: Cambridge University Press.

Chandler, Alfred D. 1977. *The Visible Hand: The Managerial Revolution in American Business*. Cambridge, MA: Belknap Press.

Chetty, Raj, David Grusky, Maximilian Hell, Nathaniel Hendren, Robert Manduca, and Jimmy Narang. 2017. "The Fading American Dream: Trends in Absolute Income Mobility since 1940." *Science* 356 (6336): 398–406.

Chetty, Raj, Nathaniel Hendren, Maggie R. Jones, and Sonya R. Porter. 2020. "Race and Economic Opportunity in the United States: An Intergenerational Perspective." *Quarterly Journal of Economics* 135 (2): 711–83.

Collins, William J., and Marianne H. Wanamaker. 2015. "The Great Migration in Black and White: New Evidence on the Selection and Sorting of Southern Migrants." *Journal of Economic History* 75 (4): 947–92.

Coorak, Miles. 2004. *Generational Income Mobility in North America and Europe*. Cambridge: Cambridge University Press.

Curtis, Matthew, and Peter H. Lindert. n.d. *Global Price and Income History Group*. http://gpih.ucdavis.edu.

Degler, Carl. 1980. *At Odds: Women and the Family in America from the Revolution to the Present*. New York: Oxford University Press.

Domar, Evsey D. 1970. "The Causes of Slavery or Serfdom: A Hypothesis." *Journal of Economic History* 30 (1): 18–32.

Donovan, Sarah A. 2015. *A Guide to Describing the Income Distribution*. CRS Report, Washington, DC: Congressional Research Service.

Du Bois, W. E. B. 2015. *The Souls of Black Folk*. New Haven, CT: Yale University Press.

Ellis, Joseph J. 2018. *American Dialogue: The Founders and Us*. New York: Alfred A. Knopf.

Ferrie, Joseph. 2005. "The End of American Exceptionalism? Mobility in the United States since 1950." *Journal of Economic Perspectives* 19 (3): 199–215.

Freeman, Richard B. 1998. "Spurts in Union Growth: Defining Moments and Social Processes." In *The Defining Moment: The Great Depression and the American Economy in the Twentieth Century*, edited by Michael D. Bordo, Claudia Goldin, and Eugene White, 265–95. Chicago: University of Chicago Press.

Goldin, Claudia. 1990. *Understanding the Gender Gap: An Economic History of American Women*. New York: Oxford University Press.

Goldin, Claudia. 1998. "America's Graduation from High School: The Evolution and Spread of Secondary Schooling in the Twentieth Century." *Journal of Economic History* 58 (2): 343–74.

Goldin, Claudia and Robert Margo. 1992. "The Great Compression: The Wage Structure in the United States at Mid-Century." *The Quarterly Journal of Economics* 107 (1): 1–34.

Goldin, Claudia and Lawrence F. Katz. 2008. *The Race Between Education and Technology*. Cambridge, MA: Harvard University Press.

Hoff, Joan. 1991. *Law, Gender, and Injustice: A Legal History of U.S. Women*. New York: New York University Press.

Horowitz, Juliana Manasce, Rith Igielnic, and Rakesh Kochhar. 2020. *Most Americans Say There Is Too Much Economic Inequality in the U.S., but Fewer than Half Call It a Top Priority.* January 9. https://www.pewsocialtrends.org/2020/01/09/most-americans-say-there-is-too-much-economic-inequality-in-the-u-s-but-fewer-than-half-call-it-a-top-priority.

Huston, James L. 2003. *Calculating the Value of the Union: Slavery, Property Rights, and the Economic Origins of the Civil War.* Chapel Hill: University of North Carolina Press.

Institute for Women's Policy Research. 2019. "The Gender Wage Gap: 2018. Earnings Differences by Race and Ethnicity." https://iwpr.org/iwpr-general/the-gender-wage-gap-2018-earnings-differences-by-race-and-ethnicity.

Isaacs, Julia, Isabel Sawhill, and Ron Haskins. 2008. *Getting Ahead or Losing Ground: Economic Mobility in America.* Washington, D.C.: Brookings Institution. https://www.brookings.edu/wp-content/uploads/2016/06/02_economic_mobility_sawhill.pdf.

Jones, Alice Hanson. 1980. *Wealth of a Nation to Be.* New York: Columbia University Press.

Jones, Stacey. 2009. "Dynamic Social Norms and the Unexpected Transformation of Women's Higher Education, 1965–1975." *Social Science History* 33 (3): 247–91.

Katznelson, Ira. 2005. *When Affirmative Action Was White: An Untold Story of Racial Inequality in Twentieth-Century America.* New York: Norton.

Kuznets, Simon. 1955. "Economic Growth and Income Inequality." *American Economic Review* 45 (1): 1–28.

Kuznets, Simon, and Elizabeth Jenks. 1953. *Shares of Upper Income Groups in Income and Savings.* Cambridge, MA: National Bureau of Economic Research.

Lamoreaux, Naomi R. 1985. *The Great Merger Movement in American Business, 1895–1904.* New York: Cambridge University Press.

Levy, Frank, and Peter Temin. 2011. "Inequality and Institutions in Twentieth-Century America." In *Economic Evolution and Revolution in Historical Time*, edited by Paul Rhode, Joshua Rosenboom and David Weiman, 357–86. Palo Alto, CA: Stanford University Press.

Lindert, Peter H. 2006. "The Distribution of Income and Wealth." In *Historical Statistics of the United States, Millennial Edition on Line*, edited by Susan B. Carter, Scott Sigmund Gartner, Michael R. Haines, Alan L. Olmstead, Richard Sutch and Gavin Wright, 2.621–2.625. Cambridge: Cambridge University Press.

Lindert, Peter H., and Jeffrey G. Williamson. 2016. *Unequal Gains: American Growth and Inequality since 1700.* Princeton, NJ: Princeton University Press.

Long, Jason, and Joseph Ferrie. 2018. "Intergenerational Occupational Mobility in Great Britain and the United States since 1850." *American Economic Review* 103 (4): 1109–37.

Lundberg, Shelly, and Robert A. Pollak. 2007. "The American Family and Family Economics." *Journal of Economic Perspectives* 21 (2): 3–26.

Main, Gloria L. 1977. "Inequality in Early America: The Evidence from Probate Records of Massachusetts and Maryland." *Journal of Interdisciplinary History* 7 (4): 559–81.

Main, Jackson Turner. 1965. *The Social Structure of Revolutionary America.* Princeton, NJ: Princeton University Press.

Margo, Robert A. 1990. *Race and Schooling in the South, 1880–1950, An Economic History.* Chicago: University of Chicago Press.

Margo, Robert A. 2006. "Female-to-Male Earnings Ratios: 1815–1987." In *Historical Statistics of the United States, Earliest Times to the Present: Millennial Edition*, edited by Susan B. Carter, Scott Sigmund Gartner, Michael R. Haines, Alan L. Olmstead, Richard Sutch, and Gavin Wright, Table Ba 4224–4233. New York: Cambridge University Press.

Margo, Robert A. 2016. "Obama, Katrina, and the Persistence of Racial Inequality." *Journal of Economic History* 76 (2): 301–41.

Margo, Robert A., and William J. Collins. 2011. "Race and Home Ownership from the End of the Civil War to the Present." *American Economic Review* 101 (3): 3355–59.

Matthaei, Julie A. 1982. *An Economic History of Women in America: Women's Work, the Sexual Division of Labor, and the Development of Capitalism.* New York: Schocken Books.

Milanovic, Branko. 2016. *Global Inequality: A New Approach for the Age of Globalization.* Cambridge, MA: Belknap Press of Harvard University Press.

Milanovic, Branko, Peter Lindert, and Jeffrey Williamson. 2011. "Pre-Industrial Inequality." *Economic Journal* 121:255–72.

Noah, Timothy. 2012. *The Great Divergence: American's Growing Inequality Crisis and What We Can Do about It.* New York: Bloomsbury Press.

Okun, Arthur M. 1975. *Equality and Efficiency: The Big Tradeoff.* Washington, DC: Brookings Institution Press.

O'Neill, June, and Solomon Polachek. 1993. "Why the Gender Gap in Wages Narrowed in the 1990s." *Journal of Labor Economics* 11 (1): 205–28.

Opportunity Insights. n.d. https://opportunityinsights.org.

Piketty, Thomas. 2015. "Putting Distribution Back at the Center of Economics: Reflections on Capital in the Twenty-First Century." *Journal of Economic Perspectives* 29 (1): 67–88.

Piketty, Thomas, and Arthur Goldhammer, trans. 2014. *Capital in the Twenty-First Century.* Cambridge, MA: Belknap Press of Harvard University Press.

Piketty, Thomas, and Emmanuel Saez. 2003. "Income Inequality in the United States, 1913–1998." *Quarterly Journal of Economics* 118 (1): 1–39.

Rosenbloom, Joshua. 2019. "Colonial America." In *Handbook of Cliometrics*, 2nd Edition, edited by Claude Diebolt and Michael Haupert, 785–810. Cham, Switzerland: Springer Nature AG.

Rosenbloom, Joshua L., and William A. Sundstrom. 2011. "Labor-Market Regimes in U.S. Economic History." In *Economic Evolution and Revolution in Historical Time*, edited by Paul W. Rhode, Joshua L. Rosenbloom and David F. Weiman, 277–310. Stanford, CA: Stanford University Press.

Ruggles, Steven. 2015. "Patriarchy, Power, and Pay: The Transformation of American Families, 1800–2015." *Demography* 52 (6): 1797–1823.

Saez, Emmanuel, and Gabriel Zucman. 2016. "Wealth Inequality in the United States since 1913: Evidence from Capitalized Income Tax Data." *Quarterly Journal of Economics* 131 (2): 519–78.

Sitarman, Ganesh. 2017. *The Crisis of the Middle-Class Constitution: Why Economic Inequality Threatens Our Republic.* New York: Alfred A. Knopf.

Smith, James P., and Finis R. Welch. 1989. "Black Economic Progress after Myrdal." *Journal of Economic Literature* 27 (2): 519–64.

Sobek, Mathew. 2006. "Labor Force Participation, by Sex and Race: 1850–1990." In *Historical Statistics of the United States, Earliest Times to the Present: Millennial Edition*, edited by Susan B. Carter, Scott Sigmund Gartner, Michael R. Haines, Alan L. Olmstead, Richard Sutch and Gavin Wright. New York: Cambridge University Press.

Soltow, Lee. 1975. *Men and Wealth in the United States, 1850–1870.* New Haven, CT: Yale University Press.

Steckel, Richard H., and Carol Moehling. 2001. "Rising Inequality: Trends in the Distribution of Wealth in Industrializing New England." *Journal of Economic History* 61 (1): 160–83.

Stiglitz, Joseph E. 2012. *The Price of Inequality: How Today's Divided Society Endangers Our Future.* New York: W. W. Norton and Company.

Stone, Chad, Danilo Trisi, Arloc Sherman, and Jennifer Beltrán. 2020. *A Guide to Statistics on Historical Trends in Income Inequality.* Washington, DC: Center on Budget and Policy Priorities.

Sutch, Richard. 2017. "The One Percent across Two Centuries: A Replication of Thomas Piketty's Data on the Concentration of Wealth in the United States." *Social Science History* 41:587–613.

Temin, Peter. 2017. *The Vanishing Middle Class: Prejudice and Power in a Dual Economy.* Cambridge, MA: MIT Press.

U.S. Bureau of Labor Statistics. n.d. "Employment Projections." https://www.bls.gov/emp/tables/civilian-labor-force-participation-rate.htm.

U.S. Census Bureau. 2012. "Statistical Abstract of the United States." https://www.bls.gov/emp/tables/civilian-labor-force-participation-rate.htm.

Wheeler, Thomas. 2018. *Who Makes the Rules in a New Gilded Age?* Washington, DC: Brookings Institution.

Williamson, Jeffrey G., and Peter H. Lindert. 1980. *American Inequality: A Macroeconomic History.* New York: Academic Press.

World Inequality Database. n.d. https://wid.world.

Wright, Gavin. 2006. *Slavery and American Economic Development.* Baton Rouge: Louisiana State University Press.

Wright, Gavin. 2013. *Sharing the Prize: The Economics of the Civil Rights Movement in the American South.* Cambridge, MA: Belknap Press of Harvard University Press.

Wright, Gavin. 2016. "Review of Unequal Gains: American Growth and Inequality since 1700." *Business History Review* 90 (4): 774–77.

Yellen, Janet L. 2016. "Perspectives on Inequality and Opportunity from the Survey of Consumer Finances." *Russell Sage Foundation Journal of the Social Sciences* 2 (2): 44–59.

SECTION I

Economic Inequality

Immigration

Over the last half century, the level of income inequality in the United States has consistently risen (U.S. Census Bureau 2019). Although there have been a number of causes cited, a key question is to what extent immigration has played a role in this increased disparity. Further, inequality can be measured in terms of employment effects as well—that is, employment and unemployment. Although the level of income itself is important, fiscal effects—the amount of income families have after taxes—is a better measure of the level of income at their disposal. Fiscal effects reflect the extent to which immigrants require government services, as well as the taxes they pay. In other words, do immigrants contribute more than they consume in terms of social welfare and other services (such as paying for roads and law enforcement)? Immigration may either increase or lighten the burden of taxes paid by the native born and, depending on the degree of progressivity, increase or decrease after-tax income equality. Lastly, immigrants' entrance into certain jobs will lower labor costs, which may in turn lower the prices consumers pay for these products or services. If higher-income individuals tend to purchase certain goods and services that are produced by firms with a larger share of immigrant labor, then the prices of these goods will fall disproportionately for this group.

IMMIGRATION TO THE UNITED STATES

Although the United States is viewed as having historically open immigration, this was not the case through much of the twentieth century. Legislation passed in the 1920s shut the relatively open door that had existed prior to that time. The immigration restrictions passed in the 1920s limited the annual influx to 150,000 immigrants. It also established preferences for immigrants from primarily Western and Northern European nations through a quota system. All of this changed with the passage of the Immigration and Nationality Act of 1965. The Act, which still provides the basic framework for the nation's immigration policy in the early twenty-first century, made two major changes. First, it dramatically increased the number of persons allowed to enter the country each year. In recent years, the

Table 1   U.S. Native-Born and Immigrant Differences in Education

Level of Education	Native Born (%)	Immigrants (%)
Dropout	11	32
High School Graduate	30	22
Some College	31	19
BA/BS or more	29	28

Source: Ashenfelter et al. (2020).

number of permanent immigrants allowed into the United States has been one million or more annually. Currently the United States is the home to more immigrants—forty-five million—than any other nation. That total includes roughly eleven million undocumented immigrants. As a share of the total population, however, the United States' percentage of immigrants is more middle of the pack among nations. One of the most important facts to consider is that immigrants make up almost 14 percent of the U.S. population in 2020, compared to approximately 5 percent fifty years ago.

The second key aspect of the Immigration and Nationality Act of 1965 is the change in the criteria for the admission of immigrants. Two-thirds of immigrants are admitted for reasons of family reunification rather than refugee status, education and skill qualifications, diversity, or other reasons. As a result, the increase in the immigrant population reflects the characteristics of the past immigration population. To the extent that immigrants compete with the native-born population, these characteristics will show us which groups are more affected by immigration and the resulting impact on inequality. An important difference between immigrants and the native-born population is the level of education.

Although college graduates make up just under 30 percent of both groups, the key difference is the share of high school dropouts. Almost one-third of the immigrant population lack a high school diploma, a rate almost three times that of the native-born population. To the extent that less-educated native and immigrant workers are competing for the same jobs, the result might be a decrease in income for those at the socioeconomic bottom. Such trends have been identified as potential contributors to income inequality in the United States as a whole.

Certainly, correlation does not prove causation, but in the minds of some, the increase in the share of the population born abroad over the last several decades and the large share of immigrants who lack a high school diploma may be seen as causes of the increase in inequality. The studies presented here, however, show the impact of immigration to be rather small.

IMMIGRATION AND INCOME INEQUALITY

Considerable research has been undertaken to assess the effects of immigration on the earnings of other members of the labor force. Although some of the earliest studies compared the earnings of workers in different areas of the nation by controlling for the share of the workforce that were immigrants, this approach had limitations. One could imagine a wave of immigrants settling in one city and depressing the wage rates there due to an increased competition for jobs. The limitation of this approach is that it would cause some workers in this city to migrate to other areas, putting downward pressure on wages there and reducing or eliminating the difference between cities entirely.

It is possible to examine the effect of immigrants at a national level. George Borjas (2013) divided the workforce of the nation into groups based on their education and experience. The reasoning was that immigrants of a certain level of education and experience would be competing with others of similar levels. He found that if immigrants increased the total number of workers in a category by 10 percent, the earnings of the group would decline by 3.7 percent. As table 1 shows, immigrants are more likely to be high school dropouts, and so the groups most impacted by their entrance into the labor force would be high school dropouts already in the labor force. Since there is a direct relation between education and income, immigration depresses the wages of less-educated, lower-income workers, and the resulting decline of earnings of those at the bottom of the earnings distribution widens the gap between high- and low-income individuals.

Given the general inability of economists to conduct experiments that examine the impact of specific types of immigration, different studies using different methods and data sets will find different results. Gianmarco Ottaviano and Giovanni Peri (2012) used a somewhat different method from Borjas and allowed for the substitution of some types of workers for others. They found a more modest effect, with the impact of immigration reducing the wages of native-born workers with no high school diploma. They estimated that over the period from 1990 to 2006, the total negative impact of immigration on the wages of this group was negligible, in the neighborhood of only 1 percent. A group that was, in fact, affected to a larger extent was previous immigrants; their wages were estimated to be almost 7 percent less than they would have been had the newer immigrants not arrived. Interestingly, the study found a 0.6-percent overall positive impact on native-born workers.

Francine Blau and Lawrence Kahn (2015) looked at the increase in wage inequality for both men and women. They found that the increase in immigration only explained 6 percent of the increase in wage inequality for men and 3 percent for women. In general, the research seems to indicate that the impact of immigration on wages is rather modest, with the negative effects being greater for native-born high school dropouts and previous immigrants with low levels of education (Card 2005, 2009).

EMPLOYMENT EFFECTS

Although the consensus is that the magnitude of the effect of immigrants on the earnings of others is small, an increase in the number of immigrants raises the supply of labor, which could conceivably reduce the demand for workers already in the United States—and thus reduce the wages and benefits that those workers can secure. To the extent that there is an impact of greater labor competition from immigration, the effect may also be seen in terms of employment. One 2010 study analyzed the extent to which immigration affected employment levels of men in the United States. A 10-percent, immigrant-induced increase in the number of workers of a specific education and experience skill group reduced the employment of Black men by almost 6 percentage points. The effect for white men was on the order of 2 percent. As Blacks tend to have lower incomes than whites to begin with, this immigration effect could further exacerbate income inequality. Further, the same 10-percent increase in the size of the labor force due to immigration was found to raise the institutionalization rate of Blacks (i.e., the share of the population residing in jail, prison, or a mental hospital) by 1.3 percent. Prison incarceration hampers future employment, and other types of institutionalization limit work experience and future earnings as well. The negative effect on the level of institutionalization on earnings was much smaller for white men (Borjas, Grogger, and Hanson 2010).

Some observers believe that higher levels of immigration may contribute to increased income inequality in another respect as well. As discussed above, immigrants (whether documented or undocumented) are more likely than nonimmigrants to lack a high school education. Although this can be a barrier to employment in many fields, it is possible for those lacking formal education to provide childcare and housekeeping services. To the extent that this lowers the cost of these services, this might enable women, who traditionally provide more of these services in the home, to enter the labor force. Such an arrangement will make sense for women who have the ability to garner greater earnings. The immigration of lower-skilled workers facilitates the ability of other women to join the labor force. If these women have more educated spouses, the result is a large increase in the income of higher-income couples. Patricia Cortés and José Tessada (2011) found that in communities with more low-skilled immigrant women, other women tended to work a bit more each week. The effect was especially strong for highly skilled nonimmigrant women, resulting in higher-income families increasing their incomes even more and widening the gap in incomes between higher-income families and others.

FISCAL EFFECTS

Immigrants, whether documented or undocumented, pay into the tax system. At the federal level, income and social security taxes will likely be taken out of their paycheck. Further, taxes on goods, ranging from federal excise taxes on gasoline to state sales taxes, are paid by all who purchase taxed items, and property taxes are paid by property-owning immigrants and native-born Americans alike. Just like native-born Americans, immigrants also use government services. *Fiscal effects*, then, is the term used to describe the net financial impact of immigration on governmental budgets. Fiscal effects depend on the number and demographic characteristics of immigrants in the population, the government services they receive, and the taxes they pay. These impacts can vary significantly from state to state. Two landmark studies were conducted in the late 1990s for California (Clune

1997) and New Jersey (Garvey and Espinshade 1996), states with large immigrant populations. California is not only the most populous state but also the one with the most immigrants. About one-quarter of the households in California were headed by a person born in another country in the late 1990s. These households tended to be younger, with an average age of the head of the household almost five and a half years younger than the native-born headed households. The immigrant households had about 25 percent lower income and were more than twice as likely to receive welfare.

While the benefits from some federal programs such as national defense are impossible to allocate to individuals or households, enrollees in social welfare programs can be identified. Although immigrants receive benefits from programs targeted at the elderly, such as Social Security and Medicare, immigrant house-holds in California are a third less likely to have members over the age of sixty-five; thus they draw on these programs to a lesser extent than the rest of the population. Given their lower average income, however, they are more likely to draw on income-dependent programs such as Medicaid, welfare, Supplemental Security Income, and others. Given the taxes they pay, and adjusting for the fact that national defense expenditures would have to be made even if they weren't in the United States, in the mid-1990s California immigrant-headed families actu-ally paid in a few dollars more in taxes than they received in federal benefits. In just examining fiscal effect at the federal level, Californians enjoyed a net benefit of four dollars per household from immigration, that is, a very small positive impact and very little impact on inequality (Smith and Edmonston 1997).

The story was different, however, for state and local expenditures during this period. Immigrant-headed households also received more financial assistance for higher education as well as other expenditures from state and local sources. The final result was that California immigrant-headed households received on average $3,463 more in benefits than they paid in taxes at the state and local level (Smith and Edmonston 1997.). This state of affairs endured into the 2010s, according to one 2017 study that found foreign-born households in California received more than twice the level of state and local expenditures for kindergarten through twelfth-grade education compared with native-born households. The higher edu-cation expenditures were due to immigrant-headed households having more than twice as many children per household compared to others (National Academies of Sciences, Engineering, and Medicine 2017).

In New Jersey, a similar analysis (Garvey and Espinshade 1996) found the net benefits to immigrants about a third as great as in California. The lower net ben-efit in New Jersey was due to the immigrant population being older, with incomes closer to the native-born population, and having fewer children per household than California immigrants did. The state and local net tax burden on native-born headed households averaged over $1,100 in California and $229 in New Jersey. Given that the nation as a whole has a level of immigration closer to New Jersey than California, the net effect nationally was on the order of $200 for each nonim-migrant household. The overall impact on inequality, though, cannot be deter-mined. Given that net benefits are being received by lower-income immigrants, this would reduce inequality. The degree of progressivity of state and local taxes raised to pay for these benefits, which varies across states and within the localities within each state, would determine the effect on inequality.

Over time, though, the effects of immigration might be different. In general, the difference between the income and educational levels of immigrants and those of the native-born population tends to dissipate with successive generations. By the third generation, these descendants of immigrants have levels of income and education similar to the rest of the population (Smith 2018). As a result, immigrants and their descendants are net contributors to federal and state and local coffers. If we figure in future generations, the net present value of admitting an immigrant to the United States is on the order of $80,000. In summary, if we only view current immigrants, there is a negative impact on native-born families at the state and local level but an overall positive effect if we view successive generations over all levels of government. The impact on inequality depends on the degree of progressivity of the tax system, something that varies from state to state and across localities.

PRICE EFFECTS

Immigrants are about three times as likely as the native-born population to lack a high school diploma (Ashenfelter et al. 2020). One 2008 study found that metropolitan areas that had a large number of these less-skilled immigrants had lower prices for the goods and services that were produced by these workers. For example, it was found that between 25 and 30 percent of the workforce in landscaping and in private household services were lower-skilled immigrants. Increases in lower-skilled immigrants did, in fact, reduce the prices of these services. The number of low-skilled immigrants affected the prices of these services, but the proportion of the labor force that was low skilled, native born did not have an effect, indicating that it is not the number of low-skilled workers but rather only the share of low-skilled immigrants in the area that have this impact (Cortés 2008).

The immigration of low-skilled workers that occurred in the last two decades of the twentieth century caused the purchasing power of high-skilled workers, who purchased the goods and services produced by the lower-skilled immigrants, to increase by a third of 1 percent (Cortés 2008.). Lower-skilled immigrants did not impact the wages of these higher-skilled native-born workers but lowered the cost of the goods they purchased. Lower-skilled, native-born workers benefited less from the lower prices of the immigrants, since they purchased less of goods such as landscaping and housekeeping services. To the extent that there were more workers competing for the jobs they were qualified for, the purchasing power of the typical native-born high school dropout fell by up to 1 percent. The effect was even more profound for low-skilled Hispanics, whose purchasing power fell by 4 percent due to low-skilled immigration (Cortés 2008). Increases to the purchasing power of high-skilled and hence higher-income workers and lower effective incomes for the less-skilled and lower-income parts of the population increase the degree of income inequality but still not to an extent to have a major impact.

An influx of immigrants into a community can also affect the price of housing. As foreign-born workers average about 17 percent less income than their native-born counterparts and will be able to spend less on housing, this increases the demand for lower-cost apartments and houses. One 2007 survey found that increases in the number of immigrants in a community raised the rental cost of apartments. To the extent that the immigrants have lower incomes, this will boost the cost of less expensive housing and disproportionately affect lower-income native-born households, thus increasing income inequality (Saiz 2007).

CONCLUSION

The last several decades have seen an increase in the degree of income inequality in the United States. In terms of incomes and earnings, the most frequently discussed measurements of inequality, the consensus is that the impact of immigration has been a small contributor. One 2009 study calculated that approximately only 5 percent of the increase in income inequality can be attributed to immigration (Card 2009). In terms of employment, one 2013 study found the overall effect of immigration on the rest of the population was relatively small for white workers but had a more substantial effect on Blacks. This was due to a higher share of high school dropouts in both the Black and immigrant populations, allowing for some substitution of their labor (Borjas 2013). The fiscal impact of immigration on the federal government was negligible in the short run but substantial and negative on state and local government. When the descendants of immigrants were added in, there was a substantial positive impact on the federal government's purse and only a small negative one for state and local governments. The change in the price of products due to immigration tended to favor upper-income consumers, as they consumed more of the services provided by immigrants.

Immigration has many positive aspects for the United States. The new arrivals bring talent, vitality, and diversity to the country, and significant numbers of immigrants bring high levels of education and valued skill sets with them. The policy of making family reunification the primary criterion for entry into the United States, however, means that immigrants will tend to be similar in terms of education and skills to their relatives already in the United States. The overall result is an influx of lower-skilled workers. Changing the mix to favor more highly skilled immigrants might decrease inequality but at a cost of keeping more families apart. Overall, however, one should bear in mind the relatively small overall impact of immigration on the various measures of inequality.

Robert J. Gitter

Further Reading

Ashenfelter, O., D. L. McFadden, A. Payne, J. Potts, R. Gregory, and W. E. Martinet. 2020. "Roundtable Discussion on Immigration." *Contemporary Economic Policy* 38 (1): 7–29.

Blau, F. D., and L. M. Kahn. 2015. "Immigration and the Distribution of Incomes." In *Handbook of the Economics of International Migration*, edited by B. R. Chiswick and P. Miller, 794–844. Oxford, United Kingdom: North Holland.

Borjas, G. 2013. "Immigration and the American Worker: A Review of the Academic Literature." Washington, DC: Center for Immigration Studies.

Borjas, G. J., J. Grogger, and G. H. Hanson. 2010. "Immigration and the Economic Status of African-American Men." *Economica* 77 (306): 255–82.

Card, D. 2005. "Is the New Immigration Really So Bad?" *Economic Journal* 115:F300–23.

Card, D. 2009. "Immigration and Inequality." *American Economic Review* 99 (2): 1–21.

Clune, M. 1997. *The Fiscal Impacts of Immigrants: A California Case Study.* Berkeley: Department of Demography, University of California.

Cortés, P. 2008, "The Effect of Low-Skilled Immigration on U.S. Prices: Evidence from CPI Data." *Journal of Political Economy* 116 (3): 381–422.

Cortés, P., and J. Tessada. 2011. "Low-Skilled Immigration and the Labor Supply of Highly Skilled Women." *American Economic Journal: Applied Economics* 3 (3): 88–123.

Garvey, D., and T. Espenshade. 1996. *Fiscal Impacts of New Jersey's Immigrant and Native Households on State and Local Governments: A New Approach and New Estimate.* Princeton, NJ: Office of Population Research, Princeton University.

Migration Policy Institute. 2019. *Frequently Requested Statistics on Immigrants and Immigration in the United States.* https://www.migrationpolicy.org/article/frequently-requested-statistics-immigrants-and-immigration-united-states.

National Academies of Sciences, Engineering, and Medicine. 2017. *The Economic and Fiscal Consequences of Immigration.* Washington, DC: National Academic Press.

Ottaviano, G. I. P., and G. Peri. 2012. "Rethinking the Effect of Immigration on Wages." *Journal of the European Economic Association* 10 (1): 152–97.

Pikkety, T., and E. Saez. 2007. "How Progressive Is the U.S. Federal Tax System? A Historical and International Perspective." *Journal of Economic Perspectives* 21 (1): 3–24.

Saiz, A. 2007. "Immigration and Housing Rents in American Cities." *Journal of Urban Economics* 6 (2): 345–71.

Smith, J. P. 2018. "Taxpayer Effects of Immigration." IZA World of Labor. https://wol.iza.org/articles/taxpayer-effects-of-immigration/long.

Smith, J. P., and B. Edmonston. 1997. *The New Americans: Economic, Demographic, and Fiscal Consequences of Immigration.* Washington, DC: National Academy Press.

U.S. Bureau of Labor Statistics. 2017. *Foreign-Born Workers Made 83.1 Percent of the Earnings of Their Native-Born Counterparts in 2016.* https://www.bls.gov/opub/ted/2017/foreign-born-workers-made-83-point-1-percent-of-the-earnings-of-their-native-born-counterparts-in-2016.htm.

U.S. Census Bureau. 2019. "Table A-4." *Income and Poverty in the United States: 2018.* https://www.census.gov/data/tables/2019/demo/income-poverty/p60-266.html.

Intergenerational Mobility

In 1831, Alexis de Tocqueville, a French sociologist, traveled to the United States on an official mission. The French government had asked him to study the prison system in the new country and report his findings to French authorities. He visited several prisons and interviewed prisoners to learn about the conditions under which they lived. But de Tocqueville's interests in the new country and the American "experiment" led him to learn more about American culture. He was especially attracted to the young nation's emphasis on "equality" and "individualism," which was for him very different from what he found in European society. He returned to France in 1832, wrote his prison report, and then proceeded to write a book about all that he learned about the "new society." His impressions were published in 1835 as *Democracy in America*, one of the most famous treatises ever written on America and its peoples, ideals, and temperament.

Alexis de Tocqueville was both impressed and troubled by what he had learned about the emphasis on equality and individualism. He wrote at length about the possible downside of what was for him very different values. How would it be possible to have the social cohesion that is necessary for all societies while extolling these new virtues? It must be remembered that de Tocqueville was part of a powerful European nation and a traditional society. With respect to mobility, it was a society where "the apple does not fall far from the tree." If one was born into a family with a small farm, it was expected that one would work on that farm and, if lucky, become the new farm owner when the parents passed on. If one was not born into a family with a farm, one would likely become a worker on the farm or in the household of the owner of a larger farm. De Tocqueville himself was born into an aristocratic family and enjoyed the opportunities to learn and grow as befitting a young person with his standing. Yet despite his qualms about the social and political sustainability of the emphasis on individualism in the new society of America, he was clearly writing about what would soon become known as the American dream.

ECONOMIC MOBILITY AND THE AMERICAN DREAM

There have been many descriptions of the American dream, and they most often describe "end states" or destinations that people would like to have at some point in their life. The specific things described in these end states change with time; for example, many of today's definitions might include graduating from college without any debt.

Specifics aside, probably the best definitions would stress "equality of opportunity" or the chance that those who are willing to work, no matter who they are, have the chance to become whatever they hope to become.

The concept of *opportunity* is a good place to start in understanding the American dream. But opportunity is a complex condition, as it is a combination of individual qualities or strengths such as talent or ability and the availability of pathways to move up, such as up the occupational structure. Moreover, to be "American dreamers," there had to be the existence of end states that defined the dream, such as a marriage mate or a home that one can afford or a job in a larger occupational structure. Those who studied the American dream, whether policy makers, politicians, or academics, would soon begin to unravel the meaning of "equality of opportunity" and to identify the barriers and pathways to opportunity.

Academic sociologists were among the first professional groups that embraced the idea that the United States was the "land of opportunity." The earliest scholarly writing on the subject focused on the dominant values and norms in a society that either fostered or hindered ambition to become something different from what was observed in the preceding generation. This literature focused on the so-called normative structure of different societies, usually those that were considered to be open and those considered to be more closed or caste societies. The favorite foci for research were the traditional European societies (Thrupp 1948; Barber 1955) and the caste-like Far Eastern countries such as India (Davis 1949). Other books examined a combination of features of both so-called open and closed societies (Cox 1948).

It must be remembered that this research was done at a time before data-processing machines and desktop computers were available, and as a result, there were few research articles based on original data. Some data-based research papers drew on U.S. Census data and documented the literacy rate from 1870 to 1950, or the number of persons attending public schools, or the number of high school and college graduates. Such data were evidence that the U.S. population was acquiring the skills and educational credentials that would lead to greater occupational achievement. Most data-based research using original data consisted of what we might call "destination studies" of social mobility. What this means is that a researcher would select an occupation of high prestige, such as the 1955 study by W. Lloyd Warner and James C. Abegglen of the educational backgrounds of business leaders (see also Glick 1954; Taussig and Joslyn 1932; Mills 1956). Despite the lack of precise measurement of the classification of occupations, the number of years of schooling completed was closely related to the prestige standing of the occupation.

Although not by plan, these early studies were documenting the important role of education in the process of mobility. These studies revealed that sons who advanced beyond their parents' generation's occupational attainments did so largely because of their educational attainments, both years of education completed and quality of colleges attended (Haveman and West 1952).

The link between occupational attainments and educational attainments became so prominent that the English sociologist Michael Young wrote a book in 1958 with the title *The Rise of Meritocracy: An Essay on Education and Inequality*, in which the idea of a meritocracy linked talent and motivation among those who made it to the top—and also implied that those on the bottom got what they deserved because they lacked the necessary talent and motivation.

Each of these studies was confronting the question, How open is the American class structure? Is it becoming more or less difficult for a young man (there were no women in these studies) to rise in social standing compared with his parents? Collection of data at two or more time periods permitted the researcher to state that it was becoming more or less difficult to achieve mobility. Other researchers argued that the openness of society was better measured by the "distance" that one traveled into a new occupational category, a phenomenon known as *intraoccupational mobility* (Perrucci 1961).

Still missing in these studies of mobility was the time-comparative analysis across a wide range of occupations at two points in time. Enter Natalie Rogoff and her study of trends in occupational mobility in a single city: Indianapolis, Indiana. Her research in the early 1950s also was innovative for the use of a statistical technique that took into account changes in the occupational structure.

Rogoff's main findings indicated that occupational inheritance was the dominant pattern. Moreover, when mobility did occur, it was modest, at least between adjacent occupational categories. However, expansion in the upper occupational categories in 1940 resulted in more upward mobility. Thus she concluded that Indianapolis had a more open occupational structure in 1940 than in 1910.

The Rogoff research occurred during the beginning of the "big science" era, meaning that research was transitioning from a practitioner working in a small lab with limited funds, to "big science" that involved research teams, extensive funding, and large-scale research hardware (De Solla Price 1963).

The first large-scale intergenerational mobility research project was conducted in the 1960s by Peter Blau and Otis Dudley. This project was funded by two research grants from the National Science Foundation and one from the National Institutes of Mental Health. Blau and Duncan were able to add a brief questionnaire to the monthly "Current Population Survey" conducted by the U.S. Bureau of the Census to obtain estimates of employment and unemployment. The new survey questionnaire obtained data on the birthplace of the respondent and the parents, and the occupation of the father and the respondent. The basic research question of this project was how social origins affected later achievements, and the research model examined four determinants of a son's occupational achievement: father's occupation, father's education, respondent's education, and respondent's first job. Although all four factors were correlated with occupational achievement, the authors concluded that "education exerts the strongest direct effect on occupational achievements" (Blau and Duncan 1967, 403). Regarding the amount of mobility, they found more upward than downward mobility because of the expansion of the occupational structure. They also found that most mobility was relatively modest, into adjacent occupational categories.

The Blau and Duncan research was replicated and extended with various other samples of employed males, with similar results (Featherman and Hauser [1952] 1978; Kerbo 2011). Yet other scholars continued to examine questions related to intergenerational mobility (Beller and Hout 2006; Mitnik, Cumberworth, and Grusky 2016). Emily Beller and Michael Hout reported in 2006 that occupational mobility increased in the 1970s compared to the period between the 1940s and 1970s but that it had declined to past levels by the 1980s and 1990s. Another study focused more on income inequality and concluded that "the incomes of parents and their adult children have become more similar" (Mitnik, Cumberworth, and Grusky 2016, 173). Both these studies reported that the changes were modest, with Beller and Hout attributing the increase in class reproduction to what they called the "top-income hypothesis," namely, the division between the professional-managerial class and all other classes.

INTERGENERATIONAL MOBILITY AMONG NONWHITES AND WOMEN

What do we know about intergenerational mobility and the pursuit of the American dream for nonwhites and women? The first large-scale study of inter-generational mobility, by Blau and Duncan (1967) discussed above, compared one minority group of men (no women in this study), African Americans, to white men. They found that whereas white men's social origins (father's education and occupation) affected their own occupation and income only indirectly, by affect-ing the amount of education, Black men's social origins affected their own success directly. Moreover, comparisons of adult Black men's income with that of white men's income found lower incomes for Black men over the decades to the present day (Hogan and Perrucci 2014; Bloome, Dyer, and Zhou 2018). Research that included men in other minority groups, such as Hispanics, often focused on the poverty in which they grew up and the lack of financial assistance from parents they received (Keister and Borelli 2014; Mattingly and Pedroza 2015). Hispanic men, moreover, had not experienced any progress in wages since the civil rights movement in contrast to several other minority groups of men—namely, African Americans, American Indians, Chinese Americans, and Japanese Americans (Sakamoto, Wu, and Tzeg 2000).

As indicated earlier, the early research on intergenerational mobility did not focus on women's opportunities compared with those of men. An important exception was Earl Wysong and David W. Wright's 2009 review of the literature of the first decade of the 2000s. Although they were only able to identify six rele-vant studies, they conducted original research of their own comparing women's intergenerational mobility to men's. One finding comparable to models for men was the importance of education. Wysong and Wright suggested that research into women's intergenerational mobility should include their mothers' socioeconomic background as well as that of their fathers.

In contrast to racial and ethnic minorities, women as a group do not come from a disadvantaged social class background. Therefore, when high prestige universities started admitting women in the 1970s, women from well-to-do backgrounds (unlike the less privileged racial and ethnic minorities discussed above) took advantage, and recently they closed the gender gap in educational attainment in general. However, most occupational positions at the top are still held by men. The occupational segregation of women into lower-paying jobs in lower-paid industries explains most of the current male-to-female wage gap. Other factors pertaining particularly to women include interrupted careers and employer discrimination due to marriage and childbearing (Hogan and Perrucci 2014). Fundamentalist religious commitments associated with traditional gender roles also lower women's income attainment by limiting their educational attainment and forcing their withdrawal from the labor market (Keister 2011; Sherkat 2005). Also important are lower rates of unionization for women workers (England, Christopher, and Reid 1999). In addition to having lower incomes, women typically have less wealth than men (Chang 2010, 2015). Their lower wealth is due not only to lower lifetime earnings but also to their greater tendency to have custody of and more financial responsibility for children. In addition, they have historically enjoyed less access to government benefits, tax breaks, and fringe benefits that facilitate asset accumulation (Chang 2010).

IS THERE AN ALTERNATIVE?

Despite the obvious advantages of having time-comparative data on father-son occupational attainment of the sort used by researchers, there is another way to answer the question, Is the United States still the land of opportunity? That approach is to examine the way in which blue-collar workers work and live, and to consider their chances, or the chances of their children, to cross over into the white-collar world. This alternative was considered in a 2008 book, *The New Class Society; Goodbye American Dream?* (Perrucci and Wysong 2008). In contrast to relying on intergenerational occupational mobility tables, the focus was on the existence and stability of resources for most middle-income Americans (who are often considered to be "middle class") and the belief that these resources are "secure." What are these resources? The following were considered: job stability, income growth, health insurance, pensions, and opportunities for job growth and continuing education. Thus the emphasis shifted from movement up and down the occupational ladder, such as moving from a skilled to a clerical and sales position (which takes one from a blue-collar occupation to a white-collar occupation), to the *resources* that may result in an improvement in one's life or that may be considered indicative of upward mobility.

Regarding income trends for full-time, full-year workers from 1970 to 2010, we found that income growth was not stable across this time period. In fact, incomes trended upward between 1947 and 1973 but then declined between 1973 and 2000 (Aaronson and Mazumder 2008). More importantly, worker productivity and wages were no longer connected in this time period. Worker productivity and wages grew together in the period from 1960 to 1973, but from 1973 to 2010, the real wages of workers declined. The decline occurred during a time when there was greater overseas investment by corporations and a reduction in job growth in the United States (Perrucci and Perrucci 2009, 2018).

In addition to declining income for full-time, full-year workers, there also was an erosion of job security. Specifically, "job stability as measured by the percentage of workers holding jobs long-term for more than ten years declined for all workers in the 1973–2006 period" (Perrucci and Wysong 2008, 90).

A third resource considered is health insurance. Employer-provided health-care plans declined between 1979 and 2010. This meant an increase in worker health-care costs that further eroded family income.

Finally, worker pensions have been essential for many Americans, given the low lifetime returns from government-based Social Security. In recent decades, however, such pension programs have diminished in both size and scale. For workers employed in medium and large private sector firms, those with defined-benefit pensions declined from 84 percent in 1980 to 50 percent in 1997 (Perrucci and Wysong 2008, 92). Moreover, there had been a shift from defined-benefit plans to defined-contribution plans. These changes represented erosion in benefits and increased costs for employees.

Thus the resources available to employees in the form of stable jobs, income, health benefits, and retirement benefits have been neither growing nor secure. Added to this decline in resources is the decline in opportunities to enter the labor force in "good-paying jobs." This decline is linked to the fact that the economy has created more low-wage jobs than jobs that were close to "middle class" compensation and benefit levels. The Bureau of Labor Statistics predicts that 11 of the 30 fastest growing jobs over the period 2019–2020 would require a high school education or less (U.S. Bureau of Labor Statistics 2019). Turning now to the supply-side of new employees, especially those college graduates who may be eligible for jobs with better incomes and benefits, the news is not good. Much of the emphasis on "going to college" in the mainstream media has been on the rising costs of doing so and declining job opportunities afterward. There have been a growing number of stories about the high cost of college attendance, and many have asked the question, Is college worth it? Much has been written about the "value" of the traditional liberal arts degree, encouraging students to think about getting degrees in majors with greater job potential, such as elementary school teaching and nursing; two-year associate degrees; and the so-called STEM majors of science, technology, engineering, and math. All of the above trends suggest that many families with sons and daughters in college will be facing declining opportunities for upward mobility.

The present state of the resources necessary to attain and maintain a middle-class life is troubling, with those resources stagnating and becoming increasingly unreliable. This suggests that the vision of the United States as the "land of opportunity" is no longer producing the same positive results that it once did.

DARK CLOUDS AHEAD FOR INTERGENERATIONAL MOBILITY?

It should be apparent from this review of research on intergenerational upward mobility that the main pathway to mobility was through education, especially higher education. There are an increasing number of signs that this pathway may not be as open as it once was, however. What are these signs? In recent years the mainstream media have been providing increasing attention to the rising costs of higher education and asking questions about the "value" of a liberal arts education. The value question is usually raised in the context of studies about postcollege employment opportunities and postcollege earnings. And who would have ever guessed that when, in 1952, scholars Ernest Haveman and Patricia Salter West discussed the economic gains flowing to graduates of Princeton University versus Podunk College, it would become general knowledge to all prospective college goers? Many cannot afford an annual cost of $50,000—for tuition only, not room or board—at Harvard or Northwestern or Stanford. Even if the postcollege payoff is better than what follows from Podunk or even a "good" state university, how many students or families can meet that price without taking on major student debt? The question of affordability of college is real, and it remains to be seen if it produces a decline in the number of high school graduates who seek admission to Princeton or Podunk. It may result in an expansion of community colleges, where the costs may be more manageable and where students can live at home while pursuing a degree.

Robert Perrucci and Carolyn Cummings Perrucci

Further Reading

Aaronson, Daniel, and Bhashkar Mazumder. 2008. "Intergenerational Economic Mobility in the United States, 1940 to 2000." *Journal of Human Resources* 43 (1): 139–72.

Baltzell, E. Digby, Jr. 1953. "The Elite and the Upper Class in Metropolitan America: A Study of Stratification in Philadelphia." PhD diss., Columbia University.

Barber, Elinor G. 1955. *The Bourgeoisie in 18th Century France.* Princeton, NJ: Princeton University Press.

Beals, Ralph L. 1953. "Social Stratification in Latin America." *American Journal of Sociology* 58:327–39.

Beller, Emily, and Michael Hout. 2006. "Intergenerational Social Mobility: The United States in Comparative Perspective." *Future of Children* 16 (2): 19–36.

Blau, Peter, and Otis Dudley Duncan. 1967. *The American Occupational Structure.* New York: John Wiley.

Bloome, Deirdre, Shawna Dyer, and Xiang Zhou. 2018. "Educational Inequality, Educational Expansion, and Intergenerational Income Persistence in the United States." *American Sociological Review* 83 (December): 1215–53.

Chang, Mariko Lin. 2010. *Short Changed: Why Women Have Less Wealth and What Can Be Done about It?* New York: Oxford University Press.

Chang, Mariko Lin. 2015. "Women and Wealth: Insights for Grantmakers." Asset Funders Network. http://www.mariko-chang.com/AFN_Women_and_Wealth_Brief_2015 .pdf (site discontinued).

Cox, Oliver C. 1948. *Caste, Class and Race: A Study in Social Dynamics.* New York: Doubleday.

Davis, Kingsley. 1949. *Human Society, New York:* Macmillan.

De Solla Price, Derek. 1963. *Little Science, Big Science.* New York: Columbia University Press.

England, Paula, Karen Christopher, and Lori L. Reid. 1999. "Gender, Race, Ethnicity and Wages." In *Latinas and African American Women at Work: Race, Gender and Economic Inequality*, edited by Ivy Browne, 139–82. New York: Russell Sage.

Featherman, David, and Robert Hauser. (1952) 1978. *Opportunity and Change.* New York: Academic Press.

Glick, Paul C. 1954. "Educational Attainment and Occupational Attainment." In *Transactions of the Second World Congress of Sociology*, 183–93. London: International Sociological Association.

Haveman, Ernest, and Patricia Salter West. 1952. *They Went to College.* New York: Harcourt, Brace.

Hogan, Richard, and Carolyn C. Perrucci. 2014. "Who Gets the Daddy Bonus and Who Pays the Cost?" *International Journal of Contemporary Sociology* 51:117–44.

Keister, Lisa A. 2011. *Faith and Money: How Religion Contributes to Wealth and Poverty.* New York: Cambridge University Press.

Keister, Lisa A., and E. Paige Borelli. 2014. "Religion and Wealth Mobility: The Case of American Latinos." In *Religion's Role in Stratification*, edited by Lisa A. Keister and Darren E. Sherkat, 119–45. New York: Cambridge University Press.

Kerbo, Harold R. 2011. *Social Stratification and Inequality, 8th Edition.* New York: McGraw Hill.

King, Charles E. 1953. "The Process of Social Stratification among an Urban Minority Population." *Social Forces* 31:352–55.

Lynd, Robert S., and Helen M. Lynd. 1937. *Middletown in Transition.* New York: Harcourt, Brace.

Mattingly, Marybeth, and Juan M. Pedroza. 2015. "Why Isn't the Hispanic Poverty Rate Rising?" In *Pathways: A Magazine on Poverty, Inequality, and Social Policy*, edited by the Stanford Center on Poverty and Inequality, 8–12. Stanford, CA: Stanford University.

McNamee, Stephen J. 2018. *The Meritocracy Myth.* Lanham, MD: Rowman & Littlefield.

Mills, C. Wright. 1956. *The Power Elite.* New York: Oxford University Press.

Mitnik, Pablo A., Erin Cumberworth, and David B. Grusky. 2016. "Social Mobility in a High Inequality Regime." *ANNALS, AAPSS* (January): 140–84.

Myrdal, Gunnar. 1944. *An American Dilemma: The Negro Problem and Modern Democracy.* New York: Harper and Row.

Perrucci, Carolyn Cummings. 1967. "Social Origins, Mobility Patterns and Fertility." *American Sociological Review* 32 (August): 615–25.

Perrucci, Carolyn Cummings. 1968. "Mobility, Marriage and Child-Spacing among College Graduates." *Journal of Marriage and the Family* (May): 273–82.

Perrucci, Carolyn Cummings. 1970. "Minority Status and the Pursuit of Professional Careers: Women in Science and Engineering." *Social Forces* (December): 245–59.

Perrucci, Robert. 1961. "The Significance of Intra-Occupational Mobility." *American Sociological Review* 26:874–83.

Perrucci, Robert, and Carolyn Cummings Perrucci. 2009. *America at Risk: The Crisis of Hope, Trust, and Caring.* Lanham, MD: Rowman & Littlefield, 2009.

Perrucci, Robert, and Carolyn C. Perrucci. 2018. "New Economy." In *Wiley Blackwell Encyclopedia of Sociology,* 2nd edition, edited by George Ritzer. Oxford, UK: John Wiley and Sons. https//onlinelibrary.wiley.com/doi/pdf/10.1002 /9781405165518.wbeos1133.

Perrucci, Robert, Carolyn C. Perrucci, and Mangala Subramaniam. 2016. "Who Publishes in Leading Sociology Journals?" In *Stress and Distress in Academe*, edited by E. Wright and T. Calhoun, 77–86. Lanham, MD: Rowman & Littlefield.

Perrucci, Robert, Carolyn C. Perrucci, and Mangala Subramaniam. 2019. "Social Closure in Four Sociology Journals, 1960–2010." *Sociological Focus* 52 (3): 171–85.

Perrucci, Robert, and Earl Wysong. 2008. *The New Class Society: Goodbye American Dream?* 3rd edition. Lanham, MD: Rowman & Littlefield.

Rogoff, Natalie. 1951. "Recent Trends in Urban Occupational Mobility." In Reader in Urban Sociology, edited by Paul Hatt and Albert Reiss, 21–8. Glencoe, IL: Free Press.

Rogoff, Natalie. 1953. *Recent Trends in Occupational Mobility.* Glencoe, IL: Free Press.

Sakamoto, Arthur, Huei-Hsia Wu, and Jessie M. Tzeg. 2000. "The Declining Significance of Race among American Men during the Latter Half of the Twentieth Century." *Demography* 37 (February): 41–51.

Sherkat, Darren E. 2005. "Religion and Economic Life." In *International Encyclopedia of Economic Sociology*, edited by Jans Berkert and Milan Zafirovski, 571–74. New York: Routledge.

Sorokin, Pitirim A. 1927. *Social Mobility,* New York: Harper and Row.

Taussig, Frank W., and Carl S. Joselyn. 1932. *American Business Leaders: A Study in Social Origins and Social Stratification*. New York: MacMillan Co.

Thrupp, Sylvia L. 1948. *The Merchant Class of Medieval London, 1300–1500.* Chicago: University of Chicago Press.

U.S. Bureau of Labor Statistics. 2019. Occupational Employment Statistics, May 2019, all data, Tables 1.3 and 5.4, https://www.bls.gov/oes/tables.htm.

Warner, W. Lloyd, and James C. Abegglen. 1955. *Big Business Leaders in America.* New York: Harper and Row.

Warner, W. Lloyd and James O. Low. 1947. *The Social System of the Modern Factory.* New Haven, CT: Yale University Press.

Wysong, Earl, and David W. Wright. 2009. "Socioeconomic Status and Gender: Recent Intergenerational Mobility Patterns in the U.S." *Journal of the Indiana Academy of the Social Sciences* XIII:112–30.

Young, Michael. 1958. *The Rise of the Meritocracy.* New York: Routledge.

Labor Markets

People receive income from a variety of sources: interest from bank accounts and bonds, dividends from common stock, rent from land, profits from the ownership of businesses (assuming things go well), and transfer payments from the government and other people. But most people receive most of their income as a reward for their labor. In recent years approximately 53 percent of gross domestic income (the other side of the coin of gross domestic product) has been compensation of employees, and inequality in labor earnings is significant. Accordingly, understanding income inequality requires careful analysis of inequality in the labor market.

Labor markets function as follows. The payment received by those who sell their labor in the labor market is typically called a *wage*. But *wage* is too narrow a term in the modern world. The term *wage* is generally thought to refer only to a monetary payment, but that is not the full range of benefits that modern workers receive. The compensation package for employees may also include fringe benefits such as health insurance, paid vacations and sick days, and bonuses for individual or company-wide performance. "Fringes" have come to constitute approximately 3 out of 10 dollars of total compensation (they amounted to 31.7 percent of total compensation in 2018) (Bureau of Labor Statistics 2018). Thinking even more broadly, the compensation package can be expanded to include the type of conditions in which employees work (e.g., time spent on feet, private vs. open plan office, and other types of workplace amenities). All these things are distributed unevenly. In what follows, the income of labor should be understood to refer to the entire compensation package.

Compensation received is determined in the marketplace by a bargaining process called *demand and supply*. Employers do not simply dictate what the wage will be. Nor does government, a labor union, or any other single institutional entity.

Employers come to the marketplace and seek to hire labor—employers demand labor. Employers want to pay as little as possible, of course, but recognize that they need to offer enough to entice the type and quality of labor they need. What sets an upper limit on what they will pay is labor's productivity. Paying labor more than it produces is a losing proposition for the employer in the long run. If there is an adequate degree of competition among employers for the available labor, then compensation is likely to get bid up to the level of the productivity of labor.

Workers come to the marketplace seeking jobs. They want to sell their labor—actually *rent* is the better term because workers never surrender the ownership of their labor, just a portion of their day to the employer—for as much as possible, of course, but recognize that they need not settle for anything less than the value of their time in its next best alternative use. Employer A must offer at least $20 per hour if the worker has a $20 per hour offer from employer B or if the worker values schooling or personally caring for children that much.

After all the haggling is done, the compensation of labor determined by demand and supply is jointly equal to the productivity of labor and the value of labor's alternative activities. If the demand for labor (in a certain industry) rises (perhaps because consumer tastes change or an overall expansion of the economy boosts members of that industry), compensation will rise, because employers are forced to compete for the now relatively scarcer supply of labor—labor is in a better bargaining position. The opposite is the case if demand falls. If the supply of labor rises (perhaps because more people seek fulfillment in paid labor, poor economic conditions produce job cuts and other labor market conditions reflecting diminished demand for workers, or the terms of a welfare program changes), compensation will fall, because more workers will be competing against each other for the available jobs—employers are in a better bargaining position. A decrease in the supply of labor will have the opposite effect.

HOW UNEQUAL IS THE LABOR MARKET?

How unequal is the distribution of labor income? In a word, the degree of inequality is substantial. There are several ways to represent this. Rakesh Kochhar and Anthony Cilluffo (2018) analyzed U.S. household income data from the Census Bureau and found that in 2016, the top 10 percent of earners earned nearly 9 times as much as the bottom 10 percent of earners (i.e., $109,578 vs. $12,523). This was up from the approximately 7 times difference seen in 1970 (i.e., $63,512 vs. $9,212).

Another way is to consider an image that can be attributed to the Dutch economist Jan Pen. He was writing about Great Britain back in 1971, but the image still works today. He asked us to imagine a parade with every person in the economy marching. All the people line themselves up by income, from lowest to highest, with the heights of the marchers proportional to their income. Marchers earning the average income will be of average height. Those earning twice the average income will be twice the average height, and so on. The parade is to last exactly one hour. What would we spectators see?

At first, we would see nothing. The lead marchers would be those who made a loss for the year—many of whom are presumably unfortunate small business owners—who would be below ground (or perhaps upside down). Then "above-ground" marchers would appear, but for about five minutes they would be only inches high. These would be people whose work was intermittent and rewarded in very modest terms of remuneration—many of them either elderly or children. Ten minutes into the march, full-time workers would appear, but they would only be of waist-high stature, and this line would continue for a long time.

After thirty minutes, the height of the marchers would only have reached about five feet. It would take until the forty-five-minute marker for the marchers to reach the same height as the spectators. From this point on, heights will start rising but still not very quickly. With six minutes to go, the top 10 percent of the income distribution arrives. At that point the heights start becoming substantial. We observe doctors and lawyers twenty feet tall. Then we start seeing top CEOs, bankers, and financial managers who are fifty-, one hundred-, and five-hundred-feet tall. With a few seconds to go, the superstars of the entertainment world and the most successful entrepreneurs make an appearance, except that they are so tall we might only be able to see their knees clearly. In the context of the contemporary United States, this parade would be similar, but the lows would be lower and the highs higher.

A third way to represent this puts a human face on things. The venerable *Parade* magazine (found in many weekend newspapers) publishes an annual report called "What People Earn." The report includes a random group of the relatively short and medium-sized people in our parade, along with a few of the really tall people. (In 2018, the article spanned two issues of the magazine.) Among the short people appearing in *Parade*'s 2018 report were Laurie Hahn, a forty-five-year-old zoo curator and vet tech who earned $33,545; Fred Lanquette, an eighty-one-year-old Uber driver who earned $25,000; and Cristen Breuer, a thirty-six-year-old dog toy maker who earned $5,000. Among the medium-height people were Cheryl Logan, a thirty-eight-year-old marine biologist who earned $86,928; Tiffany Smoth, a thirty-four-year-old police officer who earned $77,554; and Matt Lawenda, a thirty-year-old vice president of Blue Planet Eyewear, who earned $66,000. Among the giants were Kylie Jenner, a twenty-year-old reality television star and makeup mogul, who earned $41 million; Mindy Kaling, a thirty-eight-year-old actress and writer, who earned $13 million, and Bruce Springsteen, a sixty-eight-year-old musician, who earned $75 million (McCleary 2018a, 2018b).

EXPLANATIONS FOR INEQUALITY IN LABOR EARNINGS

Labor market inequality arises for a variety of reasons. Many of these reasons are "legitimate" in the sense that they are unavoidable and play a vital role in incentivizing workers to work hard, acquire skills, and take risks. Other reasons are "illegitimate" in the sense that they are based on unfair treatment. And there are some reasons that fall into a gray area.

Legitimate Reasons for Inequality in Labor Earnings

Among the legitimate reasons are the following:

A. Compensating Differentials. At least since 1776, when Adam Smith (the great-great-great-great-grandfather of modern economic analysis) published his famous *The Wealth of Nations*, economists have recognized that nonmonetary characteristics of jobs can influence the monetary compensation that a worker receives (Smith 1937, 100–106). Consider a truck driver involved in long-haul trucking (transporting shipments between cities). It is not an easy job in the United States—drivers have to combat the effects of fatigue and the frustrations of heavy traffic, among other things—but it is not an extraordinarily dangerous job. Truck drivers in the United States might earn between $35,000 and $75,000 annually depending on experience (Catmac22 2018). Take some of those truckers and transport them to a war zone—as the U.S. military did during the Iraq War, using volunteer civilian truckers to transport supplies between military bases—and the danger quotient ratcheted up considerably. Some U.S. civilians volunteered for these jobs but were compensated at a rate about twice the stateside level (Glanz 2004). The premium was a compensating differential—it compensated for and made them willing to put up with work conditions that many others would not tolerate.

The concept of compensating differentials has widespread applicability, not just to cases of risk to life and limb. It also applies to jobs that are risky in terms of variability of income: if the job does not pay a steady income, compensation for the uncertainty may be required. It applies to jobs that differ in status. Many college students aspire to jobs in the nonprofit sector, where they "help people" as opposed to jobs in the private, profit-seeking, corporate sector where they "just earn profits." They are often dismayed to find that these jobs pay noticeably less than the jobs their friends find in the corporate sector. Compensating differential theory also applies to "clean" versus "dirty" jobs (e.g., indoor vs. outdoor jobs), but here we run into some difficulty: "dirty" jobs ought to pay more than "clean" jobs, but there are scores of examples where things seem to be the exact opposite. Many "dirty" jobs, such as that of construction laborer, are not well paid. Here we run into the "other things held equal" problem. Most economic predictions assume "other things held equal." "Dirty" jobs would pay more than "clean" jobs if all the other factors influencing wages were exactly the same between them. But they seldom are. And one of those key factors is the following.

B. The Cost of Acquiring Human Capital. Human capital refers to the productive skills that workers bring to jobs. These skills are not primarily what people are born with but include skills honed through schooling and/or skill-training programs. Workers who have these skills are more productive than workers who do not. The issue workers face is that acquiring these skills is costly. There are tuition, books, and, most importantly, the opportunity cost of forgone earnings during the training process. Who would undertake this type of training unless there was some compensation premium to be had? Workers with more human capital, other things held equal, are paid more than workers with less, not only because they are more productive but also because they are relatively scarce, since many are unwilling or unable to shoulder the cost of the training.

Returning to the dirty jobs example, dirty jobs may pay more because they are dirty, but that factor can be neutralized by the fact that many dirty jobs do not require much in the way of human capital.

The Gray Area

In the gray area, we find these explanations for labor market inequality:

A. The Superstar Phenomenon. According to *Forbes* magazine (Greenburg 2016), musician Taylor Swift earned $170 million in 2016. The average musician earns about $41,000 ("Musician Salary" 2019). Swift's earnings exceeded that of the average musician by a factor of 4,146 to 1. Can we conclude Swift is 4,146 times better than the average (professional) musician? Opinions may differ on this, but many economists believe this extraordinary wage differential reflects the workings of the superstar phenomenon (Rosen 1981).

The superstar phenomenon works when two conditions are present. One, customers want to consume the product produced by the very best producer. Two—and this is probably the key factor—the product is produced under conditions that allow the best producer to serve the entire market.

Consider the market for professional musicians in the nineteenth century. The main way to earn a living as a musician in that era was to give live performances. There were no records, CDs, iTunes, or concert souvenirs that could be sold for additional income. The size of the audience was limited, because there were no microphones or electric instruments. Today, by way of contrast, Swift could conceivably perform for the entire world at the same time using some combination of radio, television, and the internet to transfer her music. If the fans want to hear the best, they can all do so at the same time. This technologically advanced environment raises Swift's earning potential phenomenally.

Superstar markets do not just exist in the world of entertainment. They also exist in sports, medicine, and the legal profession, among others. The argument goes that because of changes in technology, superstar markets have become more prominent these days, thereby exacerbating inequality. The gray aspect is that many do not begrudge Swift and other superstars their riches, and this is simply because the public gets so much enjoyment from the services they provide.

B. Labor Market Institutions.

1. Labor unions influence the pattern of compensation in the labor market. Where unions are strong, members are likely to receive a significant wage boost. By replacing individual bargaining with collective bargaining with employers, unions are able to use the power of numbers to win higher wages. Unions can also use supply-side strategies, such as controlling the supply of labor to an industry by certifying who is a skilled worker, and demand-side strategies, such as using their political power to lobby for policies increasing the demand for their members' services. The union wage effect in the United States is probably in the range of 15–20 percent, although it fluctuates greatly over time and space (Blanchflower and Bryson 2004).

2. Occupational licensing is normally a state-imposed requirement that an individual obtain a state license before practicing a particular trade or

profession. Typically, the license is granted after the individual has demonstrated some expertise in the field by any of a number of methods. In many instances, especially in health-related occupations such as doctor, dentist, nurse, or EMT, the requirement of a license is relatively noncontroversial. In other professions, such as barber or cosmetologist, manicurist, or massage therapist, the justification is less clear-cut. Occupational licensing has been on the rise in the United States, and today one in four occupations require a license of some sort (National Conference of State Legislatures 2019). Occupational licensing is restrictive, reducing the supply of labor in given occupations and reducing labor mobility, particularly across state borders. The restrictions often work to the disadvantage of minorities and the poor.

3. Labor market *monopsony* refers to a situation in which there is limited competition among the buyers of labor. This state of affairs tends to depress wages in those markets. At one time, this issue was thought to be little more than a curiosity. Today, in an era of stagnant wages, economists have begun taking a second look and noticing features of the labor market that restrict competition (Council of Economic Advisers 2016). These include rising product market concentration, which translates into fewer separate buyers of labor, and the increasing use of "noncompete" agreements, which restrict the ability of employees to leave one employer and find a job in a similar industry. Many instances of noncompete agreements applied to managerial or professional employees can be justified by the protection of trade secrets. The use of these contracts to restrict mobility among employees of fast-food restaurants and warehouses, however, seems much more difficult to justify (Council of Economic Advisers 2016, 8). There is also some evidence of collusion among employers to not hire each other's employees, which may partly shade this factor into the illegitimate reasons category.

Illegitimate Reasons for Inequality in Labor Earnings

"Illegitimate" reasons for inequality include all the various types of discrimination that groups of people (and people individually) are subject to. Despite decades of effort devoted to stamping out discrimination, it remains an important factor in U.S. labor markets (as it does in labor markets around the world). Since the word *discrimination* means different things to different people, it should be carefully defined in this context. The simple existence of wage differences between different groups of people is not by itself evidence of discrimination. Different groups of people can differ in terms of the extent and nature of their human capital, their willingness to take risks and put up with bad working conditions, and, as shown above, the resulting wage differences are economically efficient and legitimate. (This is not to deny that differences in human capital accumulation may themselves be the result of various types of discrimination, but that discrimination took place outside the labor market.) Discrimination exists when wage differences exceed what can be thought of as efficient and legitimate and seem to be related to "irrelevant" personal characteristics such as race, ethnicity, gender, sexual orientation, age, and disability status, among many others.

Discrimination affects the demand side of things by raising/lowering demand for favored/disfavored labor. Discrimination affects the supply-side by restricting access to prime occupations and crowding disfavored labor into inferior occupations. Discrimination also leads to people being judged not as individuals but as members of a group, often to the detriment of the individuals.

THE CONSEQUENCES OF "EXCESSIVE" INEQUALITY

Many people believe the degree of inequality in contemporary America exceeds what can be considered legitimate. There are two main consequences of this.

One consequence is that inequality may offend our notion of economic justice. A philosophical approach that many economists appear to accept, either explicitly or implicitly, is utilitarianism. The fundamental tenet of utilitarianism is that economic policy ought to be directed to achieving the "greatest good for the greatest number"—combined with the reasonable supposition that the more people have of something, the less they value additional increments that lead to support for a policy of redistribution. High earners would lose very little utility (happiness or satisfaction) if their high earnings were taxed, while low earners would benefit immensely from increments in income directed their way. Total utility in society would rise as a result, which is a reasonable way to represent the "greatest good for the greatest number."

Utilitarian philosophy is not airtight. Critics have pointed out that the simple process of redistribution is likely to be a source of inefficiency. Both high and low earners may be disincentivized by the tax-and-spend process: high earners because they cannot keep as much of what they worked hard to earn, and low earners because they do not have to work as hard to achieve a certain level of income. There is also the social cost of the administrative apparatus needed to collect the taxes and distribute the funds. Other critics of large wage differentials emphasize the luck element associated with being an exceptionally high earner (Frank 2016). Talent and a willingness to work hard are not all that scarce. What separates talented and hardworking people who succeed at the highest levels from similarly talented and hardworking people of more modest achievement? According to economist Robert Frank, it is nothing more than luck—for example, being born to exceptionally supportive parents, knowing the right people, and being in the right place at the right time, among others.

If, by way of contrast, riches are legitimately earned, many are loath to interfere with the judgment of the market (Mankiw 2013; Watson 2015). High earnings are simply the "just deserts" of exceptional performance, and the resulting degree of inequality should be noncontroversial. The philosophy of what constitutes "economic justice" has always been and will continue to be contentious.

Another consequence is that inequality today will have consequences for inequality in the future. Americans have always described their country as the "land of opportunity," a society where all things are possible for those with the necessary skills and work ethic. This is the essence of the American dream. What critics of American society have always contended is that the reality is much more nuanced and much less joyful and fair than that. Employing the metaphor of life as a running competition, we do not all start at the same starting line, and the less fortunate encounter a variety of obstacles on their way to the finish line that the more fortunate can bypass. In other words, individuals' position in the distribution of income is influenced by their family background (something over which the individual has no influence), and their position influences how well *their* children are likely to do when they become adults (something they had no say in).

The economic issue described above is known as *intergenerational mobility*. Do children from poor families have the same chance to be successful as the children from rich families do? The moral implications of a society where the children of the poor have equal opportunity with the children of the rich are very different from one where poor children are, with only rare exceptions, consigned to their parent's station in life—and where the children of those poor children are also limited to that station.

Despite the rhetoric of the "American dream," most Americans have always known anecdotally that being born with a "silver spoon in your mouth" conveys enormous advantages. Today, Americans do not need to rely on anecdotes for confirmation of this reality. Economists and other scholars have access to voluminous data not previously available to earlier generations that permits quantitative analysis of the extent of intergenerational mobility.

One way researchers have approached the issue is by using longitudinal data sets that contain data from parents and their children after the children have become adults. This can be used to compare their incomes. A recent finding is that if parents' income is 10 percent higher than the average income in the parental generation, then their children's income will on average be 3.4 percent higher than the average for the child's generation (Chetty et al. 2014).

What do these numbers mean? Equal opportunity would mean that instead of a 3.4-percent increase, there would be a 0.0-percent increase—the higher income of the parent would confer no advantage on the child. If there was not equality of opportunity—if we lived in a caste society with no opportunities for mobility—the 3.4 percent would be 10 percent: the advantages of the parents would fully transfer to their children. Of course, we are at neither of those extremes, but clearly some of the disadvantages of inequality can be bequeathed from generation to generation.

Another way researchers have approached the issue is by using international comparative data. The "Great Gatsby Curve" was popularized in 2011 by the late Alan Krueger, then chair of President Obama's Council of Economic Advisers. The name derives from F. Scott Fitzgerald's classic novel *The Great Gatsby*. What the curve shows is that countries with great inequality tend to have less intergenerational mobility (Corak 2013).

ADVANTAGES OF AFFLUENCE

Plotting some points on a graph does not prove a cause-and-effect relationship, but it is a simple matter to construct a logical story rationalizing that effect. Children growing up in affluent families have access to a whole package of advantages that can help them succeed—advantages that children coming from poorer families can only dream about. These advantages include:

A. Access to Better Schools. Children from families with greater financial resources have greater access to better schools. They can afford the tuition at private schools while still paying their share of the taxes to support the public schools. The opportunity cost of forgone earnings mentioned earlier is lower. They are more able to afford all the textbooks, high-technology devices and tools, and SAT prep courses necessary to continue into higher education. They can be enriched by summer camps and foreign travel.

B. Access to Better Neighborhoods. Community safety and resources also impact labor market outcomes. There is considerable research that supports the idea that people (classmates, teachers, coaches, and other parents) and institutions (businesses, churches, schools, public safety) in one's immediate sphere of everyday influence can have a significant impact on one's future income prospects (Dietz 2002).

C. Access to Better Health. Socioeconomic status affects health, which in turn impacts one's ability to learn and earn (Hearn 2021). Of particular interest is maternal health. The health of mothers and newborns for those near or below the poverty line is considerably poorer by a great number of measurables than for mothers and infants in higher-income brackets. Access to proper nutrition, birth (and contraception) services, and a healthy environment (free of environmental dangers, such as pollution in the air and water, as well as nonenvironmental dangers, such as domestic abuse and housing insecurity) for the prenatal mother play a vital role in the health and well-being of the postnatal newborn. A study of siblings found that those whose mother faced more stress during pregnancy have lower IQ levels as children and complete one fewer year of schooling (Aizer, Stroud, and Buka 2016). Maternal health transfers to the health of the newborn, which has been found to be an important predictor of later life outcomes (Aizer and Currie 2014).

D. Access to Social Capital. *Social capital* is an amorphous term referring to the connections between people in a group resulting from shared identity, norms, values, and understandings. Children born into higher socioeconomic status groups naturally internalize the identity, norms, values, and understandings of that group, which makes it easier to develop network connections with other successful people and to become more aware of opportunities. All of this makes getting a good education and high-paying job easier. Those socialized into other groups often find the process of "fitting in" at top schools or in good jobs to be arduous.

But all is not lost. Another aspect of the aforementioned Great Gatsby Curve is a blueprint for action. Countries with great equality and mobility—largely continental European, particularly Scandinavian, countries as well as Canada—are there because of conscious decisions they have made. These countries have placed greater emphasis on policies supporting the economically disadvantaged. The payoff is that these countries have higher levels of mobility than the so-called land of opportunity: the United States (Corak 2013).

CONCLUSION

Inequality in the labor market is the inevitable starting point for any analysis of economic inequality, because so much inequality stems from labor market outcomes. The extent to which this inequality is tolerable turns out to be an issue on which reasonable observers can disagree. There are legitimate and efficiency-enhancing reasons for inequality, but there are many illegitimate and efficiency-sapping reasons as well. Differences in opinion about the role of skill versus luck in determining economic outcomes also plays a role. Thinking about labor market inequality helps clarify our views about inequality in general, because most Americans have firsthand experience of multiple labor market scenarios.

Lauren DiRago-Duncan and Robert S. Rycroft

Further Reading

Aizer, A., and J. Currie, J. 2014. "The Intergenerational Transmission of Inequality: Maternal Disadvantage and Health at Birth." *Science* 344 (6186): 856–61.

Aizer, A., L. Stroud, and S. Buka. 2016. "Maternal Stress and Child Outcomes: Evidence from Siblings." *Journal of Human Resources* 51 (3): 523–55.

Black, S. E., and P. J. Devereux. 2010. *Recent Developments in Intergenerational Mobility*. No. w15889. Cambridge, MA: National Bureau of Economic Research.

Blanchflower, David G., and Alex Bryson. 2004. "What Effect Do Unions Have on Wages Now and Would Freeman and Medoff Be Surprised?" *Journal of Labor Research* 25 (3) (Summer): 383–414.

Bureau of Labor Statistics. 2018. "News Release." U.S. Department of Labor, USDL 18-1941, December 14, 2018.

Catmac22. 2018. "What You Need to Know about Being a Long Haul Trucker," *Smart-Trucking* (blog), December 3, 2018. https://www.smart-trucking.com/blog/long-haul-trucker.html.

Chetty, Raj, Nathaniel Hendren, Patrick Kline, and Emmanuel Saez. 2014. "Where Is the Land of Opportunity? The Geography of Intergenerational Mobility in the United States." *Quarterly Journal of Economics* 129 (4): 1553–623.

Corak, Miles, 2013. "Inequality from Generation to Generation: The United States in Comparison." In *The Economics of Inequality, Poverty, and Discrimination in the 21st Century*, edited by Robert S. Rycroft, 107–26. Santa Barbara, CA: ABC-CLIO.

Council of Economic Advisers. 2016. "Labor Market Monopsony: Trends, Consequences, and Policy Responses." *Council of Economic Advisers Issue Brief*, October 2016. https://obamawhitehouse.archives.gov/sites/default/files/page/files/20161025_monopsony_labor_mrkt_cea.pdf.

Dietz, R. D. 2002. "The Estimation of Neighborhood Effects in the Social Sciences: An Interdisciplinary Approach." *Social Science Research* 31 (4): 539–75.

Frank, Robert. 2016. *Success and Luck: Good Fortune and the Myth of Meritocracy.* Princeton, NJ: Princeton University Press.

Glanz, James. 2004. "Truckers of Iraq's Pony Express Are Risking It All for a Paycheck," *New York Times*, September 27, 2004.

Greenburg, Zack O'Malley. 2016. "Full List: The World's Highest Paid Celebrities of 2016." *Forbes*, July 13, 2016. https://www.forbes.com/sites/zackomalleygreenburg /2016/07/13/full-list-the-worlds-highest-paid-celebrities-of-2016/#76ce62fd9c2d.

Hearn, Gesine K. 2021. "Economic Status and Health." In *Inequality in America: Causes and Consequences,* edited by Robert S. Rycroft and Kimberley L. Kinsley. Santa Barbara, CA: ABC-CLIO.

Knowles, Jared A., and Erin E. Hill. 2021. "Labor Market Discrimination." In *Inequality in America: Causes and Consequences,* edited by Robert S. Rycroft and Kimberley L. Kinsley. Santa Barbara, CA: ABC-CLIO.

Kochhar, Rakesh, and Anthony Cilluffo, 2018. "Income Inequality in the U.S. Is Rising Most Rapidly among Asians." Pew Research Center, July 12, 2018. https://www .pewsocialtrends.org/2018/07/12/income-inequality-in-the-u-s-is-rising-most -rapidly-among-asians.

Mankiw, N. Gregory. 2013. "Defending the One Percent." *Journal of Economic Perspectives* 27, no. 3 (Summer): 21–34.

McCleary, Kathleen. 2018a. "What People Earn." *Parade*, April 22, 2018.

McCleary, Kathleen. 2018b. "What People Earn." *Parade*, April 29, 2018.

"Musician Salary." 2019. CareerExplorer. https://www.sokanu.com/careers/musician/salary.

National Conference of State Legislatures. 2019. "Occupational Licensing Legislation Database." http://www.ncsl.org/research/labor-and-employment/occupational -licensing636476435.aspx.

Pen, Jan. 1971. *Incomes Distribution*. London: Allen Lane.

Perrucci, Robert, and Carolyn Cummings Perrucci, 2021. "Intergenerational Mobility and the American Dream." In *Inequality in America: Causes and Consequences of the Rich-Poor Divide,* edited by Robert S. Rycroft and Kimberley L. Kinsley. Santa Barbara, CA: ABC-CLIO.

Rosen, Sherwin. 1981. "The Economics of Superstars." *American Economic Review* 71 (5): 845–58.

Smith, Adam. 1937. *An Inquiry into the Nature and Causes of the Wealth of Nations*. New York: Modern Library.

Watson, William. 2015. *The Inequality Trap: Fighting Capitalism Instead of Poverty.* Toronto: University of Toronto Press.

Monopolization and Rent Seeking

In the United States, income inequality has grown tremendously since the 1970s, reaching heights unseen since the 1920s. The richest 10 percent of Americans received 34 percent of all available income from labor (wages and salaries from paid employment) in 1970. By 2010, these same Americans took home approximately one-half of all labor income (Piketty 2014, 324). The rise in American inequality is a story of wage stagnation at the bottom and skyrocketing salaries at the top (Horowitz, Igielnik, and Kochhar 2020).

Two predominant narratives explain this radical takeoff in inequality in the United States. The first emphasizes *market forces*, stressing that changes to the economy have resulted in the rise of inequality. A prominent example of this narrative is the skill-biased technical change (SBTC) argument, which stresses that the rise of automation and technology increased productivity and the demand for highly skilled workers (Acemoglu 2002; Autor, Katz, and Kearney 2008). The increase in the wages of skilled and college-educated workers is largely explained by this narrative (Goldin and Katz 2008). In this narrative, income inequality is the result of a highly competitive economy that bestows its greatest financial rewards on those with the most desirable skills and tasks.

The second narrative describes inequality as generated by *market failure*—any form of corruption, supply bottlenecks caused by inefficient regulation, or collusive arrangements between firms. These nonmarket forces create a failure of the supply-and-demand mechanism to incentivize the production of goods and services in optimal amounts. The rewards from these forms of market dislocations are collectively referred to as *rents*.

RENTS, MONOPOLIZATION, AND CLOSURE

Rent is the return on an asset, such as labor, business ownership, or land, in excess of what would need to be returned to keep the asset in production in a fully competitive market (Congleton, Hillman, and Konrad [2008] 2010). In other words, rent accrues whenever social groups are able to command excess income for their services or property.

For example, rent accrues on the basis of unique natural attributes that limit competition, even without direct institutional intervention (Sørensen 1996). Height is a valuable attribute for basketball players, but there is a fixed supply of exceptionally tall players. If the sport becomes popular, and the number of teams expands to meet this increased demand from fans, the supply of players does not also expand. In order to attract these few seven-foot players who have many employment options, teams have to fiercely outbid one another in the wages they offer. Demand exceeds supply. As a result of the bidding process, these uniquely tall seven-foot players fetch a wage far higher than their similarly skilled but shorter counterparts. The resulting high salaries are a form of rent based on natural ability. Rent accrues whenever competition is limited, whether by human-made processes or natural ones.

Rents responsible for the takeoff in inequality are typically those associated with group-based monopolies. Rent of this type is not endowed by nature but rather produced artificially by occupations and institutions that constrain the supply of labor or education. A classic example is occupational licensing, in which states require workers to pass a certification process to legally work in their chosen occupation. This licensing requirement prevents some potential occupants from entering the profession and artificially narrows the overall pool of possible occupants (Redbird 2017). If the profession has high demand, the license requirement will generate rent by allowing occupational incumbents to command a higher-than-market wage due to this artificial scarcity. Therefore, rent goes hand in hand with monopolization, because rent can be generated by limiting supply or access to a demanded good, service, or other asset.

Sociologists typically view occupations as particular social groups that claim responsibility over activities and practices, and they usually attempt to establish a monopoly by claiming "jurisdiction" over these tasks (Abbott 1988). In other words, occupations seek a monopoly over a particular activity to make it "their" line of work. Only lawyers can give legal advice, only doctors are able to practice medicine, and only plumbers are equipped to fix a pipe.

Upon legitimizing claim over a jurisdiction, occupational incumbents seek to erect boundaries that will maintain their jurisdiction and limit the ability of others to lay claim to the rewards affiliated with those tasks. The process of erecting boundaries to restrict outsider access to resources is called *closure*. Common forms of occupational closure include licensure, educational credentialing, unionization, and certification. Closure also furthers the economic goals of occupational members by limiting the overall supply of new entrants (Redbird 2017; Weber [1922] 1978; Weber 1947; Weeden 2002). In this light, wage rents can be seen as the economic return or by-product to occupational closure (Grusky and Sørensen 1998). With near-total scholarly consensus, these mechanisms are thought to raise wages by both artificially limiting supply and providing a symbol of quality that enhances occupational demand (Abbott 1988; Weeden 2002; also see Redbird 2017).

Closure and rent are not always so clearly the end result of a group's direct action. For instance, if the demand for lawyers increases but law schools do not increase the number of law students, the resulting supply restriction can increase the wages of lawyers, even if they did not directly advocate for this supply "bottleneck." In this way, the rent narrative intersects with market narratives that emphasize increased returns to skill. By rationing acceptances, universities artificially limit the supply of the educated workforce (Grusky and Weeden 2011). Processes that create rent premiums for skilled labor not only increase income inequality but also waste national economic resources, as technical labor becomes more expensive to hire than it should be (Congleton, Hillman, and Konrad [2008] 2010).

RENT FROM BELOW

To understand the inequality takeoff, it is necessary to examine how rent mechanisms have changed in the United States over the last several decades. Much of the scholarship in this area has focused on the deterioration of rent-generating processes in the lower half of the earnings distribution—specifically, the decline of unions and the stagnating minimum wage.

Unionization

For much of the twentieth century, unions were a primary mechanism of rent for blue-collar and less-educated workers in the United States. In 1970, approximately 25 percent of American workers belonged to private unions, and union workers on average earned 26 percent more in weekly wages than their nonunionized counterparts (Rosenfeld 2014, 123). Today, fewer than 7 percent of workers belong to a union in the private sector (Bureau of Labor Statistics 2018). Men can expect a 26-percent increase in their salary when they belong to a union, and women 18 percent (Rosenfeld 2014, 72). Unions help raise wages for members and generally lessen other educational and occupational inequalities (Freeman 1980).

Unions also had a significant influence outside their direct membership. They increased wages for nonunion workers by standardizing wages in highly unionized industries and occupations (Western and Rosenfeld 2011). Unions, therefore, created rents for union workers and for workers at other firms who had to compete with union wages. In a sense, this was a race to the top. Each time unions were able to raise their wages, nonunionized employers within the same industry felt pressure to match unionized wage growth to attract or retain employees.

Conversely, deunionization decreases wages for both former union members and nonunionized workers in industries (Rosenfeld 2014). Many economists believe that as much as *one-third* of contemporary income inequality is explained by deunionization (Western and Rosenfeld 2011). Deunionization has affected men's earnings more substantially than women's earnings (Western and Rosenfeld 2011).

Minimum Wage

Rent destruction in the lower half of the income distribution also occurred with the stagnation of the minimum wage. The minimum wage creates rent by setting a floor for market wages, below which it is not legal for employers to pay their employees—even if the market forces would otherwise permit employers to offer a lower wage. For most of the twentieth century, the real value of the minimum wage was several dollars above the nominal value. In other words, what people received from the minimum wage was several dollars above what the market wage would pay if not for the legal protection of the Fair Labor Standards Act. Since the 1980s, however, the gap between the real and nominal wage has flipped, and the minimum wage has continually declined in relation to wages the market would otherwise bear (Neumark and Wascher 2008, 25). In other words, rather than the minimum wage being artificially higher and generating a rent premium, the minimum wage is artificially lower and no longer generates rent.

RENTS FROM ABOVE

At the same time that rent-generating mechanisms have disappeared for low-wage labor, new rent structures have appeared for the nation's high-wage workers. Because much of the inequality takeoff has been driven by increased rewards at the top (Grusky and Szelényi 2011), understanding the takeoff requires attention to the upper half of the income distribution. A growing body of research reveals that new opportunities to collect rent at the top of the class structure are emerging (Liu and Grusky 2012; Reich 2012; Stiglitz 2012).

These opportunities for "rent from above" are growing for three reasons. First, the supply of educated workers with analytical and technical skills are scarcer than current demand, allowing educated workers to accrue significant rent ("education" rent). Second, CEO and managerial salaries are skyrocketing more quickly than other wages can keep apace ("managerial" rent). Third, occupations control who is qualified to practice and can thus limit the supply of workers, artificially driving up wages as a result (licensing).

Education Rent

The education rent hypothesis is similar to the theory of skill-based technological change, because both emphasize the importance of skilled labor in an era of new technology. Scholarship in this area shows employers bidding up the price of educated occupations based in analytical skills instead of other types of skills (Liu and Grusky 2012).

However, rising returns to education have increased faster than demand for technological skill. The rent account stresses supply-side bottlenecks created by limited access to education in two ways. First, the overall supply of potential college students is artificially lowered due to stratification and poverty. Children born into poor families and neighborhoods do not get equal access to higher education (Goldin and Katz 2008), and this familial disadvantage reduces the supply of educated labor in the workforce. Second, universities artificially restrict the supply of educated labor with caps on admission rates. While the demand for educated labor has been increasing substantially, universities have not drastically increased the number of admitted students (Grusky and Weeden 2011). While universities have their own institutional autonomy, this resistance to increased admissions signals significant market failure (Grusky and Weeden 2011). Only 30 percent of each birth cohort (a *cohort* refers to a group of people born at the same time) earn a college degree, which is not significantly higher than previous birth cohorts in the 1970s (Hout 2012).

Managerial Rent

In theory, executive pay is checked by a firm's board of directors, which collectively seeks to serve shareholders' best interests by keeping managerial compensation low so as to not reduce firm profitability. This is the "arms-length" model of board and executive bargaining that executive pay is thought to follow.

However, scholarship in the area suggests that executive income compensation far exceeds performance (Marshall and Lee 2016). Executive pay tends to relate more closely to performance when the power of executives is limited by greater institutional concentration among shareholders or when the chair of the board is not appointed by the CEO (Choe, Tian, and Yin 2014; Bebchuk, Fried, and Walker 2002).

Even when executive power is limited, the personal financial interests of individual board members may not be strong enough to cause them to curb executive compensation. While board members are there to represent shareholders, board members often have personal relationships with the CEO that encourage conflict-averse decision-making. Furthermore, board members have several tools at their disposal to camouflage executive pay increases (Bebchuk and Fried 2010).

Licensing

A rising proportion of all workers are in licensed occupations, a result that is partly due to the expansion of long-licensed occupations and partly due to the diffusion of licensure to new occupations (Kleiner 2006; Kleiner and Krueger 2008; White House 2015).

Until recently, scholars regarded license-based closure as an unequivocal form of rent generated at the top of the class structure. Licensing creates closure through two processes. First, it places restrictions on who may enter an occupation, because the process of passing a licensing process is costly and prohibitive. Second, the licensing restriction places limits on certain tasks, reserving those tasks only for licensed workers. For instance, licensing laws for lawyers prohibit the practice of law without a license. Both processes restrict the availability of labor for these tasks.

Recent scholarship on state licensure laws challenges this established consensus. Using longitudinal data from 1983 to 2012, research illustrates that modern licensing restrictions do not, *on average*, restrict the supply of labor, nor do they have a bid-up effect on wage prices (Redbird 2017). In fact, occupational licensure has the *opposite* effect, creating mechanisms that help increase the supply of labor. This research from Redbird (2017) suggests that, for closure to produce rents, supply effects are necessary. The simple creation of legal restrictions is insufficient in and of itself to produce rents.

RENT AND INEQUALITY IN THE UNITED STATES TODAY

The deterioration of rent-generating mechanisms among low-wage jobs, coupled with rising rent opportunities in high-wage jobs, suggests an overall evolution in the structure of the labor market that produces inequality (Redbird 2017).

While not all forms of rent-generating mechanisms can be measured in our data, we present analyses for wage effects from *unionization, voluntary certification, college education,* and *licensing.* Because the rent-generating effect of the college premium is also closely tied to SBTC, we also included a measure of occupational skill.

We find that workers at the top of the wage distribution have consistently had higher access to rents over the entire time period, and access has increased significantly over time. In contrast, workers at the bottom generally lack access to these mechanisms—unionization, voluntary certification, college education, and licensing—and access has declined slightly in the last thirty years.

Turning attention to the specific types of rent mechanisms, workers across the distribution have experienced deunionization, but this loss has been most substantial in the middle of the wage distribution. Workers in occupations between the twenty-fifth and fiftieth percentile of wages went from a 26 percent unionization rate in 1985 to a 10-percent unionization rate in 2015. Similarly, nearly one in three workers in the fiftieth to seventy-fifth wage percentile were unionized in 1985, but today they number around 18 percent. In contrast, workers in the seventy-fifth to the ninetieth percentile of occupational wage had a 16-percent unionization rate in 1985 and a nearly identical rate of 15 percent in 2015. Overall, workers at the top of the wage distribution have not experienced a substantial loss of unionization, while the bottom categories had very little access to membership in organized labor even at the beginning of the time period. The foregoing trends are consistent with the well-known result that opportunities for rent are declining at the bottom of the class structure, with deunionization the driving force behind this decline.

The rate of unionization contrasts sharply with the rate of college attainment. Very few workers at the bottom of the occupational wage distribution have a college degree, and this dynamic has changed very little over time. For example, in 1985, only 8 percent of workers in the tenth to twenty-fifth percentile had a college degree. Thirty years later, that rate has grown only to 12 percent. The college attainment rate for workers in the seventy-fifth to ninetieth percentile, by contrast, was 45 percent in 1985, and it expanded to 60 percent by 2015.

Licensing has seen a similar growth at the top of the wage distribution. Workers at the very bottom of the wage distribution are rarely licensed, with only 2 percent required to hold a license to work in their chosen occupation. This rate has not change in thirty years. Yet in 1985, more than 20 percent of workers in the seventy-fifth to ninetieth percentile were licensed, and today that number has expanded to more than 40 percent.

The patterns are striking. While the availability of rent-generating mechanisms was rarer at the beginning of the time period, the mechanisms have nevertheless declined markedly. In contrast, the top of the wage distribution, which started with more substantial opportunities to generate wages in the first place, has enjoyed more expansive opportunities.

It is useful to conclude this section with a brief analysis of the payoff to these different types of occupational protections that generate rent. We found that earnings increase by 2.1 percent with certification, 26.9 percent with a college degree, 24.1 percent with unionization, 1.4 percent with licensure, and 72.8 percent for every 10 percent increase in occupational education. We ensured that race, gender, marital status, weekly hours worked, and employment in government office did not affect our results by statistically controlling for them. Ultimately, the analyses strongly suggest that inequality in America is explained mostly by top earners capturing rent-generating mechanisms and low earners losing such mechanisms.

KEY IMPLICATIONS

The capacity to collect rent is withering away at the bottom of the class structure while simultaneously expanding at the top of the class structure. With the exception of licensing, the wage effects to these forms of closure are significant. Thus the shifting opportunities to rent across the wage distribution are related to shifts in inequality.

The foregoing results, while suggestive, by no means demonstrate that the rapid growth in income inequality is attributable to this particular pattern of rent destruction and creation. Although a rent-based account of rising income inequality is still little more than a hypothesis, the results suggest it is worth subjecting hypotheses about closure and monopolization, as a rent-generating process, to the same causal scrutiny that competing accounts, such as the SBTC narrative, have undergone.

A proper analysis would have three important components. First, it is important to establish that wage growth has been most pronounced among occupations that either had well-developed closure mechanisms at the start of the takeoff or developed such mechanisms as the takeoff unfurled. Second, it is important to show that occupations that lack closure should not show a persistently upward wage trajectory, precisely because they lack the capacity to close off against the burgeoning supply of laborers who can secure the requisite training. Third, it is important to understand the ways in which one form of closure interacts with another. For instance, while much of the growth of licensing occurred in the service and construction occupations, where union rates have declined, the relative weakness of the licensure effect may indicate that licensing, at least among these occupations, does not have a significant enough supply effect to create monopolies and generate rents (Redbird 2017). As such, licensing is not a form of closure that has nearly the power of unionization for these occupations.

It is equally important to examine rising returns to individual-level education as a result of *both* increase in the return to skill *and* the consequence of rationing and other bottlenecks. Disentangling these two effects is necessary to understand the wage implications of both narratives.

A more thorough causal examination of the rent-based account for inequality has important consequences for our understanding of American inequality. The United States has long fashioned its public policy interventions under the assumption that inequality is an unfortunate but inevitable by-product of individual failure to compete in highly efficient competitive markets. This assumption leads to a focus on premarket intervention (e.g., education assistance) and aftermarket redistribution (e.g., through taxation and welfare policies), while deemphasizing interventions that reduce market failure. The rent-based account of inequality implies that the United States would end up with less inequality, not more, if the various forms of closure and rent-generating practices were less prevalent at the high end of the wage distribution.

Devin Wiggs and Beth Redbird

Further Reading

Abbott, Andrew. 1988. *The System of Professions: An Essay on the Division of Expert Labor.* Chicago: University of Chicago Press.

Acemoglu, Daron. 2002. "Technical Change, Inequality, and the Labor Market." *Journal of Economic Literature* 40:7–72.

Autor, David H., Lawrence F. Katz, and Melissa S. Kearney. 2008. "Trends in U.S. Wage Inequality: Revising the Revisionists." *Review of Economics and Statistics* 90:300–323.

Bebchuk, Lucian A., and Jesse M. Fried. 2010. "Paying for Long-Term Performance." *University of Pennsylvania Law Review* 158 (7): 1915–59.

Bebchuk, Lucian A., Jesse M. Fried, and David I. Walker. 2002. "Managerial Power and Rent Extraction in the Design of Executive Compensation." NBER Working Paper 9068. National Bureau of Economic Research. https://www.nber.org/papers/w9068.

Bol, Thijs, and Kim Weeden. 2014. "Occupational Closure and Wage Inequality in Germany and the United Kingdom." *European Sociological Review* 31 (3): 354–69.

Bureau of Labor Statistics. 2016. "Interest Rates Set to Rise While Wage-Growth Remains Cool." https://www.statista.com/chart/15038/interest-rates-set-to-rise-while-wage-growth-remains-cool.

Bureau of Labor Statistics. 2018. "Economic News Release: Union Members Summary." BLS. https://www.bls.gov/news.release/union2.nr0.htm.

Choe, Chungwoo, Gloria Y. Tian, and Xiangkang Yin 2014. "CEO Power and the Structure of CEO Pay," *International Review of Financial Analysis.* 35:237–48.

Congleton, Roger D., Arye L. Hillman, and Kai A. Konrad, eds. (2008) 2010. *40 Years of Research on Rent-Seeking: Theory on Rent-Seeking.* New York: Springer.

Ehrenreich, Barbara. 2001. *Nickel and Dimed: On (Not) Getting By in America.* New York: Metropolitan Books.

Freeman, Richard B. 1980. "Unionism and the Dispersion of Wages." *Industrial and Labor Relations Review.* 34:3–24.

Goldin, Claudia and Lawrence F. Katz. 2008. *The Race between Education and Technology.* Cambridge, MA: Belknap Press of Harvard University Press.

Grusky, David. B., and Erin Cumberworth. 2013. *Economic Inequality in the United States: An Occupy-Inspired primer.* In *Occupy the Future*, edited by D. B. Grusky, D. McAdam, R. Reich, and D. Satz, 13–46. Boston, MA: MIT Press.

Grusky, David B. and Jesper B. Sørensen. 1998. "Can Class Analysis Be Salvaged?" *American Journal of Sociology* 103 (5): 1187–234.

Grusky, David B., and Szonja Szelényi, eds. 2011. *The Inequality Reader: Contemporary and Foundational Readings in Race, Class, and Gender.* Boulder, CO: Westview Press.

Grusky, David B., and Kim A. Weeden. 2011. "Is Market Failure behind the Takeoff in Inequality?" In *The Inequality Reader: Contemporary and Foundational Readings in Race, Class, and Gender,* edited by David B. Grusky and Szonja Szelényi, 90–7. Boulder, CO: Westview Press.

Grusky, David. B., and Christopher Wimer. 2010. "Can Inequality Be Reduced by Building Better Markets?" In *The Inequality Puzzle,* edited by R. Berger, D. B. Grusky, T. Raffel, G. Samuels, and C. Wimer, 211–23. London: Springer Press.

Hacker, Jacob. S., and Paul Pierson. 2010. *Winner-Take-All Politics: How Washington Made the Rich Richer—and Turned Its Back on the Middle Class.* New York: Simon and Schuster.

Harrison, Bennett, and Barry Bluestone. 1988. *The Great U-Turn: Corporate Restructuring and the Polarizing of America.* New York, NY: Basic Book Publishers.

Horowitz, Juliana Menasce, Ruth Igielnik, and Rakesh Kochhar. 2020. "Most Americans Say There Is Too Much Economic Inequality in the U.S., but Fewer than Half Call It a Top Priority." Pew Research Center. https://www.pewsocialtrends.org/wp-content/uploads/sites/3/2020/01/PSDT_01.09.20_economic-inequality_FULL.pdf.

Hout, Michael. 2012. "Social and Economic Returns to College Education in the United States." *Annual Review of Sociology* 38:379–400.

Kleiner, Morris M. 2006. *Licensing Occupations.* Kalamazoo, MI: Upjohn Institute for Employment Research.

Kleiner, Morris M., and Alan B. Krueger. 2008. "The Prevalence and Effects of Occupational Licensing." NBER Working Paper 14308. National Bureau of Economic Research, Cambridge. https://www.nber.org/papers/w14308.

Liu, Yujia, and David Grusky. 2012. "The Payoff to Skill in the Third Industrial Revolution." *American Journal of Sociology* 118 (5): 1330–74.

Marshall, Ric, and Linda-Eling Lee 2016. "Are CEOs Paid for Performance? Evaluating the Effectiveness of Equity Incentives." MSCI. https://www.msci.com/documents/10199/91a7f92b-d4ba-4d29-ae5f-8022f9bb944d.

Neumark, David, and William L. Wascher. 2008. *Minimum Wages.* Cambridge, MA: MIT Press.

Organization for Economic Cooperation and Development. 2018. "Income Inequality, 2017." https://data.oecd.org/inequality/income-inequality.htm.

Piketty, Thomas. 2014. *Capital in the Twenty-First Century.* Cambridge, MA: Belknap Press of Harvard University Press.

Redbird, Beth. 2017. "The New Closed Shop? The Economic and Structural Effects of Occupational Licensure." *American Sociological Review* 82 (3): 600–624.

Reich, Robert B. 2012. *Beyond Outrage: What Has Gone Wrong with Our Economy and Our Democracy, and How to Fix It.* New York: Vintage.

Rosenfeld, Jake. 2014. *What Unions No Longer Do.* Cambridge, MA: Harvard University Press.

Shaefer, H. Luke, and Kathryn Edin. 2013. "Rising Extreme Poverty in the United States and the Response of Federal Means-Tested Transfer Programs." *Social Service Review* 87 (2): 250–68.

Sørensen, Aage B. 1996. "The Structural Basis of Social Inequality." *American Journal of Sociology* 101 (5): 1333–65.

Stanford Center on Poverty and Inequality. 2010. "Executive Pay." https://inequality.stanford.edu/sites/default/files/summer_2010.pdf.

Stiglitz, Joseph E. 2012. *The Price of Inequality: How Today's Divided Society Endangers Our Future*. New York: Norton.

U.S. Census Bureau. 2018. "Poverty Data Tables." https://www.census.gov/topics/income-poverty/poverty/data/tables.html.

Weber, Max. (1922) 1978. *Economy and Society: An Outline of an Interpretative Sociology*. Edited by G. Roth and C. Wittich. Berkeley: University of California Press.

Weber, Max. 1947. *The Theory of Social and Economic Organization*. New York: Oxford University Press.

Weeden, Kim. 2002. "Why Do Some Occupations Pay More than Others? Social Closure and Earnings Inequality in the U.S." *American Journal of Sociology* 108 (1): 55–101.

Western, Bruce, and Jake Rosenfeld. 2011. "Unions, Norms, and the Rise in U.S. Wage Inequality." *American Sociological Review* 76 (4): 513–37.

White House. 2015. "Occupational Licensing: A Framework for Policymakers." https://obamawhitehouse.archives.gov/sites/default/files/docs/licensing_report_final_nonembargo.pdf.

Technological Change

Since the shift to an information economy and the "internet age," pundits and scholars have debated the notion that advances in information technology, especially in automated robotics, will mean the end of work and perhaps the end of civilization as we know it, killing all types of jobs and income opportunities along the way (Ford 2015; Rifkin 1995). At the very least, economists and other social scientists do expect that the forces of "creative destruction" (Schumpeter 1942) will be accelerated by the spread of robotic automation, self-driving cars and trucks, autonomous delivery drones guided by GPS, fully automated shopping and product distribution, and the more widespread use of 3D printing capabilities, which may eventually replace routine manufacturing jobs with customizable product fabrication. While these new technologies "create" new products, innovations, and jobs in some industries, they also tend to "destroy" products and jobs in other industries, rendering them obsolete. As a result, heightened anxiety about job obsolescence attributable to increased technology has reached a level perhaps not seen since the Luddite uprisings in British textile factories over two hundred years ago. Will contemporary technological advances lead to rising unemployment, stagnant or declining real incomes, and eventual widespread poverty? If robots assume most or all of the former tasks once performed by workers, what might this imply about the labor force, the source of income for average households, and its distribution? If technological advances lead to the eventual obsolescence of human labor as the primary source of earnings, would anyone be left to actually buy the products and services produced?

Definitive answers to these complex questions remain elusive. However, the general consensus among most economists is that the benefits of technology have historically exceeded the adjustment costs, and that, over the long run, there is no reason to expect the current wave of technological advances in robotics or machine learning to turn out differently than in the past (Brynjolfsson and McAfee 2014; Frick 2015; Lehman 2015). Rather than reducing the total number of jobs in the economy, or rendering labor obsolete as a source of income, technological advances have historically had the more nuanced effect of altering the types of jobs people do. This means not a reduction in jobs or income per se but rather a changing composition of jobs, requiring different worker skills in a labor market adapting to the shifting structural forces introduced by new ways of producing (Kim, Hong, and Hwang 2018). In general, this has meant rapid job creation and higher incomes for workers whose skills are complementary with new forms of technology. Think of software engineers, data analysts, blockchain builders and investors, research scientists, and other "symbolic analyst" or "creative class" occupations. This has also generally coincided with equally rapid job destruction in occupations made technologically obsolete, accompanied by lower demand and declining incomes for those workers whose "routine" skills are incompatible with new technologies. Such jobs are usually eliminated as a direct consequence. Think of former workers employed in typewriter manufacturing, videocassette tape production, the analog photography industry, or even blacksmiths or wagon wheel makers in the early twentieth century.

Now consider the following questions: What if there are only a handful of supertalented workers in the labor force who possess (or who could ever hope to possess) the highly demanded skills compatible with contemporary advances in technology? What if the members of the larger, remaining workforce, both now and in the future, do not have the skills required to work alongside the technologies developed? What does this imply about the distribution of incomes? Jobs may emerge and occupations may shift in response, and the resulting change in the number of jobs may, in fact, turn out to be a net increase. Yet some observers and critics predict that automation, robotics, and machine learning will push the skill requirements of a small (and diminishing) class of jobs far above the average worker's capabilities. In their view, this could leave a relatively few, high-skilled workers earning premium wages while others experience stagnant income (Cowen 2011, 2013; Ford 2015).

Of course, this argument may overlook the possibility that, should such large and growing earnings gaps persist, and should the costs of high-skilled labor grow too great, firms may eventually respond to the relatively lower wages and greater supply of low- and moderately skilled labor by investing in physical capital and technologies that are substitutes to high-skilled and high-cost workers (known as *deskilling*). If such investments more favorable to low- and moderately skilled workers were to occur with great enough frequency across numerous industries, we could expect to see wage convergence between high- and low-skilled workers. For the moment, we ignore this possibility while acknowledging that, over the longer run, it may be a plausible and perhaps even likely outcome.

So a mark of technological innovation may be the accompanying change in the distribution of income occurring as a by-product. Rising earnings inequality is likely a feature (and not a "bug") of a labor market where the demand for analytical, quantitative, and nonroutine skills is driven higher by technological advancements, leading to large pay gaps between more-skilled and less-skilled workers (Kaplan and Rauh 2013). Indeed, historical measures of income inequality have revealed rising gaps between the top and bottom of the income distribution for the past four decades in the United States. By Census Bureau estimates, two of the most widely cited measures used to gauge levels of income inequality, the Gini

Index and the ratio of income shares of the top 20 percent to the bottom 20 percent, have increased by 24.9 percent and 64.4 percent, respectively, from their low in 1968 through 2017 (U.S. Census Bureau 2018a). Many other developed economies exhibited a similar trend in income inequality throughout this period, though perhaps not as great as in the United States (Berman, Bound, and Machin 1998; Blau and Kahn 1994; Goos and Manning 2003; Gottschalk and Smeeding 1997; Kim, Hong, and Hwang 2018).

Additionally, most developed economies experiencing a rise in income inequality since the 1970s have also exhibited varying levels of long-run (secular) economic growth (World Bank 2017). What explains this seemingly odd correlation between (mostly) rising economic growth coupled with rising wage inequality, both around the world and especially in the United States? How might rapid technological improvements since the "Microprocessor Revolution" of the 1970s be associated with both of these trends? Technological change has long been linked with improvements in labor productivity that increase economic growth (Solow 1956, 1957). But how might these same technological advances alter modern labor markets so that a persistent gap emerges between the wages of the highest- and lowest-skilled workers?

THE DEMAND SIDE: EARNINGS INEQUALITY AND SKILL-BIASED TECHNOLOGICAL CHANGE

Although changes in the tax code and adjustments to transfer payment policies beginning in the 1980s may have had some impact on after-tax income distribution, economists now accept that the rise in pretax income inequality since the 1970s is mostly a result of beneficial structural transitions in the broader economy brought on by innovation and advances in technology (Acemoglu 2002; Aghion et al. 2015; Mankiw 2013). This is often labeled "skill-biased technological change" (Autor, Katz, and Kearney 2006; Bartel and Sicherman 1999; Berman, Bound, and Machin 1998) or "routine-biased technological change" (Kim, Hong, and Hwang 2018). New technologies such as the microprocessor, production automation, and robotics raise the demand for high-skilled labor such as engineers, chemists, software developers, biotechnicians, data analysts, actuaries, and health-care and financial services professionals, all of whom work alongside technologically advanced devices and capital equipment built around the ever-faster processing speeds of contemporary microprocessor chips (Autor, Katz, and Krueger 1998; Krueger 1993; Levy and Murnane 1996). Advanced technologies are complementary to skilled and educated workers. By raising their marginal productivity as a complementary input, technological advances increase the demand for high-skilled labor and thus quickly push skilled wages higher (Autor, Katz, and Kearney 2006; Johnson 1997). Economic theory suggests that when demand for a product or service rises faster than supply, the price (in this case, wages and salaries) must rise, all else equal. So rapid technological improvements raise the demand for high-skilled workers, putting upward pressure on the earnings of the most skilled or educated workers in the labor force.

However, these same new technologies tend to reduce the demand for less-skilled or routine workers (such as those in blue-collar manufacturing jobs) for whom newer technology becomes a lower-cost substitute. By reducing the relative productivity of low-skilled labor, the substitution effects of new technology decrease the demand for the less skilled, leaving the real wages of low- or even semiskilled workers flat or declining. In these lower-skilled occupations, some jobs become automated or replaced by other forms of technology, reducing demand and pressing wages downward.

Of course, technological advances are beneficial to economies overall, as most people intuitively recognize. Along with the precursors of entrepreneurship and innovation, they are a primary source of economic growth (Schumpeter 1942; Solow 1956, 1957). They make possible much greater levels of output with the same or fewer inputs and make available a much wider and higher-quality array of goods and services than ever before. Innovative technologies accelerate the creation of wealth and enlarge the economic pie for all people in their capacity as consumers (Waldfogel 2017). However, new technologies nonetheless appear to create rising earnings inequality by driving up the demand for skilled workers faster than educational and training infrastructure can meet (Clement 2017; Goldin 2009; Goldin and Katz 2008, 2009). As the demand for skilled labor continues to outpace supply, the wage gap between skilled and unskilled workers grows and, along with it, the broader trend of rising income inequality. We can then understand rising wage inequality as a race between supply and demand for high-skilled, educated, and talented workers in an economy undergoing fundamental structural shifts where "working with your brain" is valued much more than "working with your hands."

These forces have been present throughout history (Chin, Juhn, and Thompson 2006; Goldin and Katz 1998; Katz and Margo 2014). In hindsight, their effects seem obvious. For example, during the late nineteenth and early twentieth centuries, internal combustion technology allowed trucks and tractors to replace low-skilled field hands, permitting large-scale economies in agriculture, much greater crop yields, and consequently lower food costs for consumers. But it pushed those field hands into alternate lines of work that were not always obvious at the time, most requiring adaptation. This earlier period of industrialization also exhibited skill-biased technological advances that similarly increased earnings inequality between high- and low-skilled workers, particularly increasing the wage gaps between those with a high school diploma and those without (Goldin and Katz 2008, 2009). However, rising investment in secondary and postsecondary education by state and federal governments (the "high school movement" and the GI Bill), coupled with the peak of unionization power in the manufacturing sector during the war years, led to a period of relatively low and stable earnings inequality from the 1940s until the 1970s. The supply of skilled workers rose fast enough to keep pace with demand, leaving wage inequality lower and more stable than before or since. This period came to be known as the "Great Compression" (Goldin and Margo 1992). However, beginning in the 1970s, with the rapid onset of the Microprocessor Revolution and the shift from an industrial- to a knowledge-based economy, skill bias in technology became apparent once again. The demand for educated and high-skilled labor with unique abilities and talents suitable for an information economy has risen dramatically, while the supply of that labor has been relatively stagnant (Clement 2017; Goldin 2009; Gordon 2013).

THE SUPPLY-SIDE: RELATIVE SLOWING IN EDUCATIONAL ATTAINMENT AND THE ENTITLEMENT HYPOTHESIS

Given the increasing returns to higher education and the growing earnings gap between lower-skilled and higher-skilled labor, why has the supply of higher-skilled and more educated labor been so slow to respond? Why do we not observe a bigger jump in the supply of college-educated workers as a share of the labor force, especially in fields closely linked to new technology (including science, engineering, and mathematics), in response to the technology-driven wage premiums that can be captured in these occupations? The high and rising returns to more educated workers in the first half of the twentieth century led to the "high school movement," an eventual increase in the supply of skilled workers relative to demand, and to the "Great Compression" in wages, reducing inequality by mid-century (Goldin and Katz 2008, 2009). Why is history not repeating itself this time around? Why a longer lag in response to the rising returns to human capital investment? Did immigration play a role? Or was it a change in the skill composition of native-born workers? Have the rising costs of higher education suppressed skilled labor supply relative to demand? What about shifting state and federal budgetary priorities and the emergence of transfer payments for poorer households in the second half of the twentieth century?

Perhaps the most thorough research addressing many of these questions is that of Claudia Goldin and Lawrence Katz. Upon identifying and measuring the significant increase in demand for skilled and educated workers beginning in the 1970s, they emphasize that it was the failure of the relative supply of skilled workers to keep pace with this demand that accounts for the largest increases in earnings inequality and the rising college wage premium. They first investigate the impact of immigration. If the relative increase in the supply of low-skilled immigrants following the 1965 immigration reform act led to an overall depressing of low-skilled wages at the bottom end of the income distribution, this might account for the growing skill premium and the rise in earnings inequality. On the other hand, slightly more open immigration after 1965 may have also increased the supply of high-skilled immigrants, constraining the rise in high-skilled wages at the top end of the income distribution and thus dampening the rise in earnings inequality. Because wage inequality accelerated after 1965, Goldin and Katz focus more on the first of these two hypotheses. Their models and simulations suggest that immigration explains very little of the rise in the skilled (college) wage premium since the 1980s. They put it as follows:

> But how much of the increase in the college wage premium was due to immigration? . . . Using our preferred estimate . . . the change in relative supply implies an increase in the college wage premium of . . . only 10 percent of the overall increase.

. . . Thus, the slowdown in the growth of relative college supply from the native-born was *nine* times more important than was immigration in explaining the rise of the college wage premium from 1980 to 2005. (Goldin and Katz 2009, 15–17, emphasis in original)

They emphasize that it is the slowdown in the growth rate of native-born skilled and educated workers that is responsible for the majority of the growing wage premium between higher- and lower-skilled workers:

From 1915 to 1940 supply [of skilled labor] outstripped demand by 1.41 times (3.19 percent average annually versus 2.27); from 1940 to 1960 it did so by 1.47 times (2.63 percent average annually versus 1.79). In both periods supply increased by about 1 percent per year more than demand. [There are] many reasons for the surge in education including the high school movement in the pre-1940 era and the increase in college going in the post-World War II period.

But a big reversal occurred around 1980. Had the relative supply of college workers increased from 1980 to 2005 at the same rate that it had from 1960 to 1980, the college premium, rather than rising, would have fallen. Education lost the race to technology. . . .

Our central conclusion is that when it comes to changes in the wage structure and returns to skill, supply changes have been critical, and changes in the educational attainment of the native born have driven the supply side. (Goldin and Katz 2009, 22–23)

For example, the share of seventeen-year-olds completing high school rose dramatically from just 6.4 percent in 1900 to 77 percent by 1970. But since then, it has changed little and may have declined; by one measure, it sat at 74 percent in the late 2010s (Greenspan and Wooldridge 2018, 400). Without a continued increase in the high school completion rate, the share of young cohorts eligible and prepared for a college degree has stagnated. So what accounts for this native-born slowdown in educational attainment since the 1980s? An important role was played by the rise in state and federal public education expenditures that fostered the large increase in the supply of skilled workers during the first half of the twentieth century (Goldin and Katz 2009; Clement 2017). Specifically, the push for "free" and universal public education in the late nineteenth century, the "high school movement" after 1910, and the GI Bill following World War II all accelerated public, taxpayer funding of education, lowering the cost of human capital investment to many cohorts of workers who could now afford added years of schooling (Gordon 2013). As a result, the relative supply of skilled labor increased faster than demand, bringing a decline in the skilled wage premium until the 1970s, after which it began to rise. What has changed? Why are native-born cohorts over the last four decades not generating an increase in the relative proportion of educated and skilled workers as rapidly as their predecessors?

Two related factors may provide a theory. First, since recent technological advances are more complex than those in the past, the four-year college degree has replaced the high school diploma as the minimum proximate indicator of "skill." And it is well reported that the costs of a postsecondary degree have risen dramatically since the 1970s. According to the National Center for Education Statistics (2019), real annual average tuition and fees across U.S. four-year colleges (measured in constant 2017 dollars) has increased by 220 percent from academic year 1969–1970 ($4,850) through academic year 2016–2017 ($15,512).

Second, rising costs of entitlement programs may have shifted federal and state government budget shares away from education and toward transfer payments. For example, looking only at state-level data, real per capita expenditures on higher education in the United States increased 282 percent, from about $30 per capita in 1970 to over $115 per capita in 2017. However, state-level real per capita expenditures on transfer payments for poor households in the United States increased by a much larger 1,086 percent, from about $174 per person in 1970 to over $2,061 per person in 2017 (U.S. Bureau of Economic Analysis 2018). (State-level transfer payment expenditures include annual outlays for temporary disability and workers' compensation payments, Medicaid, state-level family assistance programs, energy assistance payments, subsidies to nonprofit welfare organizations, and SSI permanent disability payments. All data are compiled by the authors from BEA National Income and Product Accounts, tables 3.12 and 3.13.)

This shift in budget priorities likely (1) increased the average out-of-pocket expense of higher education for many families, and (2) simultaneously reduced the demand for a college degree by the creation of safety nets that have buffered the decline in wages to low-skilled workers. Both factors could explain both the slowdown in college going among younger cohorts and the rise in earnings inequality since the 1970s. It is worth pointing out that during the first half of the twentieth century, prioritized government funding for secondary and postsecondary education was not simultaneously matched by increased spending on poverty programs or other transfer payments creating safety nets for lower-income households. Such transfers remained relatively rare prior to the Great Society programs after 1965. It may be that this shift in budget priorities since the 1970s has altered incentives of younger cohorts in a way that deters investment in postsecondary education in spite of the rising premium to skilled workers. If so, such shifting budgetary priorities may explain at least part of the decline in the relative supply of native-born, high-skilled labor that Goldin and Katz suggest has contributed to rising earnings inequality over the same period.

Critics of income redistribution argue that income transfers from rich to poor may dampen initiative and reduce investment in human capital or entrepreneurship (Conrad 2016; Keane 2011; Mulligan 2012; Murray 2012). If individuals receive a form of means-tested, guaranteed basic income independent of the skills they provide in the labor market, at least some fraction of these individuals may invest less in the kinds of skills and education that could raise their earnings in a technologically advanced marketplace. Reduced incentives to invest in education and skills may likewise reduce the relative supply of higher-skilled labor just as the demand for it is accelerating. This could lead to abnormally large gains in the wages and salaries of a relatively few "superstar" IT workers, engineers, CEOs, talented entertainers, and entrepreneurs (Cowen 2011, 2013, 2017; Kaplan and Rauh 2013; Mankiw 2013; Rosen 1981). If so, then rising earnings inequality may be the unintended result of income transfers to less-skilled "discouraged workers" in poorer households.

As a preliminary test of these claims, consider some simple time-series data on (1) total real state and federal per capita income transfers for the poor, and (2) the

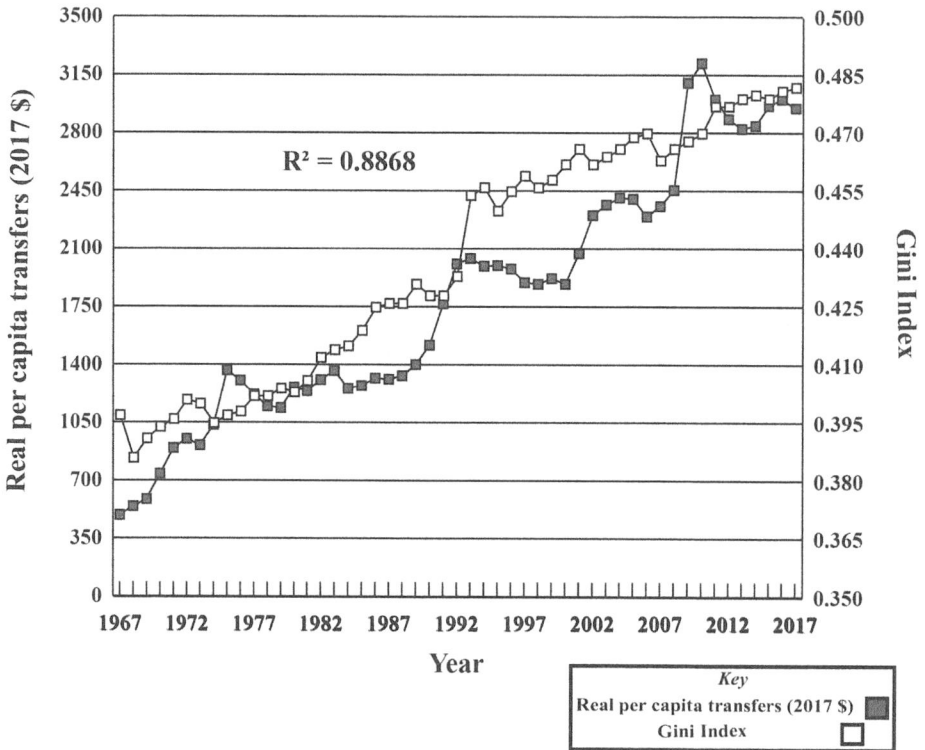

Figure 1   Real Per Capita Transfers and Gini Index (1967–2017)

Gini measure of income inequality. As shown in figure 1, these two data series are tightly correlated across recent decades ($r^2 = 0.89$, r^2 *is the coefficient of determination running from 0.0 to 1.0—the closer to 1.0 the stronger the relationship between the variables*). Despite rising per capita transfer payments to poorer households channeled through multiple means-tested programs, before-tax income inequality has continued to rise. According to estimates by the U.S. Bureau of Economic Analysis (2018) and the U.S. Census Bureau (2018b), total federal, state, and local government spending on poverty programs (excluding Social Security and Medicare benefits to retirees) equals approximately $26.2 trillion from 1950 to 2017 in inflation-adjusted 2017 dollars.

Notwithstanding these outlays, the poverty rate in the United States has remained roughly constant, between 12 and 15 percent (U.S. Census Bureau 2018b), and income inequality has risen unabated. These relatively large state and federal expenditures are not merely an artifact of the rise in population over this period. Real, annual per capita federal, state, and local government outlays on means-tested poverty programs (again, excluding retiree benefits) have increased from just over $300 per year in 1950 to $2,950 per year in 2017. The secular trends in income inequality and inflation-adjusted per capita state and federal poverty expenses have risen in lockstep since the late-1960s.

By dulling the incentive to invest in human capital, income transfers may be worsening the rise in before-tax income inequality, given the positive association between the two series. Relative declines in human capital investment may also be restraining growth and prosperity, as other authors suggest (Conrad 2016; Greenspan and Wooldridge 2018; Mulligan 2012; Murray 2012). Investing in human capital, especially in the type of higher education so greatly demanded in modern labor markets, is often costly and time consuming. Without strong incentives for human-capital investment, the supply of skilled labor may remain suppressed relative to demand, meaning larger income shares flowing to a small group of skilled and educated "superstar" workers and entrepreneurs, intensifying the rise in inequality. By providing incentives to avoid costly and often distasteful human capital investments and the hard work of higher education required to understand advanced technology, social safety nets may, in part, restrict the supply of high-skilled labor so that the income returns to technological advances are confined to a relative handful of intrepid entrepreneurs and technical geniuses. Correlation is not causation, of course, and other factors certainly play some role in restricting the supply of high-skilled labor, such as the fear of large student loan debt (Gordon 2013). Nonetheless, the positive association between per capita poverty spending, on the one hand, and rising income inequality, on the other, across four decades raises interesting and perhaps concerning questions. Further research on this correlation is warranted, and a comparison of U.S. data with other developed economy welfare states may be instructive.

CONCLUSION: THE COMPLEX CONNECTIONS BETWEEN TECHNOLOGY, INEQUALITY, GROWTH, AND PUBLIC POLICY

The relationships between technological change, income inequality, economic growth, and public policy are nuanced, complex, and perhaps even troubling. Technological advances stemming from entrepreneurial discovery, human capital, and innovation are the central forces of economic growth and more prosperous living standards in advanced economies. The Microprocessor Revolution supporting contemporary technological progress improves the lives of virtually all members of the economy, particularly in our capacity as consumers, providing lower-cost and higher-quality goods and services unavailable (and unimaginable) to earlier generations. But these same forces appear to be the source of an increasingly unequal sharing in the wealth and income gains from economic growth. By significantly increasing the demand for high-skilled labor and also reducing the demand for less-skilled workers, skill-biased technological change undoubtedly explains much of the rise in income inequality since the 1970s. The failure of the skilled labor supply to keep pace with this demand has further increased the rise in the earnings gap between the top and bottom of the education and income distributions. As Harvard economist Greg Mankiw (2013) has argued, "The story of rising inequality, therefore, is not primarily about politics or rent seeking, but rather about supply and demand."

This has put democratic governments of developed economies in something of a policy box from which it is difficult to escape. Technological advances are the lifeblood of economic growth, and most people, in their capacity as consumers, have come to expect such improvements as a matter of habit. But the gains derived from economic growth driven by these same technological improvements are shared less equally, raising demand for skilled work, reducing demand for routine jobs, creating growing wage gaps between the highest- and lowest-skilled workers. A large plurality of people, in their capacity as workers and in tension with their preferences as consumers, will tend to resist such outcomes. Modern capitalist democracies are thus at something of a policy standoff, confronted with a choice between: (1) accepting technological advances that may improve economic growth but also increase inequality and (2) imposing restraints on technological advances (and by implication on economic growth) in hopes of achieving a more equal distribution of income (Conrad 2016; Greenspan and Wooldridge 2018; Lehman 2015; Mulligan 2012; Murray 2012; Okun 1975; Piketty 2014).

It would seem that the most credible way to restrain or reduce the rise in earnings inequality is to accelerate the supply of high-skilled labor faster than demand, suppressing the wage gap between high- and low-skilled workers. That likely means a much larger outlay of government funds directed toward investments in higher education and skills development for a modern information economy, coupled with immigration reform more inviting to high-skilled immigrants. As suggested above, that may be infeasible, given the fiscal constraints and "crowding out" already imposed on state and federal spending due to large and growing entitlements (Greenspan and Wooldridge 2018), and the difficulty in shifting revenues toward education from elsewhere in public budgets. Given the somewhat glacial pace of learning and acquiring high-level cognitive skills, and apart from immigration reforms that would suddenly permit easier legal entry of vast numbers of foreign-born, high-skilled workers, demand for skilled workers is likely to outpace supply for some time to come. As such, rising income inequality is, at least for the near future, a condition we may need to adapt to rather than resist, all part of the forces of "creative destruction." This is especially so if we continue to expect technological advances to deliver the gains in living standards and economic growth to which we are accustomed.

Thomas E. Lehman and Brady W. Conn

Further Reading

Acemoglu, Daron. 2002. "Technical Change, Inequality, and the Labor Market." *Journal of Economic Literature* 40:7–72.

Aghion, Philippe, Ufuk Akcigit, Antonin Bergeaud, Richard Blundell, and David Hémous. 2015. "Innovation and Top Income Inequality." NBER Working Paper 21247. National Bureau of Economic Research. https://www.nber.org/system/files/working_papers/w21247/w21247.pdf.

Alesina, Alberto, Armando Miano, and Stefanie Stantcheva. 2018. "Immigration and Redistribution." NBER Working Paper 24733. National Bureau of Economic Research. https://www.nber.org/papers/w24733.

Autor, David H., Lawrence F. Katz, and Melissa S. Kearney. 2006. "The Polarization of the U.S. Labor Market," *American Economic Review* 96:189–94.

Autor, David H., Lawrence F. Katz, and Alan B. Krueger. 1998. "Computing Inequality: Have Computers Changed the Labor Market?" *Quarterly Journal of Economics* 113:1169–214.

Bartel, Ann P., and Nachum Sicherman. 1999. "Technological Change and Wages: An Interindustry Analysis." *Journal of Political Economy* 107:285–325.

Berman, Eli, John Bound, and Stephen Machin. 1998. "Implications of Skill-Biased Technological Change: International Evidence." *Quarterly Journal of Economics* 113:1245–80.

Blau, Francine D., and Lawrence M. Kahn. 1994. "International Differences in Male Wage Inequality: Institutions versus Market Forces." NBER Working Paper 4678. National Bureau of Economic Research. https://papers.ssrn.com/sol3/papers.cfm ?abstract_id=227965#.

Brynjolfsson, Erik, and Andrew McAfee. 2014. *The Second Machine Age: Work, Progress and Prosperity in a Time of Brilliant Technologies.* New York: W. W. Norton.

Chin, Aimee, Chinhui Juhn, and Peter Thompson. 2006. "Technical Change and the Demand for Skills during the Second Industrial Revolution: Evidence from the Merchant Marine, 1891–1912." *Review of Economics and Statistics* 88:572–78.

Clement, Douglas. 2017. "Interview with Lawrence Katz." *The Region*, Federal Reserve Bank of Minneapolis, September 25, 2017. http://minneapolisfed.org/publications /the-region/interview-with-lawrence-katz.

Conrad, Edward. 2016. *The Upside of Inequality: How Good Intentions Undermine the Middle Class.* New York: Portfolio Penguin Random House.

Cowen, Tyler. 2011. *The Great Stagnation: How America Ate All the Low-Hanging Fruit of Modern History, Got Sick, and Will (Eventually) Feel Better.* New York: Dutton Adult.

Cowen, Tyler. 2013. *Average Is Over: Powering America beyond the Age of the Great Stagnation.* New York: Plume/Penguin Group.

Cowen, Tyler. 2017. *The Complacent Class: The Self-Defeating Quest for the American Dream.* New York: St. Martin's Press.

Ford, Martin. 2015. *Rise of the Robots: Technology and the Threat of a Jobless Future.* New York: Basic Books.

Frick, Walter. 2015. "Synthesis: Technology Doesn't Always Beat Labor." *Harvard Business Review* (March): 126–27.

Goldin, Claudia. 2009. "The Future of Inequality: The Other Reason Education Matters So Much." *Milken Institute Review* (Third Quarter): 1–10.

Goldin, Claudia, and Lawrence F. Katz. 1998. "The Origins of Technology-Skill Complementarity." *Quarterly Journal of Economics* 113:693–732.

Goldin, Claudia, and Lawrence F. Katz. 2008. *The Race between Education and Technology.* Cambridge, MA: Belknap Press.

Goldin, Claudia, and Lawrence F. Katz. 2009. "The Race between Education and Technology: The Evolution of U.S. Educational Wage Differentials, 1890–2005." NBER Working Paper 12984. National Bureau of Economic Research. https:// www.nber.org/papers/w12984#.

Goldin, Claudia, and Robert A. Margo. 1992. "The Great Compression: The Wage Structure in the United States at Mid-Century." *Quarterly Journal of Economics* 107:1–34.

Goos, Maarten, and Alan Manning. 2003. "Lousy and Lovely Jobs: The Rising Polarization of Work in Britain." London School of Economics, Center for Economic Performance Discussion Papers no. DP0604. http://eprints.lse.ac.uk/20002/1/Lousy _and_Lovely_Jobs_the_Rising_Polarization_of_Work_in_Britain.pdf.

Gordon, Robert J. 2013. "The Great Stagnation of American Education." *New York Times*, September 7, 2013. https://opinionator.blogs.nytimes.com/2013/09/07/the-great -stagnation-of-american-education.

Gottschalk, Peter, and Timothy M. Smeeding. 1997. "Cross-National Comparisons of Earnings and Income Inequality." *Journal of Economic Literature* 35:633–87.

Greenspan, Alan, and Adrian Wooldridge. 2018. *Capitalism in America: A History.* New York: Penguin Press.

Johnson, George E. 1997. "Changes in Earnings Inequality: The Role of Demand Shifts." *Journal of Economic Perspectives* 11:41–54.

Kaplan, Steven N., and Joshua Rauh. 2013. "It's the Market: The Broad-Based Rise in the Return to Top Talent." *Journal of Economic Perspectives* 27:35–56.

Katz, Lawrence F., and Robert A. Margo. 2014. "Technical Change and the Relative Demand for Skilled Labor: The United States in Historical Perspective." In *Human Capital in History: The American Record,* edited by Leah P. Boustan, Carola Frydman, and Robert A. Margo, 15–57. Chicago: University of Chicago Press.

Keane, Michael P. 2011. "Labor Supply and Taxes: A Survey." *Journal of Economic Literature* 49:961–1075.

Kim, Eunha, Ahreum Hong, and Junseok Hwang. 2018. "Polarized Labor Demand Owing to Routine-Biased Technological Change: The Case of Korea from 1993–2015." *Telematics and Informatics.* https://www.sciencedirect.com/science/article/abs/pii /S0736585318308815?via%3Dihub.

Krueger, Alan B. 1993. "How Computers Have Changed the Wage Structure: Evidence from Microdata, 1984–1989." *Quarterly Journal of Economics* 108:33–60.

Lehman, Tom. 2015. "Countering the Modern Luddite Impulse." *Independent Review* 20:265–83.

Levy, Frank, and Richard J. Murnane. 1996. "With What Skills Are Computers a Complement?" *American Economic Review* 86:258–62.

Mankiw, N. Gregory. 2013. "Defending the One Percent." *Journal of Economic Perspectives* 27:21–34.

Mulligan, Casey. 2012. *The Redistribution Recession: How Labor Market Distortions Contracted the Economy.* Oxford: Oxford University Press.

Murray, Charles. 2012. *Coming Apart: The State of White America, 1960–2010.* New York: Crown Forum.

National Center for Education Statistics. 2019. "Digest of Education Statistics." Table 330.10. https://nces.ed.gov/programs/digest/d17/tables/dt17_330.10.asp.

Okun, Arthur M. 1975. *Equality and Efficiency: The Big Tradeoff.* Washington, DC: Brookings Institution.

Piketty, Thomas. 2014. *Capital in the Twenty-First Century.* Cambridge, MA: Belknap Press of Harvard University Press.

Rifkin, Jeremy. 1995. *The End of Work: The Decline of the Global Labor Force and the Dawn of the Post-Market Era.* New York: G. P. Putnam Sons.

Rosen, Sherwin. 1981. "The Economics of Superstars." *American Economic Review* 71:845–58.

Schumpeter, Joseph A. 1942. *Capitalism, Socialism and Democracy.* New York: Harper and Brothers.

Solow, Robert. 1956. "A Contribution to the Theory of Economic Growth." *Quarterly Journal of Economics* 70:65–94.

Solow, Robert. 1957. "Technical Change and the Aggregate Production Function." *Review of Economics and Statistics* 39:312–20.

U.S. Bureau of Economic Analysis. 2018. "Interactive Data—GDP and Personal Income, National Data, NIPA Tables, Tables 3.12 and 3.13 Government Current Receipts and Expenditures." https://www.bea.gov/iTable/index_nipa.cfm.

U.S. Census Bureau. 2018a. "Historical Income Tables: Households." https://www.census.gov/data/tables/time-series/demo/income-poverty/historical-income-households.html.

U.S. Census Bureau. 2018b. "Poverty Data Tables." https://www.census.gov/topics/income-poverty/poverty/data/tables.html.

Waldfogel, Joel. 2017. "How Digitization Has Created a Golden Age of Music, Movies, Books, and Television." *Journal of Economic Perspectives* 31:195–214.

World Bank. 2017. "World Development Indicators: Growth of Output." Table 4.1. http://wdi.worldbank.org/table/4.1.

Wealth Inequality

Wealth is an economic variable that influences well-being, is distributed unequally, and in recent decades has become even more unequally distributed. The bottom 90 percent of the U.S. population had 33 percent of all the wealth in 1989. The top 1 percent had 30 percent of the wealth in the same year. Over a quarter century later, in 2016, the bottom 90 percent's ownership of wealth had fallen to 23 percent of the total, while the top 1 percent had seen their ownership of American wealth increase to 40 percent (Leiserson, McGrew, and Kopparam 2019). Inequality in the distribution of wealth exceeds that of income by a substantial amount.

WHAT IS WEALTH, AND WHY DO WE WANT IT?

What is wealth? Wealth refers to the assets that people own—such as stocks and bonds, bank accounts, real estate, cars, and so on. To be precise, wealth is the value of assets owned minus liabilities, or debts, owed. The amount of an individual's assets minus the individual's liabilities is known as *net worth*. In everyday speech, wealth is often confused with income and vice versa. People with high incomes are sometimes said to be very wealthy, and people with high wealth are sometimes assumed to have high incomes. While high incomes often go with great wealth, that is not always the case. The implications of income and wealth for human well-being are not exactly the same, so keeping the meaning of the words straight is important.

In economics, wealth is what is called a *stock variable*. It is a variable that is measured at a particular point in time. Income is a *flow variable* and is one that can only meaningfully be measured over a period of time. So we can talk about a person's wealth as of November 8, 2019. We can add together the market prices of stocks and bonds, the balances in bank accounts, and the resale value of real estate and cars as they stood on November 8 (remembering, of course, to subtract out the value of debts the individual is carrying on that same day). In the case of income, we talk about money received over the course of a year or month or week or hour. Our wage rate might be $10 per hour, but that means $400 over a 40-hour work week, approximately $1,600 over a month, and approximately $19,200 over a year. Added to that is the income we receive from the interest on our bank accounts and bonds, the dividends we receive from our stocks, and the enjoyment we receive from living in a house we own and driving our own car.

The benefits of having a high income seem obvious enough. The benefits of wealth are several, but some may not be that obvious. For one thing, there are flows of income that come from wealth. Stocks pay dividends, and bonds and bank accounts pay interest. Other forms of wealth pay "income" in the form of services provided, even if there is not a flow of money. A checking account does not pay interest, but it offers the convenience of being able to manage large amounts of money by writing a check or using a debit card. You get to live in your house, play in your yard, and drive your car. If you do not own real estate or a car, you may need to rent them from someone else.

In addition, wealth is both a safety net and a way to take advantage of opportunities. With wealth we can maintain our standard of living even if the flow of income is cut off. By liquefying our wealth (turning our wealth into cash—typically by selling it), we can replace the income lost when we lose a job or get sick. If a business opportunity comes around or that perfect house comes on the market, we can jump on it by using our wealth.

THE ORIGINS OF WEALTH

Where does wealth come from? Ultimately all wealth comes from saving. Instead of consuming our income, we can put some of the money aside in bank accounts, stocks, bonds, real estate, and other assets and watch our wealth accumulate over time. Wealth will let us retire if we lose the physical ability or will to continue working. It also enables people to weather job losses or other negative financial events—and gives them the resources to take advantage of opportunities to invest (whether in the stock market or in a new home or sailboat). Wealth can also be bequeathed to heirs. The only problem with this story is that the slow, patient process of accumulating wealth by saving income does not explain the existence of billionaires (a term we will use here as a catchall for anyone with fabulous wealth).

Some people vault themselves to billionaire status by developing a new product or technology (e.g., an operating system for a desktop computer, lightweight cat litter, smartphones, or Spanx) that revolutionizes the marketplace and then making stock in their company publicly available. As investors rush to buy the stock, they push the price up to exceptional levels. With careful management and diversification, such individuals are able to accrue enormous wealth and pass it on to succeeding generations.

Of course, there are other, less reputable ways to accumulate large fortunes. Sometimes businesses "persuade" government officials to grant them a protected monopoly position. Or sometimes businesses play "hardball" with their competitors. Or sometimes there is outright theft. Some lucky people even inherit great fortunes.

Some people are more frugal than others, some people are luckier than others, some people are more talented and ambitious than others, and some people are more willing to play fast and loose with the rules of the game. Of course, government policy cannot be ignored here. The extent to which income and wealth are taxed and business is regulated also helps determine who succeeds and who fails and the degree of inequality.

THE ISSUE OF WEALTH INEQUALITY

Is wealth inequality problematic? Many Americans (generally advocates of the free market who are politically inclined toward conservative or libertarian politics) dismiss concerns with the degree of wealth inequality. They argue that if the wealth is gained legitimately, it is the product of human ingenuity and effort and should be applauded. In a capitalistic economy, the opportunity to accumulate wealth provides the incentive to work hard, save, and invest. From their perspective, limiting the rewards of such efforts would "kill the goose that laid the golden egg"—destroy one of the central drivers of the United States' powerful economic engine.

Others (generally progressive or liberal thinkers who see wealth accumulation as predicated on a broad array of factors that don't always have much to do with how talented or hardworking an individual is) find great wealth inequality to be problematic. They see inequality of wealth as a largely self-perpetuating phenomenon. Wealthy individuals have access to better schools, better neighborhoods, and a cleaner environment, and they can command political services and attention to an extent that others cannot.

An important event in the English-speaking world of economics was the publication of Thomas Piketty's *Capital in the 21st Century* in 2014 (it had been published in French in France in 2013). In the book, Piketty paints a picture of unequal development in advanced capitalistic economies, with the mechanism being largely—although not exclusively—the result of an unequal distribution of wealth.

In Piketty's model, what drives increasing inequality can be summed up in the expression $r > g$ (Piketty 2014). The symbol r stands for the rate of return on wealth. The symbol g represents the rate of growth of the economy. Based on an examination of the historical record in several advanced capitalistic economies, Piketty concludes that the long-run rate of return on capital has been approximately 5 percent per year. The long-run rate of growth of the economy has been and will continue to be approximately 1 percent per year.

Let's look at what can happen under these estimations. Take the case of an individual just starting a career who earns $100,000 per year and has wealth equal to $100,000. (That these numbers might seem fantastical for someone just entering the workforce is irrelevant to the point being made. This particular example is courtesy of Steven Pressman [2016, 65–66].) If the economy grows 1 percent per year, the individual's *income* is likely to grow at the same rate. The individual's *wealth*, however, will grow at 5 percent per year (assuming all earnings from wealth are reinvested). About 45 years later, when the worker is on the verge of retirement, the individual's labor income will be $156,481, but the individual's wealth will be $898,501.

After retirement, labor income will no longer be available, but wealth can continue to grow. If the individual in this example lives another twenty years after retiring, the individual's wealth will have grown to $2,283,990. Upon death, this wealth is bequeathed to one heir, who continues to care for the wealth. After thirty-five more years have passed, the wealth has grown to $13,150,126. If the heir (who is now an adult) then starts drawing on the wealth, say the full 5 percent rate of return for the year, the heir ends up with a cool $657,506 per year, which dwarfs anything that the heir could earn from working in most professions. (If the heir had started working when the parent retired, earning what the parent was earning, the heir would only be up to a labor income of about $268,000 55 years later.) Who would blame the heir for simply abandoning work altogether and living off the accumulated wealth?

> The main point here is that those who have wealth (and the number of families who have significant accumulations of wealth is really quite small) can continue to add to it without much difficulty, and will soon enough outdistance everybody else. The "natural" process of wealth accumulation will lead to ever-increasing wealth inequality beyond anything that can take place in the labor market. (Rycroft 2018, 359–60)

POLICIES TO ADDRESS WEALTH INEQUALITY

What is to be done about wealth inequality? For people on the right side of the political spectrum, the answer is simple. Do nothing! From their perspective, unequal accumulations of wealth are righteous in two respects. If obtained legitimately, great wealth is a reward for those who have contributed disproportionately to society. Consumers are like voters who cast ballots with their dollars, and they have approved of the new operating system, cat litter, smartphones, or Spanx by voluntarily voting for them with their dollars. And if you have accumulated great wealth in a legitimate manner, who is qualified to tell you how to dispose of it? If you choose to leave it to your heirs, that is your right and their good fortune.

For people on the left, great wealth is problematic. They assert that no one needs billions of dollars to live comfortably while many millions struggle just to get by, and wealth confers a variety of advantages mentioned earlier. They further find it difficult to justify receipt of great wealth simply because you sprang from the richest womb.

An idea from Piketty to reduce wealth inequality is to institute a global tax on wealth of 3 percent per year (Piketty 2014, 515–39). The purpose of the tax is to reduce the rate of growth of wealth, and to use the funds so acquired to finance valued social projects that benefit broad swaths of society—the "many" rather than the "few." The tax would have to be global, though, because capital is highly mobile across international boundaries. If capital is taxed in country A but not in country B, then it is likely to migrate from A to B. The practical problems of getting the nearly two hundred countries in the world to agree on such a plan, however, are clearly daunting.

A Democratic candidate for president during the 2020 election cycle, Senator Elizabeth Warren of Massachusetts, made a wealth tax one of the cornerstone policies of her platform. She proposed a two-tier tax (actually three when we consider that most people would be paying 0 percent under the plan). She proposed to tax wealth greater than $50 million at 2 percent per year. If wealth exceeded $1 billion, then she would tack on an additional percentage point. So billionaires would be paying 3 percent, a number that Piketty would understandably approve of. Warren's plan was not so ambitious as to call upon the rest of the world to do likewise.

A long-standing policy in the United States is to tax estates. The U.S. government enacted estate tax legislation in 1916 to raise revenue primarily to meet the economic demands of World War I, when the government needed to purchase huge volumes of machinery, armaments, ships, airplanes, uniforms, gasoline, and other goods and services for the war effort. Gift tax legislation was added in 1932, and then in 1976, a generation-skipping transfer tax was added. The three taxes form a unified estate and gift tax law. Over time, the revenue-raising objective of these taxes expanded to include policy goals such as wealth redistribution, and to address economic inequality. The effectiveness of these goals depends on how the policy is executed, which is generally a matter of politics. During Hillary Clinton's 2016 presidential bid, she campaigned for an increase in the tax rate on estate taxes; conversely, Donald Trump campaigned to repeal the estate tax (Lowenstein and Kisska-Schulze 2018).

The estate and gift tax exemption threshold establishes how much revenue will be raised by the government. The value of an estate is determined by the fair market value at the time of the decedent's death and is not based on what was originally paid. The items included in determining the value of an estate may include real property, cash, securities, insurance, trusts, annuities, and other assets. The estate's value may be reduced (before calculating the estate tax) for permitted deductions, such as, but not limited to, the decedent's funeral and burial expenses, donations to charities, mortgages, estate administration expenses, and property passing to surviving spouses (U.S. Department of the Treasury 2019b).

The threshold exemptions and tax rates are subject to change based on which political party controls Congress. For example, the estate and gift tax, commonly referenced by Republicans as the "death tax" (the tax only applies to individuals' property after their death) was modified in 2017, by the Tax Cuts and Jobs Act (TCJA) of 2017 (Public Law 115-97) a Republican-controlled Congress initiative. The 2017 TCJA, among other tax changes, doubled the filing threshold for the estate and gift tax from a baseline of $5 million indexed for inflation (established in 2010–2011) to $10 million (indexed for inflation). The 2017 law also established 40 percent as the top estate tax rate. By 2019, the threshold exemption was up to $11.4 million (U.S. Department of the Treasury 2019b).

Calculating taxes is a complicated endeavor and beyond the scope of this chapter, but a few simple examples may be helpful to understand the significance of the estate tax threshold exemption. To that end, if a decedent's death occurred in 2019 and the decedent's estate was valued at less than $11,400,000, the estate would pay no federal estate taxes. Should the value of the estate increase to $11,400,100, then only that last $100 above the threshold would be taxed at 40 percent (the top estate tax rate) and the estate would owe $40 for the federal estate tax.

Contrast this result with the same estate worth $11.4 million, but at a significantly lower 2011 estate tax exemption of $5 million. Had the decedent passed away in 2011 with an estate worth $11,400,000, then the estate would have owed 35 percent tax (the top estate tax rate in 2011) on all of the estate valued over $5 million (the exemption in 2011)—a total of $2.24 million (11.4 million − 5 million = 6.4 million; 6.4 million x 35 percent [0.35] = 2.24 million).

Using the 2011 estate tax threshold, the decedent's estate would pay $2.24 million for the federal estate tax, whereas if the decedent had died in 2019, the estate would pay only $40 in estate tax (U.S. Department of the Treasury 2019b). This example underscores how much less wealth may be redistributed by the government under the 2017 TCJA than when the estate tax threshold exemption was lower.

Under the current 2017 TCJA, the threshold amount for the exemption will expire in 2025, and the estate tax exemption will revert to the 2012 Tax Act level of $5 million indexed for inflation (U.S. Department of the Treasury 2019a). It is entirely possible that Congress may act before 2025 to change the estate tax law again before it reverts to the 2012 level.

The gift tax is linked to the estate tax. The annual gift tax exclusion is $15,000 per year (as of 2019). This means that individuals can gift up to $15,000 per year to as many people as they desire, with no tax consequence. For example, individual parents may gift their children up to $15,000 each without exceeding the gift tax exemption. When an individual gives a taxable gift that exceeds the gift tax exclusion (anything over $15,000 per donee per year), tax form 709 must be filed with the Internal Revenue Service (IRS). The gift is not taxed that year but rather comes into play at the time of the donor's death. For example, someone who gives a gift in the amount of $30,000 in 2019 to one donee must file tax form 709 with the IRS because the gift is $15,000 above the annual $15,000 gift exclusion amount. If the gift-giver dies in 2019, then the estate tax exemption is $11.4 million minus the amount over the gift exclusion (as evidenced by filing 709 forms) throughout the donor's lifetime. Hence, $11.4 million (the lifetime threshold exemption in 2019) minus the amount over the gift exclusion in 2019 ($30,000−$15,000) equals the decedent's allowed estate tax exemption. At this point, the estate exemption for this decedent's estate is $11,385,000, because it was reduced by the 2019 gift that exceeded the annual exclusion. If the decedent's estate is valued at more than $11,385,000, the estate will owe the federal government a tax but only for the amount over the exemption. Therefore, annual gifts that exceed the annual gift tax exclusion accumulate over a donor's lifetime and reduce the decedent's estate tax exemption.

The generation-skipping tax (GST) generally applies to gifts (that exceed the estate tax exemption) given by a grandparent to grandchildren, thereby skipping the grandparent's child. The GST allows the government to collect the gift tax revenue from each generation—grandparent, child, and grandchild—instead of only grandparent, grandchild (Herzig 2017).

Those who oppose estate and gift taxes argue that the "death tax" subjects the value of the decedent's estate to double taxation, as the money or value of the estate was already taxed at some point. Further arguments are that the estate and gift tax unfairly targets those who have worked to earn their fortunes and that the government should not divest wealthy families of the fruits of their efforts. Others claim that the estate and gift tax poses an unfair burden to farmers and small business owners. Supporters of these taxes counter that they are examples of perfectly reasonable progressive tax policy to raise revenue for the government that can be used for schools, national parks, roads, and other broad societal benefits; to reduce vast wealth that family dynasties amass; and to achieve a goal of reducing economic inequality. Another argument in favor of estate and gift tax is that special provisions in the tax code permit farmers more time to pay the estate tax, and farmers are able to value the farm's real estate by employing a farm-use value instead of the general fair-market value (Williamson and Bawa 2018, 18).

People with estates worth over $11.4 million arguably have more lawyers and accountants standing by to employ financial and accounting techniques to legally reduce or avoid the estate tax owed.

How effective is the estate and gift tax in raising revenue and mitigating inequality?

In theory, the estate tax is a progressive tax policy—one that places a higher tax burden on those more able to afford it—but today, fewer estates are subject to the estate and gift tax because of the high threshold exemption established by the 2017 TCJA. In 1936, it raised about 11 percent of America's total federal revenue. In 2015, however, only 0.6 percent of federal revenue was from the estate tax (Brunson 2019), and estate tax revenues constituted only 0.7 percent of federal receipts in 2018 (Center on Budget and Policy Priorities 2019, 2).

Proponents of the redistributive effect that the estate and gift tax promises argue that the estate tax would be more effective at mitigating inequality and raising revenue if the threshold exemption were lower, and if the wealthy were unable to easily and legally avoid paying the tax. Tax scholar Edward J. McCaffery claims that the federal estate tax could effectively mitigate economic inequality and raise revenue—but not in the manner that it is presently administered, which he sees as more symbolic (McCaffery 2017, 351) than an effective progressive tax policy.

Most states used to have an estate tax, but now only the District of Columbia and twelve states have estate taxes. Many states repealed their estate tax after Congress enacted the Economic Growth and Tax Relief Reconciliation Act (EGTRRA) of 2001. The 2001 tax law substituted a federal deduction for the more favorable dollar-for dollar federal credit allowed for state estate taxes (Maguire 2012, 6) making it significantly less favorable for states to maintain the estate tax. In some cases, the cost to administer the estate tax did not justify the revenues that the tax generated. Another reason for the decline of estate tax legislation by states was growing concern that wealthy taxpayers were opting to make their homes in states without death taxes (Juehring 2019).

Another approach to mitigate wealth inequality is to tax inheritances. Inheritances contribute about "forty percent of all wealth" (Juehring 2019, 1153) in the United States. This suggests that such accumulation of wealth can create generational dynasties. The economic significance of inheritances is rising, aided in part by laws that contribute to the growth of long-standing trusts (Kades 2019, 151). When massive amounts of wealth are sealed off from taxation in these multigenerational dynasties, heirs can be prevented from "dissipating concentrated wealth in ways that promote economic equality and socioeconomic mobility" (Kades 2019, 152). A law that requires large trusts to spend an annual percentage of the trust could offset the excessive "high savings rates by dynastic trusts" (Kades 2019, 152).

There is no federal inheritance tax, and only six states have inheritance tax laws (Juehring 2019). Proponents of installing a federal level inheritance tax to reduce economic inequality argue that an inheritance tax could potentially raise $600 billion over the next decade (2020–2030) and that many inheritances contain gains on assets that have never been taxed (Aaron 2019).

Finally, capital gains tax is another example of a government tax tool that can raise revenue and redistribute wealth. Simply put, a capital gain occurs when a taxpayer's asset sells for more than it was purchased. The law in 2020 requires a taxpayer to pay a tax on the gain that can be 0.0 percent, 15 percent, or 20 percent, depending on the taxpayer's taxable income (another 3.8-percent net investment income tax applies to capital gains for taxpayers with adjusted gross incomes over certain thresholds). Several 2020 Democratic presidential contenders, such as Bernie Sanders, Elizabeth Warren, and Joe Biden, advocated for significantly raising the tax rate on capital gains for top earners. Biden, for example, promoted raising the tax on capital gains to 43 percent for taxpayers earning more than $1 million in a given year (LaJoie 2019).

Some conservative politicians advocate for indexing capital gains to inflation, thereby reducing tax liability. To illustrate the idea, suppose that someone purchased an asset for $100 in January 1990 and sells the asset for $190 in January 2019. This is a $90 "long-term" (so designated because the asset was held for more than one year) capital gain. If the capital gains tax in this instance is 20 percent (because this taxpayer reports an ordinary income in the highest range), the capital gains tax owed is $18. But if the asset's capital gain was indexed to inflation, $100 in 1990 would have the same buying power as $197.58 in January 2019 (U.S. Department of Labor 2019). Therefore, there would not be a gain but rather a loss of $7.58. Progressives are strongly opposed to such a scheme, however. They assert that indexing capital gains to inflation without a well-constructed regulatory plan could dramatically reduce government revenue and "deliver benefits almost exclusively to those at the top of the income distribution" (Hemel and Kamin 2019, 699).

CONCLUSION

The wealth inequality issue is not simply one of who owns a better car, wears finer clothes, or takes fancier vacations. It also governs fundamental aspects of our lives, such as what neighborhoods we live in, what environmental and health hazards we are exposed to, the quality of schools our children attend, and how attentive politicians are to our concerns. Given these stakes, debate on polices to reduce wealth inequality will undoubtedly continue to occupy a central place in American politics over the next decade.

Kimberley L. Kinsley and Robert S. Rycroft

Further Reading

Aaron, Henry J. 2019. "To Reduce Inequality, Tax Inheritances Needed." Tax Policy Center, Urban Institute & Brookings Institution, November 19, 2019. https://www .taxpolicycenter.org/publications/reduce-inequality-tax-inheritances/full.

Brunson, Samuel D. 2019. "Afterlife of the Death Tax." *Indiana Law Journal* 94 (2): 355–88.

Center on Budget and Policy Priorities. 2019. "Policy Basics: Where Do Federal Tax Revenues Come From?" June 20, 2019, 1–3. https://www.cbpp.org/research/federal -tax/policy-basics-where-do-federal-tax-revenues-come-from.

Hemel, Daniel, and David Kamin. 2019. "The False Promise of Presidential Indexation." *Yale Journal on Regulation* 36:693–733.

Herzig, David J. 2017. "The Income Equality Case for Eliminating the Estate Tax." *Southern California Law* Review 90:1143–98.

Juehring, Jenny L. 2019. "Why the End Is Here for State Death Transfer Taxes and How States Should Respond." *Washington University Law Review* 96:1137–57.

Kades, Eric. 2019. "Of Piketty and Perpetuities: Dynastic Wealth in the Twenty-First Century (and Beyond)." *Boston College Law Review* 60:145–215.

LaJoie, Taylor. 2019. "Comparing Capital Gains Tax Proposals by 2020 Presidential Candidates." Tax Foundation, December 4, 2019. https://taxfoundation.org/2020-capital -gains-proposals.

Leiserson, Greg, Will McGrew, and Rakaha Kopparam. 2019. "The Distribution of Wealth in the United States and Implications for a Net Worth Tax," Washington Center for Equitable Growth. https://equitablegrowth.org/the-distribution-of -wealth-in-the-united-states-and-implications-for-a-net-worth-tax.

Lowenstein, Henry, and Kathryn Kisska-Schulze. 2018. "A Historical Examination of the Constitutionality of the Federal Estate Tax." *William & Mary Bill of Rights Journal* 27 (1): 123–51.

Maguire, Steven. 2012. "The Impact of the Federal Estate Tax on State Estate Taxes, R42788." *U.S. Congressional Research Service, CRS Report for Congress*, October 24, 2012. https://fas.org/sgp/crs/misc/R42788.pdf.

Mccaffery, Edward J. 2017. "Taxing Wealth Seriously." *New York University Tax Law Review* 70:305–75.

Piketty, Thomas. 2013. *Le Capital au XXI siècle*. Paris: Editions du Seuil.

Piketty, Thomas. 2014. *Capital in the 21st Century*. Cambridge, MA: Belknap Press of Harvard University Press.

Pressman, Steven. 2016. *Understanding Piketty's* Capital in the 21st Century. New York: Routledge.

Rycroft, Robert. 2018. *The Economics of Inequality, Discrimination, Poverty, and Mobility*. 2nd ed. New York: Routledge.

U.S. Department of Labor, Bureau of Labor Statistics. 2019. "Consumer Price Index Inflation Calculator." https://data.bls.gov/cgi-bin/cpicalc.pl?cost1=100.00&year1=199001 &year2=201901.

U.S. Department of the Treasury, Internal Revenue Service. 2019a. "Estate and Gift Tax Frequently Asked Questions." https://www.irs.gov/newsroom/estate-and-gift-tax-faqs.

U.S. Department of the Treasury, Internal Revenue Service. 2019b. "Estate Tax." https://www.irs.gov/businesses/small-businesses-self-employed/estate-tax.

Williamson, James M., and Siraj G. Bawa. 2018. "Estimated Effects of the Tax Cuts and Jobs Act on Farms and Farm Households, ERR-252." U.S. Department of Agriculture, Economic Research Service, June 2018. https://www.ers.usda.gov/webdocs/publications/89356/err-252.pdf.

Workplace Discrimination

Workplace discrimination, also known as labor market discrimination, occurs when two otherwise similar individuals are treated unequally in the labor market due to characteristics that are unrelated to their ability to work. This discrimination can occur during the hiring or firing process, through different standards for promotion, and in the payment practices of companies. Discrimination occurs in all industries and occupations. There are many explanations as to why discrimination occurs and several ways in which public policy can reduce discrimination.

WHO IS AFFECTED BY DISCRIMINATION?

Discrimination in the labor market affects a wide range of social groups. For example, women are paid less than otherwise similar men (in terms of education, experience, and skills), and minorities are paid less than otherwise similar white workers. Gay men are paid less than otherwise similar heterosexual men. Workers with disabilities confront a wage gap that is larger than the lower productivity caused by their impairments. Immigrants with darker skin tones earn less than immigrants with lighter skin tones.

Discriminatory practices extend beyond pay differences. In the application process, African Americans and Arab Americans are less likely to be offered job interviews than similarly qualified whites. Similarly, workers who identify themselves with a religion are less likely to receive interviews than workers who do not identify themselves as a member of a religious organization. Muslim Americans are the least likely to receive callbacks when their religion is identified (Wright et al. 2013). In the interview process, women are less likely to receive job offers than otherwise similar men. Older workers are often overlooked for promotions and training opportunities. Pregnant women are less likely to be recommended for hiring, even when compared to equally qualified, nonpregnant candidates.

There are many other examples of labor market discrimination. For instance, one study found that over 80 percent of older workers experience workplace discrimination in a given year (Chou and Choi 2011). Mothers were viewed as having lower competence and less commitment to work, and they had lower likelihood of getting promoted or to be offered job interviews than comparable nonmothers. In contrast, fathers and nonfathers are not viewed differently in the workplace. Women are less likely to receive promotions than similarly qualified men.

THE WAGE GAP

One of the most common forms of labor market discrimination arises from pay discrepancies. As of 2018, women make approximately 80 percent as much as their male counterparts, while African American women make 63 percent of white men's earnings, and Hispanic and Latina women make 54 percent of white men's earnings (Miller 2018).

Some of this gap is due to the different characteristics of—and choices made by—workers of different demographic groups. For example, it is expected that corporate executives have higher wages than administrative assistants. The fact that more executives are male and more administrative assistants are female therefore explains part of the gender wage gap. An additional contributor to wage gaps is worker differences in *human capital*. Human capital is the collection of attributes that increase a worker's productivity, including education, work experience, and unique talents. In addition to human capital differences, wage gaps may be the result of job location, occupation, and hours worked. The influence of differences in the characteristics of and choices made by workers constitute the *explained wage gap*. This explained wage gap makes up a large portion of the pay discrepancy. When accounting for differences in observed worker characteristics, including differences in human capital, occupation, and industry, the gender wage gap falls from 20 percent to 9 percent (Blau and Kahn 2017).

However, even after accounting for the factors that make up the explained wage gap, there still exist pay discrepancies favoring white men over women and minority workers. This remaining difference in pay is known as the *unexplained wage gap* and represents the part of the pay gap between workers of different social groups that is not explained by differences in worker attributes. For example, the higher pay of male administrative assistants relative to female administrative assistants and of male executives relative to female executives is attributed to the unexplained portion of the wage gap. Labor market discrimination contributes to the unexplained wage gap.

In the United States, overall wage gaps have generally declined over time. Part of this is due to the fact that differences in human capital between groups have declined over time. For example, in 1981, 22 percent of women and 28 percent of men graduated from college. This gender gap reversed by 2011, with 40 percent of women and 39 percent of men earning college degrees (Blau and Kahn 2017). Reductions in the differences in worker characteristics across groups decreases the size of the wage gap between those groups.

In addition, the unexplained component of racial wage gaps and gender wage gaps has generally declined over time—though increased in both racial and gender wage gaps during the 2000s. In 1970, the unexplained portion of the wage gap was just over half for Black men and one-third for Black women. By 2000, it had shrunk to a third for Black men and slightly favored Black women (i.e., Black women earned more than similar white women). However, the unexplained portion of the racial wage gap for both men and women increased in the 2000s (Mandel and Semyonov 2016). With respect to gender, the unexplained portion of the wage gap declined from just under half in 1980 to less than 40 percent in 2010. These declines in the unexplained portion of the gender wage gap occurred primarily in the 1980s (Blau and Kahn 2017). Declines in the unexplained portion of the wage gap suggest that labor market discrimination has decreased but not disappeared.

OCCUPATIONAL SEGREGATION

Another main contributor to wage gaps is *occupational segregation*. Occupational segregation is the phenomenon whereby members of different groups work in different industries and occupations. For instance, women are traditionally employed as elementary and secondary school educators, secretaries, and nurses, while men are traditionally employed as mechanics, doctors, and engineers. Occupational segregation does not only separate people of different social groups into different industries; it also separates people within an industry or firm. For example, women and minorities are underrepresented in both the managerial and executive levels of firms.

Occupational segregation is the product of many factors, some of which can be exacerbated by a history of discrimination. Intentional decisions about the types of people who can work in specific lines of work helps to reinforce cultural views of the types of work appropriate for certain social groups. Business practices, though not overtly discriminatory, may systematically overlook women and minorities for promotion.

Part of occupational segregation is most likely natural. If certain professions appeal more to members of certain social groups, there is nothing wrong or discriminatory about them entering such fields in disproportionate amounts. Much of the challenge that researchers of labor market discrimination face is determining the extent in which discriminatory factors and practices contribute to occupational segregation.

EXPLANATIONS FOR DISCRIMINATION IN THE WORKPLACE

Famed economist Gary S. Becker's theory of *taste-based discrimination* claims that discrimination is the product of preferences for people of a certain gender, race, and/or appearance when making certain market interactions (Becker 1971). In taste discrimination, there are perceived nonmonetary or nonpecuniary costs associated with employing an individual from an undesirable social group. Due to the perceived nonpecuniary costs, workers from the undesirable social group are less likely to be hired or promoted, and when hired, they receive lower wages than the preferred group. Taste discrimination originates from three distinct sources: employers, employees, and customers.

Employer Discrimination

Employer discrimination occurs when an employer assumes that hiring members of a certain social group has a nonpecuniary cost in addition to the employee's wage. A discriminatory employer takes into account the nonpecuniary costs of hiring potential employees from the minority social group. As such, the employers act as though the wage of the minority group is higher than the prevailing wage. To compensate, workers in the group facing discrimination are hired only when their wages are less than those of the preferred group. If the "distaste" is high enough, a discriminatory employer may avoid employing members from a certain social group altogether. This in turn can reinforce occupational segregation.

For example, Mr. Krabs is an entrepreneur who wishes to open a new location of his restaurant, the Krusty Krab. When attempting to staff his new restaurant, he is faced with the decision to employ candidates who are from a pool of workers that consists of sponges and squids. Mr. Krabs has a particular disdain for squids, as he finds their big noses, green skin, and propensity to spew ink unappealing. Due to this personal bias, he decides to employ squids only if he is able to pay them less than he would pay a standard worker sponge. If his disdain for squids is great enough, he may even avoid hiring squids entirely.

Claudia Goldin and Cecilia Rouse provided a real-world example of employer discrimination in a 2000 study. Positions in symphony orchestras had been dominated by male musicians. Starting in the 1970s, symphony orchestras began implementing blind auditions. Goldin and Rouse found an increase in the number of female musicians being hired to symphony orchestras in the cities that implemented blind auditions. These results suggest that employer "taste" preferences for male musicians prevented women from attaining employment in prestigious symphony orchestras. The blind auditions removed the bias of the reviewers and therefore reduced the effects of employer discrimination (Goldin and Rouse 2000).

Employee Discrimination

Employee discrimination occurs when employees of a firm find working with members of a specific gender, race, ethnicity, and/or age unfavorable. Due to this distaste, employees require additional compensation for having to work with employees from an undesirable social group. If employees' distaste for working with individuals from a certain social group is large enough, they may even take steps to prevent such individuals from entering into their firm.

Let's return to the analogy of the Krusty Krab. This time it is the sponge workers who disdain working with the squid workers. As a result, the sponges demand higher wages as compensation for working with squids. To make up for the sponges' higher wages, Mr. Krabs reduces the wages of the squid workers. If the sponges dislike their squid coworkers enough, they may also participate in discriminatory actions that affect the well-being of the squids.

Customer Discrimination

The third type of taste-based discrimination arises from customers' biases. Customer discrimination occurs when customers respond unfavorably to receiving services from employees of a particular social group. Therefore, companies find it detrimental to their profits to employ workers of the group that is perceived negatively. This form of discrimination is most prevalent in industries in which employee customer interactions are common. It also exacerbates occupational segregation, as workers of the preferred group interact with customers while workers of the unfavorable group work in jobs with little interaction with customers.

Let's return to the Krusty Krab. This time, it is the customers who do not like being served by squid employees. Mr. Krabs observes that customers are less likely to frequent restaurants if they have squid servers. Recognizing that it is less profitable to employ squids, he is hesitant to offer them employment; and when he does, he offers lower pay to offset the reduced income. Mr. Krabs, holding no bias against squid employees, may also hire squids to work in jobs that place them in the kitchen, thus out of sight of his customers, while hiring sponges to work in positions such as serving tables, in which customer interaction is prevalent.

Athletes in professional sports leagues experience customer discrimination. For instance, in the National Basketball Association (NBA) during the 1980s, white players were paid more, accounting for differences in productivity and skill, than Black players. Additionally, teams with more white players had higher fan attendance. By the 1990s, this wage gap had mostly vanished, except among higher-earning athletes, where white players were found to make more than their Black counterparts, suggesting a league preference for white star players. These results imply that fans of professional basketball have a preference for watching white players and that NBA owners respond by overcompensating white star players to boost both fan viewership and attendance. This example illustrates how the preferences of consumers can lead to labor market discrimination.

STATISTICAL DISCRIMINATION

There exists another explanation for why labor market inequalities persist. *Statistical discrimination* suggests that employers make assumptions about the productive capabilities of potential employees. To compensate for the lack of information employers have when evaluating potential employees, employers engage in stereotyping or *profiling*. Profiling can be defined as the act of assigning certain characteristics to individuals of a social group on the basis of the average traits, habits, and abilities of the social group. Statistical discrimination typically affects workers before they begin a job. In fact, as an employer learns more about a specific employee, the wage of said employee should become less reliant on easily observed attributes such as race and gender and become more influenced by individual productivity. Despite this, for employees from the minority social group, statistical discrimination may mean lower rates of training and promotion.

It is time to revisit the Krusty Krab restaurant one last time. In this scenario, Mr. Krabs is attempting to determine the quality of the job candidates presented before him, but soon realizes he does not have definitive information that would allow him to pinpoint the quality of each individual job candidate. He then turns to a consideration of his current employees. He soon realizes that he employs both a sponge (Spongebob) and a squid (Squidward) and begins to compare the work produced by both employees. He recalls that Spongebob is an employee who is energetic, optimistic, and talented. He recognizes Squidward as an employee who is rude, uninspired, and lazy. Mr. Krabs then attributes the characteristics of Spongebob to all sponge workers and the characteristics of Squidward to all squid workers. Whether these assumptions are accurate or not, the assumptions lead Mr. Krabs to value the work of sponges over the work of squids. As a result, squid job candidates will be offered employment less often and be offered lower wages on average compared to their sponge counterparts. Even if the average sponge is more productive than the average squid, a particular sponge employee may or may not be more productive than a particular squid employee. There is much more variation in ability within groups than there is between groups, so looking at the average productivity of a group ignores information about a particular employee's actual abilities.

Stereotypes of social groups are pervasive in the labor market, with workers of all demographics facing the challenge of overcoming notions that are inaccurate on an individual level. For instance, some white employers believe that Black workers, particularly Black male workers, have a poor work ethic and are difficult to manage, while Latinx workers, particularly first-generation immigrants, are viewed as having a strong work ethic and being pliable employees. These preconceived notions affect minorities in the labor market, as these workers are found to face challenges gaining employment and suffer a wage gap relative to white workers.

An example of the effects of stereotypes on minorities in the labor market can be found in a study conducted in Boston and Chicago. Resumes of varying levels of quality were randomly assigned names that were stereotypically white, such as Emily and Greg, or stereotypically Black, such as Lakisha and Jamal. Having a name that is stereotypically Black made a job candidate about 50 percent less likely to receive a callback for a job interview. Those with stereotypically Black names did not benefit from having a high-quality resume as much as those with stereotypically white names. People with a "white" name who also had a high-quality resume had an increased likelihood of receiving a callback of approximately 11 percent, while people with a "Black" name and high-quality resumes had an increased likelihood of receiving a callback of only 8 percent, a 27-percent difference in callback rates (Bertrand and Mullainathan 2004). This research suggests that stereotypes associated with Black employees lead employers to overlook them in favor of similarly qualified white job candidates.

Women also suffer from stereotypes about their labor market behavior. On average women suffer from perceptions that they are less attached to their careers and work fewer hours than their male counterparts. Much of these expectations of female workers can be attributed to the societal belief that female workers carry a larger responsibility for childcare and home obligations. Employers faced with the decision of hiring a female job candidate will often offer the candidate a lower salary than they would a male candidate. This is especially true for women who are mothers; they may be subject to wage reduction penalties from employers who see them as more likely to miss work due to maternity leave or childcare. The wages of men who are fathers, however, do not suffer. In fact, married men experience a bonus to their wages, as they are assumed to have the burden of providing financial support for their families. Labor economists refer to this phenomenon as the "fatherhood premium."

There exist a multitude of stereotypes of older workers. Surveys of managerial employees found a belief that older workers are hard to train, below average at using and learning to use technology, and overly cautious in decision-making. As a result, older workers are trained and nominated for promotions less often than their younger coworkers.

Stereotypes of a variety of social groups pervade society. These stereotypes often affect the way workers are treated and viewed by employers in the labor market, putting them at a disadvantage when it comes to obtaining employment and maximizing wages. Due to this, statistical discrimination can create inefficiencies in production, since employers do not tap into a potential pool of effective workers. Statistical discrimination also reinforces the existence of occupational segregation; when employers will only hire certain types of workers for particular jobs, social groups segregate into different professions.

INDIRECT DISCRIMINATION

Not all labor market inequalities are the product of overt discrimination. In fact, inequalities in the labor market often occur from behavior that many would deem innocent and perhaps unavoidable. One example of such behavior is the tendencies people display when making decisions to form "mentor-mentee relationships." Mentor-mentee relationships typically involve high-ranking authorities, such as business executives or professors, forming a relationship with less experienced and typically younger employees or students to provide them with insight and advice for their future careers. Such relationships often involve personal dedication on the part of the mentor, so potential mentors typically choose individuals who remind them of themselves. Since most high-ranking business executives in lucrative fields (e.g., law, medicine, and finance) are heterosexual white men, it is only natural that they are most likely to choose other heterosexual white men as their mentees. Since such behavioral tendencies tend to overlook women and minorities as potential mentees, this leaves women and minorities at a disadvantage when attempting to advance their careers.

Another factor that likely contributes to inequality in the labor market is the tendency of people from the same social group to interact with one another more frequently during non-work-related activities, forming *informal networks*. Though these informal networks are formed and typically meet outside of workplace environments, they often act as a vehicle for the transmission of information regarding job opportunities, work-related skills, and professional contacts. Thus workers who are outside informal networks can find themselves at a disadvantage to workers who are in informal networks. Men and women typically belong to their own informal networks, for instance, men's golf outings or women's book clubs. The benefit men receive from their networks on average outweigh the benefits women receive from their informal networks. This is largely due to the fact that women are less likely to have people within their informal network who are highly influential and connected in the professional world in comparison to men.

People seeking an example of informal networks in their own lives may need to look no further than their own educational institution. There is much literature regarding the spatial segregation of Black students at predominantly white schools, outlining how cultural differences among students lead students of different races to associate with members of their own race almost exclusively in their social interactions, typically beginning around the sixth or seventh grade. Many authors have documented how Black students at majority white schools often sit together in the cafeteria, join clubs together, and participate in the same extracurricular activities.

THE COST OF DISCRIMINATION

There are numerous moral motivations that argue against discriminatory practices; there are many practical and financial arguments against discrimination as well. For instance, statistical discrimination is inefficient: statistical discrimination lowers the potential productivity of a firm by causing it to overlook high-skilled workers that belong to a social group that is statistically viewed as inferior. Ending the practice of taste-based discrimination and hiring workers of the lower-paid but equally productive minority group may also lower a firm's costs and therefore increase the firm's profits.

Another business-oriented argument against discrimination comes from the belief that discrimination is likely to lead to lower levels of diversity within firms. This lack of diversity may very well be detrimental to firms; diversity is beneficial to the quality of work produced by the employees of a firm. Groups with more gender and racial diversity brainstorm more feasible and more effective ideas than groups that are not diverse. Higher levels of firm diversity are associated with a higher level of sales, an increase to the number of consumers that buy from a firm, a larger market share, and greater profits. Some studies have also found evidence that greater firm diversity can be associated with higher levels of employee conflict. Despite such findings, many authors argue these higher levels of conflict can still be a potential benefit, claiming that conflict between employees can lead to more creative business solutions that have overcome higher scrutiny before they are adopted.

POLICIES TO FIGHT DISCRIMINATION

The federal government has made numerous attempts to redress the effects of discrimination. In 1963, Congress passed the Equal Pay Act, making it illegal to pay workers differently on the basis of gender if they complete the same work.

Title VII of the Civil Rights Act of 1964 disallowed discriminating against workers in terms of hiring, firing, and promotional practices on the basis of race, sex, religion, or nationality. The Age Discrimination in Employment act, passed in 1967, made discriminatory practices against older workers, such as mandatory retirement, illegal.

Discrimination on the basis of sexual orientation and gender identity has been a highly contested policy space and currently exists in a legal gray area. As of 2020 the U.S. Congress had not passed any federal law protecting the rights of LGBT workers directly, and only twenty-two states have enacted legislation that prohibits discrimination against members of the LGBT community. The U.S. Equal Employment Opportunity Commission (EEOC) uses Title VII of the Civil Rights Act of 1964 to argue cases of discrimination based on sexual orientation and gender identity in the federal circuit court system, regardless of local or state laws. To date, courts in only six states have adopted the EEOC's interpretation of Title VII on the basis of sexual orientation. The EEOC has had slightly more success arguing their stance on gender identity, with federal courts in twenty states adopting the stance that Title VII prohibits workplace discrimination on the basis of gender identity.

Despite the implementation of a multitude of federal policies, the extent of their effectiveness has often been called into question. Academic studies have noted the unlikelihood for success in court for plaintiffs who file cases of labor market discrimination. Many researchers also point out that the gains in employment and wages made by disadvantaged workers may be the result of greater educational attainment and labor force attachment. Such findings highlight the importance of not relying solely on litigation or legislation to end labor market discrimination.

Jared A. Knowles and Erin E. George

Further Reading

Altonji, Joseph G., and Charles R Pierret. 2001. "Employer Learning and Statistical Discrimination." *Quarterly Journal of Economics* 116 (1): 313–50.

Arrow, Kenneth J. 1998. "What Has Economics to Say About Racial Discrimination?" *Journal of Economic Perspectives* 12 (2): 91–100.

Becker, Gary. S. 1971. *The Economics of Discrimination*. Chicago: University of Chicago Press.

Bertrand, Marianne, and Sendhil Mullainathan. 2004. "Are Emily and Greg More Employable Than Lakisha and Jamal? A Field Experiment on Labor Market Discrimination." *American Economic Review* 94 (4): 991–1013.

Blau, Francine D., and Jed DeVaro. 2006. "New Evidence on Gender Differences in Promotion Rates: An Empirical Analysis of a Sample of New Hires." NBER Working Paper 12321. National Bureau of Economic Research. https://www.nber.org/papers/w12321.

Blau, Francine D., Marianne A. Ferber, and Anne E. Winkler. 2014. *The Economics of Women, Men, and Work*. 7th ed. Edited by Donna Battista. Upper Saddle River, NJ: Pearson.

Blau, Francine D., and Lawrence M. Kahn. 2007. "The Gender Pay Gap: Have Women Gone as Far as They Can? Executive Overview." *Academy of Management Perspectives* 21 (1): 7–23.

Blau, Francine D., and Lawrence M. Kahn. 2017. "The Gender Wage Gap: Extent, Trends, and Explanations." *Journal of Economic Literature* 55 (3): 789–865.

Carpenter, Christopher. 2004. "New Evidence on Gay and Lesbian Household Incomes." *Contemporary Economic Policy* 22 (1): 78–94.

Carter, Dorinda J. 2007. "Why the Black Kids Sit Together at the Stairs: The Role of Identity-Affirming Counter-Spaces in a Predominantly White High School." *Journal of Negro Education* 76 (4): 542–54.

Chou, Rita Jing-ann, and Namkee G Choi. 2011. "Prevalence and Correlates of Perceived Workplace Discrimination among Older Workers in the United States of America." *Ageing & Society,* 1051–70.

Clermont, Kevin M., and Stewart J. Schwab. 2009. "Employment Discrimination Plaintiffs in Federal Court: From Bad to Worse?" Cornell Law Faculty Publications Paper 109. https://scholarship.law.cornell.edu/cgi/viewcontent.cgi?article=1108& context=lsrp_papers.

Correll, Shelley J., Stephen Benard, and In Paik. 2007. "Getting a Job: Is There a Motherhood Penalty?" *American Journal of Sociology* 112 (5): 1297–1338.

Cunningham, Jennifer, and Therese Macan. 2007. "Effects of Applicant Pregnancy on Hiring Decisions and Interview Ratings." *Sex Roles* 57:497–508.

Darity, William A., Jr., and Patrick L. Mason. 1998. "Evidence on Discrimination: Codes of Color, Codes of Gender." *Journal of Economic Perspectives* 12 (2): 41–62.

DeLeire, Thomas. 2001. "Changes in Wage Discrimination against People with Disabilities: 1984–93." *Journal of Human Resources* 36 (1): 144–58.

EEOC. 2008. "What You Should Know About EEOC and the Enforcement Protections for LGBT Workers." https://www.eeoc.gov/eeoc/newsroom/wysk/enforcement_ protections_lgbt_workers.cfm.

EEOC. 2018. Federal Laws Prohibiting Job Discrimination: Questions and Answers. https://www.eeoc.gov/laws/types/age.cfm.

Goldin, Claudia D. 1991. "The Role of World War II in the Rise of Women's Employment." *American Economic Review* 81 (4): 741–56.

Goldin, Claudia, and Cecilia Rouse. 2000. "Orchestrating Impartiality: The Impact of 'Blind' Auditions on Female Musicians." *American Economic Review* 90 (4): 715–41.

Hamilton, Barton Hughes. 1997. "Racial Discrimination and Professional Basketball Salaries in the 1990s." *Applied Economics* 29:287–96.

Herring, Cedric. 2009. "Does Diversity Pay? Race, Gender, and the Business Case for Diversity." *American Sociological Review* 74 (2): 208–24.

Hersch, Joni. 2011. "The Persistence of Skin Color Discrimination for Immigrants." *Social Science Research* 40:1337–49.

Kahn, Lawrence M. 2000. "The Sports Business as a Labor Market Laboratory." *Journal of Economic Perspectives* 14 (3): 75–94.

Kahn, Lawrence M., and Peter D Sherer. 1988. "Racial Differences in Professional Basketball Players' Compensation." *Journal of Labor Economics* 6 (1): 40–61.

Mandel, Hadas, and Moshe Semyonov. 2016. "Going Back in Time? Gender Differences in Trends and Sources of the Racial Pay Gap, 1970 to 2010." *American Sociological Review* 81 (5): 1039–68.

Martell, Michael E. 2013. "Differences Do Not Matter: Exploring the Wage Gap for Same-Sex Behaving Men." *Eastern Economic Journal* 39:45–71.

McGuire, Gail M. 2002. "Gender, Race, and the Shadow Structure: A Study of Informal Networks and Inequality in a Work Organization." *Gender and Society* 16 (3): 303–22.

McLeod, Poppy Lauretta, Sharon Alisa Lobel, and Taylor H. Cox. 1996. "Ethnic Diversity and Creativity in Small Groups." *Small Group Research* 27 (2): 248–64.

Miller, Kevin. 2018. "The Simple Truth about the Gender Pay Gap." American Association of University Women. https://www.aauw.org/research/the-simple-truth-about-the-gender-pay-gap/.

Neumark, David. 2003. "Age Discrimination Legislation in the United States." *Contemporary Economic Policy* 21 (3): 297–317.

Neumark, David, Roy J. Bank, and Kyle D. Van Nort. 1996. "Sex Discrimination in Restaurant Hiring: An Audit Study." *Quarterly Journal of Economics* 111 (3): 915–41.

Out & Equal. 2017. "2017 Workplace Equality Fact Sheet." http://outandequal.org/2017-workplace-equality-fact-sheet.

Posthuma, Richard A., and Michael A. Campion. 2009. "Age Stereotypes in the Workplace: Common Stereotypes, Moderators, and Future Research Directions." *Journal of Management* 35 (1): 158–88.

Sandberg, Sheryl. 2013. "Are You My Mentor?" In *Lean In*, 64–76. New York: Alfred A. Knopf.

Schwab, Stewart. 1986. "Is Statistical Discrimination Efficient?" *American Economic Review* 76 (1): 228–34.

Selmi, Michael. 2001. "Why Are Employment Discrimination Cases So Hard to Win?" *Louisiana Law Review* 61 (3): 555–75.

Tatum, Beverly Daniel. 2017. *Why Are All the Black Kids Sitting Together in the Cafeteria?* New York: Basic Book.

Widner, Daniel, and Stephen Chicoine. 2011. "It's All in the Name: Employment Discrimination against Arab Americans." *Sociological Forum* 26 (4): 806–23.

Wright, Bradley R. E., Michael Wallace, John Bailey, and Allen Hyde. 2013. "Religious Affiliation and Hiring Discrimination in New England: A Field Experiment." *Research in Social Stratification and Mobility* 34:111–26.

SECTION II

Educational Services

Early Childhood Education

All children in the United States deserve a quality early childhood education. As the income divide in the United States has widened, however, persistent inequities in early childhood education have been amplified. Income-level disparities can create barriers to childcare accessibility, options, programming, quality, and affordability. These inequities can negatively affect children's well-being during their early critical years of life. Quality educational opportunities support social, cognitive, and physical development. Therefore, families' access to safe nurturing learning environments for their children is a social justice issue.

This chapter details how early childhood education is a critical issue with widespread systemic inequalities. It describes efforts for more equitable childcare and early education opportunities, obstacles facing low-income families, factors that influence the quality of a child's experience, and the long-term impacts of early learning opportunities.

CURRENT STATE OF EARLY CHILDHOOD EDUCATION

The term *early childhood education* is used to describe programs for children from birth to about six years old, before they enter primary education or elementary school. Historically in the United States, the necessity of childcare programs developed when the men left home during times of war as well as during periods of rapid industrialization. In both of these cases, mothers needed to work outside the home to support their families. During the course of the twentieth century, the role of women dramatically changed in American society. Mothers more often operated as heads of households, became more highly educated, and were more likely to pursue careers and employment in order to improve the family's socioeconomic standing. Meanwhile, the range of ages described when referring to early childhood education has changed. Just a few decades ago, educational programs for children under eight years of age meant focusing on social and physical development through play. Now, children are introduced to complex concepts at much younger ages in education programs and are expected to begin academic learning in kindergarten.

Educator Friedrich Froebel first established *kindergarten*, translating to "a child's garden," in Germany. As the name indicates, kindergarten was a setting for young children to play outdoors with music, movement, and free exploration. Kindergarten in the United States has changed drastically over the years. Just as recently as the late 1960s, less than half of children were in school at the age of five. By the late 2010s, by contrast, 87 percent of children were enrolled in either half-day or full-day kindergarten at age five. Seventeen states and the District of Columbia have compulsory school attendance for children five years of age (NCES 2018). Currently, many school districts across the nation have established full-day kindergarten options for parents.

Early childhood education is a full spectrum of learning opportunities that can include parental care, informal care, and center care. They vary in setting, funding, and programming, from profit to nonprofit, homes to centers, public to private, as well as part day to full day. Early childhood education programs also can be found across a wide range of childcare options, including day care, nursery school, preschool, Head Start, kindergarten, and more. Parents look for convenience, affordability, shared values, quality, focus, loving staff, supportive policies, and connection to family. Although choices are limited, parents try to be deliberate in their selection of environments in hopes of providing enriching experiences for their children to develop to their fullest potential.

One out of five families have one parent stay home to care for young children. Up to 75 percent of parents arrange their schedules to spend some part of their workweek at home with their children. Although many families elect to have a parent or relative care for their young children, a greater number of survey responses from low-income families indicated their reasons for staying home were based on need rather than choice (Livingston 2018). Although it is important for families to decide on optimal childcare that they trust, the choices for many families are limited or nonexistent because of barriers to access, affordability, or location. According to a U.S. Census Bureau survey, the primary-care arrangement of children with employed mothers has shifted over the years from a relative providing caregiving to a day-care center arrangement (NCES 2018).

According to the U.S. Census Bureau, 61 percent of children spend an average of thirty-three hours per week in childcare. American families are heavily reliant on childcare centers. Of those children enrolled in childcare centers, 18 percent come from families in poverty, while 72 percent are from families of a higher-income level (FIFCFS 2017). Typically, they are operated out of large commercial spaces that are either privately owned or federally funded. Despite high variability in quality, parents value the structure, regulation, and security of childcare centers. Childcare centers also provide a collaborative atmosphere allowing for a variety of interactions with other children.

Families in poverty do not have as many childcare options as families with means. More low-income families (16 percent compared to 4 percent of middle- and high-income families) choose private homes that are licensed as day-care facilities (Bromer and Porter 2017). The more expensive home option selected by

13 percent of families include hiring a nanny, babysitter, or au pair (FIFCFS 2017). In 2016, one study found that 68 percent of parents with incomes over $100,000 felt they had good choices for childcare, compared to 48 percent of low-income parents (McFarland et al. 2018).

Early childhood education can make a big difference in the life of a child who lives in poverty. Statistics show that 22 percent of children in the United States live in households that are classified as poor. There are 4.7 million children under the age of six living in poverty, creating clear economic inequalities. The federal poverty level threshold for a family of four in 2018 was $24,600. These families were also classified as food insecure and at risk for homelessness. Furthermore, 41percent of children in the United States live in "low-income" households, defined as a family of four earning less than $48,678 annually (Koball and Jiang 2018, 2).In the United States, "about three million children live in families trying to survive on two dollars a day per person, which rivals child poverty in some of the world's poorest countries" (Children's Defense Fund 2017, 6).

ACCESS TO EARLY CHILDHOOD EDUCATION

Many working families in the United States have limited options for early childcare due to barriers of high cost, location, and cultural capital. Families with low socioeconomic status often work multiple jobs and make sacrifices to provide childcare. There are more limited options for the most vulnerable children of families with fewer resources.

Many middle-class and disadvantaged families cannot afford the kind of care that they would like to provide their children. In the United States, the average cost of high-quality childcare is over $10,000 a year. On average, one in four families pays more than 10 percent of their income on childcare (Children's Defense Fund 2017). In Mississippi, the average childcare cost is $5,000, which calculates to 10 percent of the median income in that state. By comparison, in Washington, DC, where the cost of living is much higher, the average annual cost is $23,000, which equates to 37 percent of the median income (Child Care Aware of America 2019). Families with infants and more than one young child are especially challenged, making childcare the most significant expense in the budgets of many families. In many urban areas, monthly childcare can cost more than rent or a mortgage payment. In some cities, annual childcare costs three times as much as a year of public college tuition.

In addition to high costs, another significant barrier for families is finding early childhood programming in a convenient location. Centers that are near their job, home, or public transportation afford parents more ease when dropping off and picking up their children. Underserved communities are especially susceptible to shortages of neighborhood centers. There are areas of the United States that have even been identified as "child care deserts" (Malik and Hamm 2017). Although many states try to predict and meet the demand for educational needs, there are entire low-resourced communities that are isolated and struggling to find care for their young. Unavailability of childcare is prevalent in large urban areas as well as rural areas of the country, especially for marginalized communities. The obstacle of finding childcare because of location was three times more difficult for families in poverty (18 percent reported difficulty) than for families of financial means (6 percent reported difficulty), according to one 2018 study (McFarland et al. 2018).

Many parents with nontraditional work schedules and without local extended family turn to unlicensed childcare options. Parents will often use personal networks or walk around their neighborhood to find nearby childcare. Many families are unaware of government offices or local chambers of commerce that can assist them in their search. Parents often lack adequate information on options or tools to help them evaluate quality programs. Meanwhile, childcare centers that do exist in these areas are often filled to capacity, forcing parents to add their names to long waiting lists (Ho 2018).

FEDERAL CHILDCARE PROGRAMS

Knowing the importance of early childhood education and recognizing the inequalities affecting low-income households, many government programs have been launched to support struggling families, such as Head Start and Universal Preschool programs.

The National Head Start initiative was developed in 1965 as part of President Lyndon B. Johnson's "War on Poverty," an ambitious slate of policies and programs designed to combat poverty conditions across the United States. Through the Department of Health and Human Services, this federally funded initiative continues to serve low-income families with free access to beneficial educational, nutritional, and social development programming for their young children. Despite its recognized benefits, this high-quality early childhood service was only accessed by 31 percent of eligible three- and four-year-old children in the late 2010s. Because of complex regulations and tight budgets, there are not enough Head Start programs to serve all eligible children. Furthermore, the specialized, comprehensive program for younger children in need, called Early Head Start, only reaches 7 percent of eligible families (Dowd 2019).

A more recent federal initiative, Universal Pre-K, allows young children residing in the United States who meet certain eligibility requirements the opportunity to attend a free, federally funded preschool program. Georgia was the first state to introduce Universal Pre-K programs, and now many other cities and states have followed suit. Universal Early Education originally started for children at age four and now includes three-year-old children in some regions. Unlike Head Start, which is specifically designed to serve low-income families, a Pre-K program can only receive classification as Universal Pre-K and receive Title 1 funding if 40 percent of the children come from low-income families, and all children are entitled to the program.

Federal subsidies began with the Child Care and Development Block Grant (CCDBG) of 1990, allocating state agencies to provide childcare vouchers to struggling families. The 2014 reauthorization of CCDBG added funds to improve quality and support informing families. However, this grant only serves 16 percent of families who are in poverty and eligible for assistance. Over the past decade, participation has decreased, serving 370,000 fewer children (Child Care

Aware of America 2019). In 2015, the Every Student Succeed Act (ESSA) included early childhood programming in public education federal funding. These federal grants not only support low-income families but also guide funded centers to meet state performance guidelines, prioritize children with special needs, and pass an on-site review every three years. States use a variety of measurement tools to provide baseline standards for childcare providers and licensing criteria.

INEQUITIES IN QUALITY

The quality of early childhood centers, preschools, and programs varies widely. Parents look for a variety of measures that are important to their family in selecting an education program or facility for their young child. Often the parents' education, worldview, culture, or religion influences the type of programming desired for their child. Generally speaking, however, the most sought-after educational environments for young children focus on development, age-appropriate learning, emotional growth, safety, and preparation to ease into the next phase of learning. Families seek compassionate, skilled caretakers working in enriching age-appropriate early learning environments.

Early childhood education has many quality indicators to determine if a program meets standards. Rating scales such as the QRIS, NAAEE, ERS, and ECECRS-R support measuring systems to improve programs. Some accrediting bodies for programs across the nation include the National Association for the Education of Young Children, National Early Childhood Program accreditation, the National Accreditation Commission for Early Care and Education programs, the National Association for Family Child Care, the Council on Accreditation, and the American Montessori Society.

According to the National Institute of Child Health and Human Development, fewer than 10 percent of childcare programs are considered high quality (Workman and Ullrich 2017). "High-quality" early childhood education programs are those that meet or exceed accreditation and licensing standards. They are identified as providing the broadest range of features designed to care for children and prepare them for overall success. Children from low-income families are most likely to experience lower-quality services from their caregivers (Chaudry et al. 2017). Poor-quality educational services in programs leave many children underserved and at risk.

One of the most essential aspects of a high-quality early childhood education program is safety. In addition to conducting thorough employee background checks, a high-quality program ensures that caretakers are skilled in first aid and developmentally appropriate practices. Facilities, meanwhile, are fully compliant with fire, health, cleanliness, and food-handling codes and have established sound safety, emergency, and equipment plans. Quality programs take care of the basic needs by feeding, cleaning, and nurturing the children in their care (FIFCFS 2017).

Another aspect of high-quality education dictated by guidelines is a low adult-to-child ratio (which typically adjusts depending on the age of the children). Studies have shown that there are measurable benefits of a low adult-child ratio, such as better-observed quality of care and better developmental outcomes, especially with younger students (NICHD 2006). With better ratios, children receive more individual attention as they learn to cooperate and gain stronger academic skills.

According to the Statewide Early Education Study, the foundational aspects of high-quality early childhood education programs are primarily centered around infrastructure and classroom design (Mashburn et al. 2008). Infrastructure includes the curriculum, daily agenda, routines, planned activities, and time for free play. Predictable routines support the developing child's natural rhythms. Classroom design is an observable criterion that measures the extent to which an environment is inclusive, inviting, and child-friendly.

Inclusive early learning environments consider age appropriateness and suitability to the needs of the children. Furniture and facilities designers consider accessibility, color, flooring, noise, lighting, and movement. Classrooms are resourced with developmentally appropriate materials to explore curriculum and activities that are grounded in child development. High-quality programs support the learning needs of all children by incorporating stimulating sensory materials within the curriculum. Well-resourced learning spaces are organized and labeled to include books, puzzles, blocks, and learning materials that spark imagination and creativity. High-quality programs can be creative in providing stimuli to promote language and literacy skills and allow for exploration of the natural world.

At a high-quality childcare center, a child's well-being is supported from a holistic perspective. Children who can explore both indoors and outdoors in safe spaces build large motor skills and balance when playing on well-designed equipment. Cognitive and emotional development is learned through play. When students engage in directed and nondirected activities, they foster skills for creative problem solving. Experiences provided in high-quality programs are described as more joyful and interactive. Children are encouraged to explore and ask questions, dress up, and learn through dramatic play. Caregivers in these settings listen and respond to the children; they praise, tell and read stories, sing, and laugh with the children. A quality educator knows the children, has creative ideas for learning, and utilizes all resources to stimulate the minds of the children. Despite this, many centers cannot afford materials for such learning opportunities nor a safe outside space where children can run. Therefore, there are evident disparities between what some children experience when they are in early childhood education programs and what is developmentally ideal.

Scholars point to the professional staff and teachers as the most critical determinant for high-quality early childhood education. Minimal qualifications of staff include formal post-high school training and licensing. Expert teachers often have a college degree in child development or early childhood education. With the expansion of Universal Pre-K, schools are scrambling for state-certified early childhood teachers. Ongoing professional development opportunities are essential to support teachers and staff. Studies show a direct correlation between caregiver education and high-quality instruction, leading to greater developmental learning outcomes (NICHD 2006).

Teachers who work with young children in public schools are paid on par with the educators in their district. However, the average childcare teacher is only paid ten dollars per hour, or fifteen thousand dollars a year. Not surprisingly, this dismal level of compensation results in high employee turnover rates at many facilities (Children's Defense Fund 2017).

Education advocates and experts emphasize that an early education approach known as *positive caregiving* has been strongly linked to exceptional student outcomes and indicates a high-quality early childhood setting (NICHD 2006). When adults who work with young children display sensitivity and encouragement, they are better able to deliver important developmental benefits, such as stronger verbal skills, to the children in their care. Positive caregiving is characterized by a compassionate attitude, encouraging smiles, comforting connections, and authentic praise. Warm, respectful interactions best meet the emotional needs of young children and build empathy in responsive care.

Relationships between early childhood teachers and their young students are also essential for developing language. Centers that encourage children's interaction with both adults and peers build linguistic and social skills (NICHD 1998). Meaningful interaction between children and caregivers is important, as is the development of relationships among teachers, parents, and children. High-quality early childhood settings are purposeful in their outreach to engage families in children's learning. Clear communication, mutual goals for child success, discussions around their interests, sharing of strengths, and attention to specific needs or concerns indicate strong family engagement. These trusting relationships strongly influence developmental progress.

Quality of early childhood settings can also be measured by how prepared the program is to reach and nurture all students. Recent studies capture a disturbing trend of expelling children in preschool programs. Children from low-income families, between the ages of three and four, are the highest group of children prone to exclusionary discipline. Overwhelmingly, statistics point to the suspension and expulsion of predominantly poor Black boys, which creates long-term negative repercussions for those children (Children's Defense Fund 2017).

Punitive and exclusionary practices create hostile environments that undermine a child's social and emotional development. The disproportionate rates of disciplinary actions for young children living in poverty have rippling effects, as their parents often cannot afford financially to take time off from work to care for children who have been suspended or expelled.

According to the Yale Study Center, a teacher's implicit biases can play a significant role in high rates of early childhood expulsion and suspension. *Implicit bias* describes the unconscious attitudes and stereotypes that individuals hold. Implicit biases in teachers can negatively affect behavior, communication, decision-making, and the ability to connect with students and their families (Gilliam et al. 2016). Boys are expelled 4.5 times more than girls are. African American children are two times more likely to be expelled than white or Hispanic children.

When children are suspended, the opportunity for teachable moments, such as the ability to understand their behavior or actions in a positive, meaningful manner are lost. Their absences can mark the beginning of lifelong negative attitudes about school and their capabilities (Martin, Bosk, and Bailey 2018). Such children are often labeled at this young age and become part of a system that will fail them.

Preschoolers expelled from early childhood settings are three times more likely to be suspended and expelled later, in higher-grade levels. By contrast, a study by Schuyler Center for Analysis and Advocacy indicated that children from low-income families who received a high-quality early education experience proved to have more productive formative years and positive thoughts pertaining to school (Schuyler Center for Analysis and Advocacy 2012). Such findings have led programs such as Head Start to prohibit expulsions and suspension of any child.

Higher-quality care is predictive of more positive interactions among children. Programs that meet accreditation standards report fewer behavior problems at age three than centers that did not meet standards (NICHD 2006). Teachers at these programs can redirect challenging behaviors and teach social and emotional skills that are essential for positive early childhood development. Programs that support children's social and emotional needs can help develop turn taking, listening skills, and caring. The supportive response to children when they feel angry or dysregulated can teach self-control and appropriate response to intense emotions. Studies show that children from high-quality settings are more cooperative in future educational settings (NICHD 1998). When compared to peers, children who experienced high-quality programs are less likely to engage in criminal behavior and more likely to hold down a job.

IMPACT OF INEQUALITY IN EARLY EDUCATION EXPERIENCES

Early childhood education has been widely researched, leading to an increased understanding of the importance of high-quality opportunities. The amount of time young children are engaged in play, communication, and exploration makes a difference. Sociologist Meredith Phillips found that young children from more affluent families experienced 1,300 more hours of enrichment activities than children from low-income families did (Duncan and Magnuson 2011). Stimulating experiences in these early years are fundamentally critical in a child's development. A young child's rapidly developing brain is extremely malleable and sensitive to environmental enrichment (Nelson and Sheridan 2011). Conversely, the developing brain is extremely vulnerable to the effects of deprivation of stimulating experiences. When physical or emotional needs are not met during this foundational time, it has a lasting impact on future success, health, and well-being.

Children's environment and their relationship to caregivers both tremendously influence their neurological, social, emotional, physical, and cognitive development. High-quality early childhood programs can build a foundation for learning and positive attitudes about school. Conversely, poor-quality early childhood programs can undermine the ability to learn, disrupt social connections, and produce negative feeling toward school. The inequalities of early childhood experiences have both immediate and lifelong impacts for children.

By the time children enter kindergarten, there already exists an achievement gap between low-income children and their more affluent peers. Even though, as a nation, great strides have been made in programs such as Head Start, Universal Pre-K, and full-day kindergarten, less than half of poor children enter first grade "ready to learn." Of all the demographic factors, low socioeconomic status makes children most vulnerable for entering school far behind their peers (Janus and Duku 2007). Several intensive early childhood interventions have been studied. Researchers targeted low-income communities to see if children's early experience can mitigate the adverse effects of poverty to close the achievement gap and lead to success in adulthood.

The most cited longitudinal study on positive effects from quality early childhood education is the Perry Preschool program. In the early 1960s, the Perry Preschool project randomly selected an intervention group of children in the low-income community of Ypsilanti, Michigan. The intervention group was given an additional 2.5 hours a day of specialized education. After one year of the study, the children of the intervention group increased their IQ scores an average of fifteen points in comparison (one standard deviation) to the children in the control group who went to the neighborhood center without an intervention. The researchers continued to measure effects of the selected "treatment" children compared to their nonselected peers with follow-up impact studies when the children were twenty-seven and again at forty years old (Barnett 1996; Barnett et al. 2013; Belfield et al. 2006). The children who had the advantage of the early intervention entered school with stronger reading and math skills, laying a foundation for school success and increasing their likelihood to finish high school (Deming 2009). The researchers found that the children in the intervention group grew up to be adults with higher earnings and less likelihood of engaging in at-risk behaviors such as criminal activity (Clarke and Campbell 1998).

Opportunities to develop language in the early years of childhood are of the utmost importance. Language exposure in early childhood settings can have substantial benefits for children, especially from lower socioeconomic backgrounds. Research has found significant differences in the language development of children in economically advantaged and disadvantaged families from as early as eighteen months (Fernald, Marchman, and Weisleder 2013). This disadvantage disproportionately affects children from low-income families who are exposed to fewer vocabulary words and less complex language. This disadvantage has a compounding effect throughout development and can lead to stark gaps in vocabulary knowledge and use by high school (Hart and Risley 1995). Early childhood educators can design experiences that promote conversation, develop language-processing skills, and cultivate a broad vocabulary. Language acquisition is cumulative. Interaction with language supports neurological development, leading in turn to stronger linguistic skills (Romeo et al. 2018).

In a longitudinal effects study of the Abbott Preschool Program, children in low-income communities in New Jersey were given the intervention of high-quality preschool. One year in preschool showed gains in literacy, math, and science achievement. Even more significant gains were noticed in children who had two years of preschool. The study also found throughout the children's education a decrease in identifying special needs and lower grade retention rates compared to children in the control group (Barnett et al. 2013).

A similar study was conducted in 1972. Called the Carolina Abecedarian Project, it offered year-round, full-day services starting from infancy for families who demonstrated need. This model emphasized language development as well as health development, resulting in long-term educational advantages (Campbell et al. 2012).

As surmised from the studies above, a focus on health development results in academic advantages. Young students engaged in outdoor play develop physically healthier and stronger brain architecture. Fresh air and sunshine have been shown to positively impact health, increase immune system function, and inhibit future obesity. Outside play develops motor skills such as directionality, balance, and laterality as well as establishing healthy behaviors for life. Neurological pathways are organized with the repetition of movement patterns. Kinesthetic gross motor movements such as swinging, running, and skipping strengthen cognitive and physical development. When muscles move, they produce proteins and endorphins. Swedish researchers found "restorative potential" when children played in outdoor environments. Play increased the children's ability to focus and attend (Mårtensson et al. 2009).

It is vital to ensure that young children participate in positive experiences such as playing outdoors. Adverse childhood experiences along with a lack of early learning opportunities put children at risk of not developing needed neurological connections for cognitive and social development. Supportive, nurturing caregivers have the potential to inspire more self-confidence, increased curiosity, and greater impulse control (Phillips and Shonkoff 2000). Early childhood education builds foundational reading and math concepts, language and vocabulary facility through everyday discussions, and the ability to develop healthy relationships with peers and caregivers.

The long-term impacts of safe, nurturing, and loving experiences in early childhood are profound. Secure relationships and supportive interactions experienced in early settings develop the ability in children to build other bonds that lead to later successful relationships and self-reported happiness (Thompson and Happold 2002). By establishing secure attachments with caregivers, young children develop a sense of self, build an ability to relate socially, and strengthen the facility to understand their own emotions, a skill needed for self-regulation. Neurological images illustrate that the more pleasurable social attention a young child receives, the more active connections are formed in the limbic structures of the brain (Gerhardt 2014). On the other hand, poor early care combined with adverse experiences, no attention, or insecure relationships lead to future social problems. Brain scans of children who endured early and chronic stress displayed altered functional connections that undermined the children's social interactions persisting into adulthood (Chugani et al. 2001).

Attention skills and emotional self-regulation are present in children before they turn three, and they develop significantly in the preschool years (Posner and Rothbart 2000). The well-known "Marshmallow Study," which measured impulse control of four-year-old children, found that the longer a child could wait to eat the marshmallow, the more likely the child would be to score higher on SATs and secure a college degree years later (Mischel, Shoda, and Rodriguez 1989).

The intervention studies corroborate that the negative impacts of living in poverty can be mitigated by high-quality early childhood education. Developmental psychologists, neuroscientists, and educators concur that early childhood experiences have the potential to benefit or negatively impact young children, determining the trajectory for future academic success. All children can grow up to be successful in school and in life. A high-quality early childhood education can make this more likely.

CONCLUSION

As author and minister Robert Fulghum famously said, "All I really need to know I learned in kindergarten." Early childhood education has the potential to gift children with the joy of learning and positive lifelong habits of mind. Conversely, low socioeconomic status often limits the educational opportunities families can give their children. Providing access, resources, quality educators, and programming to these families will foster better prepared, happier, and healthier children as they enter elementary school with a more equitable educational start.

Despite popular narratives, socioeconomic status is the most significant predictor of gaps found in both academic and social-emotional skills. High-quality early childhood education programs have been successful in mitigating this divide. Therefore, the answer is clear: all children need opportunities for high-quality care.

Patricia Crain de Galarce and Anna Maria Jones

Further Reading
Barnett, W. Steven. 1996. *Lives in the Balance: Age-27 Benefit-Cost Analysis of the High/Scope Perry Preschool Program.* Monographs of the High/Scope Educational Research Foundation, Number 11. Ypsilanti, MI: Monograph Series, High/Scope Foundation.

Barnett, W. Steven, Kwanghee Jung, M. Youn, and Ellen C. Frede. 2013. *Abbott Preschool Program Longitudinal Effects Study: Fifth Grade Follow-Up.* National Institute for Early Education Research 20. http://nieer.org/wp-content/uploads/2014/09/APPLES205th20Grade.pdf.

Belfield, Clive R., Milagros Nores, Steve Barnett, and Lawrence Schweinhart. 2006. "The High/Scope Perry Preschool Program Cost–Benefit Analysis Using Data from the Age-40 Followup." *Journal of Human Resources* 41 (1): 162–90.

Bromer, J. P. T., and Toni Porter. 2017. *Staffed Family Child Care Networks: A Research-Informed Strategy for Supporting High-Quality Family Child Care.* Washington, DC: National Center on Early Childhood Quality Assurance, Office of Child Care, Administration for Children and Families, U.S. Department of Health and Human Services.

Campbell, Frances A., Elizabeth P. Pungello, Margaret Burchinal, Kirsten Kainz, Yi Pan, Barbara H. Wasik, Oscar A. Barbarin, Joseph J. Sparling, and Craig T. Ramey. 2012. "Adult Outcomes as a Function of an Early Childhood Educational Program: An Abecedarian Project Follow-Up." *Developmental Psychology* 48 (4): 1033.

Chaudry, Ajay, Taryn Morrissey, Christina Weiland, and Hirokazu Yoshikawa. 2017. *Cradle to Kindergarten: A New Plan to Combat Inequality.* New York: Russell Sage Foundation.

Child Care Aware of America. 2019. *The US and the High Price of Child Care: An Examination of a Broken System.* https://www.childcareaware.org/our-issues/research/the-us-and-the-high-price-of-child-care-2019.

Children's Defense Fund. 2017. *The State of America's Children, 2017.* Washington, DC: The Fund. https://www.childrensdefense.org/reports/2017/the-state-of-americas-children-2017-report.

Chugani, Harry T., Michael E. Behen, Otto Muzik, Csaba Juhász, Ferenc Nagy, and Diane C. Chugani. 2001. "Local Brain Functional Activity Following Early Deprivation: A Study of Postinstitutionalized Romanian Orphans." *Neuroimage* 14 (6): 1290–1301.

Clarke, Stevens H., and Frances A. Campbell. 1998. "Can Intervention Early Prevent Crime Later? The Abecedarian Project Compared with Other Programs." *Early Childhood Research Quarterly* 13 (2): 319–43.

Deming, David. 2009. "Early Childhood Intervention and Life-Cycle Skill Development: Evidence from Head Start." *American Economic Journal: Applied Economics* 1 (3): 111–34.

Dowd, Nancy E. 2019. "Equality, Equity, and Dignity. 2019." *Law and Inequality: A Journal of Theory and Practice* 37 (1): 1–16.

Duncan, Greg J., and Katherine Magnuson. 2011. "The Nature and Impact of Early Achievement Skills, Attention Skills, and Behavior Problems." In *Whither Opportunity: Rising Inequality, Schools, and Children's Life Chances,* edited by Greg J. Duncan and Richard J. Murnane, 47–69. New York: Russell Sage Foundation.

Fernald, Anne, Virginia A. Marchman, and Adriana Weisleder. 2013. "SES Differences in Language Processing Skill and Vocabulary Are Evident at 18 Months." *Developmental Science* 16 (2): 234–48.

FIFCFS (Federal Interagency Forum on Child, and Family Studies), eds. 2017. *America's Children: Key National Indicators of Well-Being, 2017.* Washington, DC: Government Printing Office.

Fulghum, Robert. 2003. *All I Really Need to Know I Learned in Kindergarten: Reconsidered, Revised & Expanded with Twenty-Five New Essays.* New York: Random House Digital, Inc.

Gerhardt, Sue. 2014. *Why Love Matters: How Affection Shapes a Baby's Brain.* London: Routledge.

Gilliam, Walter S. 2005. *Prekindergarteners Left Behind: Expulsion Rates in State Prekindergarten Systems.* New York: Foundation for Child Development.

Gilliam, Walter S., Angela N. Maupin, Chin R. Reyes, Maria Accavitti, and Frederick Shic. 2016. *Do Early Educators' Implicit Biases regarding Sex and Race Relate to Behavior Expectations and Recommendations of Preschool Expulsions and Suspensions.* Research Study Brief. New Haven, CT: Yale University, Yale Child Study Center.

Hart, Betty, and Todd R. Risley. 1995. *Meaningful Differences in the Everyday Experience of Young American Children.* Baltimore, MD: Paul H. Brookes Publishing.

Ho, Sally. 2018. "Latest Hurdle in Grueling US Daycare Hunt: Waitlist Fees." AP News, September 29, 2018. https://apnews.com/article/dded5ace250b4de89d60376cbb6c143a.

Janus, Magdalena, and Eric Duku. 2007. "The School Entry Gap: Socioeconomic, Family, and Health Factors Associated with Children's School Readiness to Learn." *Early Education and Development* 18 (3): 375–403.

Koball, Heather, and Yang Jiang. 2018. "Basic Facts about Low-Income Children: Children under 18 Years, 2016." National Center for Children in Poverty. New York: Columbia University Mailman School of Public Health. http://www.nccp.org/wp -content/uploads/2018/01/text_1194.pdf.

Leschied, Alan, Debbie Chiodo, Elizabeth Nowicki, and Susan Rodger. 2008. "Childhood Predictors of Adult Criminality: A Meta-Analysis Drawn from the Prospective Longitudinal Literature." *Canadian Journal of Criminology and Criminal Justice* 50 (4): 435–67.

Livingston, Gretchen. 2018. "Stay-at-Home Moms and Dads Account for about One-in Five U.S. Parents." Pew Research Center, September 24, 2018. https://pewrsr.ch /2xzW0x9.

Magnuson, Katherine, and Greg J. Duncan. 2016. "Can Early Childhood Interventions Decrease Inequality of Economic Opportunity?" *RSF* 2, no. 2 (May): 123–41.

Malik, Rasheed, and Katie Hamm. 2017. *Mapping America's Child Care Deserts.* Washington: Center for American Progress. https://www.americanprogress.org /issues/early-childhood/reports/2017/08/30/437988/mapping-americas-child -care-deserts.

Mårtensson, Fredrika, Cecilia Boldemann, Margareta Söderström, Margareta Blennow, J.-E. Englund, and Patrik Grahn. 2009. "Outdoor Environmental Assessment of Attention Promoting Settings for Preschool Children." *Health & Pace* 15 (4): 1149–57.

Martin, Karin A., Emily Bosk, and Denise Bailey. 2018 "Teachers' Perceptions of Childcare and Preschool Expulsion." *Children & Society* 32 (2): 87–97.

Mashburn, Andrew J., Robert C. Pianta, Bridget K. Hamre, Jason T. Downer, Oscar A. Barbarin, Donna Bryant, Margaret Burchinal, Diane M. Early, and Carollee Howes. 2008. "Measures of Classroom Quality in Prekindergarten and Children's Development of Academic, Language, and Social Skills." *Child Development* 79 (3): 732–49.

McFarland, Joel, Bill Hussar, Xiaolei Wang, Jijun Zhang, Ke Wang, Amy Rathbun, Amy Barmer, Emily Forrest Cataldi, and Farrah Bullock Mann. 2018. *The Condition of Education 2018. NCES 2018-144.* National Center for Education Statistics. https:// nces.ed.gov/pubs2018/2018144.pdf.

Mischel, Walter, Yuichi Shoda, and Monica I. Rodriguez. 1989. "Delay of Gratification in Children." *Science* 244 (4907): 933–38.

NCES (National Center for Education Statistics). 2018. "Table 5.3: Types of State and District Requirements for Kindergarten." https://nces.ed.gov/programs/stateref orm/tab5_3.asp.

Nelson, Charles A., and Margaret A. Sheridan. 2011. "Lessons from Neuroscience Research for Understanding Causal Links between Family and Neighborhood Characteristics and Educational Outcomes." In *Whither Opportunity: Rising Inequality, Schools, and Children's Life Chances*, edited by Greg J. Duncan and Richard J. Murnane, 27–46. New York: Russell Sage Foundation.

NICHD Early Child Care. 1998. "Early Child Care and Self-Control, Compliance and Problem Behavior at 24 and 36 Months." *Child Development* 69:1145–70.

NICHD Early Child Care Research Network. 2006. "The NICHD Study of Early Child Care and Youth Development." U.S. Department of Health and Human Services. https://www.nichd.nih.gov/sites/default/files/publications/pubs/documents /seccyd_06.pdf.

Parker, Emily, Bruce Atchison, and Emily Workman. 2016. "State Pre-K Funding for 2015–16 Fiscal Year: National Trends in State Preschool Funding. 50-State

Review." Education Commission of the States. https://www.ecs.org/state
-pre-k-funding-for-2015-16-fiscal-year.

Phillips, Deborah A., and Jack P. Shonkoff, eds. 2000. *From Neurons to Neighborhoods: The Science of Early Childhood Development*. Washington, DC: National Academies Press.

Posner, Michael I., and Mary K. Rothbart. 2000. "Developing Mechanisms of Self-Regulation." *Development and Psychopathology* 12 (3): 427–41.

Romeo, Rachel R., Julia A. Leonard, Sydney T. Robinson, Martin R. West, Allyson P. Mackey, Meredith L. Rowe, and John D. E. Gabrieli. 2018. "Beyond the 30-Million-Word Gap: Children's Conversational Exposure Is Associated with Language-Related Brain Function." *Psychological Science* 29 (5): 700–710.

Schuyler Center for Analysis and Advocacy. 2012. "Quality: What It Is and Why It Matters in Early Childhood Education." Schuyler Center. http://www.wvecptf.org/docs/Quality-in-early-childhood-education.pdf.

Thompson, Ross A., and C. A. Happold. 2002. "The Roots of School Readiness in Social and Emotional Development." In *Set for Success: Building a Strong Foundation for School Readiness Based on the Social-Emotional Development of Young Children*, edited by the Kauffman Early Education Exchange, 8–29. Kansas City, MO: The Ewing Marion Kauffman Foundation.

U.S. Census Bureau. 2017. https://www.census.gov.

U.S. Department of Health and Human Services, and U.S. Department of Education. 2014. "Policy Statement on Expulsion and Suspension Policies in Early Childhood Settings." https://www2.ed.gov/policy/gen/guid/school-discipline/policy-statement -ece-expulsions-suspensions.pdf.

Workman, S., and R. Ullrich. 2017. "Quality 101: Identifying the Core Components of a High-Quality Early Childhood Program." Center for American Progress. https://www.americanprogress.org/issues/early-childhood/reports/2017/02/13/414939/quality-101-identifying-the-core-components-of-a-high-quality-early-childhood -program.

Higher Education

Education creates opportunities and paves the path to social mobility. It is one of a few options available for individuals from families with limited resources to pursue more desirable occupations and a brighter financial future. Higher education in particular plays a central role in fostering social mobility. Among college graduates (i.e., individuals with bachelor's degrees), there is little, if any, association between the income of the family in which one grew up and one's own income in adulthood (Hout 1988; Torche 2011). These findings suggest that college education allows individuals to break the link between the circumstances of their childhood and their own financial futures, dubbing higher education "the great equalizer."

Despite those encouraging patterns, some studies have questioned the equalizing power of a college degree today (Manzoni and Streib 2019; Witteveen and Attewell 2017). More importantly, even if a college degree plays an equalizing role, its impact is limited given that only a small proportion of students from socioeconomically disadvantaged backgrounds complete college (NCES 2016, 2017). In addition to inequalities in completing a college degree, students from different family backgrounds have unequal experiences during college and disparate outcomes afterward, such as attending graduate school and getting elite jobs. Moreover, there are disparities in students' experiences within college, and higher education fosters inequalities in student outcomes such as graduation school attendance. And while college may provide a hope for mobility to individuals, it is creating a growing chasm in the nation as a whole due to large income disparities between the college educated and those without college degrees (Goldin and Katz 2018). Thus higher education both holds the promise of mobility and reflects the challenges of a highly unequal society.

GAINING ACCESS TO COLLEGE

To benefit from the equalizing potential of college, individuals must first gain admission to an institution of higher education and then complete a bachelor's degree. Both entry and completion are characterized by large inequalities by family background. When sociologists study family background, they often consider various characteristics such as parental income, education, and/or occupational standing. Some scholars use those characteristics to classify individuals into categories such as "middle class" and "working class" while others combine them into a measure of *socioeconomic status* (*SES*), which is the term we will use to represent different dimensions of family background.

Today, most students enroll in higher education immediately following high school graduation (NCES 2016). However, there are significant enrollment gaps by family background. Among high school sophomores in 2002, virtually all students (96 percent) from the highest SES quartile enrolled in higher education by 2012, but only 71 percent of students from the lowest SES quartile did so (NCES 2017). The gaps are even more pronounced when considering enrollment in four-year institutions. Among students who enrolled in postsecondary education, only approximately one-third (32 percent) of students from the bottom SES quartile enrolled in four-year institutions compared to almost three-quarters (74 percent) of students from the highest SES quartile.

Many factors contribute to these disparities. One of the often-discussed factors is academic preparation. Students from socioeconomically disadvantaged backgrounds on average attend lower performing schools, which in part contributes to their lower performance on standardized tests as well as lower enrollment in advanced high school tracks and courses (Adelman 2006; Lucas 1999). While these factors contribute to disparities in college enrollment, the gaps remain even when students from different family backgrounds have the same levels of academic preparation (Roksa et al. 2007; Karen 2002). Moreover, recent work suggests that many highly academically qualified students from socioeconomically disadvantaged backgrounds undermatch, which means that they either do not enroll in higher education or enroll in less selective institutions than they are academically prepared to attend (Bowen, Chingos, and McPherson 2009; Roderick, Coca, and Nagaoka 2011).

Academic preparation is thus only part of the puzzle of unequal access to higher education. Social and cultural capital also play an important role. Social capital includes a range of resources that can be obtained through social networks or interpersonal relationships (Coleman 1988). Cultural capital refers to one's familiarity with the culture of those in power (Bourdieu 1986) and has been conceptualized as knowledge, habits, and practices that support success in social institutions such as schools (Lareau and Weininger 2003). These forms of capital often get blurred as one acquires information and understanding of social systems through relationships with others: parents, teachers, counselors, and peers. Likewise, having certain kinds of cultural resources can help students forge valuable relationships with authority figures, such as teachers and administrators. Indeed, part of the role of social capital is to build cultural capital and vice versa.

Children develop their original cultural understandings in the family through early childhood socialization (Bourdieu 1986). Students from socioeconomically advantaged backgrounds grow up in an environment in which their eventual enrollment in college is expected and where they can learn valuable information and habits that will help them in the transition into higher education. Without adequate or accurate information about college, parents from socioeconomically disadvantaged backgrounds face challenges in facilitating their children's pursuit of higher education (Cabrera and LaNasa 2001; Plank and Jordan 2001). Socioeconomically disadvantaged parents thus often leave college-related decision-making to their children, while more advantaged parents are highly engaged in their children's college search and application process (Lareau 2011).

Beyond the family, high school contexts play an important role in shaping inequality in college access. High schools attended by students from socioeconomically advantaged backgrounds are much more likely to have a strong college-going culture (McDonough 1997; Roderick et al. 2011). In schools with an established college-going culture, counselors tend to have lower advising loads, spend more time on college counseling, provide resources such as college fairs, and assist with financial aid. In part reflecting their lower likelihood of attending high schools with a strong college-going culture, students from socioeconomically disadvantaged backgrounds are less likely to see a counselor and get relevant information regarding college application and enrollment, even though they are more likely to benefit from such information (Belasco 2013; Robinson and Roksa 2016).

COMPLETING A BACHELOR'S DEGREE

Even after students enter college, notable inequalities persist. Starting in the first year, socioeconomically disadvantaged students are more likely to leave college in each year than their more advantaged peers are (Bowen et al. 2009), which leads to large gaps in degree completion. Among high school sophomores in 2002 who enrolled in postsecondary education, only 20 percent of students from the bottom SES quartile completed a bachelor's degree by 2012, while students from the highest quartile were three times as likely (62 percent) to do so (NCES 2017). Even when students have similar academic preparation, those from socioeconomically disadvantaged backgrounds are less likely to stay in school and complete bachelor's degrees (Bowen et al. 2009).

Social and cultural capital play an important role in helping students navigate college. Both academic and social engagement require substantial know-how, which many socioeconomically disadvantaged students do not have and institutions do not provide (Armstrong and Hamilton 2013). Students from socioeconomically disadvantaged backgrounds encounter challenges in many areas, from getting into specific majors and communicating with professors to interacting with peers and participating in the social life of college (Mullen 2011). The social networks of more advantaged students link them to information about how to become engaged and help them configure their involvement in ways that facilitate their sense of belonging (Silver 2020a; Stuber 2011). Meanwhile, socioeconomically disadvantaged students are more likely to struggle to find suitable opportunities for engagement (Pascarella et al. 2004). This is consequential, since social and academic engagement are related to students' adjustment to college, academic performance, and degree completion (Kuh et al. 2006; Tinto 1992).

Postsecondary institutions also play a role in whether students complete bachelor's degrees. Research indicates that students who begin their higher education at a two-year institution—which socioeconomically disadvantaged students are more likely to do—are less likely to obtain a bachelor's degree than students who initially enroll at a four-year institution (Alfonso 2006; Reynolds 2012). In addition, attending a more selective four-year institution is related to a higher probability of graduation (Bowen et al. 2009; Titus 2004); socioeconomically disadvantaged students, however, are underrepresented at these more selective institutions.

It is not only the institutions students enter but also how they enter them that matters for degree completion. Students who delay college entry, many of whom come from socioeconomically disadvantaged backgrounds, have a lower probability of completing bachelor's degrees (Bozick and DeLuca 2005; Roksa and Velez 2012). Further, students from disadvantaged family backgrounds are more likely to attend college part-time, often because of their need for jobs to pay for school or other family obligations (Pascarella et al. 2004). They are also more likely to switch schools (Adelman 2006; Goldrick-Rab 2006). Overall, following less direct routes through higher education makes graduation more difficult, and socioeconomically disadvantaged students are more likely to follow these more complex pathways.

Complex college pathways are associated in part with more extensive nonacademic obligations. Students from socioeconomically disadvantaged backgrounds are more likely to be employed and tend to work more hours each week (Pascarella et al. 2004; Roksa and Velez 2010). This is in part because their families have fewer resources to contribute to their education. While families across the socioeconomic spectrum share a similar proportion of material resources with their children, large inequalities in family income translate into large disparities in the resources that youth receive to pay tuition, room and board, and other expenses (Wightman, Schoeni, and Robinson 2012). Students from socioeconomically disadvantaged backgrounds also frequently contribute time and energy as well as emotional and financial support to their families (Goldrick-Rab 2016; Roksa 2019). Receiving limited support from the family while at the same time having substantial obligations to contribute at home can reduce students' likelihood of staying in school (Kinsley 2014) as well as constrain students' planning for life after college (Silver and Roksa 2017).

Students from socioeconomically disadvantaged families often rely on financial aid to meet the cost of college. In addition to providing means to pay tuition and fees, financial aid can reduce the number of hours students work (Goldrick-Rab, Harris, and Trostel 2009). Recent research indicates that need-based grants facilitate college persistence and completion (Castleman and Long 2016; Dynarski and Scott-Clayton 2013). These programs are more effective when they are easy to access, minimizing hurdles related to application. Rising tuition and increasing reliance on loans (NCES 2016), however, mean that grants cover a decreasing proportion of college expenses (Long and Riley 2007). For many socioeconomically disadvantaged students, the burden of student debt will follow them well beyond college.

INEQUALITY BEYOND A BACHELOR'S DEGREE

The role of higher education in shaping inequality does not end with the bachelor's degree but extends to graduate school enrollment and access to elite occupations. While a bachelor's degree may help to equalize the labor market opportunities of individuals across a range of family backgrounds, that is not the case for graduate degrees (Torche 2011). Graduate degree holders from more socioeconomically advantaged families have more desirable jobs and higher incomes. The path to a graduate degree is also characterized by inequality. Students from socioeconomically disadvantaged families are less likely to apply to and enroll in graduate school, in part because of inequalities in prior experiences, including academic preparation and selectivity of four-year institutions attended (Posselt and Grodsky 2017). Inequality is particularly pronounced in attainment of professional and doctoral degrees: children of parents with professional and doctoral degrees are substantially overrepresented among individuals who earn those types of degrees.

Moreover, while a bachelor's degree may on average eliminate the association between one's family background and labor market outcomes, elite occupations and elite firms within certain industries remain more exclusive. Access to these elite employment opportunities is frequently easier for graduates from the most advantaged backgrounds. Through exposure to elite campus culture, affluent students attending highly selective universities learn about some of the most prestigious and high-paying jobs in financial, consulting, and technical fields (Binder, Davis, and Bloom 2016). And given the similarity between affluent students' college experiences and those of hiring authorities, they often have an easier time gaining employment offers from elite firms (Rivera 2016).

Higher education also contributes to broader economic inequalities in the United States. The comparative wage advantage of college graduates relative to their peers with high school diplomas is often described as the *college wage premium*. The college wage premium in the United States is high and has grown since the 1950s (Brand and Xie 2010; Goldin and Katz 2018). As the returns to a high school diploma stagnated and fell, the gap in earnings between those with and without a college degree grew. Notably, because of the poor labor market prospects of those without college degrees, the economic returns to college are even higher for the less-advantaged individuals who, on average, are the least likely to attain a degree (Brand and Xie 2010).

These inequalities are amplified when considering families, not just individuals. Today, couples increasingly marry others with similar educational attainment, a phenomenon referred to as *educational homogamy* (Mare 2016). As college graduates marry other college graduates and those without bachelor's degrees marry others with similar levels of education, disparities in combined family resources are amplified. Further, young people whose parents were educationally similar are themselves more likely to marry others with similar education levels (Mare 2016), perpetuating inequality across generations and contributing to growing income inequality in the United States.

CONCLUSION

Higher education plays a contradictory role in social inequality. It provides a crucial avenue for social mobility. Individuals from socioeconomically disadvantaged families can attain desirable labor market outcomes, often comparable to those of their more socioeconomically advantaged peers, if they complete a bachelor's degree. But at the same time, both access to higher education and rates of degree completion are highly unequal. Thus, among those over twenty-five years of age, just one-third of individuals who grew up in low-income families hold bachelor's degrees, compared to two-thirds of individuals from more affluent families (Bailey and Dynarski 2011).

While attaining a college degree is valuable for one's standing in the labor market, there are hidden costs to both individuals and society. The experience of acclimating to the middle-class culture dominant in many colleges and universities can be an emotionally fraught one for students from socioeconomically disadvantaged backgrounds (Lee and Kramer 2013; Lehmann 2014). These students frequently come to feel tension, conflict, or distance in their relationships with friends and family from home communities who are unfamiliar with college experiences and pressures. At the same time, many socioeconomically disadvantaged students feel out of place in their new social and cultural contexts during and after college. Moreover, the high college wage premium and strong patterns of marital homogamy contribute to large and growing income inequality in the nation as a whole.

It is important to note, however, that in addition to socioeconomic background, students' experiences and outcomes are also shaped by other characteristics, including race/ethnicity and gender. All three characteristics—socioeconomic status, race/ethnicity, and gender—intersect to produce unique experiences for specific groups (Arum et al. 2018; Bowen et al. 2009; Silver 2020b). The intersectional nature of students' experiences and outcomes underscores the complexity of the relationship between higher education and inequality.

Josipa Roksa and Blake R. Silver

Further Reading

Adelman, Clifford. 2006. *The Toolbox Revisited: Paths to Degree Completion from High School through College.* Washington, DC: U.S. Department of Education.

Alfonso, Mariana. 2006. "The Impact of Community College Attendance on Baccalaureate Attainment." *Research in Higher Education* 47 (8): 873–903.

Armstrong, Elizabeth A., and Laura T. Hamilton. 2013. *Paying for the Party.* Cambridge, MA: Harvard University Press.

Arum, Richard, Josipa Roksa, Jacqueline Cruz, and Blake Silver. 2018. "Student Experiences in College." In *Handbook of the Sociology of Education in the 21st Century*, edited by B. Schneider, 385–403. New York: Springer.

Bailey, Martha J., and Susan M. Dynarski. 2011. "Gains and Gaps: Changing Inequality in US College Entry and Completion." NBER Working Paper 17633. National Bureau of Economic Research. https://www.nber.org/papers/w17633.

Belasco, Andrew S. 2013. "Creating College Opportunity: School Counselors and Their Influence on Postsecondary Enrollment." *Research in Higher Education* 54 (7): 781–804.

Binder, Amy J., Daniel B. Davis, and Nick Bloom 2016. "Career Funneling: How Elite Students Learn to Define and Desire 'Prestigious' Jobs." *Sociology of Education* 89 (1): 20–39.

Bourdieu, Pierre. 1986. "The Forms of Capital." In *Handbook of Theory and Research for the Sociology of Education*, edited by J. Richardson, 241–58. New York: Greenwood Press.

Bowen, William G., Michael M. Chingos, and Matthew S. McPherson. 2009. *Crossing the Finish Line: Completing College at America's Public Universities*. Princeton, NJ: Princeton University Press.

Bozick, Robert, and Stefanie DeLuca. 2005. "Better Late than Never? Delayed Enrollment in the High School to College Transition." *Social Forces* 84 (1): 531–54.

Brand, Jennie E., and Yu Xie. 2010. "Who Benefits Most from College? Evidence for Negative Selection in Heterogeneous Economic Returns to Higher Education." *American Sociological Review* 75 (2): 273–302.

Cabrera, Alberto F., and Steven M. LaNasa 2001. "On the Path to College: Three Critical Tasks Facing America's Disadvantaged." *Research in Higher Education* 42 (2): 119–49.

Castleman, Ben L., and Bridget T. Long. 2016. "Looking beyond Enrollment: The Causal Effect of Need-Based Grants on College Access, Persistence, and Graduation." *Journal of Labor Economics* 34 (4): 1023–73.

Coleman, James. 1988. "Social Capital in the Creation of Human Capital." *American Journal of Sociology* 94 (S): 95–120.

Dynarski, Susan, and Judith Scott-Clayton. 2013. "Financial Aid Policy: Lessons from Research." NBER Working Paper 18710. National Bureau of Economic Research. https://www.nber.org/papers/w18710.

Goldin, Claudia, and Lawrence F. Katz. 2018. "The Race between Education and Technology." In *Inequality in the 21st Century*, edited by David B. Grusky and Jasmine Hill, 49–54. New York: Routledge.

Goldrick-Rab, Sara. 2006. "Following Their Every Move: An Investigation of Social-Class Differences in College Pathways." *Sociology of Education* 79 (1): 67–79.

Goldrick-Rab, Sara. 2016. *Paying the Price: College Costs, Financial Aid, and the Betrayal of the American Dream*. Chicago: University of Chicago Press.

Goldrick-Rab, Sara, Douglas N. Harris, and Phillip A. Trostel. 2009. "Why Financial Aid Matters (or Does Not) for College Success: Toward a New Interdisciplinary Perspective." In *Higher Education: Handbook of Theory and Research*, edited by J. Smart, 1–45. New York: Springer Science & Business.

Hout, Michael. 1988. "More Universalism, Less Structural Mobility: The American Occupational Structure in the 1980s." *American Sociological Review* 93 (6): 1358–1400.

Karen, David. 2002. "Changes in Access to Higher Education in the United States: 1980–1992." *Sociology of Education* 75 (3): 191–210.

Kinsley, Peter M. 2014. "The Pull of Home: Family Dynamics and the Initial College Experiences of Low-Income Undergraduates." PhD diss., University of Wisconsin.

Kuh, George D., Jillian Kinzie, Jennifer A. Buckley, Brian K. Bridges, and John C. Hayek. 2006. *What Matters to Student Success: A Review of the Literature*. Washington, DC: National Postsecondary Education Cooperative.

Lareau, Annette. 2011. *Unequal Childhoods: Class, Race, and Family Life*. Berkeley: University of California Press.

Lareau, Annette, and Elliot B. Weininger. 2003. "Cultural Capital in Educational Research: A Critical Assessment." *Theory and Society* 32 (5–6): 567–606.

Lee, Elizabeth M., and Rory Kramer. 2013. "Out with the Old, In with the New? Habitus and Social Mobility at Selective Colleges." *Sociology of Education* 86 (1): 18–35.

Lehmann, Wolfgang. 2014. "Habitus Transformation and Hidden Injuries: Successful Working-Class University Students." *Sociology of Education* 87 (1): 1–15.

Long, Bridget T., and Erin Riley. 2007. "Financial Aid: A Broken Bridge to College Access?" *Harvard Educational Review* 77 (1): 39–63.

Lucas, Samuel R. 1999. *Tracking Inequality: Stratification and Mobility in American High Schools.* Sociology of Education series. New York: Teachers College Press.

Manzoni, Anna, and Jessi Streib. 2019. "The Equalizing Power of a College Degree for First-Generation College Students: Disparities across Institutions, Majors, and Achievement Levels." *Research in Higher Education* 60, no. 5 (August): 577–605.

Mare, Robert D. 2016. "Educational Homogamy in Two Gilded Ages: Evidence from Intergenerational Social Mobility Data." *Annals of the American Academy of Political and Social Science* 663 (1): 117–39.

McDonough, Patricia M. 1997. *Choosing Colleges: How Social Class and Schools Structure Opportunity.* Albany, NY: SUNY Press.

Mullen, Ann L. 2011. *Degrees of Inequality: Culture, Class, and Gender in American Higher Education.* Baltimore, MD: Johns Hopkins University Press.

NCES (National Center for Education Statistics). 2016. *Digest of Education Statistics.* Washington DC: U.S. Department of Education.

NCES (National Center for Education Statistics). 2017. *Early Millennials: The Sophomore Class of 2002 a Decade Later.* Washington DC: U.S. Department of Education.

Pascarella, Ernest T., Christopher T. Pierson, Gregory C. Wolniak, and Patrick T. Terenzini. 2004. "First-Generation College Students: Additional Evidence on College Experiences and Outcomes." *Journal of Higher Education* 75 (3): 249–84.

Plank, Stephen B., and Will J. Jordan. 2001. "Effects of Information, Guidance, and Actions on Postsecondary Destinations: A Study of Talent Loss." *American Educational Research Journal* 38 (4): 947–79.

Posselt, Julie R., and Eric Grodsky. 2017. "Graduate Education and Social Stratification." *Annual Review of Sociology* 43:353–78.

Reynolds, C. Lockwood. 2012. "Where to Attend? Estimating the Effects of Beginning College at a Two-Year Institution." *Economics of Education Review* 31 (4): 345–62.

Rivera, Lauren. 2016. *Pedigree: How Elite Students Get Elite Jobs.* Princeton, NJ: Princeton University Press.

Robinson, Karen, and Josipa Roksa. 2016. "Counselors, Information, and High School College-Going Culture: Inequalities in the College Application Process." *Research in Higher Education* 57 (7): 845–68.

Roderick, Melissa, Vanessa Coca, and Jenny Nagaoka. 2011. "Potholes on the Road to College: High School Effects in Shaping Urban Students' Participation in College Application, Four-Year College Enrollment, and College Match." *Sociology of Education* 84 (3): 178–211.

Roksa, Josipa. 2019. "Intergenerational Exchange of Support: Resource Dilution and Increased Contribution in Low-Income Families." *Journal of Marriage and Family* 81 (3): 601–15.

Roksa, Josipa, Eric Grodsky, Richard Arum, and Adam Gamoran. 2007. "Changes in Higher Education and Social Stratification in the United States." In *Stratification in Higher Education: A Comparative Study*, edited by Yossi Shavit, Richard Arum, and Adam Gamoran, 165–91. Stanford, CA: Stanford University Press.

Roksa, Josipa, and Melissa Velez. 2010. "When Studying Schooling Is Not Enough: Incorporating Employment in Models of Educational Transitions." *Research in Social Stratification and Mobility* 28 (1): 5–21.

Roksa, Josipa, and Melissa Velez. 2012. "A Late Start: Delayed Entry, Life Course Transitions, and Bachelor's Degree Attainment." *Social Forces* 90 (3): 769–94.

Silver, Blake R. 2020a. "Inequality in the Extracurriculum: How Class, Race, and Gender Shape College Involvement." *Sociological Forum* 35 (4): 1290–340.

Silver, Blake R. 2020b. *The Cost of Inclusion: How Student Conformity Leads to Inequality on College Campuses.* Chicago: University of Chicago Press.

Silver, Blake R., and Josipa Roksa. 2017. "Navigating Uncertainty and Responsibility: Understanding Inequality in the Senior-Year Transition." *Journal of Student Affairs Research and Practice* 54 (3): 248–60.

Stuber, Jenny M. 2011. *Inside the College Gates: How Class and Culture Matter in Higher Education.* Lanham, MD: Lexington Books.

Tinto, Vincent. 1992. *Leaving College: Rethinking the Causes and Cures of Student Attrition.* 2nd ed. Chicago: University of Chicago Press.

Titus, Marvin. A. 2004. "An Examination of the Influence of Institutional Context on Student Persistence at 4-Year Colleges and Universities: A Multilevel Approach." *Research in Higher Education* 45 (7): 673–99.

Torche, Florencia. 2011. "Is a College Degree Still the Great Equalizer? Intergenerational Mobility across Levels of Schooling in the United States." *American Journal of Sociology* 117 (3): 763–807.

Wightman, Patrick, Robert Schoeni, and Keith Robinson. 2012. "Familial Financial Assistance to Young Adults." NPC Working Paper 2012-10. Ann Arbor, MI: National Poverty Center.

Witteveen, Dirk, and Paul Attewell. 2017. "Family Background and Earnings Inequality among College Graduates." *Social Forces* 95 (4): 1539–76.

SECTION III

Health and Health Care

Access to Health Care

Few topics animate the American populace—and the middle class, specifically—more than the topic of health care. This is not a great surprise: physical, mental, and emotional health influence the extent to which individuals can participate meaningfully in the educational and economic responsibilities and the civic and social pleasures of everyday life. And while health-care services are hardly the only important determinant of one's overall well-being, there is no doubt that they are absolutely critical to it.

As a matter of public debate, "health care" is generally considered to consist of three components: *access* to health care, the *quality* of the care received, and the manner in which the care is *financed* (in other words, paid for). This chapter is concerned with the first of these, and approaches health-care access from a macro level.

One's ability to access comprehensive health-care services is important for promoting and maintaining health, preventing acute illness and managing chronic disease, reducing unnecessary disability and premature death, and achieving health equity (the idea that all people should be given an equal opportunity to achieve their optimal health) (U.S. Office of Disease Prevention and Health Promotion 2014). Note the use of "comprehensive" in the sentence above; too often, health-care access is reduced to needs associated with acute physical care. True access, however, encompasses mental health and substance use disorder services, oral health care, prescription drugs, long-term care for people with chronic conditions, and palliative care (which aims to relieve suffering and improve the quality of life for people afflicted with serious illness).

Furthermore, health-care access is not simply about receiving a particular service or product, regardless of the type of need being addressed. Instead, health-care access must also include (1) one's ability to gain entry into the health-care system in the first place, given that there is no universal legal right to health care in the United States; (2) geographic availability (e.g., how far must one travel to receive needed primary and specialty care?); and (3) issues pertaining to cultural competence (e.g., how easy is it for the patient and the health-care provider to communicate?).

Potential barriers abound at every step along the path to accessing comprehensive health-care services. The consequences of these barriers can range from annoying to catastrophic: delays in receiving care, unnecessary hospitalizations, unmet health needs, discriminatory or biased care, a reduced quality of life, bankruptcy, and even death. Furthermore, barriers can result in health disparities or health-care disparities. A *health disparity* exists when one population group experiences more disability or illness relative to another group; a *health-care disparity* signifies differences in access to health-care services or health insurance. These disparities are no small matter, as researchers have proven their existence based on race, ethnicity, religion, socioeconomic status, gender, age, mental health, cognitive/sensory/physical disability, sexual orientation, gender identity, geographic location, and immigration status (Smedley, Stith, and Nelson 2003). The persistence of these disparities prevents the United States from achieving wide-scale health equity.

KEY DRIVERS OF HEALTH-CARE ACCESS

Cost of Medical Care

Compared to other wealthy nations, the United States spends far more money, on a per capita basis, on health care. This disparity in spending has nothing to do with greater health-care utilization among the U.S. population but instead stems from higher prescription drug prices, higher salaries for doctors and nurses, higher hospital administration costs, and higher prices for many medical services (Anderson, Hussey, and Petrosyan 2019). In 2016 (the most recent year for which data is available), the United States spent $9,892 per capita on health care, which is approximately 25 percent higher than second-place Switzerland's $7,919, 108 percent higher than Canada's $4,753, and 145 percent higher than the median of $4,033 for member nations of the Organization for Economic Cooperation and Development (OECD) (Anderson et al. 2019).

While space does not permit anything close to a full exploration of health-care costs in the United States, a few examples of the consequences thereof will suffice. First, one-quarter of U.S. adults report that they or a family member have put off treatment for a serious medical condition because of cost, and an additional 8 percent have done the same in the case of less serious conditions (Saad 2019). This means that fully one-third of Americans find themselves in a situation where they must prioritize financial considerations over health. Second, two-thirds of Americans who file for bankruptcy each year—some 530,000 people—cite medical cost as at least a key contributor to their financial crisis (Himmelstein et al. 2019, 432). Third, because of the United States' outlier status in terms of health-care costs, there is a profound "wealth equals health" dynamic in the United States. Indeed, the literature on the connection between wealth and health overwhelmingly "demonstrates that disadvantaged groups have poorer survival chances and a higher mortality rate, die at a younger age, experience a blighted quality of life, and have overall diminished health and well-being when compared to other members of society" (Benfer 2015, 279). For example:

- Over the past three decades, life expectancy has sharply increased among people in the top half of the income distribution, while effectively flattening out for everyone else.

- The prevalence of nearly all chronic health conditions (e.g., stroke, heart disease) increases the more that income decreases.

- Compared with wealthy individuals, poor and middle-class individuals pay a larger share of their incomes toward health care, which in turn deepens inequalities in disposable income (Tobin-Tyler and Teitelbaum 2019, xii–xiii).

Health Insurance Coverage

Because health-care costs are so high, only a relative few can finance care for themselves and their families without the assistance of public or private health insurance. While the Affordable Care Act has covered approximately twenty million people since its passage in 2010, some thirty million Americans still remain uncovered, and tens of millions more are underinsured.

Having health insurance does not guarantee access to needed medical care services. For example, a particular health insurance plan may exclude from coverage the particular service, drug, or device needed by the owner of the health insurance policy, or the associated deductibles, copays, and coinsurance that are often required to take full advantage of health insurance may be prohibitively expensive. Nonetheless, having health insurance is a critically important step on the path to accessing care. A handful of facts helpfully summarize the link between health insurance and health-care access:

- Compared to insured adults, those without insurance are less likely to receive preventive and screening services, and less likely to receive these services on a timely basis.

- Largely due to delayed diagnoses, uninsured cancer patients generally have poorer outcomes and are more likely to die prematurely than persons with health insurance.

- Compared with those who have health insurance, uninsured adults with chronic diseases are less likely to receive appropriate care to manage their health conditions.

- Compared with individuals with insurance coverage, adults without insurance are less likely to receive mental health services.

- Compared with victims of trauma with health insurance, uninsured persons with traumatic injuries are less likely to be admitted to the hospital (U.S. Institute of Medicine 2002, chapter 3).

Geography

Even if medical care was more affordable in the United States, and even if the nation achieved universal insurance coverage, health-care access could not be assumed because of severe shortages of available services in many areas of the country. Both health-care workforce shortages and disparities unique to individuals in rural settings create barriers to health-care access.

Health Professional Shortage Areas (HPSAs) are federally designated geographic areas—or populations within geographic areas—that lack sufficient primary care, oral health, and/or behavioral health providers to meet the needs of the designated area or population. The scale of these workforce shortages is daunting: Approximately 77 million Americans live in primary-care HPSAs, with 14,000 additional providers needed to extinguish all these designations; more than 56 million people live in oral health HPSAs, with nearly 10,000 additional providers required to remove all these designations; and some 113 million people live in behavioral health HPSAs, with 6,000 additional providers needed to meet the nation's needs (fully 55 percent of all counties in the United States do not have *any* practicing behavioral health-care workers). While the workforce shortages that lead to HPSA designations plague all manner of counties across the country, they disproportionately affect rural areas: more than 75 percent of the nation's rural counties carry HPSA designations.

There are several causes of health-care workforce shortages. Relatively speaking, few students graduating from health professions schools want to practice in rural areas. Some fields of practice—primary care, for example—are experiencing declining interest among health professions graduates, in part because medical specialists typically earn twice as much as primary-care practitioners. And for some medical conditions, there is a lack of adequate training (e.g., pediatric behavioral health care). To top it all off, the existing health-care workforce is generally older than workers in other major U.S. industries. Some observers warn that this fact could lead to additional shortages in future years as health-care workers in these regions retire en masse.

Relatedly, Americans living in rural areas (approximately 15 to 20 percent of the U.S. population) encounter barriers to health-care access in ways not experienced by people living in urban and suburban areas (Warshaw 2017). In addition to the workforce shortages described above, disparities in rural areas are driven by compounding economic, social, racial, and ethnic factors. For example, migrant farmworkers, many of whom are Hispanic, may lack health insurance, have little flexibility to take time off from work to visit a doctor (particularly if the closest provider is hours away), may not have a way to get to the closest provider, and may not speak the same language as clinicians in the region.

Individuals living in rural areas with complex, chronic health conditions are also more likely than their urban and suburban counterparts to be hospitalized. One study found that Medicare beneficiaries in rural areas had a "40% higher preventable hospitalization rates and 23% higher mortality rates" compared to those in urban settings (Johnston, Wen, and Maddox 2019, 1998). The study found that access to specialists was an important intervention in improving health: one or more specialist visit(s) during the prior year decreased the hospitalization and mortality rates for those with chronic conditions by approximately 16 percent. Accordingly, policy makers seeking to improve health outcomes for those living in rural areas should focus on access not only to primary care but also to specialists able to help patients manage complex, chronic conditions.

OTHER IMPORTANT CONSIDERATIONS

Two other important topics bear mentioning at this moment in time: the potential long-term effects that technology may have on health-care access and the status of the Affordable Care Act.

Technology and Health-Care Access

Technology undoubtedly can help increase access to health-care services. For example, telehealth (distribution of health-care information and services via telecommunication technologies), a range of mobile applications (apps) for smartphones, augmented intelligence, and machine learning each offers ways to reach populations that may otherwise be overlooked. Caution is warranted when using such technologies, however, to ensure that the technology supplements, rather than supplants, the patient-clinician relationship and that there are sufficient safeguards in place against bias, discrimination, and invasion of privacy.

Telehealth is a prime example of how technology can help bridge gaps in care. For example, video visits allow a patient to schedule an appointment with a clinician during a lunch break at work instead of having to miss a shift. These types of visits can also make specialty care more readily available to those in rural or suburban locations lacking specialists, and make it easier for elderly individuals or others who are unable to easily transport themselves to appointments to meet with their clinicians. According to the American Medical Association (AMA), physician use of technology to provide televisits or virtual visits doubled from 2016 to early 2020, with nearly 30 percent of doctors adopting the digital health technology (AMA 2020). Lawmakers continue to work on legislation that will promote the use of digital health tools, including telehealth, and to ensure that federal health-care programs such as Medicare and Medicaid will cover such services.

Clinicians and researchers are increasingly utilizing smartphone apps to assist with remote patient monitoring and diagnosis. For example, studies have shown that monitoring of social media accounts, text messages, and voice and other biometric data can reveal a patient's proclivity toward depression, Parkinson's disease, and opioid overdose. Clearly, some apps have greater clinical validity than others, so patients and clinicians alike should use caution when evaluating the use of apps to diagnose or treat illness. Additionally, while these technologies are exciting due to their potential to catch warning signs that may not otherwise be apparent, they also raise questions around patient privacy. Specifically, concerns have been raised about whether the data collected by the apps will end up in the hands of entities not bound to use the information for altruistic purposes (e.g., health insurers who may limit coverage of services based on an individual's risk factors, or employers seeking to hire only healthy individuals). Still, these technologies are continually growing in sophistication and clinical reliability and may help individuals access care that they may not otherwise be able to obtain.

Technology developers are also employing augmented or artificial intelligence (AI) and machine learning (ML) to aid with access. Algorithms can help identify individuals who need certain services or interventions. However, because algorithms are built on large data sets, care must be given to how such data sets are compiled, and the potential for bias in AI/ML systems must be acknowledged and addressed. Studies from late 2019 reveal that bias can show up in ML/AI unexpectedly. For example, researchers at the University of Chicago Booth School of Business, the University of California, Berkeley, and Partners HealthCare in Boston found that software deciding who should receive access to high-risk health-care management programs regularly permitted healthy, white people into the programs rather than sicker Black individuals, despite the algorithm explicitly excluding race from the selection criteria. One of the study's authors explained that due to "structural inequalities in our health-care system, [some Black patients] end up generating lower costs than whites" because they do not seek care as often (Obermeyer et al. 2019). Unfortunately, the algorithm equated higher health-care costs with a greater need to access the health-care system and failed to realize that lower costs for a given population may actually represent lower access to care. The study's authors revealed that fixing the algorithm's bias more than doubled the number of Black patients admitted to the care programs.

The Affordable Care Act

The Affordable Care Act (ACA) is a 2010 federal law that, among other things, expanded health insurance coverage to more than twenty million people. The expanded coverage takes three forms: a broadened Medicaid program, new tax credits for the purchase of certain private health insurance plans, and a change that allows young adults to remain on their parents' insurance plans up to age twenty-six. The ACA is a highly politicized law, because today's United States exists in an era of hyperpartisanship, and the ACA was Democratic president Barack Obama's signature domestic policy achievement. As a result, the ACA's *durability* remains in question. A law's durability refers to its *political* strength—in other words, what are the chances a law will, over time, gain widespread acceptance and become maximally effective such that politicians would have a very challenging time eroding or repealing the law?

As of early 2020, it is fair to say that the full story of ACA durability has yet to be written. While it remains in force, it is on shaky ground as various courts, Republicans in Congress, and the Trump administration have taken steps to limit or roll back various parts of the law, with more existential challenges looming. Furthermore, a Kaiser Family Foundation poll from February 2020 found that only a small majority of Americans (55 percent) hold a favorable opinion of the ACA, with 77 percent of Republicans holding a disapproving view. Taken together, federal efforts and unsteady public opinion threaten to wipe out the health insurance coverage gains made under the ACA, which in turn would dramatically reduce health-care access options for the twenty-plus million people whose health insurance depends on a durable Affordable Care Act.

CONCLUSION

Inequality in health care is both a reflection of and contributor to inequality in the United States more broadly. It is a reflection, for example, because research shows that health outcomes are linked to the level of economic inequality within a particular population. It is a contributor in that the nation's glaring health and health-care disparities make it difficult for tens of millions of people to succeed educationally, professionally, and socially, a dynamic that further contributes to a range of inequalities. These factors braid together to create self-perpetuating inequality loops. For example, high levels of inequality negatively affect individuals' sense of well-being and social cohesion, which in turn can lead to feelings of stress and fear; toxic stress is itself a major contributor to a host of unhealthy conditions, including high blood pressure, heart disease, obesity, and anxiety. Thus, the inequality nurtures poor health, and the poor health forces people onto the lower rungs of the socioeconomic ladder. And so it continues.

These types of inequality loops may not be easy to interrupt, for two immediate reasons. First, there are many structural hurdles that would need to be overcome across sectors as diverse and vast as health, education, employment, housing, transportation, and public safety. Second, it appears that Americans generally experience less moral discomfort than people in other countries when it comes to income-based health-care disparities. In 2017, researchers examined population surveys from thirty-two high- and middle-income countries to understand whether Americans' views of health and health-care disparities were demonstrably different from those of people in similarly situated nations. Their key finding was sobering: the United States has a uniquely large share of people who do not find it unfair that many people lack access to needed health care (Hero, Zaslavsky, and Blendon 2017).

Joel B. Teitelbaum and Laura G. Hoffman

Further Reading

AMA (American Medical Association). 2020. "Physicians' Motivations and Requirements for Adopting Digital Health: Adoption and Attitudinal Shifts from 2016 to 2019." AMA Digital Health Research. https://www.ama-assn.org/system/files/2020-02/ama-digital-health-study.pdf.

Anderson, Gerard F., Peter Hussey, and Varduhi Petrosyan. 2019. "It's Still the Prices, Stupid: Why the U.S. Spends So Much on Health Care, and a Tribute to Uwe Reinhardt." *Health Affairs* 38 (1): 87–95.

Benfer, Emily. 2015. "Health Justice: A Framework (and Call to Action) for the Elimination of Health Inequity and Social Injustice." *American University Law Review* 65 (2): 275–351.

Hero, Joachim O., Alan M. Zaslavsky, and Robert J. Blendon. 2017. "The United States Leads Other Nations in Differences by Income in Perceptions of Health and Health Care." *Health Affairs* 36 (6): 1032–40.

Himmelstein, David U., S. Woolhandler, Robert M. Lawless, D. Thorne, and P. Foohey. 2019. "Medical Bankruptcy: Still Common Despite the Affordable Care Act." *American Journal of Public Health* 109 (3): 431–33.

Institute for Policy Studies. https://inequality.org.

Johnston, Kenton J., Hefei Wen, and Karen E. Joynt Maddox. 2019. "Lack of Access to Specialists Associated with Mortality and Preventable Hospitalizations of Rural Medicare Beneficiaries." *Health Affairs* 38 (12): 1993–2002.

Obermeyer, Ziad, Brian Powers, Christine Vogeli, and Sendhil Mullainathan. 2019. "Dissecting Racial Bias in an Algorithm Used to Manage the Health of Populations." *Science* 366 (6464): 447–53.

Reinhardt, Uwe E. 2019. *Priced Out: The Economic and Ethical Costs of American Health Care.* Princeton, NJ, and Oxford: Princeton University Press.

Saad, Lydia. 2019. "More Americans Delaying Medical Treatment Due to Cost." Gallup, December 9, 2019. https://news.gallup.com/poll/269138/americans-delaying -medical-treatment-due-cost.aspx.

Smedley, B. D., A. Y. Stith, and A. R. Nelson, eds. 2003. *Unequal Treatment: Confronting Racial and Ethnic Disparities in Health Care.* Washington, DC: National Academies Press.

Tobin-Tyler, E., and J. Teitelbaum. 2019. *Essentials of Health Justice: A Primer.* Burlington, MA: Jones & Bartlett Learning.

U.S. Institute of Medicine, Committee on the Consequences of Uninsurance. 2002. *Care Without Coverage: Too Little, Too Late.* Washington, DC: National Academies Press.

U.S. Office of Disease Prevention and Health Promotion. 2014. *Healthy People 2020.* https://www.healthypeople.gov.

Warshaw, Robin. 2017. "Health Disparities Affect Millions in Rural U.S. Communities." *Association of American Medical Colleges*, October 31, 2017. https://www.aamc .org/news-insights/health-disparities-affect-millions-rural-us-communities.

Economic Status and Health

Many factors and mechanisms have been associated with poor health outcomes among low-income groups. Individual social characteristics shape the conditions of daily life and, consequently, impact health. For example, for people over the age of sixty-five, chronic diseases and mortality increase significantly. Men and women have different disease patterns, different diseases, and different life expectancies due to biological differences, gender roles and resulting health habits, and occupational differences. Minorities tend to be more disadvantaged and tend to have worse health and disease outcomes. Apart from these population differences in health and disease patterns, other social, economic, cultural, and political factors influence health: access to and utilization of health services, lifestyle, physical environment, working conditions, social networks, discrimination, literacy levels, and legislative policies. Of all these factors, socioeconomic status (SES) most consistently impacts health. Researchers Bruce Link and Jo Phelan argued that SES is "the fundamental cause" of differences in health and illness. A fundamental cause involves "access to resources that can be used to avoid risk or to minimize the consequences of disease once it occurs" (Link and Phelan 1995, 87). The association between SES and health is enduring because

> SES embodies an array of resources, such as money, knowledge, prestige, power and beneficial social connections that protect health no matter what mechanisms are relevant at any given time. (Phelan, Link, and Tehranifar 2010, S28)

To further understand how economic status influences health, it is necessary to define the concepts of health, health care, and socioeconomic and economic status. According to the World Health Organization (WHO), *health* is a state of complete physical, mental, and social well-being, an ambitious definition that defines health more broadly as well-being. Health care denotes the provision of health services. Socioeconomic status is a "composite measure that typically incorporates economic, social, and work status. Economic status is measured by income. Social status is measured by education, and work status is measured by occupation. Each status is considered an indicator. These three indicators are related but do not overlap" (WHO 2019c).

People have known for a long time that certain occupations and living locations and conditions affect health. For example, hatmakers often went "crazy." It was later found that the mercury used in the production of hats in Europe starting in the seventeenth century caused these symptoms (Genuis 2008). River blindness is a common occurrence along fast-flowing rivers in tropical countries. The cause for the disease is a parasitic worm (Gaware et al. 2011). Industrialization and urbanization also brought on changes in work as well as social and living conditions. As crowded industrial cities were beset with public health threats, there arose a pressing need to better understand the causes and distribution of diseases. The British epidemiologist Sir Michael Marmot and his colleagues first confirmed the systematic differences in morbidity and life expectancy between different SES groups. In the Whitehall study of British civil servants, Marmot and his research team analyzed data over a ten-year span beginning in 1967 and found an inverse association between employment grade and pay, on the one hand, and mortality (death rate) and morbidity (prevalence of disease), on the other: the higher the grade and pay, the lower the morbidity and mortality rates (Marmot et al. 1978). The main findings of the Whitehall study have been replicated in numerous studies since then. A 2017 study using data from 1.7 million people from different Western countries found that people with lower SES compared to people of higher SES were 46 percent more likely to die early. On average, low SES lowered life expectancy by 2.1 years (Stringhini et al. 2017).

MEASURING HEALTH OUTCOMES

Difference in health by SES are measured using several key outcomes: morbidity (rates of disease), mortality, life expectancy (the average number of years a member of the population can expect to live), infant mortality rate (number of infant deaths per one thousand live births), and self-reported health. Populations within nations and across the world differ immensely on these measurements. For example, in 2016, the average global life expectancy was 72 years. However, the life expectancy in several African nations was below 50. Swaziland, with a life expectancy of 49.2 years, had the lowest life expectancy worldwide. Japan had the longest life expectancy at 83.3 years (WHO 2019a). Also, sub-Saharan African countries have the highest rates of HIV infection and newly infected populations. Sixty-six percent of all HIV-infected people in the world live in this region, and 77 percent of all new infections occur here (UNAIDS 2015).

Self-reported health is measured by asking people about their health: Would they describe their health as poor, fair, good, or excellent? Self-reported health has been shown to correspond to the person's actual, objectively assessed health status. Rating one's health low is indicative of worse health and mortality (Foraker et al. 2011). Low-income groups report worse health than higher-income groups (McFadden et al. 2008; Orgera and Artiga 2018).

Socioeconomic status has also been linked to higher likelihood of functional limitations with regard to basic activities of daily living, such as eating or bathing, among people ages fifty-five to eighty-four. For people ages fifty-five to sixty-four whose income was below the poverty line, the odds of reporting functional limitations were six times higher than that of people whose income was well above the poverty line (Minkler, Fuller-Thomson, and Guralnik 2006).

HOW DOES SOCIOECONOMIC STATUS AFFECT HEALTH?

"The richest 1 percent of men now live about 15 years longer than the poorest 1 percent, like the difference between being born in Germany and being born in Rwanda" (Thompson 2016). This reality reflects how health is negatively impacted by a lifelong accumulation of disadvantages combined with limited resources. However, while this cascade of events takes place from conception to old age, advantages of higher SES level off at the oldest age. At this point, health advantages simply have maxed out (Smith 2007).

> Poverty creates ill-health because it forces people to live in environments that make them sick, without decent shelter, clean water or adequate sanitation. Poverty creates hunger, which in turn leaves people vulnerable to disease. Poverty denies people access to reliable health services and affordable medicines, and causes children to miss out on routine vaccinations. Poverty creates illiteracy, leaving people poorly informed about health risks and forced into dangerous jobs that harm their health. (WHO 2019b)

A variety of factors account for the differences in health between different SES groups: income, education, occupation, health literacy, nutrition, decent and safe housing community characteristics, coping resources, support networks, health insurance, access and utilization of quality health care, health behavior, stress, and race and ethnicity are all factors that play an important role in health outcomes. It is not entirely clear which factors matter the most. What is clear is that these factors are interrelated.

Income

Income is a major determinant of SES and today is typically a function of occupation. As first observed in the Whitehall study of British civil servants, even a slight increase in income has been linked to better health outcomes. While overall life expectancy for people over 65 increased in the United States, the life expectancy of the top half of earners increased by 6 years since 1970; by contrast, the life expectancy of the bottom half of earners increased by only 1.3 years. Also, people with lower income (below $35,000 annual family income) were five times more likely to report poor or fair health (22.8 percent) than people with family income over $100,000 (5.6 percent) (Woolf et al. 2015). Higher income enables people to access quality health care, safer environments, better nutrition, and adequate resources to maintain health and counter health problems.

Occupation

In addition to occupation determining income, different occupations are also linked to different health risks and different resources. Occupations at lower levels of education or income often entail higher rates of work-related injuries. Also, access to sick leave or paid family leave differs by kind of employment and employer (BLS 2019).

Education

Education is also a major component of SES. Educational credentials are often needed for higher-paying jobs. But education also gives people important resources in relation to health over the life span such as knowledge, problem-solving skills, access to economic resources, character development, and health literacy. The health benefits from education can be seen at the individual level, at the community level, and in the larger social context. The statistics are stark: people without a high school diploma die nine years earlier than people who earned a college degree. In 2011, 15 percent of adults without a high school degree had diabetes, while only 7 percent of college graduates were diagnosed with diabetes. Between 1990 and 2008, the life expectancy for white men in the United States without high school degrees fell by more than three years and more than five years for women without high school degrees (Zimmerman, Woolf, and Haley 2015).

Stress

A significant factor related to health outcomes is the experience of stress. Stress can damage physical and mental health. Low-income groups, racial and ethnic minorities, young people, and women experience stress more often. The negative effects of stress can be alleviated with a sense of mastery, high self-esteem, and social support—coping resources that are limited among lower-status groups (Thoits 2010). Lower SES groups experience a variety of chronic stressors daily due to lack of economic resources, unemployment, marital disruption, discrimination, social exclusion, and a sense of powerlessness. Unemployment can cause considerable stress, with significant negative health outcomes. In order to cope with ongoing stressors, people often engage in a variety of unhealthy behaviors, including smoking or drinking (Björntorp 2001; Marmot 2004). Stress at work puts people at risk for chronic health conditions such as cardiovascular disease, hypertension, diabetes, or musculoskeletal and back problems. Workload demands and resulting fatigue and lack of sleep, lack of sense of control, safety hazards, less work flexibility, and a negative work atmosphere often create stress. Lower-wage workers often have part-time jobs with low pay and few benefits, which can in turn create stressful conflicts, especially for families and single parents (Richman, Johnson, and Buxbaum 2006). Higher-wage earners typically have more resources to alleviate these conflicts, such as quality childcare or eldercare, paid vacations, or sick days.

Social Exclusion

Unequal power relationships lead to economic, political, social, and cultural exclusion, which in turn diminishes access to resources at individual, household, group, community, country, and global levels. Exclusion restricts participation in economic, social, political, and cultural relationships and can thus result in unemployment, low income, poor nutrition, or other deprivations closely associated with negative health outcomes (WHO 2019c). On the other hand, trust between community members, reciprocity, and cooperation for mutual benefit tends to be greater among high-SES groups, which also explains differences in health behavior between communities (Kawachi 1999). Which groups we belong to and the characteristics of the people in our communities affect health behaviors (Kawachi, Subramanian, and Kim 2008). Family, friends, or neighbors who are health oriented support healthy behavior, sanction unhealthy behavior, and provide important health information. People of high-SES status tend to live healthier; they also tend to associate with other high-SES people and motivate those who might not care much about healthy behaviors (Freese and Lutfey 2010).

Race and Ethnicity

Racial and ethnic minorities are disproportionally affected by economic hardship, which also is related to higher crime rates, hazardous residential environments, and negative effects of residential segregation. These negative impacts include limited work opportunities and lack of access to quality health care, quality nutrition, or healthy recreational options. Discrimination has been identified as a major cause of stress, which has known negative effects on health. In the United States, African Americans, American Indians, and Alaska Natives report higher rates of chronic health conditions such as asthma, diabetes, and heart disease than whites do. AIDS and HIV diagnoses and mortality from AIDS are significantly higher among Blacks than among whites. Infant mortality rates are higher among African Americans, American Indians, Alaska Natives than among whites. Black males have the shortest life expectancy compared to any other group. Racial and ethnic groups also differ with regard to health insurance rates: the rate of uninsured individuals among whites is 6.3 percent. The uninsured rate for Blacks is 10.6 percent and for Asians is 7.3 percent. At 16.1 percent, Hispanics have the highest uninsured rate (U.S. Census Bureau 2018).

While the association between minority status and health has been consistent and persistent, Hispanics and some recent immigrant groups in the United States tend to enjoy better health and lower mortality rates than non-Hispanic whites, despite having higher poverty rates, lower incomes, and lower levels of education. This phenomenon has been labeled the immigrant paradox. Cultural factors such as better health habits or strong social networks might explain the better health outcomes. But it has also been suggested that those who immigrate tend be healthier than those who stay behind, as well as the fact that deaths or returns to the original countries are underreported (Teruya and Bazargan-Hejazi 2013).

Physical Environment

Lack of social cohesion, lack of activity spaces, lack of access to quality food and health care, and high crime rates differ by neighborhoods and can affect the health of the whole community. However, it is not only the difference in social relationships or available services but also the "built environment" that impacts living conditions and opportunities. Substandard housing with mold, lead paint, or pest infestations can affect health negatively. On the flip side, neighborhoods with well-maintained housing, traffic-calming measures, well-lit sidewalks, and safe parks can have positive health effects by providing a safer environment and outdoor exercise options (Cubbin et al. 2008).

Health Care

In the United States, significant differences in health-care access, utilization, and quality exist between various population groups and regions. Low-SES groups, ethnic minority groups, and immigrants are the most disadvantaged in the American health-care system. Blatant health-care deficiencies exist in rural areas and inner-city districts of large cities. Despite spending more money on health care than any other country, the United States fares worse with regard to health outcomes. It has a lower life expectancy, higher infant mortality rate, higher prevalence of chronic conditions, and higher mortality rate from heart disease compared to several other high-income countries. High rates of obesity, a large number of uninsured people, lifestyle factors, and high rates of accidents and violence are among the reasons for poorer health outcomes in the United States (Squires 2015).

In addition, many physicians do not accept patients with Medicaid or Medicare because of the lower payments from these federal public health programs. (Medicare is a federal health insurance program for people age sixty-five and older, younger people with disabilities, and people with permanent kidney failure. Medicaid insurance covers people with low income and people with disabilities.) Evidence also suggests that physicians view and treat patients of lower SES differently from patients from higher-SES status groups. Patients of lower SES tend to receive fewer diagnostic tests and fewer medications for chronic conditions from physicians. The perception that patients of lower-SES status are less intelligent, less independent, less responsible, less rational, and less likely to comply with physicians' orders leads many physicians to delay diagnostic tests, avoid referral to specialist, and use generic drugs instead of original prescription drugs. Patients have the impression that their SES status impacts the health care they receive, particularly with regard to treatment, access to care, and patient-provider interaction. Generally, patients of low-SES status feel they receive worse care than their higher-SES counterparts (Arpey, Gaglioti, and Rosenbaum 2017).

Health Insurance

The United States is the only high-income country without universal health coverage, despite the fact that it has the most expensive health-care system in the world. WHO defines universal health coverage as "when all people and communities can use the promotive, preventive, curative, rehabilitative and palliative health services they need, of sufficient quality to be effective, while also ensuring that the use of these services does not expose the user to financial hardship" (WHO 2016). In his first term, President Barack Obama supported and signed a new law—the Patient Protection and Affordable Care Act (ACA), also known as "Obamacare"—to address shortcomings of health insurance and health-care delivery in the United States. The legislation included provisions to reduce high costs of health care and health insurance, reduce the high number of uninsured and underinsured individuals (eighty-one million adults—44 percent of the adult population—were either uninsured or underinsured at that time), increase limits on what health insurance covers, force insurance carriers to accept patients with preexisting conditions, and outlaw other detrimental health insurance practices (Schoen et al. 2011). In the years immediately following the passage of the ACA, the overall rate of uninsured Americans decreased by 6 percent. The rate of uninsured children, uninsured poor children, and uninsured young adults was cut significantly. Still, a lot of people in the United States do not have health insurance coverage. The uninsured rate for children who live in poverty is still significantly higher compared to children who live above the poverty line.

Health Behavior

Socioeconomic status impacts lifestyles and health behaviors. Numerous behaviors have been associated with negative health outcomes, such as smoking, alcohol consumption, illegal drug use, sleep deprivation, lack of exercise, risky sexual activity, and unhealthy diet (Cockerham 2005; Pampel, Krueger, and Denney 2010). In addition, health behaviors such as adhering to checkup schedules, compliance with physicians' orders, and interaction with health-care professionals also impact health outcomes. Differences have been found between lower- and higher-SES groups, with education having the most significant impact on some negative health behaviors such as smoking, lack of exercise, and obesity. High school dropouts have much higher odds of smoking and lack of exercise than college graduates do. Low income and lower-ranked occupations also have higher odds of smoking and lack of exercise. However, the effects were smaller than the impact of educational attainment (Zhang and Wang 2004). Cockerham speculated that adhering to healthy lifestyles among high-SES groups might represent a form of social distinction as much as it serves to improve health outcomes (Cockerham 2005).

CONCLUSION

Socioeconomic status and health are interrelated. While the equation seems pretty clear—lower SES impacts health negatively—the causation can also go the other direction: disease and functional limitations can cause lower income. Poverty can be the cause and consequence for ill health.

Several outcomes are used to measure the impact of low SES on health, and a variety of factors contribute to ill health among lower-SES groups. Stress, health behavior, health care and health insurance, income, education, occupation, social exclusion, and the physical environment all differ between higher- and lower-SES groups and have been shown to negatively impact the health of lower-SES groups. In the end, it comes down to differences in socioeconomic status. With higher income, educational attainment, and a better occupation, people can afford to live in better housing and neighborhoods, receive quality health care, have good health insurance, exercise and eat a good diet, cope better with stress, and be included in supportive social networks. This is why people have called for a logical solution to the issue: address SES as a cause of ill health (Stringhini et al. 2017). Addressing SES, so goes the argument, would benefit not only individuals but whole communities, because better health increases economic well-being.

Gesine K. Hearn

Further Reading

American Psychological Association. 2019. "Work, Stress, Health and Socioeconomic Status." http://www.apa.org/pi/ses/resources/publications/fact-sheet-references.aspx.

Arpey, Nicholas C., Anne Gaglioti, and Marcy Rosenbaum. 2017. "How Socioeconomic Status Affects Patient Perceptions of Health Care: A Qualitative Study." *Journal of Primary Care & Community Health* 8 (3): 169–75.

Björntorp, Per. 2001. "Do Stress Reactions Cause Abdominal Obesity and Comorbidities?" *Obesity Review* 2 (2):73–86.

BLS (Bureau of Labor Statistics). 2019. "Access to Paid and Unpaid Family Leave in 2018." https://www.bls.gov/opub/ted/2019/access-to-paid-and-unpaid-family-leave-in-2018.htm.

Clark, A. M., M. DesMeules, W. Luo, A. S. Duncan, and A. Wielgosz. 2009. "Socioeconomic Status and Cardiovascular Disease: Risks and Implications for Care." *Nature Reviews Cardiology* 6:712–22.

Cockerham, William C. 2005. "Health Lifestyle Theory and the Convergence of Agency and Structure." *Journal of Health and Social Behavior* 46 (1): 51–67.

Cubbin, C., V. Pedregon, S. Egerter, and P. Bravemen. 2008. "Where We Live Matters for Our Health: Neighborhoods and Health." Issue Brief 3, September 2008. Robert Wood Johnson Foundation. https://folio.iupui.edu/bitstream/handle/10244/638/commissionneighborhood102008.pdf.

Foraker, R. E., K. M. Rose, P. P. Chang, A. M. McNeill, C. M. Suchindran, E. Selvin, and W. D. Rosamond. 2011. "Socioeconomic Status and the Trajectory of Self-Rated Health." *Age and Ageing* 40:706–711.

Freese, Jeremy, and Karen Lutfey. 2010. "Fundamental Causality: Challenges of an Animating Concept for Medical Sociology." In *The Handbook of the Sociology of Health, Illness, and Healing*, edited by Bernice A. Pescosolido, Jack K. Martin, Jane McLeod, and Ann Rogers, 67–84. New York: Springer.

Gaware, Vinayak M., Kiran B. Dhamak, Kiran B. Kotade, Ramdas T. Dolas, Sachin B. Somwanshi, Vikrant K. Nikam, and Atul N. Khadse. 2011. "Onchocerciasis: An Overview." *Pharmacologyonline* 1:1012–22. https://pharmacologyonline.silae.it/files/newsletter/2011/vol1/095.gaware.pdf.

Genuis, Stephen J. 2008. "Toxic Causes of Mental Illness Are Overlooked." *NeuroToxicology* 29 (6): 1147–49.

Kawachi, Ichiro. 1999. "Social Capital and Community Effects on Population and Individual Health." *Annals of New York Academy of Sciences* 896:120–30.

Kawachi, Ichiro., S. V. Subramanian, and Daniel Kim, eds. 2008. *Social Capital and Health*. New York: Springer.

Link, Bruce G., and Jo C. Phelan. 1995. "Social Conditions as Fundamental Causes of Disease." *Journal of Health and Social Behavior* 35 (extra issue): 80–94.

Lutfey, Karen, and Jeremy Freese. 2005. "Toward Some Fundamentals of Fundamental Causality: Socioeconomic Status and Health in the Routine Clinic Visit for Diabetes." *American Journal of Sociology* 10 (5): 1326–72.

Marmot, M. G., G. Rose, M. Shipley, and P. J. Hamilton. 1978. "Employment Grade and Coronary Heart Disease in British Civil Servants." *Journal of Epidemiology and Community Health* 32:244–49.

Marmot, Michael. 2004. *Status Syndrome. How Your Social Standing Directly Affects Your Health and Life Expectancy.* London: Bloomsbury Publishing.

McFadden, E., R. Luben, S. Bingham, N. Wareham, A.-L. Kinmonth, and K.-T. Khaw. 2008. "Social Inequalities in Self-Rated Health by Age: Cross-Sectional Study of 22,457 Middle-Aged Men and Women." *BMC Public Health* 8:230. https://bmcpublichealth.biomedcentral.com/articles/10.1186/1471-2458-8-230.

Minkler, Meredith, Esme Fuller-Thomson, and Jack M. Guralnik. 2006. "Gradient of Disability across the Socioeconomic Spectrum in the United States." *New England Journal of Medicine* 355:695–703.

Orgera, Kendal, and Samantha Artiga. 2018. "Disparities in Health and Health Care: Five Key Questions and Answers." Kaiser Family Foundation. https://collections.nlm.nih.gov/catalog/nlm:nlmuid-101740322-pdf.

Pampel, Fred C., Patrick M. Krueger, and Justin T. Denney. 2010. "Socioeconomic Disparities in Health Behaviors." *Annual Review of Sociology* 36:349–70.

Phelan, Jo C., Bruce G. Link, and P. Tehranifar. 2010. "Social Conditions as Fundamental Causes of Health Inequalities: Theory, Evidence, and Policy Implications." *Journal of Health and Social Behavior* 51:S28–40.

Richman, Amy, Arlene Johnson, and Lisa Buxbaum. 2006. *Workplace Flexibility for Lower-Wage Workers.* Washington DC: Corporate Voices for Working Families.

Schoen, C., M. M. Doty, R. H. Henderson, and S. R. Collins. 2011. "Affordable Care Act Reforms Could Reduce the Number of Underinsured US Adults by 70 Percent." *Health Affairs* 30:1762–71.

Smith, James P. 2007. "The Impact of Socioeconomic Status on Health over the Life-Course." *Journal of Human Resources* 42 (4): 739–64.

Squires, David. 2015. "U.S. Health Care from a Global Perspective: Spending, Use of Services, Prices and Health in 13 Countries." Commonwealth Fund, October. http://www.commonwealthfund.org/publications/issue-briefs/2015/oct/us-health-care-from-a-global-perspective.

Stringhini, Silvia, Cristian Carmeli, Markus Jokela, Mauricio Avendaño, Peter Muennig, Florence Guida, Fulvio Ricceri, et al. 2017. "Socio-Economic Status and the 25-25 Risk Factors as Determinants of Premature Mortality: A Multicohort Study and Meta-Analysis of 1.7 Million Men and Women." *The Lancet* 389:1229–37.

Teruya, S. A., and S. Bazargan-Hejazi. 2013. "The Immigrant and Hispanic Paradoxes: A Systematic Review of Their Predictions and Effects." *Hispanic Journal of Behavioral Sciences* 35 (4): 486–509.

Thoits, P. 2010. "Stress and Health: Major Findings and Policy Implications." *Journal of Health and Social Behavior* 51:S41–53.

Thompson, Derek. 2016. "Why the Poor Die Young." *The Atlantic*, April 12, 2016. https://www.theatlantic.com/business/archive/2016/04/why-the-poor-die-young/477846.

UNAIDS. 2015. "Aids Info." http://aidsinfo.unaids.org.

U.S. Census Bureau. 2018. *Health Insurance Coverage in the United States: 2017.* Washington, DC: U.S. Census Bureau.

WHO (World Health Organization). 2016. *World Health Statistics 2016: Monitoring Health for the SDGs, Sustainable Development Goals.* Geneva: World Health Organization.

WHO (World Health Organization). 2019a. "Global Health Observatory (GHO) Data." https://www.who.int/gho/mortality_burden_disease/life_tables/situation_trends/en.

WHO (World Health Organization). 2019b. "Poverty and Health." https://www.who.int/hdp/poverty/en.

WHO (World Health Organization). 2019c. "Social Determinants of Health." https://www.who.int/social_determinants/en.

Woolf, Steven H., Laudan Aron, Lisa Dubay, Sarah Simon, Emily Zimmerman, and Kom Luk. 2015. *How Are Income and Wealth Linked to Health and Longevity?* Washington, DC: Urban Institute and Virginia Commonwealth University.

Zhang, Q., and Y. Wang. 2004. "Socioeconomic Inequality of Obesity in the United States: Do Gender, Age, and Ethnicity Matter?" *Social Science and Medicine* 58 (6): 1171–80.

Zimmerman, Emily, Steven Woolf, and Amber Haley. 2015. "Understanding the Relationship Between Education and Health: A Review of the Evidence and an Examination of Community Perspectives." Agency for Healthcare Research and Quality, Rockville, MD. http://www.ahrq.gov/professionals/education/curriculum-tools/population-health/zimmerman.html.

Substance Abuse

When looking at the relationship between inequality and substance abuse, there are two issues to consider. The first of these is actual patterns of use. The second is the relationship between (social) inequality and social control efforts. The latter include arrests, prosecutions, and incarcerations of offenders, as well as substance abuse prevention and rehabilitation efforts.

In a now-classic paper, sociologist Robin Room (2004) introduced the concepts of stigmatization and marginalization to the discussion of substance use disorders, thus broadening the consideration of social inequality beyond its traditional focus on socioeconomic status (SES). Socioeconomic status has usually been measured in various ways, including education, occupation, income, and reputation as determined by a panel of community residents (Hollingshead 1949). How SES is defined may account for differences in findings among research studies (Patrick et al. 2012). Room's contribution is that factors such as race, gender, homelessness, and unemployment may be considered in examining the relationship between substance use disorders and social inequality.

PATTERNS OF SUBSTANCE USE

Data from the National Survey on Drug Use and Health (SAMHSA) for 2017–2018 indicate that substance use is related to SES as measured by employment status (SAMHSA 2019b). Those respondents who are aged twenty-six and older and are unemployed reported a greater use of illicit drugs in the year of study than did those with full-time jobs (SAMHSA 2019b). The relationship between employment status and yearly illicit substance use holds for marijuana, cocaine, crack, stimulants, sedatives and tranquilizers, hallucinogens, methamphetamines, and opioids (SAMHSA 2019c, 2019d, 2019e, 2019f, 2019g, 2019h, 2019i, 2019j). The relationship between education and substance use, however, is not so clear. Use of illicit substances in the year studied increases with education, from less than high school through some college, and then it dips slightly for college graduates, but it is still higher than use by non-high school people (SAMHSA 2019b). Yearly mari-juana use increases slightly with education, but cocaine use is slightly higher for college graduates than for those with less than a high school education (SAMHSA 2019c, 2019d). The use of crack drops significantly (from 0.6 percent to 0.2 per-cent) with an increase in education (SAMHSA 2019e). Opioid use increases for those with a high school education to those with some college, but use by college graduates drops below the percentage of non-high school graduates using them (SAMHSA 2019j). Hallucinogen use increases with education, but methamphet-amine use decreases (SAMHSA 2019f, 2019g).

Social inequality and substance abuse are also related to race, especially as it reflects SES. The SAMHSA data on lifetime use of illicit substances shows whites reporting a higher percentage of drug usage (56.8 percent) than Blacks/African Americans (47.2 percent) and Hispanics/Latinx (36.7 percent). However, the group with the highest rates of reported lifetime drug use is American Indian/Alaskan Natives, with 65.6 percent reporting such use (SAMHSA 2019a). When only the year of study is considered, survey respondents from that group again had the largest reported percentage of drug use (SAMHSA 2019b). The same holds true for methamphetamine use in the year of study, with 2.6 percent of American Indian/Alaskan Natives reporting having used meth compared with 0.8 percent of whites, 0.2 percent of Blacks, and 0.8 percent of Hispanics (SAMHSA 2019g). American Indian/Alaskan Natives also were more likely to use marijuana, fol-lowed by Blacks, whites, and Hispanics (SAMHSA 2019c). Hispanics and Asians were the least likely to report cocaine use, followed in increasing order by Ameri-can Indian/Alaskan Natives, whites, and Blacks (SAMHSA 2019d). The highest percentage of crack use was reported by Blacks, which was three times higher than that admitted to by whites and American Indian/Alaskan Natives, and four and a half times that of Hispanics (SAMHSA 2019e). Native Americans/Alaskan Natives had the highest percentage of reported opioid use, followed by whites, Blacks, and Hispanics (SAMHSA 2019j).

The higher reported use of substances by Black respondents and American Indian/Alaskan Natives has been linked in many studies to their lower income levels, with Blacks having the lowest median annual income and American Indian/Alaskan Natives just above them (U.S. Census Bureau 2016). Journalist Maia Sza-lavitz (2011) succinctly summarized the widespread understanding of linkages between poverty and substance abuse when she said, "We need to admit the truth: addiction is disproportionately concentrated among the poor, and, consequently, among blacks and Hispanics."

One longitudinal survey of substance use and mental health of students in ten sociodemographically diverse Los Angeles area high schools found that "markers of socioeconomic status (SES) such as level of parental education are inversely associated with substance use in adolescents" (Andrabi, Khoddam, and Leventhal 2016, 176).

While substance abuse is more common at lower SES levels, this does not nec-essarily mean that there is a causal relationship between the two variables. Other factors that may come into play include educational level, genetics, and mental health status (Foundations Recovery Network n.d.).

Some researchers have found, for example, that alcohol consumption appears to be positively correlated with income and education (Hart 2015; Patrick et al. 2012; Sunrise House 2019), although heavy or binge drinking may be more characteristic of those of lower SES (Sunrise House 2019). In a Norwegian study of students ages fourteen to seventeen years old, Pape et al. (2018) found that "low socioeconomic status (SES) is related to hazardous alcohol use in adults, and the association seems to be stronger for more deviant and harmful drinking behavior" (Pape et al. 2018, 132). Hart (2015) notes, "It is well established that alcohol-related harm is disproportionately prevalent among low SES drinkers," although they drink less than those in higher strata (Hart 2015, 148). Patrick et al. (2012) used three indicators of family SES during childhood (income, wealth, and parental education) to examine their influence on smoking, alcohol, and marijuana use during young adulthood. They found that "alcohol use and marijuana use in young adulthood were associated with higher childhood SES" (Patrick et al. 2012, 772). Young people in the higher socioeconomic levels were most likely to drink and to engage in binge drinking. The apparent contradiction in the literature, which indicates that lower-SES adults are more likely than higher-SES adults to indulge in binge drinking but that higher-SES youth are likely to engage in binge drinking requires explanation. One possible explanation for this finding is that more affluent people can afford more alcohol and are more likely than poorer people to attend alcohol-related social activities (Sunrise House 2019). Another possibility is that higher-SES youth are more likely to attend college, where binge drinking is more prevalent (Research Institute on Addictions 2014; Weinberg, Falk, and Adler Falk 2017) and that they eventually modify their youthful drinking practices as they graduate and leave that youth culture (SAMSHA 2019k).

An alternative way in which social inequality and substance abuse can be viewed is by considering the effect of marginalization and stigma and their relationship to social inequality and substance abuse (Room 2004). Stigma and its resulting marginalization are often part of what Becker (1963) has termed a "career" and Goffman (1959, 1961, 1963) called a "moral career," which refers to changes in how deviant individuals view themselves and others as they pass through various stages, including commission of a deviant act, the development of deviant motives and interests, being publicly labeled, and joining a deviant subculture such as, for example, the heroin subculture (Bourgois 1998a, 1998b; Hoffer 2006; Weinberg, Falk, and Adler Falk 2017).

These stages can come in any sequence. When someone is labeled as a deviant, there is a drastic change in that person's public identity. In Goffman's terms, that individual is now stigmatized, and with stigmatization comes marginalization. The qualities that others believed that the individual possessed as part of what Goffman termed a "virtual social identity" are now replaced by others less favorable, as that person's "actual social identity" is revealed (Goffman 1963).

As people become more marginalized, they often engage in behavior in an attempt to cope with their situation. Some of this behavior has been termed "secondary deviance," as it is supportive of their primary deviance. For example, heroin addicts may steal, sell drugs, prostitute themselves, and practice con games to support their habit.

Some people with substance use disorders who find themselves ostracized from "respectable" society seek out others in the same situation and become members of a drug-using subculture. These subcultures facilitate the obtaining of drugs and often provide participants with rationales that enable them to cope with their marginal social status. However, not all drug and alcohol abusers find support among others and may remain solitary users (Weinberg et al. 2017).

Among those who are most severely marginalized are the homeless. According to the Substance Abuse and Mental Health Services Administration (SAMHSA), drug use is common among the homeless. One SAMHSA study from 2003 found about 26 percent of homeless had drug use disorders and 38 percent struggled with alcohol addictions (SAMHSA 2003). The National Coalition for the Homeless (2009) notes that substance abuse can be both a cause and effect of homelessness. Ethnographies of homeless heroin addicts in San Francisco (Bourgois 1998b; Pearson and Bourgois 1995) and Denver, Colorado (Hoffer 2006), describe their day-to-day lives and how marginalization negatively affects them. In both of these studies, it is clear why drug subcultures have such a powerful hold on their members. They provide a sense of belonging and an alternative status system, which enables those who have access to drugs—and who are thus at the top of that subculture's drug-using hierarchy—to maintain a positive sense of self.

Mental illness is another factor affecting both homelessness and substance use disorders. The mentally ill are stigmatized, and when their situation is known, they often become marginalized (Goffman 1959, 1961, 1963; Hinshaw 2007; Kranke et al. 2010; Mannarini and Rossi 2019). According to the National Coalition for the Homeless, "for many homeless people, substance abuse co-occurs with mental illness. Often people with untreated mental illnesses use street drugs as an inappropriate form of self-medication" (National Coalition for the Homeless 2009).

SOCIAL INEQUALITY AND SOCIAL CONTROL

Social control over the use of alcohol and illicit substances by the justice system and other American institutions takes two very different approaches, the punitive and the therapeutic (the latter of which includes prevention and rehabilitation). Often the same individual is subjected to both punitive interventions (in the form of arrests and incarcerations) and therapeutic interventions (in the form of rehabilitation and treatment). When dealing with drug law violators and alcoholics, our society appears to be ambivalent about how best to respond. On the one hand, they are viewed as responsible for their behavior and unwilling to change; that is, they are seen as criminals. On the other hand, substance abusers are also seen as victims, whose drug and alcohol use is beyond their control, their behavior being a manifestation of an illness, so from that perspective they are treated as patients.

The punitive approach has often been applied to the homeless. Anthropologist James Spradley's classic study *You Owe Yourself a Drunk: An Ethnography of Urban Nomads* (1988) details the experience of skid row denizens with the police, drunk courts, and the lockup. These men, most of whom have drinking problems, view the police as determined to arbitrarily arrest them. The powerlessness of the men after they are pulled into the orbit of the legal system is shown by the amount of time each man spends in front of the judge: typically two to three minutes, a remarkably short time to determine a person's immediate future.

The FBI's publication, *Crime in the United States* (2018), also known as the Uniform Crime Reports, has some interesting data on arrests for various drug and alcohol violations. For example, in 2018, there were 1,654,282 arrests for drug abuse violations, 1,001,329 arrests for driving while intoxicated, 173,152 arrests for violation of liquor laws, and 328,772 arrests for drunkenness. (United States Department of Justice 2019).

When arrests for drug and alcohol violations are broken down by race, there are a number of noteworthy findings related to social inequality. While whites account for slightly more than 70 percent of arrests for drug abuse violations according to 2018 statistical data, about 27 percent of arrests for these crimes are made on Blacks, which is about twice their representation in the U.S. population (United States Department of Justice 2019; Adegboye 2020). Arrests of Blacks for driving while intoxicated, violation of liquor laws, and drunkenness are each about 14 percent, which is close to their proportion in the general population. The other racial group whose arrest percentages are greater than one would expect are Native Americans, based on their representation of 1.3 percent of the country's population, but these percentages are only for drunkenness, accounting for slightly less than 11 percent of the total (United States Department of Justice 2019; Adegboye 2020). How might these findings be explained? While some writers account for the higher rate of arrests of minorities for drug-related offenses in terms of racial discrimination (e.g., Stanton, n.d.), a number of researchers have determined that SES, not race, is the primary factor in arrests (e.g., Palamar et al. 2015). For example, the explanation for the eighteen-to-one disparity in arrests between powdered cocaine and crack is that crack is more likely to be used by the poor, including minorities, who are more vulnerable to discovery and arrest than those of higher SES.

Some writers take a *symbolic interactionist* approach when looking at social inequity and social control. Symbolic interactionists believe that people act in terms of the meanings situations hold for them. In other words, it is people's perceptions that are most important in understanding their behavior (Thomas and Thomas 1928). One 2014 study examined the relationship between the *perceptions* of racial discrimination among African American youth, their use of marijuana and alcohol, and symptoms of depression and post-traumatic stress. The authors concluded that "the most proximal effect of perceptions of racial discrimination in African American youth is depressive symptoms . . . [which] . . . are related to the more distal effect of increased use of alcohol and marijuana" (Sanders-Phillips et al. 2014, 286).

The other face of social control is prevention and rehabilitation. It is here that the effects of social inequality on substance use are most visible. Those with fewer resources are less likely to get treatment for substance abuse problems because they cannot afford it, or they have to settle for the cheapest treatment, which may not serve their needs (Foundations Recovery Network n.d.). Room noted that studies in health services indicate that individuals recognized as skid row alcoholics are likely to get inferior care (Room 2004). This situation is exacerbated by mental illness, since many treatment programs for substance use disorders often do not accept clients with mental illnesses, and treatment facilities for mental illness do not usually deal with substance use issues (National Coalition for the Homeless 2009). Another issue is the reluctance of marginalized individuals with substance use issues to enter rehabilitation programs even if they are aware of them, because the individuals give higher priority to other needs such as food and shelter; the belief that they can help themselves; suspicions and fears about legal consequences, negative judgments, and motivations of others; privacy concerns; and refusal to believe that they need treatment (Sunrise House 2019). Even when marginalized individuals enter treatment programs and are successful, long-term rehabilitation is not assured, because they often do not have access to supportive individuals to motivate and encourage them (Sunrise House 2019; Wiseman 1970).

Thomas S. Weinberg

Further Reading

Adegboye, Adewebs. 2020. "American Population by Race 2020 [Updated Statistics]-All You Need to Know, Total American Population." Kenya Prime, City of Information. May 14, 2020. https://kenyaprime.com/american-population-by-race-2020-updated-statistics-all-you-need-to-know/.

Andrabi, Nafeesa, Rubin Khoddam, and Adam M. Leventhal. 2016. "Socioeconomic Disparities in Adolescent Substance Use: Role of Enjoyable Alternative Substance-Free Activities." *Social Science & Medicine* 176:175–82.

Becker, Howard S. 1963. *Outsiders: Studies in the Sociology of Deviance.* New York: Macmillan.

Bourgois, Philippe. 1998a. "Just Another Night in a Shooting Gallery." *Theory, Culture & Society* 15 (2): 37–66.

Bourgois, Philippe. 1998b. "The Moral Economies of Homeless Heroin Addicts: Confronting Ethnography, HIV Risk, and Everyday Violence in San Francisco Shooting Encampments." *Substance Use & Misuse* 33 (11): 2323–51.

Foundations Recovery Network. n.d. "Economic Status and Abuse." https://www.dualdiagnosis.org/drug-addiction/economic-status.

Goffman, Erving. 1959. "The Moral Career of the Mental Patient." *Psychiatry: Journal for the Study of Interpersonal Processes* 22:123–35.

Goffman, Erving. 1961. *Asylums: Essays on the Social Situation of Mental Patients and Other Inmates.* New York: Anchor Books.

Goffman, Erving. 1963. *Stigma: Notes on the Management of Spoiled Identity.* Englewood Cliffs, NJ: Prentice-Hall.

Hart, Aaron. 2015. "Assembling Interrelations Between Low Socioeconomic Status and Acute Alcohol-Related Harms among Young Adult Drinkers." *Contemporary Drug Problems* 42 (2): 148–67.

Hinshaw, Stephen P. 2007. *The Mark of Shame: Stigma of Mental Illness and an Agenda for Change.* New York: Oxford University Press.

Hoffer, Lee D. 2006. *Junkie Business: The Evolution and Operation of a Heroin Dealing Network.* Belmont, CA: Wadsworth.

Hollingshead, August B. 1949. *Elmtown's Youth, The Impact of Social Classes on Adolescents.* New York: John Wiley & Sons.

Kranke, Derrick, Jerry Floersch, Lisa Townsend, and Michelle Munson. 2010."Stigma Experience among Adolescents Taking Psychiatric Medication." *Children and Youth Services Review* 32 (4): 496–505.

Mannarini, Stefania, and Alessandro Rossi. 2019. "Assessing Mental Illness Stigma: A Complex Issue." *Frontiers in Psychology* 9. https://doi.org/10.3389/fpsyg.2018 .02722, accessed November 24, 2020.

National Coalition for the Homeless. 2009. "Substance Abuse and the Homeless." National Coalition for the Homeless, July 2009. https://www.nationalhomeless.org/fact-sheets/addiction.html.

Palamar, Joseph J., Shelby Davies, Danielle C. Ompad, Charles M. Cleland, and Michael Weitzman. 2015. "Powder Cocaine and Crack Use in the United States: An Examination of Risk for Arrest and Socioeconomic Disparities in Use." *Drug and Alcohol Dependence* 149, no. 1 (April): 108–116.

Pape, Hilde, Ingeborg Rossow, Jasmina Burdzovic, and Thor Norstrom. 2018. "Social Class and Alcohol Use by Youth: Different Drinking Behaviors, Different Associations?" *Journal of Studies on Alcohol & Drugs* 79 (1): 132–36.

Patrick, Megan E., Patrick Wightman, Robert F. Schoeni, and John E. Schulenberg. 2012. "Socioeconomic Status and Substance Use among Young Adults: A Comparison across Constructs and Drugs." *Journal of Studies on Alcohol and Drugs* 73 (5): 772–82.

Pearson, Charles, and Philippe Bourgois. 1995. "Hope to Die a Dope Fiend." *Cultural Anthropology* 10 (4): 587–93.

Research Institute on Addictions. 2014. "RIA Reaching Others: Alcohol and Sexual Assault." http://www.buffalo.edu/cria/news_events/es/es11.html.

Room, Robin. 2004. "Thinking About How Social Inequalities Relate to Alcohol and Drug Use and Problems." Center for Social Research on Alcohol and Drugs. Stockholm University. http://www.robionroom.net/inequal.htm.

SAMHSA (Substance Abuse and Mental Health Services Administration). 2003. *Homelessness: Provision of Mental Health and Substance Abuse Services.* http://mentalhealth.samhsa.gov/publications/allpubs/homelessness.

SAMHSA (Substance Abuse and Mental Health Services Administration). 2019a. *Results from the 2018 National Survey on Drug Use and Health:* Detailed Tables, Table 1.22B: Illicit Drug Use in Lifetime among Persons Aged 12 or Older, by Age Group and Demographic Characteristics: Percentages, 2017 and 2018.

SAMHSA (Substance Abuse and Mental Health Services Administration). 2019b. *Results from the 2018 National Survey on Drug Use and Health:* Detailed Tables, Table 1.23B: Illicit Drug Use in Past Year among Persons Aged 12 or Older, by Age Group and Demographic Characteristics: Percentages, 2017 and 2018.

SAMHSA (Substance Abuse and Mental Health Services Administration). 2019c. *Results from the 2018 National Survey on Drug Use and Health:* Detailed Tables, Table 1.26B: Marijuana Use in Past Year among Persons Aged 12 or Older, by Age Group and Demographic Characteristics: Percentages, 2017 and 2018.

SAMHSA (Substance Abuse and Mental Health Services Administration). 2019d. *Results from the 2018 National Survey on Drug Use and Health:* Detailed Tables, Table 1.29B: Cocaine Use in Past Year among Persons Aged 12 or Older, by Age Group and Demographic Characteristics: Percentages, 2017 and 2018.

SAMHSA (Substance Abuse and Mental Health Services Administration). 2019e. *Results from the 2018 National Survey on Drug Use and Health:* Detailed Tables, Table 1.32: Crack Use in Past Year among Persons Aged 12 or Older, by Age Group and Demographic Characteristics: Percentages, 2017 and 2018.

SAMHSA (Substance Abuse and Mental Health Services Administration) 2019f. *Results from the 2018 National Survey on Drug Use and Health:* Detailed Tables, Table 1.35B: Hallucinogen Use in Past Year among Persons Aged 12 or Older, by Age Group and Demographic Characteristics: Percentages, 2017 and 2018.

SAMHSA (Substance Abuse and Mental Health Services Administration) 2019g. *Results from the 2018 National Survey on Drug Use and Health:* Detailed Tables, Table 1.41B: Methamphetamine Use in Past Year among Persons Aged 12 or Older, by Age Group and Demographic Characteristics: Percentages, 2017 and 2018.

SAMHSA (Substance Abuse and Mental Health Services Administration). 2019h. *Results from the 2018 National Survey on Drug Use and Health:* Detailed Tables. Table 1.47B: Misuse of Stimulants in Past Year among Persons Aged 12 or Older, by Age Group and Demographic Characteristics: Percentages, 2017 and 2018.

SAMHSA (Substance Abuse and Mental Health Services Administration). 2019i. *Results from the 2018 National Survey on Drug Use and Health:* Detailed Tables. Table 1.51B: Misuse of Tranquilizers or Sedatives in Past Month among Persons Aged 12 or Older, by Age Group and Demographic Characteristics: Percentages, 2017 and 2018.

SAMHSA (Substance Abuse and Mental Health Services Administration). 2019j. *Results from the 2018 National Survey on Drug Use and Health:* Detailed Tables. Table 1.60B: Misuse of Opioids in Past Year among Persons Aged 12 or Older, by Age Group and Demographic Characteristics: Percentages, 2017 and 2018.

SAMHSA (Substance Abuse and Mental Health Services Administration). 2019k. *Results from the 2018 National Survey on Drug Use and Health:* Detailed Tables, Table 2.18B: Alcohol Use in Past Year among Persons Aged 12 or Older, by Age Group and Demographic Characteristics: Percentages, 2017 and 2018.

Sanders-Phillips, Kathy, Wendy Kliewer, Taqi Tirmazi, Von Nebbitt, Takisha Carter, and Heather Key. 2014. "Perceived Racial Discrimination, Drug Use, and Psychological Distress in African American Youth: A Pathway to Child Health Disparities." *Journal of Social Issues* 70 (2): 279–97.

Spradley, James P. 1988. *You Owe Yourself a Drunk: An Ethnography of Urban Nomads.* New York: University Press of America.

Stanton, Garrett. n.d. "Crack v. Cocaine: The Issue Is Black & White." *The Issue.* https://sites.google.com/a/utexas.edu/crack-vs-cocaine-a-black-and-white-problem.

Sunrise House. 2019. "Evaluating an Individual's Treatment Needs: Addiction among Socioeconomic Groups." https://sunrisehouse.com/addiction-demographics/socioeconomic-groups.

Szalavitz, Maia. 2011. "Yes, Addiction Does Discriminate." The Fix. https://www.thefix.com/content/economic-inequality-and-addiction8202.

Thomas, W. I., and D. S. Thomas. 1928. *The Child in America: Behavior Problems and Programs.* New York: Knopf.

U.S. Census Bureau. 2016. "Median Household Income in the Past 12 Months (in 2016 Inflation-Adjusted Dollars) by Household Size." *American Community Survey.* https://data.census.gov/cedsci/table?q=B19019&tid=ACSDT1Y2016.B19019&hidePreview=false.

United States Department of Justice, Federal Bureau of Investigation. 2019. *Crime in the United States, 2018.* https://ucr.fbi.gov/nibrs/2018.

Weinberg, Thomas S. 1994. *Gay Men, Drinking, and Alcoholism.* Carbondale: Southern Illinois University Press.

Weinberg, Thomas S., Gerhard Falk, and Ursula Adler Falk. 2017. *The American Drug Culture.* Los Angeles: Sage Publishers.

Weitzman, Michael. 2015. "Powder Cocaine and Crack Use in the United States: An Examination of Risk for Arrest and Socioeconomic Disparities in Use." *Drug and Alcohol Dependence* 149, no. 1 (April): 108–16.

Wiseman, Jacqueline P. 1970. *Stations of the Lost: The Treatment of Skid Row Alcoholics.* Englewood Cliffs, NJ: Prentice Hall.

SECTION IV

Housing and Communities

Food Deserts

A comprehensive examination of inequalities in the United States is incomplete without examining food environments. Food is essential to health and quality of life and integral to the livelihood of economies, but wide disparities in access to healthy food exist in every region of the United States. Neighborhoods with limited access to healthy, nutritious, and affordable foods, referred to as *food deserts*, have been associated with poorer diet and health outcomes, including obesity, type 2 diabetes, cardiovascular disease, other diet-related chronic conditions, and neighborhood disadvantage. *Neighborhood disadvantage* is frequently described as having poor access to healthy and nutritious foods and other factors related to health behaviors and health outcomes (Macintyre 2007, 2). Policies that make food more affordable for low-wage workers and low-income households are imperative.

EVOLUTION OF FOOD DESERTS

The phrase *food desert* first appeared in a government report in Scotland in the early 1990s (Cummins and Macintyre 2002, 436). In the nearly three decades since the introduction of the phrase, this nomenclature has been used to characterize communities with little or no access to healthy, nutritious, and affordable foods. The U.S. Department of Agriculture (USDA) characterizes food deserts as neighborhoods within urban cities and rural towns that do not have access to supermarkets. Rather, these areas tend to have a greater density of fast-food restaurants and convenience stores that, historically, offer less healthy and nutritious foods (Wright et al. 2016, 171). The USDA added language to its definition of a food desert, to include income and access as criteria for food desert status. Specifically, the USDA categorizes urban food deserts as low-income areas based on the poverty rate or median household income of the community in which approximately one-third of the residents live more than one mile from the nearest supermarket (Wright et al. 2016, 171). It can be argued that higher-income groups can also reside in food deserts, but personal vehicle ownership affords higher-income households the opportunity to access supermarkets, thereby eliminating the access barrier of living in a food desert.

Urban food deserts resulted in part from the expansion and relocation of super-markets to suburban areas, where larger parcels of land provided increased food variety, more competitive pricing, and better parking options (Wright et al. 2016, 172–73). Consequently, neighborhoods in some major cities were left without ade-quate supermarket access and a greater percentage of fast-food restaurants and cor-ner stores with few if any nutritional options. Additionally, demographic shifts of middle-income families from inner cities to suburbs in the 1970s and 1980s forced supermarkets in urban areas to close, as the limited purchasing power of lower-income households that remained in these communities proved insufficient to keep those urban supermarkets afloat (Nyden et al. 1998, 2; Wright et al. 2016, 171).

ECONOMIC AND RACIAL FACTORS IN FOOD DESERTS

Researchers have identified disparities in the location of food deserts based on individual and neighborhood socioeconomic status, racial/ethnic composition of the neighborhood, and geographic region (urban and rural).

Socioeconomic status (SES) is a well-documented contributor to adverse health outcomes by influencing access to resources including education, employment, and food. Socioeconomic status is frequently studied as a composite variable that com-prises factors such as income, education, economic resources/wealth, and power or prestige (Braveman et al. 2010, 186–87). The overwhelming majority of studies examining the association between food access and neighborhood SES report that compared to higher-SES communities, lower socioeconomic communities have fewer supermarkets—and higher concentrations of convenience stores. These find-ings suggest that the diets of residents of lower-SES communities can be nutrition-ally compromised if there is sole reliance on their local food environment

Food deserts are also more likely to be found in communities with higher popu-lations of racial/ethnic minority groups (Williams, Priest, and Anderson 2016, 407). It has been widely documented that racial/ethnic minority communities have fewer supermarkets, more convenience stores, and more fast-food restaurants, and they are farther away from a supermarket, compared to their white counterparts (Block, Scribner, and DeSalvo 2004, 213–14; Moore and Diez-Roux 2006, 327–29; USDA 2009, 1, 17, 47; Zenk et al. 2005, 662).

RURAL AND URBAN FOOD DESERTS

Challenges to addressing food access in urban and rural communities are inher-ently different. As previously discussed, demographic shifts and the mass exodus of supermarkets from the inner city left these communities devoid of adequate food access. In rural communities, factors including geographical isolation, low population density, and low tax base have made it difficult for them to attract supermarkets that stock fresh, healthy, and nutritious foods (which also may be more expensive to purchase as a result). This highlights the need for interventions to provide affordable, healthy, and nutritious foods for residents in the most vul-nerable communities in the United States.

FOOD DESERT DEBATES

Despite the evidence of disparities in food access, many scholars question whether food deserts exist. Inconsistencies in the definition and measurement of food deserts, questions surrounding supply versus demand (i.e., stores' reluctance to offer healthier options versus residents' food preferences), incomplete data sources, and failure to consider the entire food landscape have all contributed to the debate.

Low-income residents primarily obtain food conveniently located within their immediate communities due to time constraints, transportation limitations, and spending priorities This dynamic has been linked to poor diet/nutrition and adverse diet-related health outcomes. In fact, individuals in these communities have been described as living not in a food desert but rather a *food swamp*, which is a metaphor used to describe communities with an abundance of unhealthy food outlets in predominantly low-income communities (Cooksey-Stowers, Schwartz, and Brownell 2017, 2). There is an increasing debate on whether, on the one hand, poor access to affordable, healthy, and nutritious foods is the main culprit in addressing food access, or, on the other hand, increased access to nutrient-poor and high-energy-dense foods (e.g., deep-fried foods and sweets) is of more importance. This distinction is of utmost public health importance given the food landscape (i.e., high fast-food restaurant density, limited access to supermarkets, etc.) in many communities.

STRATEGIES FOR COMBATING FOOD DESERTS

Many strategies to improve food access and diet-related health outcomes for American communities with limited options for purchasing healthy and nutritious foods have failed to result in meaningful and sustainable changes. Improving supermarket access through opening new stores has shown modest improvements in fruit and vegetable consumption and diet quality (Abeykoon, Engler-Stringer, and Muhajarine 2017, 2240–43; Cummins, Flint, and Matthews 2014, 286–89), and a considerable number of these ventures have ended with supermarkets closing their doors (Engler-Stringer et al. 2019). Relatedly, a study that evaluated a zoning regulation passed in 2008 in Los Angeles prohibiting the opening of "stand-alone fast-food restaurants" showed that fast-food restaurant bans (or bans from one type of unhealthy food outlet) did not reduce the consumption of unhealthy foods in those communities. In fact, the study found increased consumption of fast foods after the zoning regulation was implemented (Sturm and Hattori 2015, 206, 209–12). Another recommendation that is often met with resistance and critique is the taxation of unhealthy food items. Proponents of this intervention view taxation of unhealthy foods as comparable to taxing tobacco and sugar-sweetened beverages. Conversely, opponents view taxation as paternalistic and disproportionately impacting lower-income households (Block and Subramanian 2015, 6).

Interventions improving community-based (e.g., community gardens, farmers markets, food pantries, and soup kitchens) and governmental food assistance programs are believed to be the most impactful. On the community level, a recommendation to address limited food access in food deserts is the creation and financial support of agricultural initiatives such as community gardens and farmers markets, and emergency food assistance programs including food pantries and soup kitchens. Some reforms have also advocated for modifying the terms, conditions, and allowances of the USDA's Supplemental Nutrition Assistance Program (SNAP), commonly referred to as the "food stamp" program. As of April 2019, SNAP benefits totaling more than $4 billion were being used by nearly thirty-six million people (USDA n.d.).

Recommendations to lower food costs in lower-income and urban and rural communities (Hardin-Fanning and Rayens 2015, 389–90) and increasing the living wage among low-income workers (Brown and Brewster 2015, 203) have been cited as promising interventions for improving healthy food consumption. Examples of recommendations to lower food costs include policy changes in the allocation of SNAP benefits and introducing incentives for families to grow their own produce (Hardin-Fanning and Rayens 2015, 390). Often, low-income workers do not have the necessary financial resources to feed themselves and their families a nutritionally adequate diet. This is especially important given that more than half (52 percent) of minimum-wage workers receive public assistance (Brown and Brewster 2015, 203).

In summary, food deserts are complex and multifaceted environments. Many experts believe that improving nutritional quality and health outcomes among residents of food deserts needs to include both short-term solutions, such as expansion of government food assistance programs, with long-term strategies and policies that make healthy and nutritious food more affordable and accessible for the United States' most vulnerable populations.

Renee E. Walker and Tamicah Gelting

Further Reading

Abeykoon, Am Hasanthi, Rachel Engler-Stringer, and Nazeem Muhajarine. 2017. "Health-Related Outcomes of New Grocery Store Interventions: A Systematic Review." *Public Health Nutrition* 20 (12): 2236–48.

Bitler, Marianne, and Steven J. Haider. 2011. "An Economic View of Food Deserts in the United States." *Journal of Policy Analysis and Management* 30 (1): 153–76.

Block, Jason P., Richard A. Scribner, and Karen B. DeSalvo. 2004. "Fast Food, Race /Ethnicity, and Income: A Geographic Analysis." *American Journal of Preventive Medicine* 27 (3): 211–17.

Block, Jason P., and S. V. Subramanian. 2015. "Moving beyond 'Food Deserts': Reorienting United States Policies to Reduce Disparities in Diet Quality." *PLoS Medicine* 12 (12). https://doi.org/ 10.1371/journal.pmed.1001914.

Braveman, Paula A., Catherine Cubbin, Susan Egerter, David Williams, and Elsie Pamuk. 2010. "Socioeconomic Disparities in Health in the United States: What the Patterns Tell Us." *American Journal of Public Health* 100 (Suppl. 1): 186–96.

Brown, David R., and Luther G. Brewster. 2015. "The Food Environment Is a Complex Social Network." *Social Science & Medicine* 133:202–4.

Cooksey-Stowers, Kristen, Marlene B. Schwartz, and Kelly D. Brownell. 2017. "Food Swamps Predict Obesity Rates Better than Food Deserts in the United States."

International Journal of Environmental Research and Public Health 14 (11): 1366–86.

Cummins, Steven, Ellen Flint, and Stephen A. Matthews. 2014. "New Neighborhood Grocery Store Increased Awareness of Food Access but Did Not Alter Dietary Habits or Obesity." *Health Affairs* 33 (2): 283–91.

Cummins, Steven, and Sally Macintyre. 2002. "Food Deserts—Evidence and Assumption in Health Policy Making." *BMJ* 325 (7361): 436–38.

Engler-Stringer, Rachel, Daniel Fuller, A.M. Hasanthi Abeykoon, Caitlin Olauson, and Nazeem Muhajarine. 2019. "An Examination of Failed Grocery Store Interventions in Former Food Deserts." *Health Education and Behavior.* (Published online ahead of print [June 2019].)

Glanz, Karen, James F. Sallis, Brian E. Saelens, and Lawrence D. Frank. 2007. "Nutrition Environment Measures Survey in Stores (NEMS-S)." *American Journal of Preventive Medicine* 32 (4): 282–89.

Hardin-Fanning, Frances, and Mary Kay Rayens. 2015. "Food Cost Disparities in Rural Communities." *Health Promotion Practice* 16 (3): 383–91.

Larson, Nicole, and Mary Story. 2009. "A Review of Environmental Influences on Food Choices." *Annals of Behavioral Medicine* 38 (Suppl. 1): s56–s73.

Macintyre, Sally. 2007. "Deprivation Amplification Revisited: Or, Is It Always True That Poorer Places Have Poorer Access to Resources for Healthy Diets and Physical Activity." *International Journal of Behavioral Nutrition and Physical Activity* 4 (32): 1–7.

Moore, Latetia V., and Ana V. Diez-Roux. 2006. "Associations of Neighborhood Characteristics with the Location and Type of Food Stores." *American Journal of Public Health* 96 (2): 325–31.

Nyden, Phillip, John Lukehart, Michael T. Maly, and William Peterman. 1998. "Chapter 1: Neighborhood Racial and Ethnic Diversity in U.S. Cities." *Cityscape: A Journal of Policy Development and Research* 4 (2): 1–17.

Pechey, Rachel, and Pablo Monsivais. 2015. "Supermarket Choice, Shopping Behavior, Socioeconomic Status, and Food Purchases." *American Journal of Preventive Medicine* 49 (6): 868–77.

Powell, Lisa M., Sandy Slater, Donka Mirtcheva, Yanjun Bao, and Frank J. Chaloupka. 2007. "Food Store Availability and Neighborhood Characteristics in the United States." *Preventive Medicine* 44 (3): 189–95.

Schafft, Kai A., Eric B. Jensen, and C. Clare Hinrichs. 2009. "Food Deserts and Overweight Schoolchildren: Evidence from Pennsylvania." *Rural Sociology* 74 (2): 153–77.

Short, Anne, Julie Guthman, and Samuel Raskin. "Food Deserts, Oases, or Mirages?" *Journal of Planning Education and Research* 26:352–64.

Sturm, Roland, and Aiko Hattori. 2015. "Diet and Obesity in Los Angeles County 2007–2012: Is There a Measurable Effect of the 2008 'Fast-Food Ban'?" *Social Science & Medicine* 133:205–11.

USDA (U.S. Department of Agriculture). 2009. *Access to Affordable and Nutritious Food: Measuring and Understanding Food Deserts and Their Consequences: Report to Congress.* By Michele Ver Ploeg, Vince Breneman, Tracey Farrigan, Karen Hamrick, David Hopkins, Phillip Kaufman, Biing-Hwan Lin, Mark Nord, Travis A. Smith, Ryan Williams, Kelly Kinnison, Carol Olander, Anita Singh, and Elizabeth Tuckermanty. AP-036. Washington, DC: U.S. Department of Agriculture, Economic Research Service. https://www.ers.usda.gov/webdocs /publications/42711/12716_ap036_1_.pdf.

USDA (United States Department of Agriculture). n.d. "SNAP Data Tables." https:// www.fns.usda.gov/pd/supplemental-nutrition-assistance-program-snap.

Ver Ploeg, Michelle, Paula Dutko, and Vince Breneman. 2015. "Measuring Food Access and Food Deserts for Policy Purposes." *Applied Economics Perspectives and Policy* 37 (2): 205–25.

Walker, Renee E., Jason Block, and Ichiro Kawachi. 2012. "Do Residents of Food Deserts Express Different Food Buying Preferences Compared to Residents of Food Oases? A Mixed-Methods Analysis." *International Journal of Behavioral Nutrition and Physical Activity* 9: 41–8.

Walker, Renee E., Christopher Keane, and Jessica G. Burke. 2010. "Disparities and Access to Healthy Food in the United States: A Review of Food Deserts Literature." *Health & Place* 16 (5): 876–84.

Williams, David R., and Chiquita Collins. 2001. "Racial Residential Segregation: A Fundamental Cause of Racial Disparities in Health." *Public Health Reports* 116 (5): 40416.

Williams, David R., Naomi Priest, and Norman B. Anderson. 2016. "Understanding Associations among Race, Socioeconomic Status, and Health: Patterns and Prospects." *Health Psychology* 35 (4): 407–11.

Wright, James D., Amy M. Donley, Marie C. Gualtieri, and Sara M. Strickhouser. 2016. "Food Deserts: What is the Problem? What is the Solution?" *Social Science and Public Policy* 53: 171–81.

Zagorsky, Jay L. and Patricia K. Smith. 2017. "The Association of Socioeconomic Status and the Adult Consumption of Fast-Food in the U.S." *Economics & Human Biology* 27 (Part A): 12–25.

Zenk, Shannon N., Amy J. Schulz, Barbara A. Israel, Sherman A. James, Shuming Bao, and Mark L. Wilson. 2005. "Neighborhood Racial Composition, Neighborhood Poverty, and the Spatial Accessibility of Supermarkets in Metropolitan Detroit." *American Journal of Public Health* 95 (4): 660–67.

Housing and Neighborhoods

As a shelter, housing is a basic human need. Its physical structure provides protection, security, and privacy. The structure also provides a place to eat, sleep, and store belongings. In addition, housing has many other attributes that people value. Location and neighborhood are two important housing attributes. The location of a dwelling determines access to jobs, shopping, parks, schools, and other local amenities. Some local public goods such as elementary and secondary education are only accessible to those who reside in the designated school attendance zones, while other goods such as recreational parks and public libraries are mostly utilized by local residents. Walking or driving to a public library in a neighborhood other than the local one could be costly in terms of money and time. Being close to public parks, employment centers, or living in a high-performing school district are all valued as benefits, and they positively affect housing prices and rents. Air pollution, noise, and crime, on the contrary, are considered undesirable attributes, and their effects on housing prices and rents are all negative.

In urban housing markets, housing market participants bid for various housing characteristics and access to neighborhood amenities. Residents move to the neighborhoods where both the quality and the quantity of the available local public goods bundle match their preferences—provided they can afford to do so. Each household's income and wealth jointly determine the type of housing and neighborhood characteristics it can afford to pursue. Higher-income residents outbid lower-income residents and as a result, they can secure housing in neighborhoods with superior public services. The movement of residents across neighborhoods is called *sorting*, and through the sorting process, neighborhoods become unequal in terms of income, education, racial composition, safety, air quality, and wealth. In an urban area, a change in income inequality affects housing prices, average income, and demographic compositions of its neighborhoods.

For example, the recent surge in income and wealth inequalities in the larger urban areas of the United States made neighborhoods more dissimilar with respect to income, wealth, and racial composition. Neighborhood inequalities, in turn, widened the housing price gap between higher-income and lower-income neighborhoods. Since the quality and quantity of local public services are directly related to housing prices and the amount of property taxes collected, the neighborhoods with expensive houses can provide higher-quality public services and consequently attract wealthier residents. In the extreme sorting case, all residents in higher-income neighborhoods will have almost identical incomes. Conversely, this phenomenon can further widen the socioeconomic gap between neighborhoods. The rise in neighborhood income inequality and sorting negatively affects lower-income neighborhoods by shrinking their local property tax bases and deteriorating the quality of their local public goods.

DRIVERS OF HOUSING AND NEIGHBORHOOD INEQUALITY

Recent studies document that increases in housing and neighborhood inequalities have been driven by the change in homeownership from smaller to larger housing, geographic and spatial inequality between cities and metro areas, and economic segregation between the rich and poor within metro areas (Albouy and Zabek 2016). Starting in the 1970s, as manufacturing industry firms moved their production facilities to low-wage countries, away from the smaller and medium-sized industrial cities in the United States, most of these urban areas lost their younger and more educated population to the larger metropolitan areas, where new technology- and knowledge-based industries increasingly congregated. To some extent, inequalities within and between metropolitan areas and communities have been driven by technology, free trade, and globalization of the information economy. The rise of high-tech industries, many of which offered good salaries and benefits, in the larger metropolitan areas increased demand for college graduates, especially those with degrees in computer science, mathematics, statistics, and financial services. The influx of a younger and more educated population in larger metropolitan areas increased housing rents and prices and triggered gentrification in some inner-city neighborhoods. The supply of affordable housing did not keep pace with the rise in demand, because developers have started to build larger housing units in urban areas. The supply of affordable units further decreased as federal and local governments reduced funding for lower-income rental housing. The average home price-to-income ratio has increased from about 3.2 to 4.2 between 1988 and 2017 in the United States (State of the Nation's Housing 2019). It shows that housing has become less affordable, especially for the lower-income population. Higher house prices mean higher down payments and closing costs. Since income growth has not kept pace with the growth in housing prices, homeownership has become more difficult to attain for working-class and middle-class Americans. Moreover, those who do become homeowners are more often forced to set their sights on more modest homes or take on hefty monthly mortgage payments.

When housing prices change without a commensurate change in incomes, affordability changes as well. *Housing affordability* is defined as the share of income spent on a fixed bundle of housing attributes (Quigley and Raphael 2004). Housing costs have been rising for both owners and renters in larger urban areas of the United States. For the lowest-income groups, the share of income spent on rent has consistently risen, increasing from 47 percent to 55 percent between 1960 and 2000 (Quigley and Raphael 2004). More recent studies link cross-generation income and wealth mobility to neighborhood quality (Chetty et al. 2014). That is, compared to their parents, children who grew up in the neighborhoods that offered higher-quality public goods did better in terms of income and wealth. On the other hand, children who grew up in lower-income neighborhoods fared worse than their parents when their relative places in income and wealth distributions are considered.

Housing markets in the larger urban areas of the United States have been expanded primarily to meet the demand for expensive housing units, making it even more difficult for residents with modest financial resources to find homes or apartments to purchase or rent. Furthermore, urban economists have partly attributed the recent increase in housing prices in some urban areas of the United States to stricter building code regulations (Glaeser and Gyourko 2018). Restrictions on land supply and excessive regulations raise costs and housing prices. While restrictions on land supply reduce the development of new housing units, stricter building codes increase construction costs (Sinai and Souleles 2005).

As renters are forced to pay a higher share of their income on housing, they spend less on nonhousing goods and services and save less income toward a future down payment on a house or apartment of their own. The increase in economic hardship, driven by increases in housing prices, negatively affects the creditworthiness and saving ability of the renters. Without a good credit score and enough savings to make the 20-percent down payment, a home seeker cannot secure a thirty-year fixed mortgage loan. The amount and the interest rate of a mortgage loan are determined by the applicant's current income and creditworthiness. Hence, increases in housing prices not only raise rents but also diminish renters' abilities to become homeowners in the future.

To attract and retain businesses and residents, city governments engage in various urban development projects. The rise of the information economy and diversity in consumer goods and services has generated increased demand for the land around downtown areas. When a surge in demand is not met with a similar increase in the supply, housing prices rise. Lower-income populations living close to central business districts have been more adversely affected by increases in housing costs. Through redevelopment and urban renewal projects, many local governments have subsidized new economic activities and commercial developments that have made these neighborhoods less affordable for lower-income residents, many of whom have been in those neighborhoods for years or decades. As the share of higher-income population rose, these places attracted more affluent residents and new businesses, which tend to cater to the tastes of the newcomers. Eventually these places became unaffordable for their longtime, lower-income residents.

The effect of gentrification transcends the boundaries of the gentrified places. As the number of affordable neighborhoods declined in larger urban areas, the displaced lower-income population moved to the remaining lower-income neighborhoods. This increased congestion thus caused jumps in housing rents even in nongentrifying neighborhoods.

HOMEOWNERSHIP AND ACCESS TO WEALTH

Homeownership rate is an important determinant of neighborhood quality and wealth accumulation. Empirical studies show that homeownership rate in a given community or neighborhood is correlated with the quality of neighborhood amenities and housing prices (O'Sullivan 2018). Homeowners tend to stay longer in the same residences than renters do, and they are more likely to participate in the political and economic activities that improve the quality of life in their neighborhoods (DiPasquale and Glaeser 1999). The quality of local public goods and services is positively correlated with the quality of schools and other amenities.

Compared to renting, homeownership not only gives household members a higher likelihood of living in a better neighborhood but also offers private benefits. First, by securing fixed-interest mortgage loans, homeowners are less vulnerable to changing housing costs. Second, unlike renters, homeowners can build wealth by accumulating equity through monthly mortgage payments toward the interest and principal. For most Americans, home equities constitute the largest source of household wealth (Quigley and Raphael 2004). Third, homeowners can leverage their home equities to borrow at lower interest rates and pay for spending in education, home improvements, and health care.

Income, family wealth, credit history, and discrimination are the key factors for access to homeownership. In the United States, the first steps to homeownership are securing a 30-year fixed-interest mortgage loan and making a down payment. Without this down payment, the mortgage interest rate would be higher, as the borrower would be viewed as riskier. In fact, the likelihood of being able to secure a bank loan to buy a house plummets if the buyer does not have a significant sum to use as a down payment (20 percent of the total price of the home is typical for a 30-year mortgage loan). To reduce their risks, mortgage lenders either charge higher interest rates or require applicants to purchase mortgage insurance. With or without mortgage insurance, the cost of borrowing will be higher. To decide on whether a loan applicant will be able to afford monthly mortgage payments, financial institutions and banks use income and credit scores as measures of creditworthiness. Income and past borrowing patterns determine the amount and interest rate of the mortgage loan an applicant is qualified to obtain.

Younger homebuyers with limited savings typically cannot make down payments on a mortgage for a home without getting help from their parents and other relatives (Charles and Hurst 2002). Family wealth can also help younger homeowners move on more quickly from their "starter home" (a term used to describe a modestly sized and inexpensive first home) to a more expensive home and a better neighborhood. Meanwhile, another household with a comparable income and credit score might be unable to secure a down payment for a home purchase. Hence, two households with similar income, age, and education attainments can be on completely different wealth accumulation paths.

Earlier access to homeownership speeds up wealth accumulation and provides better education opportunities for future generations. In the United States, the persistence of the wealth-gap between white and Black residents has been attributed in part to long-standing and widespread differences in white-Black homeownership rates. Average homeownership rates for white and Black residents in the United States were approximately 74 percent and 47 percent, respectively, in 2006 ("American Community Survey" n.d.). They were about 71 percent and 41 percent in 2016. The Great Recession of 2008 widened the white-Black homeownership gap (State of the Nation's Housing 2019). Moreover, compared to the white population, fewer Black households are homeowners, and more Black adults hold temporary jobs. Consequently, Black homeowners are more likely to be foreclosed during economic downturns.

DISCRIMINATION IN HOUSING MARKETS

Persistence of discrimination in labor, housing, credit and consumer markets has been well documented (Oh and Yinger 2015). Those who are discriminated against in labor and housing markets have fewer employment and housing choices. Housing discrimination causes neighborhoods to be more segregated with respect to race and ethnicity. The persistence of a white-Black wealth gap coupled with discrimination in credit and housing markets have forced African American and, to some extent, Hispanic populations to live in de facto segregated neighborhoods (Yinger 1998).

To protect the victims of discrimination in housing and other markets, the U.S. government has enacted a variety of new laws and regulations since the mid-twentieth century. The Civil Rights Act of 1968 and its later amendments provide protections for the victims of discrimination when they engage in attending school, using a public place/facility, seeking employment or housing, voting, or serving as a juror in a state court. Title VIII of the Civil Rights Act of 1968 (also known as the Fair Housing Act of 1968) attempts to prevent the unequal treatment of persons belonging to "protected classes" when they seek housing to rent or purchase. Any group that is treated unfairly based on race, religion, national origin, sex, disability, and family status is designated as a "protected class" by this act. The Fair Housing Act defines discrimination in housing based on two standards: disparate treatment and disparate or adverse impact (Yinger 1998). Disparate treatment occurs if economic agents apply different rules depending on whether a consumer belongs to a protected group or not. Different rules range from charging higher prices or denying service to not providing information about the available housing units that may meet the consumer's preferences. Disparate or adverse-impact discrimination occurs if a housing market practice has an indirect negative effect on the protected groups even if it does not explicitly apply different rules depending on a person's group membership (Yinger 1998). In addition to the Fair Housing Act, consumers are protected against discrimination in mortgage loan markets by another law, the Equal Credit Opportunity Act (ECOA). While both Acts overlap by outlawing similar discriminatory practices, the ECOA also prohibits discrimination based on age and sex.

Housing market agents use many rules that do not directly discriminate but they may adversely affect the housing outcomes of persons belonging to the protected groups. For example, homeowners may prefer tenants from higher-income occupations because these groups may be viewed as less risky. If home seekers in the protected groups are underrepresented in these occupations, they will be denied housing based on a group characteristic, not on the creditworthiness of each applicant. Studies on housing discrimination document that African American and Hispanic home seekers continue to face discrimination at many stages of purchasing or renting a housing unit. Consequently, they incur substantial search costs in terms of time and effort and end up with inferior housing outcomes (Yinger 1998).

Discrimination in housing markets delays or prevents homeownership by increasing the victim's housing cost and limiting housing options. Mortgage interest rate is an important factor as far as housing cost is concerned. Discrimination occurs either when the mortgage applications of the individuals belonging to the protected groups are rejected or when these applicants are steered toward riskier and higher-interest-rate mortgage loans. In some cases, home seekers from the protected groups are steered toward neighborhoods where housing prices are in stagnation or decline. Housing discrimination not only works as a barrier against homeownership but it also slows down or, in some cases, decreases the rate of housing capital accumulation for the homeowners who reside in lower-income and segregated neighborhoods that feature either stagnant home values or do not increase in value at the same rate as economically healthy residential areas.

GOVERNMENT PROGRAMS TO AID HOMEOWNERS

Municipal governments such as counties and incorporated cities collect property taxes to provide a wide range of local public goods, including water and sewer services, law enforcement and fire protection, education, health services, road and highway construction, and other services. Even though local governments try to equalize per capita spending on their public schools, parks, public libraries, and others, there are significant variations in the quality of public goods across neighborhoods. There are variations in school performance even within the same school district. These quality variations exist in central city school districts as well as in suburban school districts (Persky and Kurban 2003). Even within a municipality where local property taxes are shared by different local tax districts, neighborhoods may be unequal in terms of school quality, safety, air quality, and cleanliness. Additionally, higher-income neighborhoods have greater political power to secure more funding from the local and state government and to block any attempt to diversify their communities and schools to include greater numbers of people from minority and/or lower-income populations.

Federal and local governments reduce housing costs through subsidies built into income and property tax systems (Persky and Kurban 2003). By either directly supplying public housing for eligible home seekers or indirectly increasing the supply of rental housing, these government programs try to keep housing rents more affordable for lower-income populations who would otherwise be priced out of the rental market. Some local governments also implement "rent controls" to set more affordable rental prices for housing in some high-cost neighborhoods.

Indirectly, local governments also influence the supply of housing through setting zoning regulations and subsidies that encourage affordable housing developments. The demand-side policies are intended to reduce the cost of housing for buyers and renters. The government provides mortgage insurance to mortgage applicants who do not qualify for a thirty-year fixed mortgage loan. The eligible borrower pays higher mortgage interest rates to cover the cost of the mortgage insurance. This policy has an ambiguous effect on wealth building. On the one hand, it provides access to homeownership for those without the ability to afford a 20-percent down payment, but on the other hand, mortgage lenders may also steer borrowers from the protected groups toward purchasing mortgage insurance even if they do not need it.

To reduce discrimination in housing markets, both state and federal governments must be committed to provide funding to enforce fair housing laws and regulations on a continuous basis. In the United States, the enforcement of antidiscrimination laws and regulations also depends on the political views of the president and the political party controlling the U.S. Congress. Lack of political will to confront housing discrimination as well as within and across-community inequality, budget cuts that reduce funding for fair housing programs, and conservative hostility toward various federal regulations of any type have all combined to weaken the enforcement of antidiscrimination laws and regulations (Clozel 2019).

Furthermore, many city governments have implemented tax increment finance (TIF) systems to finance urban renewal and redevelopment projects. The proponents of this system claimed that TIF-funded new developments would improve the quality of life and expand the local tax base by providing new goods and services for local residents and nonlocal residents. The empirical evidence (Lester 2014) indicates that TIF systems did not increase the local tax base but instead further reduced the quality of public education in lower-income neighborhoods by diverting local property tax revenues from education and other public services.

LOCAL INITIATIVES TO REDUCE NEIGHBORHOOD INEQUALITY

Income distribution, wealth distribution, and discrimination play important roles in determining the type of housing and neighborhood a buyer or renter can afford. As explained in previous sections, access to housing and neighborhood is largely determined by income and wealth distributions. A rise in inequality indicates that housing becomes inaccessible for more people. Discrimination in housing markets further reduces access to affordable housing for the members of the protected groups.

Fair housing advocates have expressed concern about escalating housing inequality in the years to come as well. The Trump administration has been less willing to enforce antidiscrimination laws and regulations. Attempts to weaken fair housing regulations (Jan 2018) coupled with the worsening of income and wealth inequalities in many sectors of American society have contributed to the continued rise in neighborhood inequalities.

Some local governments have designed and implemented housing programs to directly supply more affordable housing and improve neighborhood integration by race and income. For example, to enhance neighborhood integration by income and race, Montgomery County in Maryland designed an Inclusive Zoning (IZ) program to increase residential density, further fair housing, and decrease income and racial segregation (Diagne, Kurban, and Schmutz 2018). Like other local IZ programs, the Montgomery County IZ program, which was started in 1974, allows developers to build additional units beyond the limit set by regular zoning regulations. In return, a certain share of the units in the housing development is required to be set aside for lower-income populations. An important goal of the program is to create mixed-income neighborhoods. The Montgomery County IZ program developed eligibility criteria to ensure that the available units are allocated to the home buyers and renters who meet income and household size requirements. Home prices and rents in this program are set by the county. The Montgomery County IZ program screens all applicants in the purchase program based on established eligibility criteria. The applicants who are certified as eligible by the program are required to attend homeownership-counseling classes. The program also helps the certified applicants to complete a mortgage application and get a mortgage offer letter from a financial institution (Diagne et al. 2018).

Compared to previously mentioned laws and policies, Montgomery County–type IZ programs can be more effective at mitigating the negative effects of income and wealth inequality as well as across-neighborhood inequalities in locally provided goods and services, including education, safety, and air quality. These IZ programs specifically target the achievement of income and wealth integration by providing housing to the eligible renters and owners at below-market prices. The successful participants of the program have access to higher-quality amenities and local public goods in middle-class neighborhoods. Local IZ programs are very small, and therefore they have negligible effects in mitigating the housing affordability problem in urban areas. If extended to cover a larger part of urban areas, local IZ programs could potentially decrease inequalities in education, safety, and other amenities across neighborhoods.

PEOPLE-ORIENTED AND PLACE-ORIENTED POVERTY PROGRAMS

Policies to address neighborhood and racial inequality are divided into two groups: "people-oriented" and "place-oriented." Policies that aim to move people, particularly young individuals, out of economically disadvantaged places and relocate them to neighborhoods with better schools and public services are labeled as *people-oriented*. As their name implies, they target specific population groups. The Section 8 housing-voucher program is one of the most well-known and well-utilized people-oriented programs. Through the Department of Housing and Urban Development (HUD), the federal government provides housing vouchers to residents in economically disadvantaged communities for relocation to better neighborhoods.

On the other hand, *place-oriented* programs target a specific place and seek to make them more financially viable or pleasant places to live. All urban renewal and redevelopment projects that target lower-income neighborhoods are considered place-oriented. Ironically, even though these programs are often touted as a pathway for revitalizing lower-income communities and improving the quality of life for existing residents, they may instead attract higher-income groups who subsequently crowd out lower-income residents. Neighborhood revitalization causes displacement when the income gap between higher-income and lower-income groups widens and neighborhoods are unequal with respect to income, wealth, and education levels.

CONCLUSION

Surges in income and wealth inequality across the world since the late twentieth century are driven by similar economic forces. Free trade and technological innovations have caused the spatial concentration of economic activities in larger urban areas. The agglomeration of economic activities also amplified income and wealth inequalities between and within metropolitan areas. Income and wealth segregation in larger metro areas made housing less affordable for renters and lower-income populations. For instance, in 2009, the 6.7 million lowest-income households in the United States were paying more than 50 percent of their income for housing (Collinson 2011). The persistence of income and wealth inequalities also amplified income and wealth segregation in the local neighborhoods. Without government intervention at the federal and local levels, across-neighborhood inequalities in the provision of local public goods will further limit the housing outcomes for lower-income residents. Education outcomes are determined by per-pupil spending and by an array of other factors, including peer effects, social networks, teacher quality, safety and other neighborhood-level income and demographic characteristics. When income and wealth inequalities rise, higher-income residents segregate themselves by income and wealth, and the housing price premium between a higher-income and a lower-income neighborhood widens.

Any public policy effort toward reversing neighborhood inequality, whether it is undertaken at a federal or local level, needs to use income and wealth integration as main policy goals. Local IZ policies, although they are small, seem to be better equipped to achieve income and racial integration and reduce neighborhood inequality. Fair housing laws and regulations are designed to prevent discrimination of individuals belonging to protected groups by housing market participants. These laws and regulations cannot stop sorting of higher-income residents into segregated neighborhoods. Many housing advocates believe that to attain income integration and racial integration goals, fair housing regulations must be supplemented with IZ-type inclusive zoning initiatives.

Haydar Kurban

Further Reading
"American Community Survey." n.d. Washington, DC: U.S. Census Bureau. https://www
.census.gov/programs-surveys/acs.

Albouy, David, and Mike Zabek. 2016. "Housing Inequality." NBER Working Paper 21916. National Bureau of Economic Research. https://www.nber.org/papers /w21916.

Charles, Kerwin Kofi, and Erik Hurst. 2002. "The Transition to Home Ownership and the Black-White Wealth Gap." *Review of Economics and Statistics*, 84 (2): 281–97.

Chetty, Raj, Nathaniel Hendren, Patrick Kline, Emmanuel Saez, and Nicholas Turner. 2014. "Is the United States Still a Land of Opportunity? Recent Trends in Intergenerational Mobility." *American Economic Review* 104 (5): 141–47.

Clozel, Lalita. 2019. "HUD Proposal Raises Bar on Housing Discrimination Complaints." *Wall Street Journal*, August 19, 2019.

Collinson, Rob. 2011. "Rental Housing Affordability Dynamics, 1990–2009." *Cityscape* 13 (2): 71–103.

Diagne, Adji F., Haydar Kurban, and Benoit Schmutz. 2018. "Are Inclusionary Housing Programs Color-Blind? The Case of Montgomery County MPDU Program." *Journal of Housing Economics* 40:6–26.

DiPasquale, Denise, and Edward L. Glaeser. 1999. "Incentives and Social Capital: Are Home-owners Better Citizens?" *Journal of Urban Economics* 45 (2): 354–84.

Glaeser, Edward L., and Joseph Gyourko. 2018. "The Economic Implications of Housing Supply" *Journal of Economic Perspectives* 32 (1): 3–30.

Haurin, Donald R., Robert D. Dietz, and Bruce A. Weinberg. 2002. "The Impact of Neighborhood Homeownership Rates: A Review of the Theoretical and Empirical Literature." *Journal of Housing Research* 13 (2): 119–51.

Jan, Tracy. 2018. "Ben Carson's HUD Dials Back Investigations into Housing Discrimination." *Washington Post*, Business Section, December 24, 2018.

Lester, William T. 2014. "Does Chicago's Tax Increment Financing (TIF) Program Pass the 'But-For' Test? Job Creation and Economic Development Impacts Using Time-Series Data." *Urban Studies* 51 (4): 655–74.

Oh, Sun J., and John Yinger. 2015. "What Have We Learned from Paired Testing in Housing Markets?" *Cityscape* 17 (3): 15–60.

O'Sullivan, Arthur. 2018. *Urban Economics*. 9th edition. New York: McGraw-Hill Education.

Persky, Joseph, and Haydar Kurban. 2003. "Do Federal Spending and Tax Policies Build Cities or Promote Sprawl?" *Regional Science and Urban Economics* 33 (3): 361–78.

Quigley, John M., and Steven Raphael. 2004. "Is Housing Unaffordable? Why Isn't It More Affordable?" *Journal of Economic Perspectives* 18 (1): 191–214.

Sinai, Todd, and Nicholas S. Souleles. 2005. "Owner-Occupied Housing as a Hedge against Rent Risk." *Quarterly Journal of Economics* 120 (2): 763–89.

"The State of the Nation's Housing 2019." 2019. Joint Center for Housing Studies of Harvard University. https://www.jchs.harvard.edu/state-nations-housing-2019.

Yinger, John. 1998. "Evidence on Discrimination in Consumer Markets." *Journal of Economic Perspectives* 12 (2): 23–40.

SECTION V

Family Life and Inequality

Marriage, Cohabitation, and Divorce

Not long ago, the family lives of Americans, regardless of their class background, were very similar. Although some families were rich and others were poor, the basic structures of family life, including intimacy, companionship, and childbearing, were largely the same. Today, however, families from one end of the class hierarchy to the other look very different. This emergent family class divide is evident not only in differing rates of marriage, divorce, and other family-related patterns but also in how people from different classes experience and practice family life.

This chapter seeks to better understand the relationship between American family life and social class and how it has changed over time. It focuses on three areas where the family class divide has become most apparent: marriage, divorce, and cohabitation. It begins with an examination of how recent trends in the U.S. economy have effected family inequality. It continues with an exploration of growing class differences in family life, including variations in marriage, divorce, and cohabitation. It then concludes with a discussion of causes and effects of the family class divide, and possible solutions.

FAMILY INEQUALITY

Economic inequality has become a growing problem in the United States. In fact, in a rare sign of bipartisanship, members of both major political parties talked about the issue of income inequality in the 2016 election—although they touted very different policies for addressing it. The United States also has seen a number of social movements in recent years focused on economic inequality, including efforts to increase the minimum wage, fast-food and big-box store workers going on strike, and the Occupy Wall Street movement, which popularized the phrase "We Are the 99 Percent" to draw attention to growing income disparity in the United States and beyond. Of course, economic inequality is not exactly a new issue. The gulf between the haves and the have-nots has been widening since the 1970s. The present situation is simply a more extreme version of what has been happening for a number of decades. The rich and near rich are getting richer. The middle class is shrinking. And the poor are barely getting by—or failing to do so.

The recent growth of economic inequality can be seen among family households as well. Consider, for example, how earnings among U.S. families at different income levels grew apart between 1980 and 2011. Well-to-do families (the top 20 percent on the income scale) saw their earnings jump by about 55 percent, from an average of $127,983 in 1980 to $197,932 in 2011. People in the middle of the population also saw income gains, but they were much more modest. The 20 percent with the lowest income saw an 8.3-percent decrease in earnings (adjusted for inflation). Meanwhile, for families even higher up on the income scale (the highest 5 percent), recent decades have brought a windfall. These families, with an average income of about $182,000 in 1980, were making $345,000 in 2011—almost twice as much (U.S. Census Bureau [2012] 2019). Of course, the biggest winners over the past few decades have been the families of the richest 1 percent. Inequality between the richest 1 percent and the other 99 percent has reached levels not seen since 1929, just before the Great Depression.

Several factors help to explain the growth of family inequality. Of particular importance is the restructuring of the U.S. economy, which can be traced to large-scale organizational changes beginning in the 1970s. These include the movement of jobs in industrial production to developing nations, where wages are lower and working conditions are poorer, and the use of new technologies, including automation and computers, which allow companies to replace workers with machines. For the most part, these changes have hurt people without college degrees: blue-collar workers, pink-collar workers, and other members of the industrial working class, as well as some in the lower-middle class. This is because the number of full-time jobs that offer good wages with fringe benefits (such as health-care coverage and paid vacation or sick days) to workers that do not have a college degree—the kind that less-educated men used to rely on to support their wives and children—has dwindled. Instead, semiskilled and low-skilled workers are now increasingly forced to find work in the service sector, where the pay is usually lower and there are fewer fringe benefits.

At the other end of the spectrum, college-educated Americans—white-collar workers, professionals, and other members of the upper-middle class—have benefited from globalization and automation. This is because economic restructuring has increased the importance of education. Since the 1970s, the amount of education that people obtain has become a pivotal factor in predicting how much they earn and how much income their families have. Before, education played a much smaller role in determining a family's economic status. For example, in 1950, a family whose head had a college degree earned just about twice as much as a family whose head had not completed high school. In 2000, that same family earned about three times as much (Fischer and Hout 2006). Thus families headed by college grads have seen their incomes rise in recent decades, while families headed by those without a college degree have seen their incomes either stagnate or, in the case of high school dropouts, decline. In both cases, the gap between families with a college-educated head and those without one has widened.

There is another important reason why family inequality is rising: families headed by college graduates are now significantly more likely than their less-educated peers to have two parents in the household. Married-couple, two-parent households used to be the predominant family form in the United States, regardless of one's education level or other class characteristics. But due to higher rates of divorce and to more childbearing outside of marriage, single-parent families have become increasingly common, especially among the less educated. For example, in 2015, 13 percent of all families with children whose heads had a college degree were headed by a single mother. In contrast, 31 percent of all families with children whose heads did not have a college degree were headed by a single mother (U.S. Census Bureau [2015] 2019). Most single-parent families rely on just one income, and most single-parent families are headed by women, whose average earnings are lower than that of men. Two-parent families, in contrast, can pool the incomes of both adults. Moreover, since 1980, married-couple households have seen their incomes rise at a higher rate than single-parent households, a trend that has further contributed to the increase in family inequality. Finally, there are many more single-mother households than there were in 1980, which has also worked to widen inequality.

MARRIAGE AND SOCIAL CLASS

The family lives of Americans with and without college degrees have diverged in other ways as well. This is evident when looking at marriage rates. Marriage has historically been an important and esteemed institution in the United States. Since colonial times, Americans have viewed marriage as the bedrock of healthy families and communities and vital to functioning of democracy itself (Cott 2000). And until recently, marriage was a near-universal feature of adult life, even among the poor. In fact, among adults between the ages of twenty-five and thirty-four, those with a high school degree or less actually had higher marriage rates before 1970 than those with a bachelor's degree or more (U.S. Census Bureau [2010] 2019). However, since the 1970s, marriage rates have fallen for all education groups, and starting around 1980, rates began falling faster among those without a college degree. Today, those without a college degree have a significantly lower lifetime probability of marrying than those with a college degree.

These general trends hold among young adults as well. Marriage rates among twenty-five- to thirty-four-year-olds have dropped significantly in recent decades. Today, less than half of adults aged twenty-five to thirty-four are married. In fact, between 2000 and 2010, the share of young adults aged twenty-five to thirty-four who were married dropped ten percentage points, from 55 percent to 45 percent. During the same period, the percentage who have never been married increased sharply, from 34 percent to 46 percent. Thus, in a dramatic reversal, the proportion of young adults in the United States who have never been married now exceeds those who are married. The decline, however, is mostly concentrated among young adults without college degrees. Data show that those with only a high school diploma (or less) have experienced a steep decline in marriage during the first decade of the 2000s—from 54 percent to 44 percent. In contrast, marriage rates have held fairly steady for those with at least a bachelor's degree—from 56 percent to 52 percent (U.S. Census Bureau [2010] 2019). This divergence in trends has led to a growing marriage gap between those at different ends of the educational scale. In fact, some scholars characterize marriage as a "luxury item"—a family form that class-disadvantaged Americans increasingly can no longer afford. Instead, the poor and working are disproportionately likely to cohabit or become single parents, the "budget" approaches to family formation (Furstenberg 1996).

Several factors have contributed to the steady decline in marriage. These include rising divorce rates, a rise in nonmarital cohabitation as a precursor or an alternative to marriage, and an increase in women's educational attainment and labor force participation. Of course, people are also getting married later than they used to; the median age of first marriage in 2010 was around 29 for men and 27 for women, compared to 23.5 and 21 in 1970 (U.S. Census Bureau [2010] 2019). Sociologists Kathryn Edin and Maria Kefalas (2005), who interviewed 162 unwed, low-income mothers, offer another explanation for the decline of marriage, especially among class-disadvantaged Americans. The authors claim that contrary to popular stereotypes, few poor single mothers outright reject the institution of marriage. Instead, most claim to revere marriage, so much so that they are unwilling to marry just anyone, including the fathers of their children, whom they frequently describe as untrustworthy, controlling, financially unstable, and/or in legal trouble. For these women, marriage is no longer an essential institution or a necessity for intimacy, companionship, and childbearing. Rather, marriage is now an elective means of achieving personal fulfillment. In this respect, the authors argue that poor women are very similar to their middle-class counterparts. Both the poor and the middle class view marriage as having a great deal of symbolic significance but relatively little practical significance. The difference, however, is that the poor do not have the same material resources as the middle class, nor the same marriage pool, and the gap is growing. Thus while poor women may desire to put marriage before motherhood, they are less likely than their middle-class peers to reach their "white picket fence dream" (Edin and Kefalas 2005, 130).

DIVORCE AND SOCIAL CLASS

The trends in divorce show a similar divergence by class. The United States' divorce rates, for both the rich and the poor, rose sharply between 1960 and 1980. Since then, however, the overall risk of divorce has declined. And the decline has been greater among college graduates. Consequently, college graduates now have a substantially lower lifetime risk of divorce than their less-educated peers do. Meanwhile, over the same period, the risk of divorce actually increased among individuals who did not complete high school. Thus, as in the case with marriage, the risk of divorce also seems to be stratified, with a college-educated group at one end, a middle group consisting of high school graduates and people with some college in the middle, and people without high school degrees at the other end.

Reasons for the widening divorce gap are complex. It may stem partly from the fact adults without a college degree are more likely than their college-educated peers to get married as teenagers or young adults. For example, in 2016, the share of never-married adults among non-college grads aged twenty-two to twenty-four was 15.1 percent. In contrast, the share among college grads of the same age was 9.6 percent (U.S. Census Bureau [2016] 2019). Marriages formed at younger ages tend to be less stable than those formed at older ages. For example, roughly 50 percent of marriages end in divorce for those who marry before age twenty; 35 percent for those twenty to twenty-five; and just 26 percent for those over the age of twenty-six (Ueker and Stokes 2008). Young couples may lack maturity in handling work and family responsibilities or selecting suitable spouses. They also have restricted opportunities for college and tend to have more financial difficulties, especially if they have children. Early marriages also are more likely to include couples who marry in response to an unplanned pregnancy.

Moderately educated and less-educated couples also tend to have fewer economic resources, including lower incomes. A lack of economic resources can be burdensome for intimate relationships. Economic stress also may interfere with parenting and other family practices, adversely affecting family members, which, in turn, can create emotional stress. Sudden financial difficulties, such as unemployment, also increase the probability of marital dissolution. In fact, low income is one of the main reasons for the high probability of teen and young adult marriages ending in divorce. Unfortunately, divorce does little to solve the financial difficulties that may be at the root of many couples' marital problems.

Studies also find that the reasons people give for divorce vary by social class (Amato and Previti 2003). For example, class-advantaged individuals are more likely to complain about a lack of communication, a lack of love or intimacy, sexual problems, unhappiness, changes in interests or values, and incompatibility. In contrast, the class-disadvantaged individuals are more likely to attribute their unhappiness with their spouse to financial problems, physical abuse, drinking problems, neglect of housework, gambling, criminal activities, and unemployment. These differences suggest that as one's class status increases, one is less likely to report extrinsic motivations for divorce and more likely to report intrinsic or relationship-centered motivations.

COHABITATION AND SOCIAL CLASS

One family-related trend that has increased across the class spectrum is nonmarital cohabitation. Just because more young adults are delaying marriage today does not mean they are delaying marriage-like relationships. According to census data, there were less than 500,000 unmarried, cohabiting households in 1960. But by 2010, there were more than 7.5 million (Sassler and Miller 2017). That is a fifteenfold increase over a fifty-year time period. This represents a profound change. Prior to the 1970s, most Americans deemed living together outside of marriage to be an immoral act. Cohabitation was referred to as "living in sin" or "shacking up." It was actually illegal in many states. For middle-class young people in the 1950s and 1960s, getting married was considered the only way to become full-fledged adults—that is, to set up a household, to have sexual relations, and to raise children. In the 1950s and 1960s, men over the age of thirty who were not married were sometimes ridiculed and seen as perverts or sexual deviants. Unmarried women, even as young as twenty-five, were often treated even worse, labeled as "sluts," "whores," or "old maids." Today, however, the options for full-fledged adulthood appear to include cohabitation. For example, cohabiters no longer attract as much parental disapproval or punitive housing discrimination as they once did.

People may choose cohabitation as a living arrangement or lifestyle for a number of reasons. For many couples, cohabitation is simply an alternative way of being single. These types of couples have not yet thought about marriage and would consider themselves single and not necessarily looking for a spouse. Many of these couples may be in the early phase of figuring out the seriousness of their relationship and simply want the benefits of being in a relationship without the binding commitments. Others may choose cohabitation as way to save money, to escape their parents' home, or because of an eviction. Still, for other couples, cohabitation may be a testing ground for marriage. In fact, most cohabiters say that they plan to marry their partners, and most eventually do marry. The rest either end their relationship, usually within a few years, or else remain in a cohabitating arrangement for an indefinite time period. Currently, about two-thirds of marriages begin as cohabiting relationships (Sassler and Miller 2017).

In some Western nations, cohabitation has become an alternative to marriage—that is, as a way of living that is similar to marriage but does not involve a legal commitment. In France, for example, about 25 percent of all children live with cohabiting parents who have been together for ten years or more. In Sweden, about half of children are living with cohabiting parents, an indication that cohabitation is seen as another way of constructing viable family units (Kierner 1999). It is unclear, however, whether the United States is heading in the same direction. On the one hand, people in the United States still place more importance on getting married than many of their peers do in other Western countries (Cherlin 2009). On the other hand, the number of cohabiting unions that act as trial marriages in the United States is declining. For example, in 1990, 60 percent of cohabiters married; in 2000, only 55 percent did so. More cohabiting couples also are having children—and increasingly several children—without marrying. About 40 percent of cohabiting couples have children, and the rate is even higher among those without a college degree. In most cases (70 percent), these are the children of only one partner. But in about 30 percent of these couples, the children are the biological offspring of both partners (Sassler and Miller 2017). Further, for certain demographic groups, including the most economically disadvantaged, cohabitation has already become a substitute for marriage. In fact, among the most class-disadvantaged Americans, serial cohabitation—defined as having multiple premarital cohabiting relationships—is also becoming increasingly common.

There is some debate about whether premarital cohabitation increases the risk of subsequent marital dissolution. Older studies found that couples who have cohabited before marriage have, on average, a higher rate of divorce than those who do not cohabit. However, more recent research suggests the relationship between cohabiting before marriage and divorce risk is more complex. For example, findings show that a premarital cohabiting relationship that is limited to one's eventual spouse does not affect the risk of marital disruption, but having at least one other cohabiting relationship prior to marriage is linked to an increased risk of divorce. In other words, people who have had several premarital cohabiting relationships are actually the ones who are more likely to divorce. There may be a few other qualifications. For example, premarital cohabiting relationships that are postponed until age twenty-three or older appear to have less of an effect on the risk of marital disruption. By this age, most adults are done with school and have some financial independence. And short-term (six months or less) or engagement cohabitation also appears to have little or no effect on divorce risk (Teachman 2003).

Although cohabitation has increased in recent decades across population groups, rates differ by social class. For example, among those who have ever cohabited, rates are lower among more educated Americans than among the less educated (Sassler and Miller 2017). Thus moderately educated and less-educated young adults, not college grads, are the cultural vanguard of this family trend. Further, the meaning of cohabitation—that is, what individuals who are living together think that their relationship signifies—also varies among college-educated, moderately educated, and less-educated young adults. For the college educated, cohabitation is closely linked to marriage. They usually use it as a "testing ground" and are less likely to have children while cohabiting. Their experience of cohabitation tends to be short-lived, and many are already engaged when they begin cohabiting. For them, cohabitation is a step in the family-building process. For the moderately educated, cohabitation is less closely linked to marriage. Many wish to marry eventually but do not believe it is feasible for the time being. Many drift into cohabitation without giving much thought to what the relationship might become in the future. For many, cohabitation occurs quickly following the formation of a relationship. Moderately educated couples also are more likely to have a child together before marrying. In fact, many cohabit in response to an impending birth. For the moderately educated, cohabitation represents a short-term alternative to marriage, because most eventually do get married. For the less educated, cohabitation is virtually no longer linked to marriage. The less educated are more likely to serial cohabit or serial date. They often enter cohabiting relationships in response to a pregnancy, but their relationships are rarely stable. They may cohabit for financial need. For the less educated, cohabitation is often a long-term—maybe even lifelong—alternative to marriage.

FAMILY CLASS DIVIDE

As the discussion above suggests, a variety of family patterns, including marriage, divorce, and cohabitation, have diverged by class in recent decades. In general, the family lives of Americans without a college degree have become less connected to marriage. Compared to several decades ago, they are less likely to get married, stay married, and have children within marriage. Although many of them do live with unmarried partners, these relationships are more likely to break up than marital relationships are. Instead of the conventional path in which people finish school, get a job, find a partner, get married, and then have kids—the so-called success sequence—people without a college degree are starting to follow a different path. For those with low to moderate education, the life course may involve having children well before marrying, even before they have a job. In fact, for many of them, having children may be the reward of adulthood that they know they can get, as opposed to a good-paying and meaningful job or a long-lasting and fulfilling marriage.

Meanwhile, those with a college degree typically start out by getting their degree, marrying someone else who is also a college graduate, and then having kids. College grads often delay marriage but ultimately have a higher lifetime probability of marrying than those without a college degree. The college-educated also are less likely to have a child outside of marriage. Their chances of divorce are lower and declining. And the college-educated also have lower rates of non-marital cohabitation. In short, the family lives of Americans with a college degree more closely resemble those found in the past, as they continue to be strongly linked to marriage. Perhaps the only major difference is they now typically take much longer to get married.

Observers have attributed the growing class divide in family life to a number of factors. According to the conservative scholar Charles Murray, cultural changes are the main culprit. Echoing sentiments previously used to explain marriage decline among African Americans, Murray contends that members of the white working class have begun to forsake traditional values that have historically contributed to family stability. In particular, working-class men no longer value "industriousness," which he defines as the "bone-deep American assumption that life is to be spent getting ahead through hard work, making a better life for oneself and one's children" (Murray 2012, 135). Instead, Murray and some other observers assert that they appear to be not only less willing to work as hard as their class-advantaged peers work but also less willing to work as hard as previous generations of working-class men worked. This apparent retreat in industriousness and other traditional values has led to a decline of marriage and stable families.

Sociologist Andrew Cherlin (2014), on the other hand, argues that while cultural forces matter, the family culture of the working class is actually quite similar to that of the upper-middle class, including their attitudes toward marriage. Where there are class differences is in their attitudes toward practices that take place outside of marriage, including premarital sex, nonmarital living arrangements, and unwed fertility. Here, however, it is working-class people who appear to be more traditional. In general, they are less accepting of nonmarital sex, cohabitation, divorce, and unwed childbearing than are their upper-middle-class peers. Thus, according to Cherlin, the growing family class divide cannot be explained by culture alone. In his view, economic forces play a much bigger role. Recent economic changes, which have increased inequalities between families with and without college degrees, have left the working class and increasingly the lower-middle class less protected against the uncertainties of daily life that contribute to family instability and complexity.

Other scholars, notably qualitative researchers influenced by the sociology of Pierre Bourdieu (1984), have offered a more nuanced explanation for the growing family class divide, one that combines both economic and cultural components of class inequality. According to this view, class differences in family life are rooted in distinct, class-based cultural styles (also called *strategies* or *logics*) and thus in the different implications that these styles have for how people navigate the landscape of everyday personal and family life. This research suggests that well-educated, upper-middle-class adults and their children have developed an approach to their daily lives that involves a fair amount of planning, monitoring, organizing, and overseeing. Conversely, the poor and working class, and to a lesser extent those from the lower-middle class, have more of a go-with-the-flow, present-oriented, laissez-faire style. Consequently, the upper-middle class possesses a cultural style that is anchored toward the future and the reduction of risks, including ill-timed, out-of-sequence, and other unscheduled life-course events, while members of less privileged classes have adopted an approach that may, in fact, increase the likelihood of unscheduled events, such as unwed childbearing and marital and relationship dissolution. While scholars who take this position acknowledge that evidence of class differences in family attitudes and actions is not exactly new, they argue that such differences now have new significance due to growing economic inequality and uncertainty.

The emergence of distinct, class-based cultural styles appears to exist across the life course, including in how young people navigate sexuality, form intimate relationships, and approach fertility, as well as in how adults approach their roles as spouses and parents. For example, sexualities scholars have observed that class-advantaged teenagers are less likely than their less-advantaged peers to engage in risky sexual behavior, including vaginal intercourse. This is not because they are more religious than other teens and thus opposed to premarital sex on moral grounds. Rather, their approach to sexuality is more about safeguarding their future and thus limiting the possibilities of unplanned pregnancies and sexually transmitted diseases. In fact, most middle-class virgins, including those who use masturbation, oral sex, and/or anal sex as substitutes, have no moral objection to vaginal intercourse. They simply think that it is a risk not worth taking (Regnerus 2009).

Similarly, gender scholars have observed that social class and concerns about it also shape college women's relationship to sexuality, including their willingness to participate in the campus hookup culture and/or to pursue romantic relationships. In general, class-advantaged college women are more likely to hook up with sexual partners than their less-advantaged peers are. In fact, many, if not most, prefer hookups over romantic relationships. This is because the informality and relative ease of hooking up is more compatible with their educational and career goals. Relationships, on the other hand, can be time consuming, especially for women, who are expected to be nurturing and caretaking; and relationships can be deeply damaging if they involve violence, emotional abuse, or power imbalances. Conversely, class-disadvantaged college women are more likely to express discomfort about the hookup scene and less likely to see serious relationships as incompatible with college life. In fact, many are already looking forward to settling down and starting a family (Hamilton and Armstrong 2009).

Class also shapes how more mature adults approach their roles, including spousal and parental roles. For example, sociologist Jessi Streib (2015) found that among spouses in cross-class marriages, those who grew up middle class differ from those who grew up working class in how they spend and budget money, think about paid work, organize housework, and even manage their emotions. Similarly, sociologist Annette Lareau (2003) found class differences between the middle class and working class in parenting styles. Middle-class parents are more likely to cultivate the talents, opinions, and skills of their children through organized, adult-guided activities using a parental style she calls "concerted cultivation"; while working-class parents tend to focus more on providing safe and loving environments for their children and letting them grow up on their own, a parental style that she calls the "accomplishment of natural growth." In everyday life, these different styles affect children's time use, language use, and family ties. Middle-class parents fill their children's weeks with various formal activities, such as lessons, sports, tutoring, and playdates; whereas working-class parents are more content to let their children hang out at home or in the neighborhood. Further, middle-class parents talk to their kids more and reason with them rather than telling them what to do; while kids from working-class and poor families tend to have closer ties to uncles, aunts, cousins, and siblings than their middle-class peers do. Lareau argues that both parenting styles have value but that the middle-class style is more consistent with dominant institutions; thus middle-class parents are able to transmit to their children hidden class advantages that will benefit them in later life.

Scholars who study family and class have different views about how to best reduce the family class divide. Some, such as Murray (2012), believe that the upper-middle-class people have a moral responsibility to actively engage the working class in promoting their way of life, including moral values. Others, such as Cherlin (2014), advocate for employment and wage growth, expanded access to education at all levels, a higher minimum wage, and institutional reforms such as tax code reform and financial regulation to keep the wealthiest from further widening the financial distance between themselves and other Americans. Still others advocate for the adoption of middle-class cultural approaches to family and personal life. Such arguments assume that the working class can simply adopt the cultural practices of the middle class. However, as history shows, such approaches may not be possible without the addition of structural changes. For example, prior to the 1940s, when the economy saw an increase in the number of manufacturing jobs that paid family wages, most members of the industrial working class could not afford to adopt family practices that had long been prevalent among the industrial middle class, such as having a full-time breadwinning husband, a full-time homemaking wife, and children who went to school rather than worked. On the other hand, some scholars, including Lareau (2003), argue that there is value in both middle-class and working-class family cultural styles and that Americans should learn to appreciate and adopt aspects of both. In fact, Streib (2015) found in her study of cross-class married couples that many Americans may actually be drawn to class differences in how they were raised when it comes to selecting partners suitable for marriage.

CONCLUSION

A half century ago, most families with children, regardless of class, were headed by two married parents. Although differences existed between rich and poor families, the likelihood of parents being married was not one of them. Since then, however, the family patterns and practices of people across the class hierarchy have moved in different directions. Future research should continue to explore how class characteristics, such as education and economic status, affect family life, as well as how family patterns and practices may affect class status.

Chris Wienke

Further Reading

Amato, Paul R., and Denise Previti. 2003. "People's Reasons for Divorcing: Gender, Social Class, the Life Course, and Adjustment." *Journal of Family Issues* 24:602–26.

Armstrong, Elizabeth A., and Laura T. Hamilton. 2009. "Gendered Sexuality in Young Adulthood: Double Binds and Flawed Options." *Gender and Society* 23 (5): 589–616.

Bourdieu, Pierre. 1984. *Distinction: A Social Critique of the Judgement of Taste.* Cambridge, MA: Harvard University Press.

Cherlin, Andrew. 2009. *The Marriage-Go-Round: The State of Marriage and the Family in America Today.* New York: Alfred A. Knopf.

Cherlin, Andrew. 2014. *Labor's Love Lost: The Rise and Fall of the Working-Class Family in America.* New York: Russell Sage Foundation.

Cott, Nancy. 2000. *Public Vows: A History of Marriage and the Nation.* Cambridge, MA: Harvard University Press.

Edin, Kathryn, and Maria Kefalas. 2005. *Promises I Can Keep: Why Poor Women Put Motherhood before Marriage.* Berkeley: University of California Press.

Fischer, Claude, and Michael Hout. 2006. *Century of Difference: How America Changed in the Last One Hundred Years.* New York: Russell Sage Foundation.

Furstenberg, Frank. 1996. "The Future of Marriage." *American Demographics* 18 (6): 34–40.

Kierner, Katherine. 1999. "Cohabitation in Western Europe." *Population Trends* 96:25–32.

Lareau, Annette. 2003. *Unequal Childhoods: Class, Race, and Family Life.* Berkeley: University of California Press.

Murray, Charles. 2012. *Coming Apart: The State of White America, 1960–2010.* New York: Crown Forum.

Regnerus, Mark. 2007. *Forbidden Fruit: Sex & Religion in the Lives of American Teenagers.* New York: Oxford University Press.

Sassler, Sharon, and Amanda Jayne Miller. 2017. *Cohabitation Nation: Gender, Class, and the Remaking of Relationships.* Berkeley: University of California Press.

Streib, Jessi. 2015. *The Power of the Past: Understanding Cross-Class Marriages.* New York: Oxford University Press.

Teachman, Jay D. 2003. "Premarital Sex, Premarital Cohabitation, and the Risk of Subsequent Marital Dissolution among Women." *Journal of Marriage and Family* 65:444–55.

Ueker, Jeremy E., and Charles E. Stokes. 2008. "Early Marriage in the United States." *Journal of Marriage and Family* 70 (4): 835–46.

U.S. Census Bureau. (2010) 2019. "2010 American Community Survey 1-Year Estimates."
        https://www.census.gov/programs-surveys/acs/technical-documentation/table
        -and-geography-changes/2010/1-year.html.

U.S. Census Bureau. (2012) 2019. "2012 American Community Survey 1-Year Estimates."
        https://www.census.gov/programs-surveys/acs/technical-documentation/table
        -and-geography-changes/2012/1-year.html.

U.S. Census Bureau. (2015) 2019. "2015 American Community Survey 1-Year Estimates."
        https://www.census.gov/programs-surveys/acs/technical-documentation/table
        -and-geography-changes/2015/1-year.html.

U.S. Census Bureau. (2016) 2019. "2016 American Community Survey 1-Year Estimates."
        https://www.census.gov/programs-surveys/acs/technical-documentation/table
        -and-geography-changes/2016/1-year.html.

Parenting Styles

There is substantial anxiety around parenting in the United States. Any trip to a bookstore or internet search on parenting practices will yield an overwhelming amount of information being sold to parents (or soon-to-be parents) on how to raise a child. This concern stems not simply from the fear of the unknown for first-time parents but also from the social pressure placed on parents to set their children up for success. Parents believe that skilled child rearing can equip their children with the tools and resources to successfully navigate the many challenges of life. This parental anxiety and related intervention are not new phenomena but have been exacerbated since the 1980s as a result of globalization and the rapidly changing U.S. and global economy (Honoré 2010). Whether parents are seeking class preservation or class mobility in their children, they make choices about how to parent their children with future outcomes in mind.

In fact, parenting styles are often a proxy for the (re)production of social class inequalities that shape parents' fears that their children will not be successful. The focus in the United States on economic success as a measure of adult success rather than well-being or happiness (alongside having basic needs met) has yielded a cauldron of unrealistic expectations on parents. The parenting styles literature has captured much of this unease through investigation into the children's outcomes of how parents parent.

This chapter reviews research on the evolution of parenting styles as a concept and then documents how these styles are connected with social (especially class) stratification and race/ethnicity in the United States. It concludes with a brief discussion of research documenting differential outcomes among children based upon parenting styles.

DEFINING PARENTING STYLES

Early literature on parenting styles came to construct various classifications of parenting styles, such as the highly influential "prototypic" parenting styles of Diana Baumrind (1927–2018). While her early work (Baumrind 1966, 1967) differentiated three parenting styles, Baumrind's later work, influenced by psychologists Eleanor E.

Maccoby and John A. Martin (1983), extended the typology to four parenting styles (e.g., Baumrind 1991), based on parents' balance of responsiveness and demandingness: permissive, authoritarian, authoritative, and rejecting-neglecting. This typology reflected the kind of power dynamic that existed between parents and their children. Authoritarian parents were described as parents that combined high demands with low responsiveness. These parents told children what to do and punished when their children did not respond accordingly. Permissive parents combined low demands with a high responsiveness: they allowed for the power to rest in the hands of the children, allowing children to guide their own direction. Authoritative parents were responsive to and engaged with their children but still maintained high demands and therefore power in the relationship. The latter style is referred to as supportive rather than punitive, as opposed to the authoritarian style. The rejecting-neglecting parenting style is neither responsive nor demanding; parents who fit in this classification rejected or neglected their parenting responsibilities (Baumrind 1991).

This approach was widely used and elaborated on to describe and classify parenting styles (e.g., Darling 1999; Darling and Steinberg 1993; Leyendecker et al. 2005; Reitman et al. 2002) as well as to research their influence on children's outcomes, such as educational outcomes, psychological well-being, and behavioral problems. The authoritative parenting style has been found to be most consistently linked with positive outcomes (Givertz 2015).

In her influential book *Unequal Childhoods*, Annette Lareau (2003) offers a different way of understanding parenting styles by using her ethnographic work. Rather than focusing on the power wielded within the relationship, Lareau categorized parenting styles by the intersection of parental motivations and behaviors. The configurations that emerged were twofold: (1) the accomplishment of natural growth and (2) concerted cultivation.

Parents facilitating the accomplishment of natural growth are characterized by setting boundaries and using directives for crucial responsibilities, which are generally considered legitimate by the child and unquestioned. Within this setting, a natural growth approach allows children to grow and direct their own time and play with little adult interference. Parents practicing a concerted cultivation approach, on the contrary, focused on maximizing individual development by structuring and organizing children's lives and leisure time with extracurricular activities. Additionally, concerted cultivation puts reasoning and negotiation with children, rather than directivity, central.

Lareau's (2003) work examined parenting styles at the intersection of class with race and gender, an approach that has become more important as American society has become more economically and culturally diverse (Garcia Coll and Pachter 2002; Leyendecker et al. 2005; Weis and Toolis 2010). Consequential in both Lareau's and Baumrind's typologies is the process through which parenting styles lead to differential outcomes for children.

PARENTING STYLES AND SOCIAL CLASS DYNAMICS

Researchers using either Baumrind's typology or Lareau's classification of parenting styles do so with an eye toward understanding whether and how differences in parenting practices are associated with children's outcomes that are connected to social class in the United States.

Lareau's research (2003, 2011) documented how social class dynamics in the family shape parenting styles and children's daily lives. Lareau's work demonstrated that middle-class parents engaged mostly in a concerted-cultivation parenting style, while working-class families focus on natural growth.

Parents typically want their child to be "future proof"—able to navigate life's challenges successfully and to prosper. What is considered future proof may, however, differ from individual to individual. It is argued, for example, that parents occupy different, socially stratified jobs that value different qualities in employees. These differences in social context influence parenting styles. For example, some researchers assert that independence, self-direction, and initiative taking are, generally speaking, more prominent in jobs occupied by the middle class, and obedience and conformity are more prominent in jobs occupied by working class. Therefore, parents employed in different socially stratified jobs may encourage different behavior in their offspring, as they are confident that the lessons that they have accrued will help their child navigate future life (Crouter and McHale 2005; Kohn 1969, 1979).

In line with this, Lareau (2011) argues that child rearing is considered as a project among the middle class, where parents work to create opportunities for their children to accumulate human, cultural, and social capital in order to be able to utilize those acquisitions for future advancement. Middle-class parents are, therefore, providing many extracurricular experiences to nurture their talents and develop their cognitive and social skills. All these formal activities in leisure time are scheduled in order to secure better outcomes for children. While engaging in these activities, children develop skills and insights, such as growing to understand their own abilities, learning how to interact with adults, and mastering how to prioritize and perform multiple activities (Leyendecker et al. 2005). Researchers warn, however, that this approach can veer into "hyperparenting," in which children are badly overscheduled, leading to fatigue in parents as well as in children (e.g., Honoré 2010; Lareau 2011; Levine 2006). Working-class (and working-poor) parents, on the other hand, are more likely, according to a number of studies, to focus on providing children with the necessary basic support for children, which facilitates the natural growth of the child. The children learn, within the boundaries set by adults, to be independent and informally manage their own time. Parents do not question institutional practices where their children were concerned, as they value and count on professionals such as educators and doctors. Parenting in working-class families is often characterized by a higher focus on discipline and obedience to hierarchy (Crouter and McHale 2005; Hill 2006; Hoff, Laursen, and Tardif 2002; Leyendecker et al. 2005). Children therefore learn how to manage their own time but not how to navigate and advocate for themselves in institutional settings (Lareau 2011).

Additionally, social differences noticed in child-rearing practices are also rooted in differences in access to economic, time, and educational resources. As extracurricular experiences are central in a concerted cultivation approach, economic resources (e.g., registration fees and transportation), time resources (e.g., work-schedule flexibility), and educational resources (e.g., negotiation skills, broad vocabulary, and understanding and negotiation with [educational] professionals) all contribute to facilitate extracurricular experiences for their children (Okagaki and Luster 2005; Lareau 2011). These financial, human capital, and social resources are generally more available for middle-class families (Hill 2006; Lareau 2003, 2011; Leyendecker et al. 2005).

PARENTING STYLES AMONG DIFFERENT RACIAL AND ETHNIC GROUPS

The importance of understanding racial and ethnic differences in parenting styles and children's outcomes within the United States came to the foreground in the 1990s and early 2000s. This focus on ethnic minority parenting comes from recognizing a growing diversity within the United States and how the distinct value systems of these groups, combined with their socioeconomic status, influence their parenting styles (Garcia Coll and Pachter 2002; Harwood et al. 2002).

Some minority ethnic groups are overrepresented in working-class or working-poor communities in the United States, so parents within those groups have fewer economic resources in which to raise their families than their counterparts in more affluent communities do. This reduced access to economic resources may result in adherence to parenting styles that may have less beneficial outcomes in children (Leyendecker et al. 2005). Thus the economic situations of some ethnic minority groups—rather than prevailing ethnocultural values and priorities—may actually be the root of many struggles experienced by children in such communities (rather than their ethnicity, as some critics—typically of other races—claim) (Harwood et al. 2002; Hill 2006; Leyendecker et al. 2005).

In her work, Lareau found similar parenting patterns in racially different groups when they were from similar social classes: "[W]hite and black parents engaged very similar, often identical, practices with their children" (Lareau 2011, 641–42). These similarities in parenting styles within socioeconomic background status and across racial and ethnic groups are consistent with other scholarship (Hill 2006; Leyendecker et al. 2005).

This does not, however, mean that no cultural differences are present; parenting styles do vary across ethnic groups due to ethnocultural differences, such as some ethnic groups centralizing interdependence instead of independence in parenting, such as Asian American (Chao and Tseng 2002), Latin American (Harwood et al. 2002; Leyendecker et al. 2005), and African American parents (Hill 2006). Robert Weis and Erin E. Toolis found that ethnic differences in parenting styles are more prominent between people from lower socioeconomic background; they indicate that "as SES increased, differences in maternal warmth as a function of ethnicity was reduced. . . . many apparent ethnic differences in parenting behavior may be partially attributable to differences in SES" (Weis and Toolis 2010, 862).

It should be noted, too, that the social context or minority status of ethnic minority parents contributes to parenting differences. Ethnic minority parents navigate society and social relationships that expose them to structural barriers, power imbalances, and discrimination (Garcia Coll and Pachter 2002), irrespective of their socioeconomic position (McAdoo 2002). Thus ethnic minority parents also need to prepare their children for discrimination and for being bicultural, on top of preparing for success in adulthood (Garcia Coll and Pachter 2002; McAdoo 2002). This behavior was also prevalent in the research of Lareau (2011). She found that middle-class parents of color seek to avoid situations wherein their child is the only person of color and are attentive to potential racial incidents. Many parents of color also invest in efforts to develop a positive racial identity in their children, next to investing in a concerted-cultivation parenting style.

ETHNOCENTRIC APPROACHES TO RESEARCHING PARENTING

Parenting styles may be ethnically different, but parenting styles may also be differently perceived by and result in different outcomes for children of different societal groups (Garcia Coll and Pachter 2002). Differences in parents' perceptions about parenting styles across racial/ethnic groups may be the result of how those groups have experienced social life in the United States (Chao 1994; Leyendecker et al. 2005). Authoritarian parenting styles, for example, are differently perceived by African American and white families (e.g., Hill 2006; Hill and Bush 2001) and parental control is differently perceived by Asian Americans (Chao 1994; Chao and Tseng 2002). Parents seem to choose parenting styles, to include the exertion of parental control, that are consistent with how they think children need to be prepared for the world. If parents believe that their children will have to work to gain advantages in the world and therefore must be taught how to handle disadvantage, they may be more inclined to use more authoritarian styles. Racial/ethnic differences in the effects of parenting styles may also be a result of the social and economic conditions of racial/ethnic groups. Psychological control, for example, has shown to be inversely related to prosocial behavior for African American but not white children (Clark, Dahlen, and Nicholson 2015), and positive parenting yields more prosocial behavior among white children relative to African American children (Gryczkowski, Jordan, and Mercer 2018).

Researchers thus caution against taking an ethnocentric, normative approach to parenting styles, presuming not only a hierarchy of appropriate parenting styles but that one more closely connected to Western cultural values of independence should be the most optimal for families. Past research tended to focus on white respondents' parenting styles and children's outcomes, with an overrepresentation of families from middle to high socioeconomic backgrounds (Garcia Coll and Pachter 2002). The literature therefore tends to universalize results with a bias toward white respondents, often comparing broadly defined ethnic minority groups (e.g. Asian, African American, and Latinx) with the white ethnic majority group. This approach often takes a deficit perspective toward ethnic minority groups, presuming that the white families' behaviors are the standard by which others should be compared. Cultural values, social context and the interaction between socioeconomic status and ethnicity can no longer be ignored in researching parenting styles and their outcomes in children within ethnically diverse groups in the United States. Parenting style and children's outcomes may vary across different cultures and contexts (Chao 1994; Hill 2006). Some outcomes, such as independence in children, may be more central to social mobility in the United States and may give some children an advantage in this country, but those same outcomes would not necessarily lead to upward social mobility in other societies.

PARENTING STYLES AND CHILDREN'S EDUCATION

Parenting styles are not only embedded within social class and ethnicity but also produce different outcomes in children; as such, they have the power to reproduce social differences. Educational attainment is a key mechanism through which upward social mobility is attained.

The work of Pierre Bourdieu (1930–2002) on social reproduction explains the relationship between educational inequalities, on the one hand, and child-rearing practices, on the other. Bourdieu argues that educational institutions prerequire certain forms of language and cultural competencies. The acquisition of these language and cultural competencies are often linked to specific ways of parenting. Therefore, children start school on unequal footing depending on the parenting style they have experienced. Bourdieu argues that social inequality accumulates through education: "[I]t is difficult to break the circle in which cultural capital is added to cultural capital" (Bourdieu [1973] 2018, 77). That is to say, not only do children start school with different amounts of cultural capital but school is also easier to navigate for more privileged students, as the parenting they experienced used language and cultivated competencies that are rewarded within school. This process aligns with Lareau's (2011) findings regarding the concerted-cultivation parenting style, which is linked to more middle-class families, suggesting it offers tools to navigate in institutional settings that set children up for a successful adulthood.

Other scholarship has connected parenting styles with different educational outcomes (e.g., Hill 2006; Spera 2005), also noting clear connections between academic performance, on the one hand, and parental social class, on the other. Christopher Spera's (2005) review of the literature on parenting and adolescent school achievement, for example, highlights this connection. However, the outcomes of children are not monolithic based on class and parenting styles. Josipa Roska and Daniel Potter (2011) document the importance of concerted cultivation for parents moving from the working class to the middle class in shaping children's academic achievement, while noting that middle-class children overall consistently have higher academic achievement relative to their working-class peers. Further, the link between authoritative parenting styles and academic performance varies by ethnicity, especially among families with immigrant parents (e.g., Chao and Tseng 2002).

PARENTING STYLES AND SOCIAL INTEGRATION

Access to educational opportunities is tied to other ways in which children and adolescents are integrated into their communities. *Prosocial* behaviors, or behaviors that benefit others, such as volunteering, are positively correlated with educational attainment (Gerbino et al. 2018) while negative social outcomes (such as delinquency and incarceration) reduce opportunities to gain access to educational benefits (Ward and Williams 2015). As a result, both positive and negative social outcomes are associated with parenting styles. Adolescent social responsibility and other prosocial behaviors have also been documented to be connected to parenting styles. Prosocial behavior is more frequent when parents exhibit consistent discipline without corporal punishment (Gryczkowski, Jordan, and Mercer 2018). Social responsibility and other prosocial behaviors are more frequent among children who experienced primarily authoritative parenting (Gunnoe, Hetherington, and Reiss 1999; Roth 2008; Spinrad and Stifter 2006).

A large review study in 2009 found that while the researchers could not make overall claims about differences in parenting styles, supportive parenting behaviors were moderately linked to a reduction in delinquency, while parenting with higher levels of neglect, hostility, and rejection were strongly associated with more delinquency in adolescents. There were also small associations between authoritarian and authoritative control and increases in delinquency (Hoeve et al. 2009). More recent research has also found that authoritarian parenting is correlated with negative behavioral outcomes, even once cultural characteristics and variability are taken into consideration (Pinquart and Kauser 2018; Smetana 2017).

CONCLUSION

The changing global economy ties the economic conditions of people around the world together in ways that would have been unthinkable even one generation ago. Economic anxiety regarding social position and employment possibilities for oneself and one's children is unlikely to abate. Therefore, it would not be surprising to see middle- and upper-middle-class parents continuing to focus their energies on maintaining at least the status quo among their children. They do so at least in part through the parenting styles they choose to deploy when raising their children, positioning them to be able to navigate changing institutions and interact with a diverse set of individuals and within diverse contexts. When authoritative parenting styles (or those more consistent with concerted cultivation) are used, providing guidance without being controlling, fewer negative behavioral problems (e.g., delinquency) and more positive social behaviors seem to follow, setting children up for greater opportunities in the future. Conversely, working-class and poor parents are generally less equipped to prepare their children to interact with institutional settings as effectively. Further, more authoritarian and controlling parenting styles lead to children being more likely to engage in behaviors that have negative social consequences (such as incarceration). These negative consequences often reduce their access to educational and employment opportunities, which can in turn thwart upward social mobility. Therefore, one way to level the playing field for children is not only to increase opportunities available to them but also to provide opportunities for parents to secure better paying jobs and educational opportunities for themselves. Improve job outcomes for parents, and social outcomes for children can also improve. It is difficult to see how future generations can reduce socioeconomic inequality in the United States without meaningful economic and social support for working-class parents.

Shannon N. Davis and Myriam Halimi

Further Reading

Baumrind, Diana. 1966. "Effects of Authoritative Parental Control on Child Behavior." *Child Development* 37 (4): 887–907. https://www.jstor.org/stable/1126611.

Baumrind, Diana. 1967. "Child Care Practices Anteceding Three Patterns of Preschool Behavior." *Genetic Psychological Monographs* 75 (1): 43–88.

Baumrind, Diana. 1991. "The Influence of Parenting Style on Adolescent Competence and Substance Use." *Journal of Early Adolescence* 11 (1): 56–95.

Bourdieu, Pierre. (1973) 2018. "Cultural Reproduction and Social Reproduction." In *Knowledge, Education and Cultural Change: Papers in the Sociology of Education*, edited by Richard Brown. New York: Routledge. Citations are to the 2018 reprint.

Chao, Ruth K. 1994. "Beyond Parental Control and Authoritarian Parenting Style: Understanding Chinese Parenting through the Cultural Notion of Training." *Child Development* 65 (4): 1111–19.

Chao, Ruth K., and Vivian Tseng. 2002. "Parenting of Asians." In *Handbook of Parenting Volume 4: Social Conditions and Applied Parenting*, edited by Marc H. Bornstein, 59–94. Hillsdale, NJ: Lawrence Erlbaum Associates.

Clark, Caitlin M., Eric R. Dahlen, and Bonnie C. Nicholson. 2015. "The Role of Parenting in Relational Aggression and Prosocial Behavior among Emerging Adults." *Journal of Aggression, Maltreatment & Trauma* 24 (2): 185–202.

Crouter, Ann C., and Susan M. McHale. 2005. "The Long Arm of the Job Revised: Parenting in Dual-Earner Families." In *Parenting: An Ecological Perspective*, 2nd edition, edited by Tom Luster and Lynn Okagaki, 291–312. Hillsdale, NJ: Lawrence Erlbaum Associates.

Darling, Nancy. 1999. *Parenting Style and Its Correlates*. ERIC Digest ED427896.

Darling, Nancy, and Laurence Steinberg. 1993. "Parenting Style as Context: An Integrative Model." *Psychological Bulletin* 113 (3): 487–96.

Garcia Coll, Cynthia, and Lee M. Pachter. 2002. "Ethnic and Minority Parenting." In *Handbook of Parenting Volume 4: Social Conditions and Applied Parenting*, edited by Marc H. Bornstein, 1–20. Hillsdale, NJ: Lawrence Erlbaum Associates.

Gerbino, Maria, Antonio Zuffianò, Nancy Eisenberg, Valeria Castellani, Bernadette Paula Luengo Kanacri, Concetta Pastorelli, and Gian Vittorio Caprara. 2018. "Adolescents' Prosocial Behavior Predicts Good Grades beyond Intelligence and Personality Traits." *Journal of Personality* 86 (2): 247–60.

Givertz, Michelle. 2015. "Parenting Styles/Disciplines." *International Encyclopedia of Interpersonal Communication*. https://doi.org/10.1002/9781118540190.wbeic037.

Gryczkowski, Michelle, Sara Sytsma Jordan, and Sterett H. Mercer. 2018. "Moderators of the Relations between Mothers' and Fathers' Parenting Practices and Children's Prosocial Behavior." *Child Psychiatry & Human Development* 49 (3): 409–19.

Gunnoe, Marjorie Lindner, E. Mavis Hetherington, and David Reiss. 1999. "Parental Religiosity, Parenting Style, and Adolescent Social Responsibility." *Journal of Early Adolescence* 19 (2): 199–225.

Harwood, Robin, Birgit Leyendecker, Vivian Carlson, Marysol Asencio, and Amy Miller. 2002. "Parenting among Latino Families in the US." In *Handbook of Parenting*

Volume 4: Social Conditions and Applied Parenting, edited by Marc H. Bornstein, 21–46. Hillsdale, NJ: Lawrence Erlbaum Associates.

Hill, Nancy E. 2006. "Disentangling Ethnicity, Socioeconomic Status and Parenting: Interactions, Influences and Meaning." *Vulnerable Children and Youth Studies* 1 (1): 112–24.

Hill, Nancy E., and Kevin R. Bush. 2001. "Relations between Parenting Environment and Children's Mental Health among African American and Euro-American Mothers and Children." *Journal of Marriage and the Family* 63 (4): 954–66.

Hoeve, Machteld, Judith Semon Dubas, Veroni I. Eichelsheim, Peter H. Van der Laan, Wilma Smeenk, and Jan R. M. Gerris. 2009. "The Relationship between Parenting and Delinquency: A Meta-Analysis." *Journal of Abnormal Child Psychology* 37 (6): 749–75.

Hoff, Erika, Brett Laursen, and Twila Tardif. 2002. "Socioeconomic Status and Parenting." In *Handbook of Parenting, Volume 2: Biology and Ecology of Parenting,* edited by Marc H. Bornstein, 231–52. Hillsdale, NJ: Lawrence Erlbaum Associates.

Honoré, Carl. 2010. *Under Pressure: Rescuing Our Children from the Culture of Hyper-Parenting.* London: Orion Books.

Kohn, Melvin L. 1969. *Class and Conformity: A Study in Values.* Homewood, IL: Dorsey.

Kohn, Melvin. L. 1979. "The Effects of Social Class on Parental Values and Practices." In *The American Family: Dying or Developing,* edited by David Reiss and Howard Hoffman, 45–68. New York: Plenum.

Lareau, Annette. 2003. *Unequal Childhoods: Class, Race and Family Life.* Berkeley: University of California Press.

Lareau, Annette. 2011. *Unequal Childhoods: Class, Race and Family Life.* 2nd edition. Berkeley: University of California Press.

Levine, Madeline. 2006. *Price of Privilege: How Parental Pressure and Material Advantage Are Creating a Generation of Disconnected and Unhappy Kids.* New York: HarperCollins.

Leyendecker, Birgit, Robin L. Harwood, Lisa Comparini, and Alev Yalcinkaya. 2005. "Socioeconomic Status, Ethnicity, and Parenting." In *Parenting: An Ecological Perspective,* 2nd edition, edited by Tom Luster and Lynn Okagaki, 319–42. Hillsdale, NJ: Lawrence Erlbaum Associates.

Maccoby, Eleanor E., and John A. Martin. 1983. "Socialization in the Context of the Family: Parent-Child Interaction." In *Handbook of Child Psychology: Socialization, Personality and Social Development,* edited by E. Mavis Hetherington, 4:1–101. New York: John Wiley and Sons.

McAdoo, Harriette P. 2002. "African American Parenting." In *Handbook of Parenting Volume 4: Social Conditions and Applied Parenting,* edited by Marc H. Bornstein, 47–58. Hillsdale, NJ: Lawrence Erlbaum Associates.

McLanahan, Sara, and Christine Percheski. 2008. "Family Structure and the Reproduction of Inequalities." *Annual Review of Sociology* 34 (1): 257–76.

Okagaki, Lynn, and Tom Luster. 2005. "Research on Parental Socialization of Child Outcomes: Current Controversies and Future Directions." In *Parenting: An Ecological Perspective,* 2nd edition, edited by Tom Luster and Lynn Okagaki, 275–96. Hillsdale, NJ: Lawrence Erlbaum Associates.

Pinquart, Martin, and Rubina Kauser. 2018 "Do the Associations of Parenting Styles with Behavior Problems and Academic Achievement Vary by Culture? Results from a

Meta-Analysis." *Cultural Diversity and Ethnic Minority Psychology* 24 (1): 75–100.

Reitman, David, Paula C. Rhode, Stephen D. A. Hupp, and Cherie Altobello. 2002. "Development and Validation of the Parental Authority Questionnaire–Revised." *Journal of Psychopathology and Behavioral Assessment* 24 (2): 119–27.

Roska, Josipa, and Daniel Potter. 2011. "Parenting and Academic Achievement: International Transmission of Educational Advantage." *Sociology of Education* 84 (4): 299–321.

Roth, Guy. 2008. "Perceived Parental Conditional Regard and Autonomy Support as Predictors of Young Adults' Self-versus Other-Oriented Prosocial Tendencies." *Journal of Personality* 76 (3): 513–34.

Smetana, Judith G. 2017. "Current Research on Parenting Styles, Dimensions, and Beliefs." *Current Opinion in Psychology* 15:19–25.

Spera, Christopher. 2005. "A Review of the Relationship among Parenting Practices, Parenting Styles, and Adolescent School Achievement." *Educational Psychology Review* 17 (2): 125–46.

Spinrad, Tracy L., and Cynthia A. Stifter. 2006. "Toddlers' Empathy-Related Responding to Distress: Predictions from Negative Emotionality and Maternal Behavior in Infancy." *Infancy* 10(2): 97–121.

Ward, Shannon, and Jenny Williams. 2015. "Does Juvenile Delinquency Reduce Educational Attainment?" *Journal of Empirical Legal Studies* 12 (4): 716–56.

Weis, Robert, and Erin E. Toolis. 2010. "Parenting Across Cultural Contexts in the USA: Assessing Parenting Behavior in an Ethnically and Socially Diverse Sample." *Early Child Development and Care* 180 (7): 849–67.

SECTION VI

Environment

Environmental Justice

Social inequality in the United States (as well as globally) is heavily intertwined with differential access to environmental amenities ("goods") and exposure to environmental problems ("bads"). The term *environmental justice* (EJ) reflects the fact that certain groups of people, such as racial minorities and the poor, are less likely to have access to environmental goods (e.g., parks) and are more likely to be exposed to environmental bads (e.g., pollution). These groups often lack the political or social power to address these inequities, and authorities typically disregard them.

Social activism and academic study of environmental justice (or, rather, environmental *in*justice) within the United States has proliferated since the early 1980s. Environmental justice concerns have revolved heavily around inequalities based on race and social class (specifically, income), with activists and scholars debating which of these characteristics is a more significant factor. Discussions have also centered on how and why environmental injustice occurs. Over time, EJ concerns have increasingly widened, incorporating additional interlocking sources of social and environmental injustice and expanding beyond the local focus of much of early EJ activism.

As a social movement, EJ activism fits into both the continuing civil rights movement and the environmental movement. EJ issues have readily been adopted into contemporary civil rights activism. However, EJ activists, at least initially, found it more difficult to get the mainstream environmental movement to pay attention to EJ issues. Ultimately, the EJ movement defines the environment even more broadly than has often been the case within the environmental movement, with the latter's traditionally heavy focus on protection of wilderness, wildlife, and national parks. To the EJ movement, the environment goes beyond pristine landscapes, many of which have limited accessibility (especially to minorities and the poor); rather, the environment includes all of the things that people have to deal with every day. A common refrain of EJ activists is that the environment is "where we live, work and play."

EJ issues are both a cause of and a consequence of social inequality in the United States. Because a decent living environment is of vital importance for all people (and all life—a concern increasingly discussed by EJ activists), EJ issues are fundamental to any discussion of social inequality. This chapter presents a history of the idea and movement surrounding EJ issues in the United States and then turns to theoretical and empirical discussions that have been at the center of EJ issues, namely: (1) the relative importance of race versus social class and (2) how or why environmental injustice comes about. The characteristics of EJ as a social movement are also discussed, devoting particular attention to how it compares to the mainstream environmental movement and how EJ concerns have broadened over time.

HISTORY OF ENVIRONMENTAL JUSTICE IN AMERICA

In 1982, the governor of North Carolina, Jim Hunt, made the decision to bury thirty-two thousand cubic yards of soil contaminated with PCBs (polychlorinated biphenyls) in Warren County, which had the highest proportion of Blacks in the state—and was also one of its poorest counties. While many similar burials of toxic waste had occurred elsewhere in the United States before this point, and many had led to local-level protest, this particular decision resulted in the first national-level protest against what became known as *environmental racism*. Local residents' protests gained national media attention, which in turn led to support from civil rights, environmental, and labor activists and officials from around the country. While the residents were unable to prevent the burial of PCBs in Warren County, their protest is commonly considered the beginning of the U.S. environmental justice movement.

The Warren County protests led to calls for research into a possible connection between the demographic makeup (i.e., race and social class) of communities and the siting of hazardous waste sites. In conducting research regarding the four largest hazardous waste landfills in the southern part of the United States, the U.S. General Accounting Office noted that in each case, the communities with the landfills had disproportionate numbers of Blacks. Following this report, the Commission for Racial Justice of the United Church of Christ (UCC) began research of its own, resulting in a groundbreaking national level study: *Toxic Wastes and Race in the United States*. The UCC study, published in 1987, found a definitive connection between the racial composition of a community and the presence of hazardous waste facilities: communities near such facilities were significantly more likely to have higher proportions of racial minorities. Race was found to be an even better predictor of which communities had such a facility than was income or social class.

The UCC report has been extremely influential. Not only did it originally define the terms *environmental racism* and *environmental justice* but also its meticulous and comprehensive study clearly exposed the extent of environmental injustice in the United States. Contemporary studies, including a follow-up report by the UCC in 2007 (*Toxic Wastes and Race at Twenty, 1987–2007*), using even more sophisticated methods and more refined data, continue to corroborate and strengthen the basic findings of the original UCC report. While the UCC report addressed hazardous waste sites specifically, numerous studies since that time have shown that other environmentally noxious facilities or threats (also known as LULUs or "locally unwanted land uses") also have a higher chance of occurring or being sited in communities that are disproportionately populated by racial minorities and/or people of low income.

Shortly after the UCC report was published, a conference was convened at the University of Michigan to further study the issues it raised. The 1990 Michigan Conference on Race and the Incidence of Environmental Hazards brought together public officials and scholars who had been working on these issues. This conference, coupled with the UCC report, was vital to bringing the issue of EJ to the attention of the U.S. Environmental Protection Agency (EPA). In 1992, the agency developed an Office of Environmental Equity (now the Office of Environmental Justice), and one year later, the agency established the National Environmental Justice Advisory Council. In 1994, President Bill Clinton issued an executive order (12898) mandating that all federal agencies make EJ part of their missions by "identifying and addressing, as appropriate, disproportionately high and adverse human health or environmental effects of its programs, policies, and activities on minority populations and low-income populations."

The 1980s and 1990s also saw significant growth in EJ activism and attention to EJ issues in academia. In 1990, Robert Bullard's seminal work *Dumping in Dixie: Race, Class, and Environmental Quality* was published. In 1991, activists involved in EJ issues from around the country came together in the First National People of Color Environmental Leadership Summit and drafted a list of fundamental principles of EJ (see table 1).

The two decades following the first national-level EJ protest revealed substantial promise for those concerned with EJ issues. However, progress on these issues slowed in the early 2000s. Authors of the 2007 UCC report indicated that the EPA within the George W. Bush presidential administration actively undercut the policies of EJ that came out of the 1990s. While the Barack Obama administration was generally quite supportive of and active on EJ issues, the Donald Trump administration has substantially undermined EJ considerations, targeting the EPA and its Office of Environmental Justice with severe budget cuts and focusing much of its energy on deregulation of polluting corporations.

Regardless of national administrations, however, local and regional environmental injustice problems continue. A particularly glaring example was the "Flint Water Crisis," which has been described as "the nation's most egregious" example of environmental injustice to date (Mohai 2018, 27). In the spring of 2014, through the culmination of various decisions made by state officials, the water supply of Flint, Michigan (a midsize city with about one hundred thousand residents), became contaminated with lead. According to the U.S. Census Bureau, approximately 55 percent of the population of Flint in 2014 was Black, and just under 42 percent of the population had incomes below the poverty level. In comparison, the population of Michigan overall in 2014 was 14 percent Black, and only about 17 percent of the population was below the poverty level.

While the decisions that led to the contamination were largely for cost-cutting purposes (Flint was operating at the time under a state-controlled "emergency management" authority due to financial stress), the effect of these decisions had a

Table 1   The Principles of Environmental Justice

1. **Environmental Justice** affirms the sacredness of Mother Earth, ecological unity and the interdependence of all species, and the right to be free from ecological destruction.

2. **Environmental Justice** demands that public policy be based on mutual respect and justice for all peoples, free from any form of discrimination or bias.

3. **Environmental Justice** mandates the right to ethical, balanced, and responsible uses of land and renewable resources in the interest of a sustainable planet for humans and other living things.

4. **Environmental Justice** calls for universal protection from nuclear testing, extraction, production and disposal of toxic/hazardous wastes, and poisons and nuclear testing that threaten the fundamental right to clean air, land, water, and food.

5. **Environmental Justice** affirms the fundamental right to political, economic, cultural, and environmental self-determination of all peoples.

6. **Environmental Justice** demands the cessation of the production of all toxins, hazardous wastes, and radioactive materials, and that all past and current producers be held strictly accountable to the people for detoxification and the containment at the point of production.

7. **Environmental Justice** demands the right to participate as equal partners at every level of decision-making, including needs assessment, planning, implementation, enforcement, and evaluation.

8. **Environmental Justice** affirms the right of all workers to a safe and healthy work environment without being forced to choose between an unsafe livelihood and unemployment. It also affirms the right of those who work at home to be free from environmental hazards.

9. **Environmental Justice** protects the right of victims of environmental injustice to receive full compensation and reparations for damages as well as quality health care.

10. **Environmental Justice** considers governmental acts of environmental injustice a violation of international law, the Universal Declaration On Human Rights, and the United Nations Convention on Genocide.

11. **Environmental Justice** must recognize a special legal and natural relationship of Native Peoples to the U.S. government through treaties, agreements, compacts, and covenants affirming sovereignty and self-determination.

12. **Environmental Justice** affirms the need for urban and rural ecological policies to clean up and rebuild our cities and rural areas in balance with nature, honoring the cultural integrity of all our communities, and provided fair access for all to the full range of resources.

13. **Environmental Justice** calls for the strict enforcement of principles of informed consent, and a halt to the testing of experimental reproductive and medical procedures and vaccinations on people of color.

14. **Environmental Justice** opposes the destructive operations of multinational corporations.

15. **Environmental Justice** opposes military occupation, repression and exploitation of lands, peoples and cultures, and other life-forms.

(continued)

Table 1   The Principles of Environmental Justice (continued)

16. **Environmental Justice** calls for the education of present and future generations which emphasizes social and environmental issues, based on our experience and an appreciation of our diverse cultural perspectives.

17. **Environmental Justice** requires that we, as individuals, make personal and consumer choices to consume as little of Mother Earth's resources and to produce as little waste as possible and make the conscious decision to challenge and reprioritize our lifestyles to ensure the health of the natural world for present and future generations.

Source: Delegates to the First National People of Color Environmental Leadership Summit 1991.

disproportionate impact on poor and minority families. Furthermore, state officials' initial responses to Flint residents' expressions of concerns about their water were largely dismissive and derogatory. While residents were largely ignored early on, state and corporate actors were taking steps to protect state officials in Flint as well as manufacturing processes from water contamination. Purified water coolers were secretly installed in state office buildings in Flint, and General Motors' Flint Engine Operations facility switched its water source due to concerns of corrosion in the manufacturing process. It was not until a year and a half after the contamination began—after extensive resident activism, several studies documenting contamination, and investigative reporting—that the state publicly acknowledged the problems with the Flint water supply. Despite the resulting local, state, and national declarations of emergency, attempted remedies have been "piecemeal and incomplete" (Mohai 2018, 30). According to the Flint Water Advisory Task Force (cited in Mohai 2018, 31), which was created by Michigan governor Rick Snyder to investigate the Flint water situation,

> The facts of the Flint water crisis lead us to the inescapable conclusion that this is a case of environmental injustice. Flint residents, who are majority Black or African American and among the most impoverished of any metropolitan area in the United States, did not enjoy the same degree of protection from environmental and health hazards as that provided to other communities. Moreover, by virtue of their being subject to emergency management, Flint residents were not provided equal access to, and meaningful involvement in, the government decision-making process.

While the Flint water crisis is a particularly blatant example of environmental injustice, there is ample evidence that similar incidents are occurring across the United States. From the contested siting of the Dakota Access Pipeline on the Standing Rock Sioux tribal reservation to disproportionate exposure to toxic pollutants, chemicals, and pesticides among Latin and Asian Americans, environmental injustice remains a pernicious and intractable problem. Racial minorities (also known as "people of color" or POC) and poorer communities are affected more by environmental problems, with documented higher average levels of exposure to air and water pollutants, higher rates of lead poisoning (particularly in children), and a greater likelihood of being selected as the site for environmentally harmful facilities. Studies have further shown that POC and poorer communities will be (or already are) more likely to suffer the negative consequences of climate change (e.g., extreme heat, flooding, and dislocation). In addition to having greater exposure to environmental bads, these communities also have more limited access to environmental goods such as accessible green space or clean rivers, lakes, and other waterways.

The unequal distribution of environmental goods and bads (what is referred to as *distributive justice*) is, however, only one layer of environmental injustice. Another layer is that of *procedural justice*. Environmental justice activists and researchers assert that the concerns of people and communities faced with environmental hazards and threats are typically dismissed or treated with indifference by regulatory or corporate actors; they are often denied adequate procedures for voicing their concerns. Additionally, these communities lack *corrective justice*: when problems are acknowledged by authorities, there is often a lack of urgency, and responses are often more limited than what would be the case for white and more affluent communities. The fact that POC and lower-income households and communities are less likely to have all of these forms of justice is inherently linked to the fact that these households and communities face a whole host of other types of inequalities, including more limited access to quality education, food, housing, and economic opportunities (referred to more broadly as *social justice*).

RACE VERSUS SOCIAL CLASS

Race is a social construct with very little basis in human biology. Even so, perceptions of racial differences within a specific society or culture can have enormous effects on how people are treated. The groups/communities that have typically been at the receiving end of environmental injustice within the United States have been racial minorities or POC. These groups/communities are also more likely to be poor or of lower income than communities/groups with a heavy white presence.

Sociologically, income is only one factor underlying social class; however, because income is typically highly correlated with the other elements of social class (higher education levels, as well as jobs with higher prestige, often lead to higher incomes), income is a commonly used and relatively straightforward indicator of social class. Within the United States, there is a strong connection between minority status and income (i.e., social class), with racial minorities, on average, having higher rates of poverty and lower household and individual incomes. It is therefore difficult to separate out the effects of race and income (social class) on EJ and other issues. Even so, sophisticated statistical analyses that can tease out the effects of race versus class have generally found that while both are important, race is a more potent predictor of environmental injustice. The relative importance of race versus class has been a core issue of debate within the EJ movement and among EJ scholars. While this debate might seem trifling, determining the factor(s) that make environmental injustices more likely is important for crafting solutions to address them or prevent them in the first place. It also speaks to important aspects of the lived experience of the individuals, groups, and communities that have been victimized by environmental injustice.

When thinking about EJ, activists and scholars have readily and reasonably turned to discussions of racial inequality. The environmental issues that have prompted concern and activism among lower-income or working-class white households/communities have traditionally been considered a separate problem and were not included under the moniker of EJ, at least not initially. Organizing around these issues has typically been given a different label, including the terms *grassroots environmental movement* (GEM) or NIMBY ("Not in My Back Yard"). Just like other EJ issues, however, these issues revolved strongly around social class inequalities, with lower- and working-class communities having greater exposure to environmental bads and less access to environmental goods than their middle- and upper-class counterparts.

Just as the EJ movement had its catalyst in the 1982 protest in Warren County, North Carolina, the GEM was sparked by a 1978 case of toxic pollution of a largely white, working-class community in the Love Canal neighborhood of Niagara Falls, New York. After several years of heightened health problems in the neighborhood and numerous investigations by residents (led by mothers with mysteriously sick children), reporters, and state authorities, it was determined that toxic chemicals had been leaking out of an old chemical waste dump buried beneath the neighborhood elementary school. Outraged by what they viewed as an indifferent regulatory response to this revelation, activists went so far as to hold two EPA officials "hostage" in order to get the federal government's attention to the matter. They succeeded in getting President Jimmy Carter to declare a federal health emergency at Love Canal in August 1978. Lois Gibbs, a key figure in the fight to address the contamination at Love Canal, went on to develop an organization (initially called the Citizen's Clearinghouse for Hazardous Waste) to help other activists and communities around the United States faced with similar issues. Since then, numerous local, regional, and national organizations have been active in communities fighting environmental threats and hazards.

GEM activists and organizations have often been given the label NIMBY, with detractors arguing that activists only wish to have the pollutants or problematic facilities located elsewhere, just not in *their* backyards. In fact, there is some evidence to suggest that activism from white communities, albeit lower income or working class, has indeed meant that LULUs have increasingly been placed in lower-income/working-class communities of POC. However, various observers have noted that the GEM has generally been concerned with preventing the production of hazardous wastes and the siting of noxious facilities altogether. Rather than being NIMBY, their focus is more on NIABY (Not in Anyone's Back Yard). Furthermore, despite the early consideration of EJ and GEM as separate entities (with EJ being largely about lower-income *minority* communities and GEM being largely about lower-income *white* communities), the contemporary EJ movement readily incorporates both sets of concerns.

WHY ENVIRONMENTAL INJUSTICE?

A key question in EJ revolves around how environmental inequalities occur in the first place. Do community demographics precede the siting of LULUs? In other words, are communities with disproportionately high numbers of lower-income and/or racial minorities more likely to be targeted for noxious facilities? Or does the occurrence of environmental hazards or the siting of LULUs come first, leading to a shift in community demographics? As noted earlier, these kinds of questions are vital for determining policies and strategies aimed at intervening in or preventing cases of environmental injustice.

These questions have been difficult to answer, because they require directly following changes in a community over time (e.g., through field research) or having existing data about community dynamics from before as well as after an environmental injustice has been identified. The former type of longitudinal study can be especially costly, and it is difficult anticipating which communities should be studied over time. For the latter, usually only basic demographic data (from the Census in many cases) exist for a community. The few longitudinal studies that have been conducted, primarily using existing data, have generally been inconclusive. More recent studies utilizing sophisticated tools and analyses, however, do tend to find that the sociodemographics of a community precede the siting of LULUs. In other words, environmentally problematic facilities or technologies are typically sited in communities that already have a disproportionate number of POC and lower-income households. Such studies have also found that the siting of such facilities then typically leads to an even greater disparity in environmental impacts—racial minorities and lower-income households are more likely to remain in these areas as those with greater economic resources are able to migrate out.

Three broad, overlapping theoretical explanations have been forwarded to explain why these environmental inequalities occur. *Sociopolitical* explanations focus on differences in social and political power. Nonracial minorities and those with more income typically have more political power and the resources to devote to fighting potential LULUs. Because they have more resources, they are also better able to move out of an area that is facing an environmental threat. Additionally, companies or government authorities likely make decisions to site noxious facilities or technologies in poorer and/or minority communities because they anticipate less pushback from a community that has more limited resources and a restricted ability to fight the situation.

Economic explanations focus on how market forces determine where LULUs are sited and where people live. It is economically beneficial for companies to utilize cheap land and labor when determining where to site LULUs. Areas with cheaper land and access to cheaper labor have often also been those areas where racial minorities and people of lower income are disproportionately located. Once a LULU has been sited, property values often decrease, making it difficult for poor homeowners to leave and more enticing for more well-to-do homeowners to leave. Lower property values also attract more low-income households into the area.

While sociopolitical and economic explanations are certainly helpful in understanding how differences in power and resources contribute to environmental inequities, EJ scholars and activists repeatedly point out that racial minority status has generally been found to be an even stronger predictor of environmental injustice than either social class or income by itself. Hence, a third explanation, *racial discrimination*, cannot be ignored. The argument is not that actors involved in siting decisions are deliberately and intentionally using race as a criterion for siting decisions (although that could certainly be the case in some situations). Rather, the point is that there is a long-standing history of racism built into societal institutions, policies, and practices that continues to impact social relationships to this day. What may seem like race-neutral economic decisions often have devastatingly unequal impacts on racial minorities. In sum, all three of these explanations hold elements that can help us to understand how environmental injustice occurs.

CHARACTERISTICS OF THE ENVIRONMENTAL JUSTICE MOVEMENT

Since the 1982 protests in Warren County, North Carolina, activism on EJ issues has grown extensively. Numerous local, regional, and national organizations have emerged to address an apparently expanding array of environmental injustices in POC and white, working-class and lower-income communities in the United States. Organizations such as the Deep South Center for Environmental Justice, the Indigenous Environmental Network, the Asian Pacific Environmental Network, the United Farm Workers, and the Center on Race, Poverty & the Environment all work on various issues and use a variety of tactics. Overall, this movement and the numerous organizations working on its behalf focus on issues of social inequality, human health, and the prevention or appropriate mitigation of environmental hazards. The movement places great emphasis on providing support to local communities distressed by LULUs and in promoting citizen participation and self-determination regarding decisions that affect communities.

Compared to many contemporary movements, the EJ movement has been characterized as being very pluralistic (not dominated by a singular approach to activism), more heavily driven by volunteers, and less hierarchical in its leadership. The EJ movement has become closely aligned with the civil rights movement, with civil rights activists and organizations readily taking on the issues of environmental injustice within POC and lower-income communities. Tactically, the EJ movement has substantial parallels to the civil rights movement, with a high degree of direct action activities such as protests and rallies. As with the civil rights movement, community churches play an important role in organizing events and actions.

Although EJ issues occur at the intersection of issues addressed by the civil rights movement and those addressed by the environmental movement, the former has more readily subsumed EJ issues than the latter. Early on, EJ activists had to fight to get mainstream environmental organizations to pay attention to local environmental injustice issues and to address racial and social class inequities within the leadership and membership ranks of the mainstream organizations. Mainstream environmental organizations (e.g., the Sierra Club, Audubon Society, National Wildlife Federation) have been notorious for being disproportionately white and middle or upper class in their membership composition and, especially, in their leadership. EJ activists were often critical of the mainstream environmental movement, claiming that it was too willing to compromise on important issues (especially on issues that directly affected local communities), too little concerned about local as opposed to national and/or global issues, more concerned about issues affecting wildlife and wild lands than issues affecting human health and communities, and uninterested in issues of social inequity. However, the environmental movement and organizations have increasingly incorporated EJ issues into their workloads and concerns. Similarly, these organizations have made some substantial strides in addressing racial and social class imbalances in their ranks.

CONCLUSION

While environmental injustices have been a reality throughout American history, they have become increasingly recognized since the early 1980s, when a formally recognized EJ movement came into being. Since that time, there have been many instances of environmental hazards and threats occurring in communities heavily populated by POC and lower-income households. While race and social class (income) were the predominant focus of EJ issues, it has become clear that racial minorities and lower-income households are not the only groups disproportionately threatened by LULUs. Environmental justice activists and scholars have increasingly focused on how environmental injustice also tends to affect people differently based on gender/sex (indeed, women are often key actors in the EJ movement), sexuality, disability, age, ethnicity, and citizenship. There have been increasing calls for a truly intersectional approach to EJ issues—in addition to looking at how each of these factors plays into unequal exposure to bads and access to goods, Americans should be looking at how they work in combination (e.g., how disability exacerbates racial and class differences in exposure to environmental hazards).

In addition to interrogating an expanding set of axes upon which environmental injustice occurs (i.e., beyond race and class) and addressing how these are interconnected, EJ activists and scholars have increasingly focused on a broader set of topical issues, arguing that EJ pervades all environmental issues. Because EJ defines the environment even more broadly than has been done in the traditional environmental movement, EJ has taken on a host of additional issues, from those occurring locally or regionally to those that affect the entire globe.

Global climate change, for example, has become a key EJ issue, with EJ organizations recognizing that not only are POC, lower-income and other groups within the United States disproportionately affected by climate change but that similar communities around the world are also disproportionately affected. Because of the persistence of environmental hazards and threats, EJ activists typically have had to focus on being *reactive*, responding to environmental hazards or threats as they occur. However, EJ organizations have increasingly focused on being *proactive*, working for sustainable development and appropriate planning of communities in order to avoid environmental bads and to achieve environmental goods. While EJ issues have typically revolved around concerns of environmental impact on current human generations and their health, EJ activists and organizations are increasingly discussing and acting out of concern for the welfare of future generations of humans as well as of other species.

The broadening of EJ issues in all of these aforementioned directions comes at a particularly important time. Environmental hazards (as exemplified by the situation in Flint and elsewhere) are not going away and will likely increase in light of recent national and global events and trends. The signs of global climate change have become unmistakable, and a plethora of reports have indicated that the natural world (e.g., biodiversity) is facing unprecedented upheaval due to human activities. As is often the case, those groups and societies least responsible for creating environmental damage (e.g., poorer households and poorer societies) are often those who will be faced with the greatest environmental impact.

Angela G. Mertig

Further Reading

Bullard, Robert D. 1990. *Dumping in Dixie: Race, Class, and Environmental Quality.* Boulder, CO: Westview Press.

Bullard, Robert D., Paul Mohai, Robin Saha, and Beverly Wright. 2007. *Toxic Wastes and Race at Twenty, 1987–2007: Grassroots Struggles to Dismantle Environmental Racism in the United States.* Cleveland, OH: United Church of Christ Justice and Witness Ministries.

Delegates to the First National People of Color Environmental Leadership Summit. 1991. *Preamble, Principles of Environmental Justice.* Washington, DC: First National People of Color Environmental Leadership. http://www.ejnet.org/ej/principles .html.

Gibbs, Lois M. 1982. *Love Canal: My Story.* New York: SUNY Press.

Mohai, Paul. 2018. "Environmental Justice and the Flint Water Crisis." *Michigan Sociological Review* 32:1–41.

United Church of Christ. 1987. *Toxic Wastes and Race in the United States: A National Report on the Racial and Socio-Economic Characteristics of Communities with Hazardous Waste Sites.* Cleveland, OH: United Church of Christ, Commission for Racial Justice.

SECTION VII

Justice System

Civil Justice

In *Gideon v. Wainwright* (1963) the U.S. Supreme Court (hereinafter, the Court) unanimously held that the Sixth Amendment guaranteed a criminal defendant the right to assistance of counsel. The right to counsel in a criminal proceeding is grounded in the concern for fairness and requires the government to appoint counsel to a defendant who does not have the financial means to hire an attorney to navigate the often complex legal process. Justice Hugo L. Black wrote the opinion in *Gideon*, explaining that "in our adversary system of criminal justice, any person hauled into court, who is too poor to hire a lawyer, cannot be assured a fair trial unless counsel is provided" (U.S. Supreme Court 1963, 344). (See the "Criminal Justice" chapter in this volume for discussion of issues of inequality in the criminal justice system.)

Conversely, the same concern for fairness does not extend to civil legal matters. There is no federal constitutional right to an appointed (government-provided) attorney in civil litigation. Yet the risk of loss as a defendant or respondent in a civil case can be dramatic, such as the termination of parental rights, loss of a home, deportation, or loss of government benefits. Some civil litigants face incarceration for failing to obey a civil court order. Many *pro se* (without counsel) litigants turn to the court for protective orders, to secure custody of a child, or for a divorce. Civil legal matters may also involve fighting against wrongful termination of employment or discrimination.

PRO SE ISSUES

Many pro se litigants turn to the court for help with serious matters. In *Lassiter v. Dep't of Social Services* (1981) the Court held that the constitution does not require the state to provide a pro se litigant with counsel even in a proceeding to permanently terminate parental rights. The Court in *Turner v. Rogers* (2011) rejected a father's right to counsel in a civil contempt proceeding brought by the child's mother, where he faced incarceration for failure to pay child support.

In Maryland, 95 percent of tenants in housing cases are pro se litigants, and in California family law cases, about 80 percent of litigants are pro se by disposition of the case (Steinberg 2015, 750–51).

Pro se parties are more likely to lose their case than someone with counsel. Tenants are "two to ten times" more apt to prevail if represented by counsel, and women are "nearly twice as likely to be awarded custody of their children and two and a half times more likely to receive a protective order" when represented by an attorney (Steinberg 2015, 757).

The number of litigants representing themselves has increased since the early 2000s. More low-income people today may be turning to the courts to resolve disputes, whereas in the past, there was more reliance on family and community resources to fix problems (Steinberg 2015, 753; Buxton 2002, 111). Poverty, however, is a primary reason for the rise. Litigation is a luxury even for medium-income households. Attorneys typically bill from $125 to $300 per hour, and court filing fees can be as high as $500.

DISCRIMINATION

Women and racial minorities represent a disproportionate percentage of pro se litigants. In New York City, most litigants in housing and family law cases are racial minorities and appear pro se. Statewide research in California and Pennsylvania suggests that women and minorities are disproportionately represented in family-related cases, and most appear without counsel (Columbia Law School Human Rights Clinic 2014, 413).

A negative signaling effect may occur with pro se status. Researchers have identified a likely pro se litigant bias in sex discrimination claims where the plaintiff is female and the decision-makers are male. Law-trained men discounted the value of female sex discrimination claims more than law-trained women did, and the men "were more likely to derogate the claimant as a complainer, less competent, and to perceive her claim as less meritorious than did law-trained women" (Quintanilla, Allen, and Hurt 2017, 1118).

Title VI of the Civil Rights Act of 1964 (Title VI) prohibits federally funded programs from unlawfully discriminating, and these protections extend to litigants with limited English proficiency (LEP). But although these protections exist in theory, they are not always available in reality. For example, the Justice Department received a complaint from a non-English-speaking woman who sought a protective order from a court against her husband after he physically attacked her. The judge denied her request for an interpreter, could not understand her during the proceeding, and then refused to issue the protective order (U.S. Department of Justice 2016, 6–7). Despite Title VI, many courts lack the resources to provide free interpreters in all civil cases. Some courts, for example, suggest that non-English speakers bring a friend or relative to interpret for them (Abel 2013, 608).

WAIVER OF COURT FEES

Gladys Boddie wanted a divorce, but the state refused to waive court fees even though she was indigent. Boddie appealed, claiming that her due process rights were violated. The Court agreed, holding in *Boddie v. Connecticut* (1971) that since the state monopolized the divorce process, it could not deny Boddie a divorce only because she was poor. Similarly, in *M.L.B. v. S.L.J.* (1996), the Court held that in instances in which a parent is unable to pay for record fees necessary to defend against the termination of parental rights, the fees must be waived. Justice Ginsburg delivered the opinion holding that Mississippi could not block M.L.B's access to the court because of her poverty.

COMMON CIVIL LEGAL ISSUES IMPACTING LOW-INCOME HOUSEHOLDS

In 2017, 70 percent of low-income individuals reported being severely impacted by a civil legal problem, yet they received insufficient legal help for 86 percent of their legal issues, according to the Legal Services Corporation (LSC), a nonprofit organization devoted to helping poor Americans secure legal aid in civil justice cases (LSC 2017, 6, 25). An inadequate supply of resources drives these unmet legal needs, which span a wide range of important areas. Common civil law issues that impact low-income households include areas of health, housing, family law, domestic violence, and government benefits. Other civil law justice gaps are commonly seen in immigration-related issues and for populations living in rural areas.

A. Health

Health issues account for 41 percent of legal problems among low-income households. Health insurance–related issues and debt brought on by poor health (LSC 2017, 22) contribute to this category.

B. Housing

Nearly 30 percent of renters experience legal problems such as evictions and unsafe housing conditions (LSC 2017, 23). Studies show that evictions can lead to homelessness, declining health, and depression (Sabbeth 2018).

C. Family Law

About 27 percent of households with minor children struggle with custody issues (LSC 2017, 23) yet receive insufficient legal assistance (LSC 2017, 51). Many individuals also require legal protection from domestic violence. Studies show that an effective way to reduce domestic violence is for the victim to have meaningful access to legal assistance (Farmer and Tiefenthaler 2003, 167), yet survivors of domestic violence receive insufficient legal help for the majority of these issues (LSC 2017, 52).

D. Employment

Most employers retain counsel when sued for employment discrimination (Berrey, Hoffman, and Nielsen 2012, 9), but low-income workers more often go it alone due to the expense of securing legal representation. This puts them at a distinct disadvantage. Pro se litigants in federal employment discrimination cases rarely prevail against employers in their claims "for lost back pay attributable to unlawful discrimination, reinstatement to a prior position, promotion, or halting unlawful employer conduct" (Quintanilla et al. 2017, 1094).

E. Benefits and Financial Issues

Individuals with disabilities report legal problems concerning denial or reduction of disability services or benefits yet receive insufficient legal help in about 80 percent of cases (LSC 2017, 50). Low-income individuals seek legal assistance for denial, loss, or reduction of Veterans benefits, Social Security Survivors income, Social Security Disability income and Supplemental Security income. Over one-third of low-income households experience financial legal issues. Nearly half of these problems go unaddressed due to insufficient legal aid (LSC 2017, 22, 24).

F. Immigration and Related Issues

Individuals facing civil immigration proceedings have the right to retain an attorney on their own, but the government will not provide free counsel. Only 14 percent of detainees retain counsel for their removal hearings, according to the Legal Services Corporation. Not surprisingly, detainees with attorneys have "statistically significant" better outcomes than those without representation (Eagly and Shafer 2015, 9).

Undocumented immigrant workers can experience different treatment from the courts based on their status. For example, Jose Castro, an undocumented worker, had a viable legal claim against his employer, Hoffman Plastics Compound. Castro, along with other workers, attempted to lawfully organize a union. Hoffman laid off the employees, including Castro, in retaliation for their efforts to unionize. The National Labor Relations Board (NLRB) determined that Hoffman's actions violated federal labor laws and ordered the employer to compensate Castro $66,951 in back pay. An appellate court enforced Castro's award, but in 2002, the U.S. Supreme Court ruled in *Hoffman Plastics Compound v. NLRB* that the award did not square with federal law prohibiting employers from hiring undocumented immigrants. Therefore, Castro was not entitled to receive back pay for his employer's wrongdoing because of his undocumented status.

G. Rural Areas

Ten million Americans from rural areas have incomes less than 125 percent of the poverty guidelines. Low-income rural residents receive insufficient legal assistance for over 80 percent of their civil legal problems, according to the Legal Services Corporation, largely because there are few legal resources located in rural locations (LSC 2017, 48).

PRO BONO SERVICES

Thousands of *pro bono* (without pay) attorneys work tirelessly for nonpaying clients. But some attorneys (and the law firms that employ them) do not provide their pro bono clients with the same level of attention as would be given to paying clients (Cover 2014). Additionally, there are far fewer pro bono attorneys than there are low-income civil litigants.

LEGAL SERVICES CORPORATION

Legal Services Corporation (LSC) was established by Congress in 1974 to provide civil legal support to low-income individuals (incomes at or below 125 percent of federal poverty guidelines). The LSC provides more financial resources to legal aid organizations than any other source, but it is chronically underfunded (Columbia Law School Human Rights Clinic 2014, 421), resulting in significant unmet legal assistance needs (LSC 2017, 13).

LEGISLATION

The Equal Access to Justice Act (EAJA) (U.S. Code 1980) authorizes the government to pay prevailing parties their costs and attorneys' fees in federal cases. The EAJA was successfully applied by a U.S. Court of Appeals in *Castaneda-Castillo v. Holder* (2013), an immigration case where the respondent sought payment to cover extensive attorneys' fees and costs accrued for asylum proceedings, and in *Astrue v. Ratliff* (2010), a U.S. Supreme Court case involving Social Security benefits. In the latter case, Justice Sonia Sotomayor noted in her concurring opinion that the EAJA was established to remove cost barriers by permitting litigants to recover attorney's fees if they prevail. Sotomayor noted the success of the legislation to help recipients of Social Security benefits and Veterans benefits recover their attorney fees.

LOCAL SOLUTIONS

New York City recognized the economic and social problems associated with eviction. In 2017, it became the first jurisdiction to legislate that an indigent tenant has a right to an attorney for eviction proceedings (Sabbeth 2018, 56, 66–67).

CONCLUSION

Millions of people in the United States face significant civil legal problems every year but cannot afford an attorney, and limited free or low-cost legal services cannot fill the access gap. An obvious solution would be to extend the same right to a free attorney enjoyed by indigent criminal defendants to indigent parties involved in civil cases. This solution would likely have to come from new legislation, however, because the Court has firmly rejected extending a blanket constitutional right to counsel to civil cases. Additional *pro bono* services also would increase the supply of legal resources. The government or state bar associations could design stronger incentives for attorneys to supply more pro bono hours.

A demand-side solution suggests the creation of uniform rules to provide courts a path to play an active role in assisting pro se litigants. Pro se litigants could help themselves with more input from courts to navigate formal evidentiary and procedural rules with fewer errors (Steinberg 2015, 794, 802). Simplifying the court process for pro se litigants would also provide more meaningful access to court.

Finally, studies show that community benefits derived from government-provided legal aid often outweigh the cost (Abel and Vignola 2010). For example, the government investment is arguably low, as legal aid organizations supply free or reduced-cost services to low-income people. The return on government legal aid funding includes improvements in the welfare of children, reinstatement of employment for those wrongfully terminated, restoration of housing or benefits to low-income households, and so on. This suggests that the government could explore investing more public dollars in legal aid programs to ease the justice gap.

Kimberley L. Kinsley

Further Reading

Abel, Laura K. 2013. "Language Access in the Federal Courts." *Drake Law Review* 61 (3): 593–638.

Abel, Laura K., and Susan Vignola. 2010. "Economic and Other Benefits Associated with the Provision of Civil Legal Aid." *Seattle Journal for Social Justice* 9 (1): 139–67.

Berrey, Ellen, Steve G. Hoffman, and Laura Beth Nielsen. 2012. "Situated Justice: A Contextual Analysis of Fairness and Inequality in Employment Discrimination Litigation." *Law & Society Review* 46 (1):1–36.

Buxton, Tiffany. 2002. "Foreign Solutions to the U.S. Pro Se Phenomenon." *Case Western Reserve Journal of International Law* 34 (1): 103–47.

Columbia Law School Human Rights Clinic. 2014. "Access to Justice: Ensuring Meaningful Access to Counsel in Civil Cases: Response to the Fourth Periodic Report of the United States to the United Nations Human Rights Committee." *Syracuse Law Review* 64:409–45.

Cover, Danielle R. 2014. "Pro Bono Grievances," *Cardozo Public Law, Policy & Ethics* 12:375–422.

Eagly, Ingrid V., and Steven Shafer. 2015. "A National Study of Access to Counsel in Immigration Court." *University of Pennsylvania Law Review* 164 (1): 1–91.

Farmer, Amy, and Jill Tiefenthaler. 2003. "Explaining the Recent Decline in Domestic Violence." *Contemporary Economic Policy* 21 (2): 158–72.

Hubbard, Dana, 2021. "The Criminal Justice System." In *Inequality in America: Causes and Consequences*, edited by Kimberley L. Kinsley and Robert S. Rycroft. Santa Barbara, CA: ABC-CLIO.

LSC (Legal Services Corporation). 2017. "The Justice Gap: Measuring the Unmet Civil Legal Needs of Low-Income Americans." Prepared by NORC at the University of Chicago for Legal Services Corporation. Washington, DC.

Maryland Access to Justice Commission. 2011. *Implementing a Civil Right to Counsel in Maryland.* https://mdcourts.gov/sites/default/files/import/mdatjc/pdfs/implement-ingacivilrighttocounselinmd2011.pdf.

Quintanilla, Victor D., Rachel A. Allen, and Edward R. Hirt. 2017. "The Signaling Effect of Pro Se Status." *Law & Social Inquiry* 42 (4): 1091–121.

Sabbeth, Kathryn A. 2018. "Housing Defense as the New Gideon." *Harvard Journal of Law & Gender* 41:56–117.

S.F., CAL., ADMIN. CODE. 2011. Art. 85, §§ 58.1–58.3 (amending S.F., CAL, ADMIN. CODE).

Steinberg, Jessica K. 2015. "Demand Side Reform in the Poor People's Court." *Connecticut Law Review* 47 (3): 741–805.

U.S. Code. 1980. Equal Access to Justice Act of 1980. Pub. L. No. 96-481, 94 Stat. 2325 (codified at 28 U.S.C. § 2412 and 5 U.S.C. § 504).

U.S. Court of Appeals. 2013. *Castaneda-Castillo v. Holder*, 723 F.3d 48 (1st Cir.)

U.S. Department of Justice, Civil Rights Div., Federal Coordination and Compliance Section. 2016. *Language Access in State Courts.*

U.S. Supreme Court. 1963. *Gideon v Wainwright*, 372 U.S. 335.

U.S. Supreme Court 1971. *Boddie v. Connecticut*, 401 U.S. 371.

U.S. Supreme Court. 1981. *Lassiter v. Dep't of Social Services*, 452 U.S. 18.

U.S. Supreme Court. 1996. *M.L.B. v. S.L.J.*, 519 U.S. 102.

U. S. Supreme Court. 2002. *Hoffman Plastic Compounds, Inc. v. NLRB*, 535 U.S. 137.

U.S. Supreme Court. 2010. *Astrue v. Ratliff*, 560 U.S. 586.

U.S. Supreme Court. 2011. *Turner v. Rogers*, 564 U.S. 431.

Criminal Justice

The criminal justice system is comprised of police, judges, correctional officers, and probation and parole officers, as well as numerous other employees. Approximately 2.3 million people were incarcerated behind bars in the United States in 2018, and a total of 6.7 million were under some sort of supervision by the criminal justice system (i.e., probation through parole) (Wagner and Sawyer 2018). While the criminal justice system is supposed to operate as a fair and just system, much research suggests that treatment of people within the larger criminal justice system depends to a significant extent on such variables as the wealth, gender, race, and cultural background of the individual. This fact has prompted persistent calls for fundamental reforms of all facets of the American criminal justice system, from law enforcement to sentencing to corrections policies. For as Martin Luther King Jr. said in his famous letter from the Birmingham Jail in 1963, "Injustice anywhere is a threat to justice everywhere."

Many Americans operate under the erroneous belief that there are more African Americans in jails and prisons than there are white Americans. This is not true, but it is accurate to say that people of color are more highly *represented* in the corrections system as a proportion of their total population in the United States. While African Americans make up about 13 percent of the population of the United States, they make up 35 percent of those incarcerated. In many state systems, African Americans make up 50 percent of the incarcerated population. Latinx people are not left out of this race imbalance; for example, one in six of Latinx men will spend time in prison in their lifetimes (Rabuy and Kopf 2016). These trends prevail among women as well. While 1 in 111 white women can expect to be incarcerated in their lives, 1 in 18 Black women and 1 in 45 Latinx women can expect the same thing (Rabuy and Kopf 2016). Critics of the U.S. criminal justice system assert that these disproportionate numbers suggest overt racism by law enforcement, prosecutors, judges, and lawmakers, as well as the corrosive effects of often subtle but nonetheless systemic racism and classism in American society (e.g., police targeting African Americans and Mexican Americans in traffic stops).

Research suggests that there are police practices that target people of color more than white Americans. Numerous studies have found, for example, that police are more likely to stop and frisk African Americans than white Americans (Davis, Whyde, and Langton 2018), and research has found that people of color are more likely to be pulled over by police for discretionary stops than white drivers are (Ghandnoosh 2014). In addition, the highly publicized shootings of unarmed, young Black males such as Trayvon Martin and Michael Brown have further deepened suspicions in communities of color that law enforcement in their communities can and do utilize violence much more freely in their interactions with the public than they employ in white neighborhoods and communities. The Black Lives Matter movement emerged as a direct response to the shootings of Martin, Brown, and several other unarmed, young Black males across the country by law enforcement or self-styled vigilantes in the mid-2010s.

Researchers have found that money—or the lack of it—drives criminal justice responses and outcomes in a variety of ways. This can be found in the workings of the bail system all the way through to the application of the death penalty. For example, many of the factors that judges and other criminal justice entities use in applying bail, probation, incarceration, and the death penalty are due to such factors as whether an offender can afford bail and/or whether a defendant can afford a private attorney versus a public defender. White men on average have higher incomes and greater financial resources to, for example, secure accomplished legal representation than do women or people of color.

People who are detained prior to trial are more likely to be convicted (Rosich 2007; Dobbie, Goldin, and Yang 2018). Studies have also found that law enforcement authorities are more likely to charge people of color with more crimes than white individuals arrested under similar circumstances. This may give them an added appearance of guilt and thus make it harder for them to secure their freedom prior to facing charges. The norm in the criminal justice system is that the accused gets a bond from the judge, and then a bail bond agent pays the bond. In turn, the defendant must pay the bond agent a certain percentage to ensure that the defendant will return to face charges at a later date. People being detained in jail prior to seeing the judge are often wearing jail-provided clothes and may look more guilty. Moreover, poor defendants are often given a higher bail and are less likely to be released on bond.

Wealthy Americans can often afford private attorneys—some of whom have the resources of large firms behind them—while poor or working-class defendants often have no choice but to accept representation from a public defender. Public defenders are overworked and underpaid. They have hundreds of cases and often do not meet the defendant for the first time until they are in front of the judge.

Bias by race, gender, and social class also exists in the jury selection process. According to a 2010 report issued by the Equal Justice Initiative, both overt and covert racism was uncovered in a jury study. When the organization looked at jury selection in eight states, it found that defendants being tried in mostly Black counties nonetheless often faced all-white juries. In *Flowers v. Mississippi* (2019), the U.S. Supreme Court reaffirmed that peremptory challenges used by both prosecutors and defense attorneys to select jury members may not solely be based on race. Yet the Equal Justice staff found that in a number of jurisdictions, prosecutors were trained or encouraged by their departments to use race in choosing jurors. Some prosecutors were told to use factors such as the prospective juror's intelligence, eyesight, age, and poverty to strike a prospective juror, thereby concealing racial bias during jury selection (Equal Justice Initiative 2010).

Sentencing decisions have also been found to have racial overtones. Prosecutors often charge African Americans with crimes that are associated with harsher sentences. According to a review of research, Ojmarrh Mitchell (2018) found that Latinx people and African Americans were more likely to get harsher sentences than whites were. Similarly, the likelihood of being sent to prison or receiving the death penalty when convicted of charges is influenced by race and class. Tactics employed in the so-called War on Drugs "have affected Americans of every race," wrote one scholar, but "we find that racial disparities in drug arrests cannot be explained by differences in drug offending, nondrug offending, or residing in the kinds of neighborhoods likely to have heavy police emphasis on drug offending" (Mitchell and Caudy 2015).

Mandatory sentencing guidelines created in the 1980s to advance the U.S. "war on drugs" had a particularly severe impact on African American communities, because African Americans are more likely to be charged with these crimes.

Meeting some requirements for probation or parole can be more difficult when the defendant lacks money. For example, requirements of probation and parole require the defendant to attend regular appointments, maintain employment, pay fees, and stay away from known offenders. When a defendant has money, these things are easier. When defendants do not have transportation or a phone, meeting probation officers and finding employment are much more difficult. Even staying away from known offenders, which is a requirement for people on probation, can be difficult when defendants' financial straits give them few options but to live in housing where known offenders may also live. Yet defendants who cannot meet these conditions run the risk of having their probation or parole revoked and being returned to jail to serve out the remainder of their sentence.

Finally, after a defendant is released from prison, there are often collateral consequences. For example, in many states, felons and prisoners cannot vote, get public housing, or find suitable employment. While the criminal justice system is supposed to operate as a fair and just system for all, it does not. Far too often, the criminal justice system punishes people who do not have the resources to get through the criminal process far more severely than it does individuals from more affluent socioeconomic backgrounds.

Dana Hubbard

Further Reading

Davis, Elizabeth, Anthony Whyde, and Lynn Langton. 2018. "Contacts between Police and the Public, 2015." Bureau of Justice Statistics. https://www.bjs.gov/content/pub/pdf/cpp15.pdf.

Dobbie, Will, Jacob Goldin, and Crystal S. Yang. 2018. "The Effects of Pretrial Detention on Conviction, Future Crime, and Employment: Evidence from Randomly Assigned Judges." *American Economic Review* 108 (2): 201–40.

Equal Justice Initiative. 2010. "Illegal Racial Discrimination in Jury Selection: A Continuing Legacy." Equal Justice Initiative. https://eji.org/reports/illegal-racial -discrimination-in-jury-selection.

Ghandnoosh, Nazgol. 2014. "Race and Punishment: Racial Perceptions of Crime and Support for Punitive Policies." Sentencing Project. https://www.sentencingproject .org/publications/race-and-punishment-racial-perceptions-of-crime-and-support -for-punitive-policies.

King, Martin Luther, Jr. 1963. "Letter from a Birmingham Jail." April 16, 1963. University of Pennsylvania African Studies Center. https://www.africa.upenn.edu/Articles_Gen/Letter_Birmingham.html.

Mitchell, Ojmarrh. 2018. "The Continuing Evolution of Race and Sentencing Research and Reviews of This Research." *Journal of Criminal Justice* 59 (C): 29–31. https:// doi.org/10.1016/j.jcrimjus.2017.05.004.

Mitchell, Ojmarrh, and Michael S. Caudy. 2015. "Examining Racial Disparities in Drug Arrests." *JQ: Justice Quarterly* 32, no. 2 (April): 288–313.

Ogletree, Charles J. 1995. "An Essay on the New Public Defender for the 21st Century." *Law and Contemporary* Problems 58 (1): 81–93.

Rabuy, Bernadette and Daniel Kopf. 2016. "Detaining the Poor: How Money Perpetuates Poverty and Jail Time." Prison Policy Initiative. https://www.prisonpolicy.org/ reports/incomejails.html.

Rosich, Katherine J. 2007. "Race, Ethnicity, and the Criminal Justice System." American Sociological Association. https://www.asanet.org/sites/default/files/savvy/images/ press/docs/pdf/ASARaceCrime.pdf.

U.S. Supreme Court. 2019. *Flowers v. Mississippi* (*Flowers VI*). 139 S. Ct. 2228.

Wagner, Peter, and Wendy Sawyer. 2018. "Mass Incarceration, The Whole Pie." Prison Policy Initiative. https://doi.org/10.1016/j.jcrimjus.2017.05.004.

SECTION VIII

Consumer Issues

Consumer Credit and Payday Loans

The choice of financial products affects a household's ability to withstand economic shocks, save, and make investments in education, businesses, and purchases that enhance economic mobility. Since the late 1970s, income and wealth inequality has risen rapidly. From 1979 to 2015, income for the top 1 percent grew 233 percent while income growth for the first four quintiles grew 32 percent (CBO 2018). These trends have attracted concern, in part, because of what Alan Krueger termed the "Great Gatsby Curve": the idea that income inequality is related to economic immobility (Krueger 2012).

As inequality grew over the past three decades, rapid financial innovation created a two-tiered financial system. Today, high-income households rely on banks and credit unions while lower-income households rely heavily or exclusively on nonbank financial providers, often referred to alternative financial service (AFS) providers or "fringe banks" (e.g., pawnshops and institutions that offer high-interest loans, and car title loans).

In 2017, more than one in five households—28.6 million households—reported using an AFS product (Apaam et al. 2018). In fact, businesses that offer payday loans and check cashing exceed the total number of McDonald's and Starbucks combined, and the number of pawnshops operating in the United States in 2019 exceeded the number of credit unions and banks (CFPB 2019).

THE IMPORTANCE OF CONSUMER CREDIT

Credit is enormously valuable because it allows households to withstand economic shocks, invest, and easily purchase a wide range of goods and services. It is particularly important for households lacking savings to invest in goods and services that enhance economic mobility, including education to qualify for jobs with higher earnings, vehicle ownership to commute to employment, capital to start a business, and more.

Mainstream financial providers primarily consist of banks and credit unions. Both offer credit cards and loans. The cost of credit is given by the annualized

Table 1   Household Use of Credit over Twelve Months (2017)

No Mainstream Credit (%)	Any Mainstream Credit (%)		Any Nonbank Credit (%)	
19.7	80.4		6.9	
	Credit Card	68.7	Pawn Shop Loan	1.4
	Store Credit Card	41.6	Payday Loan	1.7
	Mortgage Home Equity Loan, or HELOC	33.8	Tax Refund Anticipation Loan	2.4
	Auto Loan	32.3	Rent-to-Own Loan	1.4
	Student Loan	16.6	Auto-Title loan	1.4
	Bank Personal Loan	6.9		
	Other Mainstream Nonbank	2.1		

Source: Apaam et al. (2018). Tabulations available at https://economicinclusion-staging. fdic.gov. Note that households may utilize more than one source of mainstream credit, so percentages may not add up to 100.

percentage rate (APR). Fringe banks offer short-term, small-dollar credit, including pawn loans and payday loans.

The National Survey of Unbanked and Underbanked Households examines credit choices. Table 1 shows the different credit sources used in 2017. Most households reported using at least one source of mainstream credit over the previous year, and many used multiple sources.

However, one-fifth of households reported not using any mainstream source of credit, and 6.9 percent of households used nonbank credit. These households experienced more financial hardship than households relying on mainstream credit. Approximately 1 percent to 2 percent of households reported using nonbank products—pawn loans, payday loans, tax refund anticipation loans, rent-to-own agreements, and auto-title loans—in the previous year. Payday loans are among the most common AFS products and garner considerable controversy.

PAYDAY LOANS

A payday borrower postdates a check or authorizes an electronic transfer for the loan amount plus fees. The lender agrees not to cash the check until an agreed-upon date, often the borrower's next paycheck date. On this date, the borrower either pays cash to redeem the check, allows the check to be cashed, or, pays a fee to renew the loan. This renewal is referred to as a rollover. The typical payday loan is a two-week loan for $300 incurring $45 to $90 in fees, which results in an APR of 400 to 1,000 percent. The average borrower takes out eight loans a year, spending $520 on interest (Bourke, Horowitz, and Roche 2012).

THE PAYDAY LOAN INDUSTRY

Payday loans have existed since the Great Depression. The industry experienced rapid growth in the 1990s, peaking in the mid-2000s with $50 billion in loan volume (CFPB 2019). Growth slowed somewhat in the 2010s.

Loans are available from storefronts as well as online. In 2016, consumers spent $3.2 billion and $2.9 billion on fees and interest from storefront payday lenders and online lenders, respectively (Wilson and Wolkowitz 2017). Payday lending is not abnormally profitable due to high operating costs (Flannery and Samolyk 2005; Huckstep 2007). The key determinant of profitability is loan volume, providing incentives for lenders to offer renewals (Flannery and Samolyk 2005).

The location of payday lenders has a notable pattern. Lenders are more prevalent in areas with more minorities, among populations with less education and lower creditworthiness, and among more conservative Christian populations in general (Bhutta 2014; Fowler, Cover, and Kleit 2014; Graves and Peterson 2008; Prager 2009).

REGULATION OF PAYDAY LOANS

Businesses that provide payday loans are controversial. Some people consider these to be "predatory lenders," trapping vulnerable households in debt (Dobbie and Skiba 2013). Others argue that payday lenders fill an unmet need for credit that can assist households at critical times, such as by enabling loan recipients to avoid eviction or repair a car needed to travel to work (Mullainathan and Shafir 2009).

Regulating this industry is challenging due both to the number of businesses and the pace of financial innovation. Federal law does not limit payday lenders, save for limits on loans made to active-duty service members. States provide the primary source of regulation. Some states allow payday lending but place some regulations on loans. Other states directly or indirectly ban the industry by limiting the APR to 36 percent, a level considered too low to be profitable. In 2019, seventeen states and the District of Columbia prohibited payday lending.

State bans dramatically curtail payday borrowing. Borrowers substitute between-payday loans and other sources, including pawn loans, bank overdrafts, delaying bill payment, or borrowing from friends and family (Bhutta, Goldin, and Homonoff 2016; Melzer and Morgan 2009; Bourke, Horowitz, and Roche 2012; Zinman 2010).

PAYDAY BORROWERS

The FDIC estimated in 2017 that 2.2 million U.S. households (2 percent) borrowed from a payday lender, a portion that has remained steady since 2011 (Apaam et al. 2018). Pew Charitable Trusts estimates a slightly larger number, with 12 million individual borrowers (6 percent) each year (Bourke, Horowitz, and Roche 2012).

The characteristics of borrowers illustrate the demand for these products. Compared with those who do not borrow, payday borrowers tend to be younger and less educated but more likely to be employed (Lawrence and Elliehausen 2008; Lusardi and Scheresberg 2013; Zinman 2010). Borrowers are more likely to be nonwhite, unmarried, and female, and to have children (Bourke, Horowitz, and Roche 2012).

The average income of borrowers is lower than that of nonborrowers; most borrowers have annual incomes below $50,000 and that vary month to month (Bourke, Horowitz, and Roche 2012; Stegman 2007; Zinman 2010). Payday borrowers are more likely to live in the Midwest and South, consistent with the location of state-level bans.

WHY BORROW FROM A PAYDAY LENDER?

Given the high costs, why do households turn to payday loans? Studies show that borrowers require extra money to cover basic living expenses and emergencies or to make up for lost income (Bourke, Horowitz, and Roche 2012; Zinman 2010). This is consistent with situations in which the price of many goods and services, ranging from housing to medical care to childcare, rises faster than incomes, especially for lower-income households.

Table 2 shows that households may choose payday loans because they have few other options. Many are denied mainstream credit, and one 2015 study found that nearly two-thirds of households using payday lenders reported falling behind on bills in the previous year; fewer than half had been able to save for unexpected expenses in the previous year (Bhutta et al. 2015). As a result, policies that improve household financial stability, ranging from health insurance to higher minimum

Table 2   Financial Characteristics of Households that Borrowed by Whether They Borrowed from Payday Lender in Previous Twelve Months, 2017

Household	Borrowed (%)	Did Not Borrow (%)
Unbanked	11.0	6.1
Did not use mainstream credit in past twelve months	25.5	19.5
Had credit card	47.6	69.2
Denied credit card or personal loan or line of credit from bank in past twelve months	11.0	2.6
Fell behind on bills in past twelve months	60.1	13.6
Saved for unexpected expenses or emergencies in past twelve months	44.6	58.0

Source: Author's calculation of Apaam et al. (2018). Payday borrowers are households that reported using a payday loan in the last twelve months.

wages, reduce reliance on payday loans (Allen et al. 2017; Dettling and Hsu 2018; Fitzpatrick and Fitzpatrick 2019).

EFFECTS OF ACCESS TO OR USE OF PAYDAY LOANS

The "big question" is whether payday loans help or harm borrowers (Caskey 2012). Their high costs and potential for debt could harm borrowers, especially those who repeatedly use loans or rollover loans or borrow for impulse purchases. For these borrowers, payday loans harm financial stability and creditworthiness. However, borrowers may use loans to overcome income shortages before additional financial hardship occurs. If so, payday loans may improve mobility by managing cash flows, smoothing financial shocks, and improving creditworthiness.

Whether a payday loan helps or hinders borrowers depends on which effect dominates. Research focuses on financial outcomes associated with payday borrowing: bankruptcy filings, late bill payment, credit scores, and material hardship. Payday loans may increase bankruptcies, an outcome that has had far-reaching financial effects (Skiba and Tobacman 2019). But payday borrowers have poor credit, and the loan has no effect on credit scores up to three years later (Bhutta et al. 2015). In fact, payday borrowing helps households manage emergencies, reducing material hardship and improving well-being when they face economic difficulties (Dobridge 2018; Fitzpatrick and Coleman-Jensen 2014; Morse 2011; Zinman 2010). On net, payday loans likely provide little harm and some short-term benefits for households. Payday loans, however, do not improve a household's prospects for economic mobility. To the contrary, reliance on nonbank credit is a consequence of the growth in inequality that has left many behind. Ensuring access to safe and effective credit will allow the economy to grow at its full capacity and encourage all Americans to realize their greatest potential.

Katie Fitzpatrick

Further Reading

Allen, Heidi, Ashley Swanson, Jialan Wang, and Tal Gross. 2017. "Early Medicaid Expansion Associated with Reduced Payday Borrowing in California." *Health Affairs* 36 (10): 1769–76.

Apaam, Gerald, Susan Burhouse, Karyen Chu, Keith Ernst, Kathryn Fritzdixon, Ryan Goodstein, Alicia Lloro, et al. 2018. *2017 FDIC National Survey of Unbanked and Underbanked Households Report*. Washington, DC: Federal Deposit Insurance Corporation.

Bhutta, Neil. 2014. "Payday Loans and Consumer Financial Health." *Journal of Banking & Finance* 47:230–42.

Bhutta, Neil, Paige Marta Skiba, and Jeremy Tobacman. 2015. "Payday Loan Choices and Consequences." *Journal of Money, Credit and Banking* 47 (2–3): 223–60.

Bhutta, Neil, Jacob Goldin, and Tatiana Homonoff. 2016. "Consumer Borrowing after Payday Loan Bans." *Journal of Law and Economics* 59 (1): 225–59.

Bourke, Nick, Alex Horowitz, and Tara Roche. 2012. "Payday Lending in America: Who Borrows, Where They Borrow, and Why." Pew Charitable Trusts. https://www

.pewtrusts.org/en/research-and-analysis/reports/2012/07/19/who-borrows-where
-they-borrow-and-why.

Caskey, John P., ed. 2012. *Payday Lending: New Research and the Big Question.* Oxford:
Oxford University Press.

CBO (Congressional Budget Office). 2018. "Distribution of Household Income, 2015."
November 8, 2018. https://www.cbo.gov/publication/54646#.

CFPB (Consumer Financial Protection Bureau). 2019. "Payday, Vehicle Title, and Certain
High-Cost Installment Loans." Notice of Proposed Rulemaking. 12 CFR Part
1041.   https://www.consumerfinance.gov/policy-compliance/rulemaking/final
-rules/payday-vehicle-title-and-certain-high-cost-installment-loans.

Dettling, Lisa J., and Joanne W. Hsu. 2018. "Minimum Wages and Consumer Credit:
Impacts on Access to Credit and Traditional and High-Cost Borrowing." Federal
Reserve Board Divisions of Research & Statistics and Monetary Affairs, Finance
and Economics Discussion Series. Washington, DC: Federal Reserve, Board of
Governors.

Dobbie, Will, and Paige Marta Skiba. 2013. "Information Asymmetries in Consumer
Credit Markets: Evidence from Payday Lending." *American Economic Journal:
Applied Economics* 5 (4): 256–82.

Dobridge, Christine L. 2018. "High-Cost Credit and Consumption Smoothing." *Journal
of Money, Credit and Banking* 50 (2–3): 407–33.

Fitzpatrick, Anne, and Katie Fitzpatrick. 2019. "Health Insurance and High Cost Borrowing: The Effect of Medicaid on Pawn Loans, Payday Loans, and other non-Bank
Financial Products." Working paper, University of Massachusetts, Boston.

Fitzpatrick, Katie, and Alisha Coleman-Jensen. 2014. "Food on the Fringe: Food Insecurity and the Use of Payday Loans." *Social Service Review* 88 (4): 553–93.

Flannery, Mark, and Katherine Samolyk. 2005. "Payday Lending: Do the Costs Justify
the Price?" Working paper, FDIC Center for Financial Research, Washington, DC.

Fowler, Christopher S., Jane K. Cover, and Rachel Garshick Kleit. 2014. "The Geography
of Fringe Banking." *Journal of Regional Science* 54 (4): 688–710.

Furman, Jason. 2016. "Financial Inclusion in the United States." Council of Economic
Advisers.   https://obamawhitehouse.archives.gov/blog/2016/06/10/financial-inclu
sion-united-states.

Graves, Steven M., and Christopher L. Peterson. 2008. "Usury Law and the Christian
Right: Faith-Based Political Power and the Geography of American Payday Loan
Regulation." *Catholic University Law Review* 57 (3): 637–700.

Huckstep, Aaron. 2007. "Payday Lending: Do Outrageous Prices Necessarily Mean Outrageous Profits." *Fordham Journal of Corporate and Financial Law* 12 (1):
203–31.

Krueger, Alan B. 2012. "The Rise and Consequences of Inequality in the United States."
Speech at the Center for American Progress, January 12, 2012.

Lawrence, Edward C., and Gregory Elliehausen. 2008. "A Comparative Analysis of Payday Loan Customers." *Contemporary Economic Policy* 26 (2): 299–316.

Lusardi, Annamaria, and Carlo de Bassa Scheresberg. 2013. "Financial Literacy and
High-Cost Borrowing in the United States." NBER Working Paper 18969. National
Bureau of Economic Research. https://www.nber.org/papers/w18969.

Melzer, Brian T., and Donald P. Morgan. 2009. "Competition and Adverse Selection in the
Small-Dollar Loan Market: Overdraft Versus Payday Credit." *Federal Reserve
Bank of New York Staff Reports.* New York: Federal Reserve Bank of New York.

Morse, Adair. 2011. "Payday Lenders: Heroes or Villains?" *Journal of Financial Economics* 102 (1): 28–44.

Mullainathan, Sendhil, and Eldar Shafir. 2009. "Savings Policy and Decisionmaking in Low-Income Households." In *Insufficient Funds: Savings, Assets, Credit, and Banking among Low-Income Households*, edited by Rebecca M. Blank and Michael S. Barr, 121–45. New York: Russell Sage Foundation.

Prager, Robin A. 2009. "Determinants of the Locations of Payday Lenders, Pawnshops and Check-Cashing Outlets," Finance and Economics Discussion Series. Washington, DC: Divisions of Research & Statistics and Monetary Affairs Federal Reserve Board.

Skiba, Paige Marta, and Jeremy Tobacman. 2019. "Do Payday Loans Cause Bankruptcy?" *Journal of Law and Economics* 62 (3): 485–519.

Stegman, Michael A. 2007. "Payday Lending." *Journal of Economic Perspectives* 21 (1): 169–90.

Wilson, Eric, and Eva Wolkowitz. 2017. "2017 Financially Underserved Market Size Study." Center for Financial Services Innovation. https://s3.amazonaws.com/cfsi-innovation-files-2018/wp-content/uploads/2017/04/27001546/2017-Market-Size-Report_FINAL_4.pdf.

Zinman, Jonathan. 2010. "Restricting Consumer Credit Access: Household Survey Evidence on Effects around the Oregon Rate Cap." *Journal of Banking & Finance* 34 (3): 546–56.

Financial Education

Financial education is an essential component in the efforts to reduce inequality in the United States. Unfortunately, it remains unclear which programs are useful, as results of various initiatives to that end have been mixed and difficult to determine. Current knowledge, socioeconomic status, demographic characteristics, financial attitude, past behavior, and many other factors affect an individual's need for financial education. Financial literacy is the ability to make appropriate financial decisions. Financial education can provide the knowledge and skills necessary to navigate increasingly complex financial products and to become financially literate.

The complexity of financial products currently available in the marketplace presents consumers with an incredibly diverse range of options, making it difficult for average individuals to choose the most appropriate and effective financial instruments for their personal situation. Many of the financial literacy resources and classes available today offer only a basic presentation of the fundamentals. The generalized financial education courses offered in schools have not produced significant results (Brown et al. 2016). Financial education, like most areas of study, cannot cover a narrow topic and expect the information to apply to every situation. Experts agree that when this information is taught in a manner that is easy to relate to specific situations, it is more likely to result in smart financial choices.

Experts also agree that the need for improvements in financial literacy is evident in any review of investment, spending, and savings trends across the United States. Due to questionable decisions and difficult circumstances, consumer habits are showing concerning trends. According to the Federal Reserve Bank of New York, total household debt in 2018 exceeded $13.5 trillion, surpassing the $12.7 trillion levels seen following the 2008 Great Recession. In 2018, college debt exceeded $1.5 trillion, and the U.S. national debt exceeded $21.5 trillion. The student loan default rate more than doubled between 2003 and 2011, and 40 percent of borrowers are expected to fall behind on their loans by 2023 (Nova 2018). The U.S. Department of Education releases official cohort default rates once per year.

In 2018, the U.S. Secretary of Education announced a default rate of 10.8 percent for loans with repayment schedules that began in 2015.

KEYS TO FINANCIAL LITERACY EDUCATION

The most effective and efficient financial literacy education is targeted, specific, practical, and repeated. According to the Consumer Financial Protection Bureau (CFPB), optimal results are achieved by applying the following five principles of financial education:

> Principle 1: Tailor information to the specific circumstances, challenges, goals, and situational factors of the individuals served. Avoid a one-size-fits-all approach.
> Principle 2: Provide just-in-time-information that is relevant and actionable to a specific situation or goal so that information and skills are more likely to be retained.
> Principle 3: Build generalizable skills, such as knowing where to find reliable information to make decisions and how to process information.
> Principle 4: Build on motivation by supporting people to focus on their own values and standards, to persevere in the face of challenges, and to build confidence that they can achieve their financial goals.
> Principle 5: Help create habits and systems so that it is easy to follow through on decisions.

Historically, financial literacy curricula and large-scale education efforts tend to view financial literacy in a vacuum, with very little consideration given to the social, political, and economic contexts affecting an individual's ability to maintain financial security and build wealth (Soroko 2015). Typically, these plans fail to give individuals the ability to effectively and efficiently address the financial issues affecting their lives. It is important to present information in a dynamic manner that can help consumers address specific financial issues. The instruction must address age, socioeconomic status, financial situation, and other unique needs of the individuals.

CONTEMPORARY LANDSCAPE OF FINANCIAL EDUCATION

While financial literacy education in the United States has been rising, its effectiveness remains unclear. Since 1957, various states have adopted mandates to include financial education in the curriculum of high school students (Bover, Hospido, and Villanueva 2018). The Council for Economic Education reviews the condition of financial education in the K-12 schools every two years. In 1998, when the reviews began, twenty-one states included personal finance in the state board educational standards, and one state required high school students to take a course. Today, forty-five states include personal finance in the state board standards, and seventeen states require high school students to take a course.

Efforts to measure the impact and adequacy of these programs are rare and have never been formalized. It is a widely held belief that more financial education leads to a better understanding of the economy, a greater propensity to save for retirement and emergencies, reduced personal debt, a lower likelihood of using high-cost methods of borrowing, and other desirable outcomes for consumers (Council for Economic Education 2018). However, there is very little empirical evidence to support these broad claims (Willis 2009).

The Fair and Accurate Credit Transactions Act of 2003 established the U.S. Financial Literacy and Education Commission. The mission of the Act was to spearhead the federal government's involvement in financial literacy education. In a 2006 report issued by the Commission, many claims were made about what financial literacy education could achieve, although the report also acknowledged that "there is little research on successful methods for financial education" (Willis 2009).

Many financial literacy programs target high school students because they are old enough to understand the underlying mathematical concepts and because many of those students are on the cusp of transitioning into worlds of increasingly independent saving and spending choices. Financial education programs, however, have also begun to include instruction in earlier grades. For example, in April 2015, the CFPB issued a report recommending that policy makers consider integrating financial education throughout the K-12 curriculum. According to the report, "[w]hen we start early with age-appropriate and relevant financial education and consistently reinforce those lessons throughout the K–12 years, we can give young people more chances to develop positive habits and behaviors" (CFPB 2015).

Research on cognitive development and economic understanding indicates that children can understand financial concepts as early as age twelve. Studies have found that experiential learning programs targeting elementary school students made a significant difference in financial knowledge, budgeting, socialization, and financial experiences after ten weeks of participation in the program (Batty et al. 2017). However, financial education that occurs earlier in life is forgotten more easily than education that occurs later in life, a phenomenon observed in some long-term studies on high school students (Brown et al. 2016).

Adult financial education tends to be more topical and targeted as opposed to providing a broad group of people with generalized education. Some state governments require debt counseling for people who declare bankruptcy, for example, and many community organizations offer classes on retirement planning, health care, and other programs focused on one financial budgeting area or another.

TYPES OF EDUCATION

Generalized classes, coaching, and targeted classes are the primary types of financial education. High school students often take generalized classes. This approach can become problematic when applied to a vulnerable population such as low-income families, who have very different financial needs and priorities than higher-income families do. Most financial literacy curricula do not address the unique challenges that these individuals face, instead opting for a prescriptive, one-size-fits-all approach (Soroko 2015).

Coaching is an individual approach to financial education in which consumers are paired with instructors whose goal is to help them accomplish their financial goals by tutoring them about various options and tools. Coaches can be financial professionals with a wealth of knowledge and experience, or they can be fellow citizens with training in motivation and empowerment (Loomis 2018). As opposed to generalized financial education, financial coaching is anchored in behavioral change instead of in transferring financial knowledge (Peeters et al. 2018). A study conducted by the U.S. Department of Housing and Urban Development found that counseling is an effective method to reduce foreclosure among distressed homeowners (Myhre and Watson 2017). According to a study of over 240,000 loans made after the Great Recession of 2008, clients who received mortgage counseling were 2.83 times more likely to receive a loan modification and were 70 percent less likely to re-default on a modified loan than were similar borrowers who did not receive counseling (Myhre and Watson 2017).

The third type of financial education involves a mixture of the two previous approaches. Small, targeted classes, where instruction occurs in a setting similar to group therapy can also be very effective. Targeted classes and coaching often produce similar results. Therefore, targeted classes are often preferable to coaching due to the lower use of resources and reduced costs (Peeters et al. 2018).

CURRICULAR CONTENT

In addition to the structure of financial education programs, the content of the programming is also a source of contention. The educational programs usually cover retirement planning, estate planning, investment planning, and other topics that are of particularly high interest to middle-income and wealthy constituencies (Soroko 2015). However, there is no consensus on which personal finance principles are universally necessary (Peeters et al. 2018). Unsurprisingly, studies have found a correlation between the content of programs and their effectiveness (Brown et al. 2016). For example, programs that had a greater focus on debt were associated with lower rates of default.

Determining the most effective content often depends upon the age, stage of life, and individual backgrounds of the participants. The cost of individualized programs has been a significant deterrent in offering targeted training to all populations in our schools, leaving the higher-risk populations without needed financial education.

FINANCIAL LITERACY FOR LOW-INCOME AMERICANS

People living in poverty are one of the most vulnerable populations and stand to benefit the most from financial literacy education. Unfortunately, participation rates are low, particularly among those with high need, and programs often fail to address the needs of low-income populations (Lara Ibarra, McKenzie, and Ruiz Ortega 2017; Willis 2009).

The basic premise behind offering financial education implies that poverty is an individualistic issue that can be solved with prudent financial decisions. "By making a client responsible for his or her financial destiny, this approach makes it appear as if the solution to poverty is discipline, agency, and access to credit, rather than a living wage, adequate social support or reparations to address centuries of racialized wealth dispossession" (Loomis 2018).

Poverty does not occur in a vacuum. There are complex social, political, and economic contexts affecting individuals' ability to maintain financial security and build wealth (Soroko 2015; Loomis 2018). These dimensions of poverty are not addressed in financial education programs. It would be difficult to adequately address poverty in financial education programs due to their limited scope. Financial education tailored to student populations whose financial education needs vary based on demographics is much more efficient and effective (McCormick 2008). For example, a program for urban low-income students may include an analysis of the benefits and drawbacks of payday loans in addition to other financial institutions and banking functions, allowing students to relate the discussion to familiar institutions.

RACE AND GENDER

An individual's racial, community, and gender identity have a complex impact on personal financial behavior. Many financial education programs subscribe to the false neutrality created by assuming there are no differences between participants in a program (Soroko 2015). A study examining racial differences in household spending, for instance, found that reducing spending, a common strategy suggested in coaching sessions, would not close the racial wealth gap between Black and white households (Loomis 2018). The reason for its ineffectiveness in this regard was that the individual behavior targeted by financial coaching is not the driving force behind income or wealth disparities.

Women consistently show lower levels of financial literacy throughout the world. Longer life spans, shorter work experience, and other factors increase the likelihood that women will become economically vulnerable and increase their need for financial education (Xu and Zia 2012). Older women in the United States, who are more susceptible to poverty after retirement because of longer life spans and lower lifetime earnings, are less financially literate than the older population as a whole. Currently, very few financial education programs focus on reaching such women and addressing their unique financial needs.

CONCLUSION

More research is needed to determine the best course of action when it comes to financial education. The majority of such programs currently in existence operate on the assumption that more education leads to improved financial behavior.

The current environment of financial literacy education is inadequate in a myriad of ways. First, many programs are generalized and focused on targeting younger groups. Although the content of these programs is not standardized, the majority of them focus on generic topics that may not apply to all participants. Even when applicable, the financial education classes taken in high school have limited lasting impact on students.

Promising research has shown that a curriculum focused on practical applications and financial attitudes can be more effective than teaching traditional financial education courses in high school (Batty et al. 2017). Teaching students financial attitudes and giving them a setting in which to apply those new concepts heighten engagement and build associations that last longer than a traditional lecture format.

Available financial resources used wisely can help navigate some financial decisions but tend to be too standardized. The importance of financial education that is delivered repeatedly through financial education programs is essential in addressing the lack of knowledge needed to address financial issues.

The world of finance is complex, driving consumers to make difficult decisions that impact the rest of their lives. Coaching can help consumers navigate these decisions. An impartial guide with a deep understanding of financial topics can help consumers make better decisions and become less susceptible to fraudulent and misleading practices.

Regardless of the program chosen, financial education remains an essential component in the efforts to reduce inequality in America. Educators must not look for history to define the future of financial literacy education but continue to move forward with their efforts, adapting methods and contents of instruction to each audience.

Ivan C. Roten, Madeline Hamiter, and Jarrod Johnston

Further Reading

Batty, Michael, Michael Collins, Collin O'Rourke, and Elizabeth Odders-White. 2017. "Experiential Financial Literacy: A Field Study of My Classroom Economy." Unpublished manuscript, April 25.

Bover, Olympia, Laura Hospido, and Ernesto Villanueva. 2018. "The Impact of High School Financial Education on Financial Knowledge and Choices: Evidence from a Randomized Trial in Spain." Banco de España Working Paper 1801.

Brown, Meta, John Grigsby, Wilbert van der Klaauw, Jaya Wen, and Basit Zafar. 2016. "Financial Education and the Debt Behavior of the Young." *Review of Financial Studies* 29 (9): 2490–2522.

CFPB (Consumer Financial Protection Bureau). 2015. "Advancing K–12 Financial Education: A Guide for Policymakers." https://www.consumerfinance.gov/data-research/research-reports/advancing-k-12-financial-education-a-guide-for-policymakers.

Council for Economic Education. 2018. "2018 Survey of the States." https://www.councilforeconed.org/survey-of-the-states-2020.

Lara Ibarra, Gabriel, David McKenzie, and Claudia Ruiz Ortega. 2017. "Learning the Impact of Financial Education When Take-Up Is Low." World Bank Policy Research Working Paper 8238.

Loomis, Jessa. 2018. "Rescaling and Reframing Poverty: Financial Coaching and the Pedagogical Spaces of Financial Inclusion in Boston, Massachusetts." *Geoforum* 95:143–52.

McCormick, Martha. 2008. "The Effectiveness of Youth Financial Education: A Review of the Literature." *Journal of Financial Counseling and Planning* 20 (1): 70–83.

Myhre, Marina, and Nicole Watson. 2017. "Housing Counseling Works." U.S. Department of Housing and Urban Development. https://www.huduser.gov/portal/publications/hsgfin/housing-counseling-works.html.

Nova, Annie. 2018. "Despite the Economic Recovery, Student Debtors 'Monster in the Closet' Has Only Worsened." CNBC, September 27.

Peeters, Nele, Kathinka Rijk, Barbara Soetens, Berenice Storms, and Koen Hermans. 2018. "A Systematic Literature Review to Identify Successful Elements for Financial Education and Counseling in Groups." *Journal of Consumer Affairs* 52 (2): 415–40.

Soroko, Agata. 2015. "Poverty in US and Canadian Financial Literacy Curriculum Frameworks: A Critical Discourse Analysis." PhD diss., Université d'Ottawa/University of Ottawa.

Willis, Lauren. 2009. "Evidence and Ideology in Assessing the Effectiveness of Financial Literacy Education." *San Diego Law Review* 46: 415–58.

Xu, Lisa, and Bilal Zia. 2012. "Financial Literacy around the World: An Overview of the Evidence with Practical Suggestions for the Way Forward." World Bank Policy Research Working Paper 6107.

SECTION IX

Public Policy

.

Cash Assistance to the Poor

Providing for the poor has always been a chief concern of government policy. Many different schemes have been conceived, the majority of which center around either "in-kind" transfers (provision of goods and services) or cash transfers, which typically involve regularly scheduled and ongoing payments. These transfers usually flow from individuals of higher socioeconomic status to those of lower. A cash transfer, in theory, is more efficient than an in-kind one—recipients can use cash to buy what they really need, instead of receiving in-kind transfers that may or may not be useful or needed. Three main paradigms exist for transferring income to those with less: social cash transfers, conditional cash transfers, and a universal basic income. A social cash transfer (or SCT) generally requires that recipients meet a certain description or set of parameters. These are often called *means-tested* programs. For instance, some SCTs restrict eligibility to those below a maximum income level, and others require that a family contain a specified number of children. These programs can also scale with the selection factors. For example, the cash transfer value could increase as income decreases, or increase as the number of children increases. Social cash transfer programs prioritize groups that need income assistance the most.

Conditional cash transfers (or CCTs) resemble SCTs, but they are conditional on some action or set of actions being fulfilled by the recipient. For instance, a CCT for low-income adults might be predicated on a work requirement. Similarly, a CCT for families with children might set a requirement that those children receive some level or form of education before any cash transfers become available.

The third broad category is the universal basic income (or UBI). Unlike the two preceding models, the UBI has no requirements. Largely theoretical and uncommon throughout history, a UBI distributes cash to an entire population. Many UBI models imagine a monthly system in which every adult receives a set amount of money regardless of any other circumstances.

All these programs exist to improve the quality of life for the poor, accelerate the economic growth of developing countries, or encourage risk taking and entrepreneurialism by providing additional economic security. The programs can also be geared toward reducing wealth inequalities. Of the 142 countries in the World Bank ASPIRE database, 70 percent have some form of SCT, and 43 percent have a CCT (Ivaschenko et al. 2018). Depending on the definition one uses, there are between 10 and 15 UBI experiments ongoing in the world today (Basic Income Earth Network n.d.).

The UBI model is less common and has been tested in fewer iterations. It is currently receiving a great deal of attention due to the potential for a UBI to reduce the persistent and growing divide between the rich and poor. The concept and theory have existed for some time, and many countries and cultures have experimented with or piloted systems resembling a basic income. As of yet, however, none has actually set a basic income and paid that amount, unconditionally, to every citizen.

HISTORY OF CASH TRANSFERS

Income assistance systems for the poor existed in countless ancient civilizations for centuries, and they persist today in the modern world. Ancient Semitic cultures—particularly Hebrews, whose influence through monotheistic texts steered much of Western development—displayed diverse systems to sustain the poor and needy. Religious texts can influence cultures as they shape their governments, and this tendency can be seen in the way governments treat their poor as well.

Exodus 22:25 stipulates that a loan made to any poor individual must be without interest. Because interest can further impoverish the borrower, the amount received for a loan was to be the amount returned, regardless of the maturity date of the loan. The chapter further states, in verses 26 and 27, that cloaks pledged as collateral in such a loan (a commonly used item in the culture) should be returned in the evening, because pledge or not, poor individuals might not have any other protection from the cold and winds. This law serves as a fine introduction to the kind of economic safety nets that the Hebrew people had; while it does not define "poor" or formally establish a system, it propagates heightened kindness and courtesy on behalf of poorer individuals.

Another ancient state with a large, clear impact on Western culture, the Roman Empire, made use of government-organized wealth transfers. The Roman grain dole, or *cura annonae*, is one notable example. In the middle of the final century BCE, the city of Rome began a public system for the distribution of grain. Perhaps prompted by the philosophy of achieving political success by satiating the public with consumption goods, the dole nonetheless served as a kind of predecessor to the UBI model. Heads of households received grain (wheat and barley) rations for their households on a monthly basis. Historians argue over the exact amount of grain dispersed to households, but most estimates seem to indicate that the supply of grain was sufficient to sustain life (Erdkamp 2013). Government provision of essential goods, such as grain, became the centerpiece of public opinion and election success, and they became a staple of Roman culture (Rickman 1980). Historians do not agree on the outcomes of the policy, however. Some argue that the unprecedented population of the city and its heavy reliance on imported grain left the private market underequipped for food supply; government distribution was the only way to sustain the citizens (Aly 2017). Others argue that the dole helped cause the empire's collapse by tying public sentiment to government provisions, creating a crippling tax burden on the middle class, and reducing the productivity of citizens (Bartlett 1994).

Steeped deeply in Jewish and Roman culture, the early Christian Church enacted similar standards for treatment of the poor. For millennia, Christian doctrine has expected Christians to tithe, or donate 10 percent of their income. It has also dictated that the portion of that tithe that does not fund the church should fund charities with an almost exclusive emphasis on helping the poor (Smith, Emerson, and Snell 2008). Some of the strongest and most explicit poor-relief efforts reveal themselves in the records of Saint John Chrysostom, who was the archbishop of Constantinople at the end of the fourth century. The works he authored reveal a strong Christian movement toward respect for and donation to the poor. He indicated that poverty ran rampant and urged wealthy Christians to offer direct donations to the impoverished in their communities (Sitzler 2009).

In the late eighteenth century, much of England adopted the Speenhamland system, a model of poor relief that resembled the grain dole in some ways (Hammond and Hammond 1912). In this time period, aggressive money printing, seigniorage (profits realized by governments when the face value of a currency exceeds the cost of producing it), and implicit inflation taxes funded many aspects of the Napoleonic and Revolutionary wars. Bread prices soared, and wages were slow to adjust. In the town of Speenhamland, local government officials produced legislation that set the wages of laborers as a multiple of the price of bread. The system quickly spread across southern England and accelerated wage growth to match inflation (or at least the price of a single vital good). This system differs from the *cura annonae* in that the guarantee of subsistence is predicated on employment. It does bear some resemblance to a UBI, and many attempts at understanding how UBI might work are educated by studies of the Speenhamland system (Spicker, Leguizamon, and Gordon 2007).

In the United States, most modern poor relief programs can trace their origins to President Franklin D. Roosevelt's New Deal programs during and immediately following the Great Depression of the 1930s. Roosevelt played a large part in starting the United States' Social Security system, and he brought about many federal programs to spend tax revenues on food and jobs for poor Americans. The programs evolved throughout the twentieth century, and they remain at the center of much political discussion and debate in the United States.

The most prominent cash assistance programs in the United States today are Temporary Assistance for Needy Families (TANF, colloquially known as "welfare"), the Earned Income Tax Credit (EITC/EIC), and Supplemental Security Income (SSI). The TANF program is a means-tested, conditional cash transfer (CCT) that provides cash assistance (routed through state agencies) to families experiencing hardship. As a CCT, this program has a work and/or job search requirement, and recipients are limited to twenty-four consecutive months of welfare and sixty months over a lifetime (U.S. Federal Government 2019).

After undertaking a sweeping review of the literature regarding TANF, economist James P. Ziliak concluded that work increased and welfare usage decreased as compared to earlier welfare programs (Ziliak 2016). However, real incomes and health outcomes appear to have worsened. Other scholars, for example, found that the health of women receiving TANF is markedly worse than those not receiving it, even after controlling for other factors. They posit that the work requirement forces females into strenuous jobs that may deteriorate health (Kaplan et al. 2005).

The EITC is also a means-tested CCT, paid through a tax refund, that encourages individuals to seek gainful employment. For those that qualify, the EITC first increases as other wages increase, then it plateaus, and then it slowly decreases as a household's income approaches the income limit. This approach means that individuals are "rewarded" for earning higher wages with a higher EITC payment, and even over the range in which it is decreasing, it is always preferable for the household to have one extra dollar of income. Unlike other cash assistance programs, there is no point where households are "punished" for earning more by the removal of the credit (IRS 2018).

Research shows that the EITC, unlike TANF, increases health outcomes for recipients and their families. Furthermore, it encourages single mothers to work, decreases the number of married mothers working, and has no effect on men (Nichols and Rothstein 2016). Child educational outcomes have been shown to improve with each additional $1,000 of credit received. Another interesting outcome of research on the EITC is that individuals prefer (have larger effects from) a single, lump-sum transfer (such as the EITC) as opposed to recurring payments (such as TANF).

Finally, SSI is a federal social cash transfer and is aimed at aged, blind, or disabled individuals who also have limited income or resources. This is the only current cash assistance program in the United States with no job requirement. Additionally, SSI includes work incentives for persons with disabilities (U.S. Federal Government 2019).

The research on SSI indicates that the program does support some of the United States' most vulnerable citizens by decreasing poverty and increasing incomes (Duggan, Kearney, and Rennane 2016). However, certain features of the program (such as asset and income limits) discourage savings and work, and encourage overconsumption. Particularly difficult are cases of parents who are unwilling to work more because of a fear that a child with a disability in their home will stop receiving benefits. These researchers conclude that the venerable program should be adjusted to eliminate these troublesome incentives.

Given the problems with the current slate of cash assistance programs in the United States, renewed interest has been given to another idea—the universal basic income (UBI).

UNIVERSAL BASIC INCOME THROUGH HISTORY

The idea of a universal basic income is not new, and it did not form in a vacuum. In 1516, the philosopher Thomas Moore published *Utopia*, wherein he suggested that providing everyone access to livelihood was the best way to combat thievery. Moore's contemporary, Juan Luis Vives, the "Father of Modern Psychology," proposed a series of poor-relief policies to the mayor of Bruges in *On Assistance to the Poor*. Among them, he offered that "even those who have dissipated their fortunes in dissolute living . . . should be given food." He believed that if the rich could live off their assets without laboring, the laboring poor should not be allowed to starve.

Nearly three centuries later, the French Revolution and its thinkers influenced Thomas Paine to step even closer to the true basic income model. Paine believed that French poor-relief was bureaucratic and inefficient. In *The Rights of Man*, he suggested replacing the then-current system with cash payments to the elderly and to the parents of young children. He claimed that the payments were not charity but a right (King and Marangos 2006). He reasoned that since rich and poor alike pay taxes, paying families and the elderly merely functioned as a dividend on their tax payment "investment." This proposal was not universal, per se, as it did not offer payments to all citizens. However, it is notable because it was unconditional; all individuals in the target group would receive a payment.

A few years later, Paine proposed something even closer to a true UBI, in *Agrarian Justice* (1797). Paine reasoned that society collectively owns all of nature. However, because of his strong belief in individual property rights, Paine clarified that collective ownership should not preclude "landowners" from exercising an exclusive right to utilize certain tracts of land. Rather, he posed an argument that these landowners should pay a rent to the community to compensate for the natural inheritance nonlandowners were not receiving. He said that this rent payment should go into a pool, and each person should receive a share when they reached adulthood. The remainder would go to the handicapped and elderly as an annual pension. Any eligible recipient who did not need the money could donate the share back into the pool. Here, Paine suggested a true universal, unconditional payment. Today's proponents of UBI generally envision periodic payments, as Paine suggested for the handicapped and elderly, to all members of society.

The famous University of Chicago economist Milton Friedman posited in *Capitalism and Freedom* (1962) that society would benefit from replacing all welfare programs with a simple negative income tax (NIT). Friedman's proposed NIT works similarly to the UBI. In the NIT model, the state sets an income threshold. Suppose, for example, the income threshold was $30,000, and the tax rate was 10 percent. Individuals making exactly $30,000 per year would pay no taxes. For every dollar earned above the threshold, the tax rate would apply. In our example, an individual who earned $40,000 would pay $1,000 in taxes (i.e., 10 percent of the $10,000 earned above the threshold). An individual earning only $20,000, however, would have a tax liability of *negative* $1,000 and would receive this amount as a payment. Since the individual is earning $10,000 less than the threshold, the individual receives 10 percent of that shortfall. In our example, someone without any income would receive $3,000 per year in negative income tax from the government.

Unlike UBI, the NIT does not provide a supplement to incomes at or above the threshold. Like UBI, it is uniform, it guarantees a minimum income, and it is unconditional.

In his last book, *Where Do We Go from Here* (1967), Martin Luther King Jr. put his voice behind UBI. King suggested that most poor assistance programs fail because they target poverty indirectly. He claimed that guaranteed income, as he called it, is superior because it is simple and cannot be inhibited by bureaucracy. King's take on UBI was markedly progressive. He proposed that the basic income level should be set at the median of citizens' income levels and adjusted to growth at regular intervals.

From 1974 to 1979, the town of Dauphin in Manitoba, Canada, was the location of a UBI "saturation site," in other words, a location where everyone received a basic income and poverty was completely eliminated. Although this program (which was named *Mincome*) ended without a formal analysis, Forget (2011) found significant increases in the health and welfare of the population using health-care data. Calnitsky and Latner (2017), however, found an 11-percentage-point decrease in labor force participation, which supported fears expressed by critics that UBI reduces the incentive to work.

Richard Nixon, who served as president of the United States from 1969 until his resignation in 1974, considered implementing a UBI during his tenure. His administration orchestrated the New Jersey Graduated Work Incentive Experiment and experiments in other states that resembled the basic income model (Watts 1971). In early December 1969, Nixon gave a speech to a food, nutrition, and health conference at the White House wherein he urged support for legislation to provide basic income to American families (Nixon 1969). He asserted that the best way to combat hunger in America was to give money to the hungry rather than provide them food on a schedule. He desired a system that provided money without grouping families or examining the circumstances of their poverty. Nixon's proposal took form as the Family Assistance Plan but never made it through Congress, and Nixon himself eventually stopped advocating the idea. The UBI model received little attention in U.S. political and economic discussions for decades afterward.

UBI VERSUS OTHER CASH TRANSFERS

What UBI offers that other forms of cash transfers do not is a partial solution to the argument that cash transfers reduce the incentive to work. This is because the payments continue to be paid to individuals at every level of income. Working more, or acquiring a higher-paying job, does not cause one to be disqualified from receiving the UBI payment. In other systems, an escape from poverty is actually "punished" by the reduction or removal of the cash transfer. In essence, it may seem as if the government is "paying" or "rewarding" people who stay poor. Thus many thinkers see UBI as the most market-friendly, incentive-neutral cash transfer system.

Additionally, a simple UBI involves fewer administrative costs than do the welfare programs found in many countries today. The cash transfer is not conditional on a certain outcome, so the administrative bureaucracy is greatly lessened. Furthermore, UBI can be easily distributed because each citizen receives the same sum. This leads to less error than that which occurs when different individuals receive different amounts based on their qualifications and circumstances.

That same fact, however, highlights a potential weakness to UBI as compared to the other cash transfer systems. If the goal of a cash transfer is only to raise the standard of living of the poorest individuals, then providing a large payment to the poorest and little, if anything, to the richest is the most effective solution—even though, as previously mentioned, this scheme provides a disincentive to working hard.

UBI can be a superior alternative to many countries' existing poor-relief programs. It requires less oversight. It does not persuade against work. It encourages risk taking and entrepreneurialism. On the other hand, UBI can be a supplement to current programs. The poor could use basic income payments to consume in any way they please, and they could live more comfortably with the continued support of existing poor relief systems.

There also exist compelling arguments against UBI. Some argue that if it aims to improve quality of life for poorer people, it should be targeted at poorer people only. Others argue that it is too expensive, and that the taxes or spending cuts necessary to implement a UBI would cost more than the program is worth. Perhaps, then, it could be said that UBI's goal is more akin to establishing a common minimum standard than establishing the highest possible minimum. The desirability of such a system is strongly dependent on one's values.

PROPONENTS OF UBI

The debate surrounding UBI intensified in the 2010s. The increasing attention has brought many proponents to the idea—including some famous billionaire entrepreneurs who cite growing trends of economic inequality and forecast substantial job losses in decades to come as a result of further advances in AI (artificial intelligence) and automation (Weller 2017). Among the ranks are Mark Zuckerberg and Chris Hughes, cofounders of Facebook; Elon Musk, the CEO of SpaceX and Tesla; Pierre Omidyar, the founder of eBay; and Richard Branson, the founder and CEO of Virgin Group.

Zuckerberg believes that securing people's necessities facilitates creativity and invention, boosting innovation and progress. In his commencement address to Harvard's Spring 2017 graduating class, Zuckerberg asserted that he would not have created Facebook if he had not felt secure in case of its failure (Zuckerberg 2017). He said he never would have started coding and programming in high school if his parents had needed him to bring home income. For these reasons, Zuckerberg argues that UBI is a necessary part of the world's future, and a morally beneficial proposal.

Zuckerberg's former colleague at Facebook, Chris Hughes, advocates for a slightly different system, for slightly different reasons. In his book *Fair Shot*, Hughes proposes a tax increase for the wealthiest Americans to fund a system that pays $500 per month to workers making $50,000 or less (Hughes 2018). Hughes makes a point of calling it a guaranteed income rather than a UBI to emphasize the differences—most notably, that not all citizens are being paid. Hughes's plan sets two requirements for recipients: they must work, and they must bring home $50,000 or less. Hughes also notes that his proposal includes a broadened definition of "work." He says that the work requirement could include unpaid care work, such as childcare or eldercare. It could also include training and formal degree studies. He ultimately suggests that any activities that benefit society should be called "work."

Hughes focuses on different reasons to advocate for his guaranteed income. He says he worked hard to make Facebook a success, but the rewards he earned were disproportionately high. He acknowledges that his experience is unusual but contends that most of the very wealthy—including the most industrious and talented of them—receive excessive windfalls for their efforts. He believes that the economy is unfairly good to the rich. His focus is not on stimulating innovation and economic growth. He wants to change the economy to balance the incentive structure for a broader population of workers.

Elon Musk advocates the UBI for still different reasons. Musk claims that both automation and artificial intelligence (AI) will displace so many jobs that there will be no alternative. Unemployment will rise until governments have no option but to pay citizens for their sustenance. Musk, who does voice concerns about the negative effect that UBI might have on workers' incentives, projects that automation and AI will make goods so cheap that implementing a UBI will cost much less than many suspect. He argues that funding everyone's barest needs will be inexpensive enough that wealthy countries should at least try (Clifford 2018).

Richard Branson supports UBI for a similar rationale. He believes that when wealthy countries can afford to sustain their citizens, it becomes imperative to do so. He is especially interested in UBI experiments and research, given the growing ubiquity of automation and AI. In his view, it may be that research will show UBI to be a good solution. Alternatively, UBI may be found wanting. Branson is optimistic about UBI because he thinks it could provide self-esteem to strugglers and encourage them to pursue their entrepreneurial interests (Branson 2017).

RESEARCH ON UBI

UBI's newfound attention has brought it more than famous supporters. It has also spurred new research and experiments. Basic income pilots currently exist, or have existed until very recently, in Canada, Finland, Kenya, the United States, Spain, Brazil, Uganda, and the Netherlands, to name a few locations. Most of these are funded by the government, but some are funded by private, charitable organizations.

Some researchers have looked to the Alaska Permanent Fund to find readily available information on UBI's effects. The Alaska Permanent Fund, which was established in 1976, pools revenues from Alaska's natural resources and pays an annual dividend from that pool to every citizen (O'Brien and Olson 1990). Since the Alaskan dividend has been in existence for more than four decades, researchers can gather long, time-series data and analyze its long-run effects. However, it is also smaller than most UBI proposals, and it is paid out less frequently. As a result, it may not imitate the effects of many UBI proposals.

The economists Damon Jones and Ioana Marinescu (2018) looked at the effects of the dividend on Alaskan labor. Their findings indicate a negligible change in employment and labor participation. That is, people did not work less after receiving the payment. They suggest the real effect of a UBI on the labor market would depend on the source of its funds and the way it interacts with existing welfare programs.

Finland's social insurance institution Kela recently began a UBI experiment of its own. The experiment targeted two thousand Finnish citizens who received unemployment insurance and randomly assigned some of them to a payment of 560 euros per month (Kela 2016). The experiment aimed to test the employment differences between UBI and unemployment benefits. The Finnish government is making efforts to simplify its welfare system and increase the incentive to find work. Kela administrators hoped to discover that UBI recipients show a higher level of employment. By excluding employed citizens, the experiment could test the work incentive more closely, but it could not provide as much useful information about the other effects of a true UBI. This experiment ended on December 31, 2018, and analysis occured in two reports, published in 2019 and 2020. Economists found that the recipients of the basic income reported higher rates of economic and mental well-being than their peers in the control group. Importantly, they also reported that the higher rate of employment observed among the basic income recipients was too small to conclude that replacing existing unemployment benefits with a basic income would result in higher employment rates.

The government of Ontario, Canada, recently administered the Ontario Basic Income Pilot. Despite its name, the pilot was structured like the negative income tax model. Beneficiaries received a cash transfer to ensure their income is at a minimum level. For those who did not earn income, the minimum level was set at 75 percent of the government's "Low Income Measure." For wage earners, the level was decremented by fifty cents for every dollar of earned income. Unlike the Finnish experiment, the Canadian pilot included employed citizens and excluded citizens living on an annual income above Can$34,000 (Segal 2016). This experiment could indicate the standard of living and consumption changes caused by a UBI better than the Finnish experiment could, but it could not indicate employment changes as accurately. Unfortunately, after the Ontario Government changed party hands in early 2019, the pilot was cut short, and the planned analysis was canceled.

While that Canadian and Finnish experiments were well poised to provide new information about some major dimensions of a UBI, their results provide little new information. The Finnish experiment's tentative conclusion that UBI could improve economic and mental well-being of recipients is not groundbreaking. Meanwhile, the lack of strong conclusion about the employment affects, and the complete cancellation of the analysis portion of the Ontario pilot leaves basic income research with a continued lack of information.

The effect of policy decisions, such as those mentioned above, is also determined by the way the program is administered. De Wispelaere and Stirton (2017) explain that the structure of administration (the source of the money, the frequency, method of receipt, etc.) can affect the outcomes, but these concerns are often ignored.

RESEARCH ON OTHER FORMS OF CASH TRANSFERS

There are approximately 175 countries worldwide with some sort of SCT or CCT. In a sweeping review published in 2017, researchers found no systematic evidence that cash transfers discourage work. They analyzed evidence from programs in Argentina, Brazil, Cambodia, China, Colombia, Mexico, Pakistan, Philippines, and Zambia, to name a few locations (Banerjee et al. 2017).

One of the most famous cash transfer programs to date is Mexico's PROGRESA (now called *Oportunidades*). This CCT pays a certain amount of cash to the mother of a household if the children attend school and visit a health clinic for a specified number of checkups. Studies have found that the program did not reduce the probability of work and that it resulted in children going to school for an additional 1.5 years on average—an increased level of education associated with a number of positive household and economic outcomes (Parker and Skoufias 2000; Parker and Vogl 2018).

The success of PROGRESA spawned a wave of similar cash transfer programs. For example, Opportunity NYC decreased food insufficiency by 33 percent and overall poverty by 16 percent among enrollees in New York City (Riccio 2010). A review of such programs in developing countries found that expenditures on food increased in twenty-two of thirty-one transfer programs. Educational attendance went up as well, but educational outcomes, on average, did not. Diet diversity increased, and malnourishment, on average, decreased (Bastagli et al. 2016).

CONCLUSION

Cash transfers have been used throughout history to aid the world's poor. Empirical evidence has shown that they do not discourage work, especially when designed as a UBI. Most socioeconomic indicators, such as health, education, and nutrition, show positive increases for individuals enrolled in these programs.

The UBI model of cash transfer is currently enjoying a great deal of popularity among policy makers, researchers, and even famous individuals. While the UBI targets poverty less directly than many means-tested welfare programs, it theoretically provides a stronger incentive to work. It is simpler than most welfare programs but could likely be more expensive. UBI has the potential to be the solution for employment problems caused by automation and artificial intelligence and could encourage people to be innovative and entrepreneurial.

Ultimately, whether the question is what kind of cash transfer program to implement or whether to implement any system at all, the deciding factor is likely to be the values of the voters. In countries that consider ambition the best solution to poverty, government social programs are less supportive in general than their counterparts in countries that see poverty as a strictly institutional problem (Banerjee et al. 2017). This same narrative plays out in the discussion surrounding cash transfers as well. For individuals and populations, however, that believe it is the government's role to reduce poverty, cash transfers provide a promising policy option.

Justin Jarvis and Garrett Lee Fiegenbaum

Further Reading

Aly, Samuel. 2017. "The Gracchi and the Era of Grain Reform in Ancient Rome." *Tenor of Our Times* 6, article 6.

Banerjee, Abhijit V., Rema Hanna, Gabriel E. Kreindler, and Benjamin A. Olken. 2017. "Debunking the Stereotype of the Lazy Welfare Recipient: Evidence from Cash Transfer Programs." *World Bank Research Observer* 32, no. 2 (August): 155–84. https://doi.org/10.1093/wbro/lkx002.

Bartlett, Bruce. 1994. "How Excessive Government Killed Ancient Rome." *Cato Journal* 14, no. 2 (Fall): 287–303.

Basic Income Earth Network. n.d. "Research Depository." https://basicincome.org/research/research-depository.

Bastagli, Francesca, Jessica Hagen-Zanker, Luke Harman, Georgina Sturge, Valentina Barca, Tanja Schmidt, and Luca Pellerano. 2016. *Cash Transfers: What Does the Evidence Say? A Rigorous Review of Programme Impact and of the Role of Design and Implementation Features.* London: Overseas Development Institute.

Bott, Claire. 2017. "Richard Branson Supports UBI." *Basic Income Earth Network.* https://basicincome.org/news/2017/08/richard-branson-supports-ubi.

Branson, Richard. 2017. "Experimenting with Universal Basic Income." Virgin.com. https://www.virgin.com/richard-branson/experimenting-universal-basic-income.

Calnitsky, David, and Jonathan P. Latner. 2017. "Basic Income in a Small Town: Understanding the Elusive Effects on Work." *Social Problems* 64, no.3 (August): 373–97. https://doi.org/10.1093/socpro/spw040.

Clifford, Catherine. 2018. "Elon Musk: Automated Jobs Could Make UBI Cash Handouts Necessary." CNBC. https://www.cnbc.com/2018/06/18/elon-musk-automated-jobs-could-make-ubi-cash-handouts-necessary.html.

De Wispelaere, Jurgen, and Lindsay Stirton. 2017. "When Basic Income Meets Professor Pangloss: Ignoring Public Administration and Its Perils." *Political Quarterly* 88:298–305.

Duggan, Mark, Melissa S. Kearney, and Stephanie Rennane. 2016. "The Supplemental Security Income Program." In *Economics of Means-Tested Transfer Programs in the United States, Volume 2*, edited by Robert Moffitt, 1–58. Chicago: University of Chicago Press.

Erdkamp, Paul. 2013. "The Food Supply of the Capital." In *The Cambridge Companion to Ancient Rome*, 262–64. Cambridge: Cambridge University Press.

Forget, Evelyn. 2011. "The Town with No Poverty." Working paper, University of Manitoba. http://nccdh.ca/images/uploads/comments/forget-cea_(2).pdf.

Friedman, Milton. 1962. *Capitalism and Freedom.* Chicago: University of Chicago Press.

Hammond, J. L., and Barbara Hammond. 1912. *The Village Labourer 1760–1832.* London: Longman Green & Co.

Hughes, Chris. 2018. *Fair Shot.* New York: Bloomsbury Publishing.

IRS (Internal Revenue Service). U.S. Department of the Treasury. 2018. *Publication 596: Earned Income Credit.* https://www.irs.gov/pub/irs-pdf/p596.pdf.

Ivaschenko, Oleksiy, Claudia P. Rodriguez Alas, Marina Novikova, Carolina Romero Robayo, Thomas Vaughan Bowen, and Linghui Zhu. 2018. *The State of Social Safety Nets 2018 (English).* Washington, DC: World Bank Group. http://documents.worldbank.org/curated/en/427871521040513398/The-state-of-social-safety-nets-2018.

Jones, Damon, and Ioana Elena Marinescu. 2018. "The Labor Market Impacts of Universal and Permanent Cash Transfers: Evidence from the Alaska Permanent Fund." SSRN working paper. https://ssrn.com/abstract=3118343.

Kaplan, George A., Kristine Siefert, Nalini Ranjit, Trivellore E. Raghunathan, Elizabeth A. Young, Diem Tran, Sandra Danziger, Susan Hudson, John W. Lynch, and Richard Tolman. 2005. "The Health of Poor Women under Welfare Reform." *American Journal of Public Health* 95 (7): 1252–58.

Kela, Social Insurance Institution of Finland. 2016. "From Idea to Experiment. Report on Universal Basic Income Experiment in Finland." Working paper 106. http://hdl.handle.net/10138/167728.

King, J. E., and John Marangos. 2006. "Two Arguments for Basic Income: Thomas Paine (1737–1809) and Thomas Spence (1750–1814)." *History of Economic Ideas* 14 (1): 55–71.

King, Martin Luther, Jr. 1967. *Where Do We Go from Here: Chaos or Community?* Boston: Beacon Press.

Marsh, Frank Burr. 1922. "In Defense of the Corn-Dole." *Classical Journal* 22:10–25.

Moore, Thomas, Saint. 1989. *Utopia.* Edited by George M. Logan and Robert M. Adams. Cambridge: Cambridge University Press.

Mott, Stephen, and Ronald J. Sider. 2000. "Economic Justice: A Biblical Paradigm." *Transformation* 17 (2): 50–63.

Nichols, Austin, and Jesse Rothstein. 2016. "The Earned Income Tax Credit." In *Economics of Means-Tested Transfer Programs in the United States, Volume 1*, edited by Robert Moffitt, 137–218. Chicago: University of Chicago Press.

Nixon, Richard M. 1969. "Remarks of the President." Speech, White House Conference on Food, Nutrition, Health, December 2, 1969. Washington, DC.

O'Brien, J. P., and D. O. Olson. 1990. "The Alaska Permanent Fund and Dividend Distribution Program." *Public Finance Quarterly* 18:139–56.

Paine, Thomas. 1797. *Agrarian Justice.* Self-published.

Parker, Susan W., and E. Skoufias. 2000. *The Impact of PROGRESA on Work, Leisure, and Time Allocation.* Washington, DC: International Food Policy Research Institute (IFPRI).

Parker, Susan W., and Tom Vogl. 2018. "Do Conditional Cash Transfers Improve Economic Outcomes in the Next Generation? Evidence from Mexico." NBER Working Paper 24303. National Bureau of Economic Research. https://ideas.repec.org/p/nbr/nberwo/24303.html.

Rawlings, Laura B., and Gloria M. Rubio. 2005. "Evaluating the Impact of Conditional Cash Transfer Programs." *World Bank Research Observer* 20 (1): 29–55.

Riccio, James. 2010. "Sharing Lessons from the First Conditional Cash Transfer Program in the United States." University of Michigan: National Poverty Center. http://www.npc.umich.edu/publications/policy_briefs/brief22/policybrief22.pdf.

Rickman, G. E. 1980. "The Grain Trade under the Roman Empire." *Memoirs from the American Academy in Rome* 36: 261–75.

Segal, Hugh D. 2016. "Finding a Better Way: A Basic Income Pilot Project for Ontario." Ontario Government. https://www.ontario.ca/page/finding-better-way-basic-income-pilot-project-ontario#section-8.

Sitzler, Silke. 2009. "Identity: The Indigent and the Wealthy in the Homilies of John Chrysostom." *Vigiliae Christianae* 63 (5): 468–79.

Smith, Christian, Michael O. Emerson, and Patricia Snell. 2008. *Passing the Plate: Why American Christians Don't Give Away More Money.* New York: Oxford University Press.

Spicker, P., A. Leguizamon, and D. Gordon, eds. 2007. "Speenhamland System." In *Poverty: An International Glossary.* 2d ed, 188. London: Zed Books.

U.S. Federal Government. 2019. "Government Benefits." https://www.usa.gov/benefits #item-213996.

Vives, Juan Luis. 1999. *On Assistance to the Poor.* Toronto: University of Toronto Press.

Watts, Harold W. 1971. "The Graduated Work Incentive Experiments: Current Progress." *American Economic Review* 61 (2): 15–21.

Weller, Chris. 2017. "Entrepreneurs Who Have Endorsed Universal Basic Income." *Business Insider.* https://www.businessinsider.com/entrepreneurs-endorsing-universal -basic-income-2017-3#pierre-omidyar-2.

Ziliak, James P. 2016. "Temporary Assistance for Needy Families." In *Economics of Means-Tested Transfer Programs in the United States, Volume 1*, edited by Robert Moffitt, 303–393. Chicago IL: University of Chicago Press.

Zuckerberg, Mark. 2017. Commencement Address, May 25. Harvard University, Cambridge Massachusetts.

Children and Family Policy

Family policies, or the lack thereof, play a critical role in shaping employment, income, and gender inequalities. These inequalities affect children's access to quality childcare, adequate nutrition, educational opportunities, safe housing, and a stable family environment. These factors, in turn, have a substantial influence on child well-being, shaping children's exposure to adverse life events and chronic conditions that impact their physical and mental health as well as long-term economic outcomes. A consideration of the dominant policies that have been designed to assist families with children is, therefore, critical for understanding the structure and persistence of larger social and economic inequalities.

WHAT IS FAMILY POLICY?

There is no single family policy. Rather, family policy includes a wide range of employment and economic policies, programs, and laws that support families and caregiving. Consequently, many scholars focus on family policy "regimes" (Engster and Stensöta 2011), "packages" (Meyers, Gornick, and Peck 2001), or "portfolios" (Daly and Ferragina 2018) to describe the collections of policies intended to support families with dependent children. Examining the full set of supports available, rather than a single policy, is useful, because policies can work in competing or supplementary ways (Thévenon and Luci 2012). For example, some family policies encourage parental employment, while others support unpaid family caregiving (O'Connor, Orloff, and Shaver 1999). Implementing complementary family policies helps prevent gaps in support for families (Adema 2012). While a wide variety of social policies impact families, family policy scholars tend to focus on those that provide direct assistance to families with children or working parents, such as child tax benefits, parental leave policies, and childcare assistance.

Comparative research is helpful for imagining family policy possibilities and also for assessing their impacts on social inequalities, family functioning, and child well-being. Scholars have generally identified three to five distinct, country-level family policy regimes (Gauthier 2002; Korpi 2000; Thévenon 2011). Dual-earner regimes (or social democratic, which includes mostly Nordic countries) encourage women's employment participation through generous support of paid parental leave and public childcare programs. General family support regimes (or conservative, which includes mostly continental European countries) support women's caregiving through generous cash and tax benefits for families with children but provide less support for paid parental leave and public childcare services. Low family support regimes (or neoliberal, typically consisting of Anglo-Saxon countries) lack family policies altogether or provide low levels of support, are more market oriented in the provision of services, and encourage families to rely on kinship networks to meet needs (Engster and Stensöta 2011).

The United States is consistently placed with low family support or market-oriented policy regimes due to the lack of federal paid parental leave and comparatively minimal investments in childcare supports that generally prevail within its borders (Olivetti and Petrongolo 2017). Nevertheless, there is quite a bit of variability across U.S. states in the inclusion criteria and benefit levels of family policies. States have been given a great deal of power in determining how they will administer federal programs and funding, and some provide much more assistance in the realms of childcare and family support than others do. In fact, five state-level family policy clusters have been identified with meaningful variations in level of income support, nutrition assistance and childcare benefits, and tax policy (Meyers, Gornick, and Peck 2001). These policy variations contribute to significant disparities in a wide range of child outcomes—especially those related to family economic well-being and health—across the states (O'Hare et al. 2013).

HOW DO FAMILY POLICY REGIMES IMPACT CHILD WELL-BEING?

Family policy objectives include combating child poverty and enhancing child well-being (Adema 2012) as well as reducing the gap in standard of living between households with children and those without (Thévenon and Luci 2012). Policy regimes accomplish this by socializing the cost of children through reducing barriers to employment and providing income supports for families with children (Mills, Compton, and Golden 2011). Regimes that provide more support for families through cash assistance, paid parenting leaves, and public childcare programs and funding show significantly better outcomes for children, including reduced child poverty and mortality (Kangas and Palme 2000; Ferrarini and Norström 2010). Dual-earner regimes tend to have the lowest levels of child poverty and mortality, whereas low family support regimes have the highest levels of child poverty and mortality (Engster and Stensöta 2011). Children in countries with more generous family support policies also rate higher on subjective measures of well-being, reporting better emotional health and more satisfaction with school life and relationships (Mínguez 2017).

Cross-national research shows countries with higher levels of income inequality have lower levels of child well-being. This same phenomenon is evident within countries; as income inequality increases within a nation, overall child well-being declines (Pickett and Wilkinson 2015). Family policies such as paid leave and public childcare have been shown to help facilitate parental employment and reduce economic inequalities among coupled households (Nieuwenhuis, Need, and van der Kolk 2019). While family policies have been critical for reducing poverty in the United States, policy changes in the 1990s, which prioritized support for working families, have actually reduced the anti-inequality effects of federal family policies (Joo 2011).

HOW DO SPECIFIC FAMILY POLICIES IMPACT CHILD WELL-BEING?

Family and Child Tax Benefits

While some countries provide direct, monthly cash allowances to families in order to ensure a universal minimum income, other countries, such as the United States, have implemented indirect financial assistance through tax relief for families with dependent children (Gauthier 2002). In 2019 the Earned Income Tax Credit (EITC) provided up to $6,557 for married families with three or more children whose incomes were less than $55,952. Families could also reduce their tax burden by up to $2,000 per qualifying child through the Child Tax Credit (CTC). These family support policies supplement the incomes of poor and moderate-income families, lifting millions out of poverty every year (Marr et al. 2015). Generous transfer policies such as direct cash assistance and tax credits are among the most effective programs in reducing child poverty (Meyers and Gornick 2001; Misra, Moller, and Budig 2007). Research also shows that these social policies are associated with better infant and maternal health, improved school performance for children, and better long-term health and economic outcomes (Marr et al. 2015).

Parental Leave Policies

Although the 1993 Family Medical Leave Act entitles eligible U.S. employees twelve weeks of unpaid leave following the birth or adoption of a child or to care for a spouse, child, or parent with a serious health condition, the United States remains the only industrialized nation that does not have a national paid parental leave policy. Some individual employers offer paid parental leave, but only 17 percent of U.S. workers have access to this benefit (National Partnership for Women and Families 2019).

Due to the lack of federal policy, states have begun exploring their own paid leave policies. Nevertheless, as of early 2019, only six states and the District of Columbia had a paid family leave policy in place—even though research shows that short or moderately well-paid family leave results in greater maternal employment and job continuity and enhances long-term earnings and career advancement (Ruhm 2011). Paid parental leave policies are particularly powerful in reducing the poverty rates of single-parent households (Misra, Moller, and Budig 2007). Such policies also impact child well-being. While there is a strong correlation between paid parental leave and reduced child poverty and mortality (Ruhm 2000, 2011), unpaid (or very low-paid) parental leave is not associated with reduced child poverty levels or mortality rates (Engster and Stensöta 2011; Tanaka 2005).

Childcare Assistance

Social policies that support access to childcare subsidies or tax credits for care are also important for reducing employment, income, and gender inequalities (Meyers and Gornick 2003). Most funding for childcare in the United States comes from the Child Care and Development Block Grant (CCDBG) program, which provides subsidies for childcare to families with incomes under 85 percent of state median income (Ruhm 2011). States also supplement CCDBG funding through Temporary Assistance for Needy Families (TANF) block grants (Mills, Compton, and Golden 2011). In 2015, nearly 13.6 million children were eligible for CCDBG childcare subsidies in an average month, but only 15 percent received these subsidies (Chien 2019). Although funding has been relatively stable in recent years, CCDBG has been serving fewer children over time due to the rising cost of care (Rice, Schmit, and Matthews 2019). States can also get funding for childcare subsidies through Social Service Block Grants, but appropriations through this program are much smaller and have been declining as well (Ruhm 2011). The Child and Dependent Care Tax Credit and flexible spending accounts for dependent care have also been useful for reducing the tax burden for more moderate-income families. Childcare subsidies help facilitate parental employment (Ruhm 2011), and higher public childcare spending is associated with lower child mortality (Engster and Stensöta 2011). Low-income and poor families' access to childcare subsidies in particular have been shown to improve the work stability and earnings of parents and have long-term positive impacts on children (Mills, Compton, and Golden 2011; Rice, Schmit, and Matthews 2019).

CONCLUSIONS

During the twentieth century, family policies—both globally and also within the United States—have expanded a great deal and are expected to continue to grow and evolve in the future (Daly and Ferragina 2018; Ooms 2019). In fact, there are many other public policies that impact families that are not addressed above. Examples include TANF, Supplemental Nutrition Assistance Program (SNAP), Women, Infants, and Children (WIC), Medicaid, state Children's Health Insurance programs (CHIP), Head Start, and the Section 8 Housing Choice Voucher Program, as well as Unemployment Insurance (UI) and Supplemental Security Income (SSI).

Despite the known benefits of these family policies in improving well-being and reducing inequality, most programs in the United States reach only a fraction of the families eligible for support (Mills, Compton, and Golden 2011), which contributes to social and economic inequalities in the United States. Although under-utilization is mostly the result of underfunding, some underutilization may be due to a lack of awareness about eligibility together with the complexity of administrative procedures (i.e., having to provide copies of certain documents and attend multiple in-person appointments, etc.), which make it especially difficult for poor and low-income families to retain benefits (Mills, Compton, and Golden 2011). Some experts argue that implementing more universal child benefits would help reduce the administrative costs of programs and also improve benefit uptake by reducing the stigmatization often associated with targeted and means-tested programs, leading to substantial increases in child well-being and outcomes (Bradshaw 2012). Given the important role of family policy in shaping inequalities in the material conditions, caregiving, health, and well-being of children in the United States, family policy researchers and advocates are committed to continuing to work toward building public and political support for expansions in a wide range of family policy programs.

Elizabeth M. Legerski

Further Reading

Adema, Willem. 2012. "Setting the Scene: The Mix of Family Policy Objectives and Packages across the OECD." *Children and Youth Services Review* 34:487–98.

Bradshaw, Jonathan. 2012. "The Case for Family Benefits." *Children and Youth Services Review* 34:590–96.

Chien, Nina. 2019. "Factsheet: Estimates of Child Care Eligibility & Receipt for Fiscal Year 2015." U.S. Department of Health & Human Services. https://aspe.hhs.gov/system/files/pdf/260361/CY2015ChildCareSubsidyEligibility.pdf.

Daly, Mary, and Emanuele Ferragina. 2018. "Family Policy in High-Income Countries: Five Decades of Development." *Journal of European Social Policy* 28:255–70.

Engster, Daniel, and Helena Olofsdotter Stensöta. 2011. "Do Family Policy Regimes Matter for Children's Well-Being?" *Social Politics: International Studies in Gender, State and Society* 18:82–124.

Ferrarini, Tommy, and Thor Norström. 2010. "Family Policy, Economic Development and Infant Mortality: A Longitudinal Comparative Analysis." *International Journal of Social Welfare* 19:S89–S102.

Gauthier, Anne H. 2002. "Family Policies in Industrialized Countries: Is There Convergence?" *Population* 57:447–74.

Joo, Myungkook. 2011. "Effects of Federal Programs on Children: Absolute Poverty, Relative Poverty, and Income Inequality." *Children and Youth Services Review* 33:1203–11.

Kangas, O., and Joakim Palme. 2000. "Does Social Policy Matter? Poverty Cycles in OECD Countries." *International Journal of Health Services* 1:335–52.

Korpi, Walter. 2000. "Faces of Inequality: Gender, Class, and Patterns of Inequalities in Different Types of Welfare States." *Social Politics* 7 (2): 127–91.

Marr, Chuck, Chye-Ching Huang, Arloc Sherman, and Brandon DeBot. 2015. "EITC and Child Tax Credit Promote Work, Reduce Poverty, and Support Children's Development, Research Finds." Center on Budget and Policy Priorities. https://www.cbpp.org/research/eitc-and-child-tax-credit-promote-work-reduce-poverty-and-support-childrens-development.

Meyers, Marcia K., and Janet C. Gornick. 2001. "Gendering Welfare State Variation." In *Women and Welfare: Theory and Practice in the United States and Europe* edited by Nancy J. Hirschmann and Ulrike Liebert, 215–43. New Brunswick, NJ: Rutgers University Press.

Meyers, Marcia K., and Janet C. Gornick. 2003. "Public or Private Responsibility? Early Childhood Education and Care, Inequality, and the Welfare State." *Journal of Comparative Family Studies* 34:379–411.

Meyers, Marcia K., Janet C. Gornick, and Laura R. Peck. 2001. "Packaging Support for Low-Income Families: Policy Variation across the United States." *Journal of Policy Analysis and Management* 20:457–83.

Mills, Gregory B., Jessica F. Compton, and Olivia Golden. 2011. "Assessing the Evidence about Work Support Benefits and Low-Income Families." Urban Institute. https://www.urban.org/research/publication/assessing-evidence-about-work-support-benefits-and-low-income-families/view/full_report.

Mínguez, Almudena Moreno. 2017. "The Role of Family Policy in Explaining the International Variation in Child Subjective Well-Being." *Social Indicators Research* 134:1173–94.

Misra, Joya, Stephanie Moller, and Michelle Budig. 2007. "Work Family Policies and Poverty for Partnered and Single Women in Europe and North America." *Gender and Society* 21:804–27.

National Partnership for Women and Families. 2019. "Paid Leave." http://www.national-partnership.org/our-work/workplace/paid-leave.html.

Nieuwenhuis, Rense, Ariana Need, and Henk van der Kolk. 2019. "Family Policy as an Institutional Context of Economic Inequality." *Acta Sociologica* 62:64–80.

O'Connor, Julia S., Ann Shola Orloff, and Shelia Shaver. 1999. *States, Markets, Families: Gender, Liberalism and Social Policy in Australia, Canada, Great Britain, and the United States.* Cambridge: Cambridge University Press.

O'Hare, William P., Mark Mather, Genevieve Dupuis, Kenneth C. Land, Vicki L. Lamb, and Qiang Fu. 2013. "Analyzing Differences in Child Well-Being Among U.S. States." *Child Indicators Research* 6:401–31.

Olivetti, Claudia, and Barbara Petrongolo. 2017. "The Economic Consequences of Family Policies: Lessons from a Century of Legislation in High-Income Countries." *Journal of Economic Perspectives* 31:205–30.

Ooms, Theodora. 2019. "The Evolution of Family Policy: Lessons Learned, Challenges, and Hopes for the Future." *Journal of Family Theory & Review* 11:18–38.

Pickett, Kate E., and Richard G. Wilkinson. 2015. "The Ethical and Policy Implications of Research on Income Inequality and Child Well-Being." *Pediatrics* 135:S39–S47.

Rice, Douglas, Stephanie Schmit, and Hannah Matthews. 2019. "Child Care and Housing: Big Expenses with Too Little Help Available." Center on Budget and Policy Priorities. https://www.cbpp.org/research/housing/child-care-and-housing-big-expenses-with-too-little-help-available.

Ruhm, Christopher. 2000. "Parental Leave and Child Health." *Journal of Health Economics* 19:931–60.

Ruhm, Christopher J. 2011. "Policies to Assist Parents with Young Children." *Future of Children* 21:37–68.

Tanaka, Sakiko. 2005. "Parental Leave and Child Health across OECD Countries." *Economic Journal* 115:7–27.

Thévenon, Olivier. 2011. "Family Policies in OECD Countries: A Comparative Analysis." *Population and Development Review* 37:57–87.

Thévenon, Olivier, and Angela Luci. 2012. "Reconciling Work, Family and Child Outcomes: What Implications for Family Support Policies?" *Population Research and Policy Review* 31:855–82.

Community Development Programs

Who can have a problem with striving to make things better in a community? On the surface, community development seems to have at its core the basic impetus of making things better, presumably for all those who live in the place where it is being applied or practiced. Indeed, there are many examples where such efforts have yielded benefits to residents, property and business owners, local and regional government, and even tourists. Yet there is another side of the story when considering inequalities in American communities. Unintended consequences are phenomena that immediately come to mind. While there are many benefits of community development, there are numerous issues and challenges that have emerged based on actions taken in the name of development, whether in the broader economic or a more localized community context. How are these outcomes intertwined and what do these connections imply for inequality?

WHAT IS COMMUNITY DEVELOPMENT?

Pause for a moment and think about an investment you may have seen in your own community, one that is open for residents to enjoy. Was it related to any sort of public program providing incentives to make the investment? Likely it had some relation to local or regional government, and more often than not, some of the funds emanated from either state or federal funds. There are exceptions to this where the private sector (either for-profit or nonprofit organizations) built a facility to benefit everyone, such as a park around a private development. Special events are often connected to community development efforts as well. They may be educational, cultural, or recreational events, including ones that are focused on the built environment to support historic preservation.

All of the above are more visible examples of community development in action. Community development is considered most simply to be efforts to improve conditions where people live. More in-depth exploration reveals that it is about residents organizing and mobilizing their capacities, talents, and resources to effect desired change in their communities. One definition that has been offered is, "a process: developing the ability to act collectively, and an outcome: (1) taking collective action and (2) the result of that action for improvement in the community in any or all realms: physical, environmental, cultural, social, political, economic, etc." (Phillips and Pittman 2015, 8). Crucial to enabling community development to occur is the existence of *community capital*. Community capital can take the form of not only social capital but also human, physical, financial, and environmental capital (Green and Haines 2011). It is practiced at the local, regional, state, and federal levels, although more policy and guidance are typically provided for the latter level.

Community development has deep roots in the social change and collective action movements of earlier eras of American history. For example, Jane Addams was an important advocate in Chicago for housing reforms starting in the late 1800s, and her efforts inspired reformers in other cities across the United States. The Progressive and City Beautiful movements of the 1890s through the 1920s were certainly about community development (although that term did not come into common usage until the mid-twentieth century). In terms of both practice and an area of scholarship, the 1960s were an intensively active period of community development, with thousands of community development corporations forming across the nation to combat poverty, address housing deficiencies, and address environmental issues. The first scholarly association in the United States devoted to community development emerged in 1969, with the founding of the Community Development Society. The roots of social change movements of that era can be seen in the Society's Principles of Good Practice, which reflected a deep belief in the power of social activism:

- Promote active and representative participation toward enabling all community members to meaningfully influence the decisions that affect their lives.

- Engage community members in learning about and understanding community issues, and the economic, social, environmental, political, psychological, and other impacts associated with alternative courses of action.

- Incorporate the diverse interests and cultures of the community in the community development process; and disengage from support of any effort that is likely to adversely affect the disadvantaged members of a community.

- Work actively to enhance the leadership capacity of community members, leaders, and groups within the community.

- Be open to using the full range of action strategies to work toward the long-term sustainability and well-being of the community. (Community Development Society n.d.)

Now more than ever, community development is needed. Much inequality has occurred and at the same time, more interest in community development is emerging. As scholars Mae Shaw and Marjorie Mayo explain, "Community development is being rediscovered as a supposedly cost-effective intervention for dealing with the social consequences of global restructuring" (Shaw and Mayo 2016, 3).

COMMUNITY DEVELOPMENT PROGRAMS

To deepen understanding of community development priorities, operations, and programs, it helps to think about how any government entity, whether at the local, regional, or national level, can influence development outcomes. Community development often involves use of public funds to build infrastructure, to provide funding for new or expanded initiatives, or to engage in public-private partnerships. Nonmonetary actions are important, too, especially in the realm of policies to support community development, and for aiding in fostering community capacities via participation and other engagement tools. Policies can incentivize outcomes in many cases, particularly if they are more regulatory in nature.

The U.S. government does not explicitly oversee local and regional decisions but certainly can influence them. The U.S. Constitution does not mention localities and sometimes not too much about states. There is an assumption that states and their localities will address their needs and desires for developing their communities. However, oversight is achieved when tied to funding sources as well as any overarching federal policies that supersede those of the state.

State-enabling legislation is another layer of policy that influences outcomes in community development. Each state has its own, and it may or may not be detailed or provide much guidance for localities regarding development. Some states have very strong enabling legislation, providing details on types of development actions and policies that can be used. Others are general in nature, with only basics covered, such as regulations around dividing parcels of land (subdivision regulations). Essentially, these type of policies at the local or regional government levels can invoke differences in how localities approach land use planning.

The advent of the federal role in policy for community development in the United States can be traced back to the 1930s. The Great Depression and its horrible economic impacts—mass unemployment and waves of bank and business closures—led the federal government under President Franklin D. Roosevelt to take a much more hands-on approach to addressing the country's woes than it had ever done before. In response to the dire economic situation across the country, programs such as the Works Progress Administration, the Civilian Conservation Corps, and others were organized to put Americans back to work. Thousands of civilians were employed to build public infrastructure across the United States in national and state parks, to build public infrastructure such as dams and waterways, and to make physical improvements within towns and cities. There were programs designed to consider the future of housing and urban development along with many other approaches to using federal funds and policy to elicit desirable outcomes for a nation in distress.

In the post–World War II era, the United States enjoyed a period of sustained economic growth. During this same time, the federal government implemented a range of programs and policies to start redeveloping many cities, both for explicit development purposes and to meet soaring demand for housing. The passage of the Housing Act of 1949 paved the way not only for the mortgage industry as we know it but also for urban renewal—perhaps the most famous or infamous of the federal policy actions. Founded on the goal of encouraging revitalization in inner cities, urban renewal instead unintentionally drove divisiveness and polarization around socioeconomic dividing lines of race, income, and ethnicity. Thousands of people were dislocated from their communities, with minority groups impacted disproportionately. Billions were spent by the federal government to clear slums in inner cities, with the definition of *slums* questionable in some cases. There was little interaction between residents of these areas and government, with decisions made in the name of economic progress.

In the 1950s, when urban renewal was fully implemented, another major policy influenced outcomes for many communities. This was the advent of the interstate highway system, developed for defense but seen in many quarters as an economic development investment. In some cases, interstates were constructed to divide neighborhoods and even entire cities by income, race, and ethnicity. Coupled with the devastation created by urban renewal slum clearance, destruction of community and social connectedness was further exacerbated in many cities. One only has to imagine the dividing lines that interstates create—between waterfronts and living spaces and other varying land uses and functions of cities. Obviously, there were cases where urban renewal accomplished positive outcomes: for example, many high-rise city centers were created during this time. And certainly, the interstate highway system is a marvel that ushered in an era of growth and access for the United States that would not have occurred in its absence.

The 1960s was a time of social unrest reflected widely in community-focused policies and programs. It is perhaps the decade that has most influenced the practice as well as the underlying ethos of community development. White flight to the suburbs and declining property taxes contributed to dire situations for many cities. This spiral of decline was so severe that the federal government intervened with several programs aimed at encouraging affordable public housing and addressing issues of poverty in both rural and urban areas of the country. These "Great Society" programs rolled out by the administration of President Lyndon B. Johnson in the 1960s aimed to ameliorate poverty and racial injustice.

In some ways, a reclaiming of citizen-based government emerged during this decade in response to negative outcomes of federal urban renewal and other programs. As mentioned, many thousands of community-based organizations arose during this period. Jane Jacobs, a journalist-turned-activist, led a famous fight to preserve the SoHo neighborhood in New York City from wholesale demolition. Paul Davidoff, an urban planning theorist and activist for social justice during this period, captured the turmoil of the times: "[T]he 'great issues' in economic organization, those resolving around the central issues of the nature of distributive justice, have yet to be settled. The world is still in turmoil over the way in which the resources of the nations are to be distributed" (Davidoff 1965, 332).

Saul Alinsky's work as a community organizer in Chicago during the 1960s influenced many and served as a primer for nonconventional means to close equity gaps. Martin Luther King Jr. adopted and refined nonviolent methods. In his famous "Letter from a Birmingham Jail," King explained why demonstrations and other nonviolent "direct actions" were needed for the civil rights movement:

You may well ask: "Why direct action? Why sit ins, marches and so forth? Isn't negotiation a better path?" You are quite right in calling for negotiation. Indeed, this is the very purpose of direct action. Nonviolent direct action seeks to create such a crisis and foster such a tension that a community which has constantly refused to negotiate is forced to confront the issue. (King 1963)

The influence of these views can still be seen decades later in terms of how community development is approached. The 1970s brought the end of urban renewal and the advent of environmental policies. Joint ventures and public-private partnerships along with a focus on enterprise ruled the day in the 1980s. The 1990s and early 2000s saw the rise of sustainable development practices, with some federal programs encouraging balanced economic development and conservation practices, such as the U.S. Environmental Protection Agency's Smart Growth programs. According to the EPA, Smart Growth "makes efficient use of land, fully utilizes urban services and infrastructure, promotes a wide variety of transportation and housing options, permanently preserves critical natural resources, and protects architectural and environmental character through compatible, high quality, and environmentally-sensitive development" (U.S. EPA n.d.). Some of these efforts have become embedded within state and local polices and approaches; others have fallen by the wayside in the current (2020) federal policy environment.

As seen throughout this journey, economic development is a closely related area of practice (and so is scholarship that holds relevance for policy implications). It focuses on job creation or retention and the monetary impacts of development. While not as outwardly explicit in relation to money and income, community development has often been considered the "soft side" (qualitative rather than quantifiable dimensions) of economic development and what some say prepares a community for subsequent economic development. It does differ vastly from economic development in that a small group of people may be the decision-makers with regard to economic development, while community development seeks to be more inclusive and has concerns with social justice.

How to reconcile the two? Not an easy task, as this is where much conflict and resulting inequality have emerged; if there are monetary dimensions (and most assuredly, economic development always has money involved), then this often drives decisions and outcomes. What is blamed on "politics" as the root of unintended or undesirable outcomes is often about the monetary aspects.

All this said, economic development as a profession and area of scholarship has made significant strides to become more broadly focused and inclusive, with discussions of quality of life and other factors beyond only those with economic dimensions. Both economic and community development integrate concepts of social capital, building on this to achieve desired outcomes. At the same time, there is a dark side to these efforts, in which all outcomes are not desirable or may have deleterious effects on residents, so assumptions need to be made carefully. Influencing social equilibriums is not without impact, be it positive or negative (Talmage, Bell, and Dragomir 2019); in other words, any changes made in a system or its subsystems (such as communities and neighborhoods) cause a change in balance between the system and its internal and external environments.

While newer efforts at the local and state levels have emerged around quality of life and community well-being, there is little response at the federal level. At the multinational level, the Organization for Economic Co-operation and Development is one of several organizations that have developed tools to gauge quality of life and well-being at the national level. Inequality can perhaps best be viewed from this vantage point of comparing the United States to other nations on a variety of socioeconomic and environmental variables. It is clear that inequality is an issue that has not been resolved, and indeed, the United States has fallen on several notable measures that impact inequality (OECD 2020).

Some variations of the following have been written about for nearly one thousand years, and it still holds true: the road to hell is paved with good intentions. In some ways, this is apropos for some of the larger federal programs. At the state and local levels, there are numerous grievances against equality, yet there are bright points as well. Some states are more aggressive with policies to aid in fighting inequalities, and some cities have developed policies and measures to gauge impact in impactful ways that are making a difference. Those communities that are striving to have inclusive processes for developing and implementing sustainable plans for community well-being are one example. Others are fostering social enterprises that are inclusive for creating community capital as well as economic opportunity.

CONCLUSION

The United States has a long tradition of community activism, which is the vital underpinning of community development. This activism is necessary because "traditional institutions and political processes have not always given sufficient voice and a 'seat at the table,' for the nation's poor and minorities" (Stein 2015, 6).

There is little doubt that modern American communities would look and operate much differently were it not for community development activists and organizations. Without community development efforts, the United States would not have as much social advocacy and as many calls to social action that emphasize equity. Without community organizers and development efforts, there would be less response at the local and state levels to issues around balancing economic needs with those of social equity. At the federal level, clearly, attempts through the years to revitalize and rehabilitate struggling communities have resulted in both positive and negative outcomes. As scholars Chris Benner and Manuel Pastor explain,

> The challenge for the nation is to lift up lessons from those places where equity, growth, and community have come together—and to do so in a manner that helps inform a new national conversation about how to secure prosperity, promote inclusion, and reweave a tattered social fabric. (Benner and Pastor 2015)

Balance to bring together all members of our communities is what is needed. Community development can indeed help foster better outcomes and ensure that federal, regional, and local government policies all reflect what is actually desired in communities.

Rhonda Phillips

Further Reading

Benner, Chris, and Manuel Pastor. 2015. *Equity, Growth, and Community, What the Nation Can Learn from America's Metro Areas*. Oakland: University of California Press.

Community Development Society. n.d. https://www.comm-dev.org/about/principles-of-good-practice.

Davidoff, Paul. 1965. "Advocacy and Pluralism in Planning," *Journal of the American Institute of Planners* 31 (4): 331–38.

Green, Gary, and Anna Haines. 2011. *Asset Building and Community Development*. Thousand Oaks, CA: Sage.

King, Martin Luther, Jr. 1963. "Letter from a Birmingham Jail." April 16. University of Pennsylvania, African Studies Center. https://www.africa.upenn.edu/Articles_Gen/Letter_Birmingham.html.

OECD 2020, "Income and Wealth." In *How's Life 2020: Measuring Well-Being*. Paris: OECD Publishing. https://doi.org/10.1787/2e9dd941-en.

Phillips, Rhonda, and Robert Pittman, eds. 2015. *Introduction to Community Development*. London: Routledge.

Shaw, Mae, and Marjorie Mayo. 2016. "One Class, Inequality and Community Development." In *Class, Inequality and Community Development*, edited by Mae Shaw and Marjorie Mayo, 3–22. Bristol, UK: Bristol University Press.

Stein, Jay. 2015. "The Underrepresented." In *Introduction to Community Development*, 2nd edition, edited by R. Phillips and R. Pittman, 5–6. London: Routledge.

Talmage, Craig, Jocelyn Bell, and Gheorghe Dragomir. 2019. "Searching for a Theory of Dark Social Entrepreneurship." *Social Enterprise Journal* 15:131–55.

U.S. EPA (Environmental Protection Agency). n.d. "What Is Smart Growth?" https://www3.epa.gov/region1/eco/uep/smartgrowth.html.

Education Reform Policies

Education is essential for economic growth. In order to create equity in economic growth and society, American students need equal access to education. The American education system has been through many educational reforms—defined as any public policies or changes designed to improve school programs or the educational outcomes of students—but many students are still receiving an inferior education and have unequal access to high quality resources.

Social, political, and economic changes across the last century continue to shape the education system in the United States. The structure of the public school system perpetuates inequalities in educational services for students and is defined by policy. The historical context of educational reform and policy is important due to political and ideological shifts in the system and how schools are formed, overseen, and funded. The history of these reforms has greatly changed the landscape of school structures, student populations, and curriculum. Education policy and funding have driven these changes. Inequities continue to exist because society, researchers, and legislators cannot agree on what constitutes equality in education.

Multiple types of public and private schools operate in the United States. Public schools are defined as schools that are publicly funded and free to attend. Most students attend a traditional public school; in 2019 there were 56.6 million K-12 students and 50.8 million of the students were enrolled in public schools, according to the Department of Education's National Center for Education Statistics (Educationdata.org, n.d.). A traditional public school operates within a defined community and is governed by local, state, and federal policies. Traditional public schools may be defined by geographical boundary lines, but many also accept students outside of their boundaries if space is available. In addition to traditional public schools, there are also various types of nontraditional public schools.

FIRST PUBLIC SCHOOLS

Puritan colonists opened the first public and Latin schools to enhance religious values, but many of these early schools were only for the elite. The first free public school opened in 1635, in Virginia Colony. Less than ten years later, Massachusetts passed a law stating that towns larger than fifty people must hire a schoolmaster and towns over one hundred people must also hire a Latin grammar schoolmaster. In 1837, Massachusetts created the first state board of education, stemming from the work of Horace Mann, a state legislator known for promoting social reform. Mann believed that public education would bridge social and class inequities (Chen 2018).

Around the same time, Henry Barnard shared a similar passion for public education in Connecticut. He became secretary of the Board of Commissioners of the Common Schools and required districts to increase standards for school resources. During the nineteenth century, most schools consisted of a single room and a female teacher who taught reading, writing, and arithmetic. In 1867, the federal Department of Education was created to collect information on individual schools, since states and localities funded schools.

At this time in history, the American economy was much more agrarian in nature, and farming was a way of life for a much higher percentage of families. Many people thus homeschooled their children due to lack of access to established schools.

EARLY PRIVATE SCHOOLS

Private schools are defined by two characteristics: first, the schools are governed by a private entity (religious or nonreligious); second, they are mostly privately funded. Private schools in the United States predate public schools. Roman Catholic missionaries in Florida and Louisiana established the first private schools in what became the United States. The northeastern colonies also set up private schools to teach classical languages, such as Latin and Greek. Early private schools separated boys and girls, and none allowed Black students (Archer 2000).

Today a wide variety of private school options exist in the United States. In 2019, there were around 5.8 million students (9.5 percent of all K-12 students) enrolled in private school (Bustamante 2019). In 2018, 69 percent of all private school students were white, whereas only 52 percent of all traditional public school students were white (Bustamante 2019). Private schools fall into two general categories: religious (7.6 percent of all K-12 students) and nonsectarian (1.9 percent of all K-12 students) (IES 2016; NCES 2019b).

Approximately 3.3 percent of families choose to homeschool their children. Each state sets its own regulations for homeschooling, with some having minimal regulations and others having strict regulations. The percentage of students who are homeschooled greatly increases for households with three or more children and is more prevalent in rural areas than in cities and suburban areas (NCES 2019b).

BACK-TO-BASICS MOVEMENT

After the Soviets launched their successful Sputnik space mission in 1957, many Americans expressed fears that shortcomings in the nation's educational system might eventually hamper the nation's national defense capabilities. This concern was so great that the first federal education funding legislation, the National Defense Education Act (NDEA), was passed in 1958. This legislation provided federal funding but also required testing in secondary schools so assessment data could inform decisions regarding students' educational paths. Many educational reforms have resulted from publicly available assessment data. The public's perception and understanding of assessment has greatly influenced educational reform and political shifts in education (Brookhart 2013).

The increase in assessment data did not go unnoticed—especially after test scores in reading, writing, and arithmetic began to decline. In the 1960s and 1970s, meanwhile, the high unemployment rate among young people was blamed in part on public schools. These two trends combined to spark a "back to basics" reform movement to counter perceptions that students were being promoted from grade to grade without knowing basic reading, writing, and mathematics (Brookhart 2013) and that schools were not placing sufficient emphasis on educational outcomes (Haertel and Herman 2005). Thus reforms designed to return to heavy instruction in the basic building blocks of education basics helped improve public support for increased investment in education.

ANTIDISCRIMINATION POLICIES

Educational segregation has a long history in the United States, but in 1954 the U.S. Supreme Court declared in *Brown v. Board of Education of Topeka* that providing separate public schools for Black and white students was unconstitutional. Proponents of segregation utilized poor assessment data to argue that desegregating schools led to poor achievement for all students. Those in favor of desegregation used the assessment data to highlight how unequal the two school systems had been (Brookhart 2013).

Meanwhile, multiple antidiscrimination laws were passed during the course of the 1960s and 1970s that had significant impacts on the American education system. In 1964, Title VI of the Civil Rights Act was passed to prohibit discrimination "on the basis of race, color, and national origin in programs and activities receiving federal financial assistance." In 1965, Title I of the Elementary and Secondary Education Act (ESEA) created a funding source to assist local schools educating socioeconomically disadvantaged children. In 1972, Section 504 of the Rehabilitation Act prohibited discrimination based on sex; followed by disability in 1973. In 1975, the Education for All Handicapped Children Act was passed. This law required public schools to provide a free, appropriate education to students with disabilities. All of these pieces of legislation were crafted at least in part to provide equal access to education for all students, and they have had significant impacts on current federal, state, and local education funding formulas.

One response to desegregation efforts was the creation of public magnet schools. Magnet schools are publically funded and set within a traditional public school district, typically within a racially or economically segregated location. Magnet schools offer specialized curriculum, such as science or humanities, in order to attract students from other parts of the district, thus voluntarily integrating students. Students must apply to attend the school and are chosen by lottery when the number of applicants exceed enrollment limits. Magnet schools often have a wait list and are intentional about maintaining diverse populations.

While racial segregation is no longer constitutional, segregation persists due to geographic boundary lines that often separate students by race and economics. Because property taxes play such a large part in funding public education, districts are forced to choose how they will spend their resources. Funding formulas attempt to provide equity for per-pupil funding, but equal funds do not cover the cost of teachers' salaries, curricula, support for students, and failing facilities, because each district has different needs in those areas. For example, districts with outdated facilities may need to spend funds on maintenance.

STANDARDS MOVEMENT

Increased, published educational outcomes created the "standards movement" in the 1980s and 1990s. The U.S. job market had an increased demand for higher-level math and literacy skills, and schools were not meeting that demand. The standards movement took on a business approach of setting goals, communicating goals, and then reporting the data. The goals that were set were the "standards." Once these standards were set, the schools became accountable for finding teaching approaches and curricula that would help their students meet these goals, especially in math and literacy. Once the state had set standards in place, schools across the state could be compared. This allowed politicians and educators to attempt to identify best practices in education.

In 1979, Congress established the cabinet-level U.S. Department of Education, which was created to coordinate federal education programs and promote equal educational opportunities. This movement was congruent among states and the federal government. States set their own standards and assessments, but federal officials remained interested in trying to establish criteria for measuring academic performance that could be applied nationwide. In 1989, President George H. W. Bush brought governors together for an Educational Summit, at which several broad student achievement goals to be attained by the year 2000 were identified. President Clinton followed the Summit with the National Educational Goals Panel in 1991 and 1994. These panels created Goals 2000: The Educate America Act, which provided states with funding to create higher academic standards (Brookhart 2013). The standards movement evolved greatly with the introduction of No Child Left Behind, discussed below.

Virtual Schools

In the search for best practices and increased standards, states also started looking at alternative school models. In 1996, the Department of Education gave a five-year grant to Hudson Public Schools in Massachusetts to offer virtual classes. Although the internet was just beginning to be incorporated into school curricula at the time, this was considered a pilot program of *virtual schools*. Since that time, the virtual school has gained popularity. It is defined as any school that delivers the majority of its curriculum online. Virtual public schools allow students to attend school on the internet, utilizing online curriculum with instruction from certified teachers. Some districts use virtual schools to supplement Advanced Placement (AP) classes in locations that otherwise would not have access to this type of curriculum. These districts blend online learning with traditional school. The students may be in a traditional school while also attending virtual classes.

While the research on virtual schools is limited, the National Educational Policy Center stated in 2019 that only 48.5 percent of virtual schools meet performance guidelines. Even more significant is that the on-time graduation rate for virtual schools has been only 50.1 percent, whereas traditional public schools claim an 84-percent on-time graduation rate. Many districts are implementing blended schools: traditional "brick and mortar"—that is, traditional physical campuses—with online components. Yet in 2019, only 44.6 percent of these schools met performance guidelines, putting blended schools behind both virtual and brick and mortar schools. Nationwide access to virtual schools varies. Some districts provide resources for students to access online classes (including a separate school building and computers), while other districts do not.

COVID-19 and Virtual Learning

However, the use of virtual school has shifted dramatically. In the spring of 2020 schools across the country and the world were forced to close their doors amid the pandemic. By April of 2020, 83 percent of parents surveyed reported that their child was engaged in some type of virtual learning (Brenan 2020). Most schools did not reopen for in-person learning in the spring of 2020 or in the fall of 2020, but instead opted for a fully virtual or a hybrid model. Many students across the country remain without the appropriate technology and internet access to engage in virtual learning. In March of 2020 the federal government passed the Coronavirus Aid, Relief, and Economic Security (CARES) Act, which included $13.2 billion in funding for K-12 public education, but these funds were only intended to address costs of addressing the virus. In addition to some schools already being underfunded, the economic downturn in many areas intensified. Many parents faced job loss, fears of catching a life-threatening virus, and stress of social isolation. In addition to the shift to virtual learning, many districts also canceled all statewide assessments in schools. Many rural and private schools did open in the fall of 2020 for in-person learning, thus further widening the gap between economically disadvantaged students in urban districts and others. While many schools and students wait for full-time in-person learning to resume, some schools have greatly increased technology resources. The technology will remain and may shift pedagogy in many educational settings long term even though many teachers and parents view virtual learning as inferior to traditional school in-person school (Brenan 2020). The impact of COVID-19 on education has not yet been measured or estimated.

NO CHILD LEFT BEHIND, CHARTER SCHOOLS, AND VOUCHERS

The No Child Left Behind (NCLB) Act of 2001, which actually was signed into law in January 2002, reauthorized 1965's ESEA. Much of the legislation was the same as that landmark 1965 law, but NCLB boosted student testing, provided resources for recruiting quality teachers, and implemented research-based education programs (NCLB 2002). States were required to annually test students in grades three and eight and once in high school. Required annual district reports presented stratified data for subgroups of students, including minority enrollment and performance and economic status. States also were obligated under NCLB to report the percentage of students who met benchmarks for proficiency in reading, mathematics, and, later, science. Districts were charged with making "adequate yearly progress (AYP)" toward student proficiency by 2014. Schools that did not meet AYP for two consecutive years were often sanctioned, requiring them to earmark money for student tutoring and allow student transfers. Schools with repeated sanctions faced the possibility of school closure, transformation into a charter school, and loss of Title I funds. Data from NCLB highlighted areas of student progress and needs. Disaggregated data, or data broken down into subcategories such as ethnicity, among others, also highlighted the needs of previously ignored and disadvantaged groups of students (Brookhart 2013).

Charter Schools

A public charter school is publicly funded and operated by a group or organization under a contract with an authorizer. While state legislators pass laws about charter schools and are accountable to the public, an authorizer ensures charter school contracts are complied with. Initially, school districts were authorizers, but now many states allow organizations to be authorizers. The contract or charter releases the school from the local school district regulations (NCES 2019a). While charter schools are publicly funded, they usually operate autonomously from the local school district. In order for charter schools to continue operation, they must meet specific performance guidelines set forth in their charter. Charter school admittance is by application, lottery, and/or a first-come, first-served basis.

Charter schools have steadily risen in popularity. This has implications for traditional public schools, because charters compete for students who would otherwise attend the traditional public school. Charter schools also consume public school funds. While charter schools only constituted 6–7 percent of public school students in the late 2010s, the number is closer to 30 percent in some cities (Prothero 2018).

Traditional public schools operate with the ideology that schools do not compete with one another, yet charters directly take funds away from public schools (Vergari 2007). Charter schools receive almost equivalent per pupil spending from taxpayer funds. Some districts also fund charter school facilities. The first law allowing charter schools was passed in 1991 in Minnesota. Since 1996, 43 states and the District of Columbia have passed charter school legislation. Seven states do not have charter school legislation as of 2019 (Kentucky, Montana, Nebraska, North Dakota, South Dakota, Vermont, and West Virginia) (U.S. DOE 2019). While public schools are not permitted to contract with private and sometimes for-profit entities to administrate their facilities and operations, charter schools do not fall under these regulations, which are highly opposed by labor unions because profits may be prioritized over students (Vergari 2007).

How do students at charter schools perform academically? The National Assessment of Educational Progress (NAEP) measures reading and math scores at grades four and eight. As of 2017, no measurable difference was seen in scores between traditional public and public charter schools (NCES 2019b). This data does not compare performances of schools before and after they become a charter school, which some researchers believe may be a better indicator of the efficacy of the charter school model. Further, a study of charter middle schools demonstrated wide variability, noting that performance of some higher-income students and higher-achieving students declined upon entering charter schools (IES 2010).

The segregation reported in charter school populations is also troubling. In the Minneapolis-St. Paul metro region, it was found that charter school segregation was greater than in the already highly segregated public schools within the same boundaries (Institute on Race and Poverty 2008). A longitudinal study in California and Texas also found that Black students were more segregated after transferring to charter schools than they were previously (Zimmer and Buddin 2006). Charters may also be separating students by socioeconomic status through their admission process and requirements for parent participation (Frankenberg, Siegel-Hawley, and Wang 2011). This type of segregation continues today. A longitudinal study from 1998 to 2015 found that eliminating charter schools would decrease segregation by 5 percent. Overall, there is a 0.5-percent increase in segregation within a school district when charter schools are integrated within the school district. However, school district lines are often highly segregated from one area within a city to another (Monarrez, Kisida, and Chingos 2019). Charter schools may continue to see an increase in segregation until admissions policies change. One change that could increase desegregation efforts would be to weight admissions by ethnicity.

Vouchers

In addition to charter schools, NCLB also increased the number of school voucher programs in the United States. A school voucher is "a government-supplied coupon that is used to offset tuition at an eligible private school" (Epple, Romano, and Urquiola 2017). Some of the first school vouchers were issued in the 1960s as "tuition grants" designed to promote desegregation. Today, school vouchers operate in a variety of ways, depending on the preferences of state and local school districts. The majority of voucher programs are funded by tax revenues, tax credits, and/or private foundations (Epple, Romano, and Urquiola 2017). As of 2020, thirty states utilize some form of school choice program. State legislation is constantly changing (EdChoice 2019).

The majority of all tax revenue–funded U.S. voucher programs (with the exception of Ohio and Florida) target students in households earning from 150 percent to 300 percent above the poverty line. These voucher programs include students in such far-flung cities as Milwaukee, Racine, Cleveland, New Orleans, and

Washington, DC, as well as all students in the state of Indiana. Florida and Ohio have implemented voucher programs in areas with failing or underperforming schools. School admission is determined by lottery or private school admission criteria, depending on state and locality. In all programs reviewed, these vouchers can be used at religious schools, with requirements that students take the same standardized tests as students in public schools. Voucher use at religious schools has become an important issue since it means public funds are being used to support a religious institution. Critics assert that such arrangements violate church-state separation provisions of the U.S. Constitution (Epple, Romano, and Urquiola 2017).

Milwaukee started vouchers in 1990 and serves as a model for many other tax revenue voucher programs. In 2019, the city had over 120 schools and 28, 978 students participating in the voucher program (EdChoice 2019). Initially students at 175 percent of the poverty level were given vouchers, but that has recently increased to 300 percent. Religious schools have been eligible for the voucher program since 1998. Vouchers at the standard district allocation may be applied to private school tuition; since 2011, private schools have been allowed to charge additional tuition beyond the voucher value. The program includes student transportation within a predetermined distance to the chosen school. Although early assessment results lagged behind Milwaukee's public schools, since 2006, student assessment results between voucher schools and public schools have been comparable (Epple, Romano, and Urquiola 2017).

Some voucher programs are funded by providing tax credits to businesses. The credit is limited, and the vouchers go to eligible students through lotteries. The following states have tax-credit-financed programs: Florida, Georgia, Indiana, Iowa, Oklahoma, Pennsylvania, and Rhode Island. With the exception of Georgia (where all public school students are eligible), these states require that household income of eligible students must be less than 260 percent of the poverty line (nationally) or that the student applicant attends an underperforming school. Vouchers under these programs can be used at religious private schools. However, when achievement results from these programs are compared with the national average for public schools, only Florida and Indiana show similar results as good as the national average for public schools (Epple, Romano, and Urquiola 2017).

Florida is one of the earliest adopters of a tax-credit-funded program and has the largest voucher program in the United States. The Florida Corporate Income Tax Credit Scholarship program is funded with corporate contributions. While their total contributions are capped at $559.1 million, donors receive a 100-percent corporate income tax credit for contributions (not to exceed 75 percent of their liability). There are limitations for Florida's vouchers: Students are not guaranteed admission to their chosen school, since private schools maintain selectivity and are only regulated by antidiscrimination statutes. Additionally, the average Florida voucher of $6,195 (in 2020) may not cover full private school tuition, leaving a gap that families must pay (EdChoice 2019) Voucher programs are continually changing by program and state. For current programs and eligibility and funding levels, please see https://www.edchoice.org.

In 2017, it was estimated that around fifty privately funded school voucher programs existed, but that number is on the rise. The Children's Scholarship Fund (CSF) was founded in 1998, with founding contributions from the Walton Family Foundation (Epple, Romano, and Urquiola 2017). The CSF is a major contributor to private/individually funded programs throughout nineteen states. Students of color and students from low-income families receive special attention from CSF and several other privately funded voucher programs. Privately funded programs often work within states that also have tax-revenue or tax-credit vouchers. These privately funded programs provide student scholarships for tuition at participating private schools.

Per-Pupil Spending and Vouchers

Consistent with much of the research on educational reform movements, voucher programs show mixed results on academic achievement (Epple, Romano, and Urquiola 2017). However, voucher programs have recently entered the political spotlight. When families use vouchers to take their students out of public schools and put them into private schools, the public funding allocations follow the students. School districts count on those funds to supplement services within the system. The individual amount set forth in the per-pupil spending does not mean that each student is receiving equal monetary services. The per-pupil spending is an average cost of educating all students within a school system. However, the cost of educating students with special needs far exceeds that of educating general education students. For example, a student who is enrolled in an English-language-learning (ELL) program or a student receiving special education will require a significantly greater financial outlay than students in the general education classroom. Schools rely on a mix of students in order to support all students as legally required.

Funding issues are magnified by the fact that most private schools accepting vouchers must only abide by antidiscrimination statutes in setting their admittance policies. Many private schools are not equipped with the resources to serve students with special needs and will therefore deny admission to those students. Serving students with special needs is costly, and many private schools make the choice not to serve these students. In turn, this leads to unbalanced student populations within public schools, which are legally obligated to serve all students. School vouchers were designed to give families choice, but given how many of the voucher schools operate, families with special-needs children actually have no choice but to keep their children in the public school system.

RACE TO THE TOP INITIATIVE

While NCLB focused on accountability and exposed inequities and achievement gaps, it also highlighted challenges with the goal of raising student test scores. In 2009, Congress and the Obama administration responded by introducing two major educational reforms. The first was the American Reinvestment and

Recovery Act, which earmarked over $90 billion for education. This legislation included the Race to the Top initiative, which was designed to spur educational reform through $4.35 billion in competitive grant funds. States were encouraged to submit educational reform plans that would target low-achieving schools, adopt benchmarked standards and assessments to prepare students for college, recruit and retain teachers in high-needs areas, and create data systems that would track student improvement and guide instruction (U.S. DOE 2009a).

In 2009, one of the largest and most unified assessment reforms was the adoption of the Common Core State Standards (CCSS). The roots of the CCSS can be traced back to the 1980s, when there was a call for more nationally standardized assessments of subject proficiency. The CCSS provided a unified system of standards and assessment across states. Over 46 states adopted the CCSS before the American Reinvestment and Recovery Act was signed. The grants competition for Race to the Top Initiative funds incentivized states to adopt the CCSS through points added to their proposal-rubric scores. Although the incentives were small, some critics nonetheless viewed the program as an indication that the federal government was overstepping by interfering with state and local control of their education policies (Whitman 2015).

EVERY STUDENT SUCCEEDS ACT

In 2012, at the end of NCLB, states were permitted to design their own plans to address achievement gaps, promote equity, and increase standards. In 2015, the Every Student Succeeds Act (ESSA) was reauthorized (ESSA, NCLB, and ESEA all refer to the same law). Critical protections were put into place for disadvantaged and high-need students (often English-language learners). ESSA seeks to advance equity by upholding protections for students, requiring all students to be held to high academic standards, supporting local school district plans, and providing accountability (U.S. DOE 2019).

ESSA requires states to submit plans that include academic standards, annual testing, school accountability, academic achievement goals, plans for supporting and improving struggling schools, and state and local report cards. States are required to present plans to parents for feedback. ESSA is designed to give states more flexibility in how they will provide equitable access of education for all students (U.S. DOE 2019). However, equality across districts and states assumes equal and adequate school funding, which does not occur.

SCHOOL FUNDING

States now have a variety of school types available to students, including the following: traditional public schools, magnet schools, private schools, charter schools, and virtual schools. The number and types of students who attend these schools directly compete with the traditional public school model and the funds available. The federal government has traditionally provided funds to supplement states and districts. In 2018, approximately $71 billion in federal funding was distributed to K-12 education, about 9 percent of all school funding nationally. States and local revenue make up the remaining 91 percent, with states contributing about 1 percentage point more than local revenue (U.S. Census Bureau 2015). How state and local revenue is accrued and divided among schools varies.

Federal Education Funding

Federal funding is provided through grants and programs that are earmarked for specific educational goals. The following is an example of how federal funds are actually distributed to individual schools. Title I funds are distributed to schools after the annual budget is submitted. The president submits a budget request, Congress files a budget resolution (setting funding for the next fiscal year, which begins in October), and state education agencies (SEAs) submit plans to the federal government detailing planned learning outcomes and progress measures. Next, the government awards Title I funds to SEAs based on income formulas. The SEAs then allocate money to school districts, or local education agencies (LEAs), according to the district's Title I families. LEAs are responsible for allocating funds in accordance with Title I student enrollment formulas. For example, schools with fewer than 40 percent Title I–eligible students must fund targeted assistance programs. Schools with more than 40 percent Title I–eligible students may use funds for schoolwide improvement.

The goal of the federal budget, SEAs, and LEAs is to give equitable funding to students in all districts. However, ways to define and measure equity are still debated. Should equity be measured by the amount spent on each student? While school funding goals should promote equitable experiences for all students, the definition of equality remains murky: Should per-pupil expenditures match across schools within a district, or should schools serving students with greater needs be provided more funds to boost educational attainment? The current systems for funds allocation are challenging to measure and are further complicated by varied funding streams. Since federal monies account for just 9 percent of school funding, SEAs and LEAs are responsible for the rest, and disparities are clear. The wealthiest districts and schools spend 21 percent more per pupil than the national average, while the poorest spend 11 percent less.

On the surface, average expenditures appear equitable, but students who need more resources to be successful remain disadvantaged—a phenomenon that has come to be known as "ghettoization" (Books 1999). Similarly, localities that have lost businesses also lose tax-derived school funding. For example, tax incentives intended to woo corporations to less wealthy, job-needy localities can further undercut school funding (White and Johnston 1997).

State and Local Funding

The majority of school funding comes from states and localities, and each state is responsible for deciding how to distribute funds. Most states use one or some combination of three types of funding formulas.

The first type of funding formula is student based; it uses the number of students to devise a calculation of per-pupil spending. Generally, there is a base amount that reflects the cost to educate each student, with further adjustments for low-income students, special-education services, and English-language learners.

The second type, a resource-based funding formula, is calculated by the cost of resources, and the third, a program-based formula, is calculated to fund specific programs. As of 2020, thirty-eight states use student-based formulas or a hybrid formula blending student-based funding with resource- or program-based formulas. Nine states use a solely resource-based funding formula, and eight states include resource-based funding in their formulas. As of 2020, Wisconsin is the only state that solely uses a program-based formula, but Montana, South Carolina, and North Carolina also rely partially on program-based formulas (Edbuild 2020).

Kansas has struggled to meet state funding formulas for decades. Kansas's state education budget was left with a tremendous funding gap after Governor Sam Brownback cut income taxes by the largest percent in the state's history, leaving the state with a major deficit. Even though the tax cuts were repealed in 2017, Kansas is still struggling to fund the budget. In 2017, the Kansas Supreme Court ruled that the state's funding formula was unconstitutional because it left schools without the necessary financial resources to provide Kansas K-12 students with a basic education. In 2019, after a prolonged court battle between the state and various families and education advocates, Kansas added $90 million in funding to its education budget. It may be years before Kansas feels the effects of this decision. Massachusetts faced a similar ruling in 1993. Massachusetts increased funding in all districts but dramatically raised funding in poorer districts, which increased the required amount all districts would receive by the state. In addition to the extra funds, new curriculum standards, which increased learning time, were also implemented. In less than a decade, Massachusetts was able to increase its national assessment data based on student test scores across the board.

Most states expect that local school districts will contribute funds to these formulas, but how do localities raise funds, and what do they get in return? Localities are responsible for raising around 45 percent of funds for local schools (U.S. Census Bureau 2015). In forty-seven states, funding is drawn from property taxes (Edbuild 2020). In return for raising funds, local communities have a say in how their local schools operate and what curricula they follow. Taxpayers can see how their tax funds are applied. There is also more accountability for locally elected officials: School board officials are in charge of budgets. Voters in a district may reelect or replace members based on public budget sentiment. While such scrutiny may have benefits, taxpayers in the district may disagree on expenditures. For example, childless residents may see some expenses as extravagant.

School funding formulas are different for each state, and exact dollar amounts are constantly changing. The goal of funding formulas is to provide equity among students, but due to economic inequities, this does not always occur. Wealthy localities are able to provide significant funding through property taxes, while others are not able to turn to this for meaningful funding.

With school choice generated by charter schools and vouchers, it is even harder to determine equal funding and equitable schooling opportunities. One study published in 2007 showed that urban minority children are exposed to elevated poverty rates because of three factors: "the under representation of more affluent children in neighborhood-based public schools, the tendency for wealthier students to withdraw from public schools serving economically balanced areas, and the differential withdrawal of poor and non-poor children from schools serving neighborhoods that are predominantly black or Hispanic" (Saporito and Sohoni 2007, 1247). Schools are segregated by income further when wealthier students attend charter or private schools.

Not all geographic areas have equal access to funding, quality teachers, new facilities, and school choice. Researchers Jin Lee and Christopher Lubienski (2016) defined the term *spatial inequality* as geographical disparity in access to necessary resources and services, and they noted that within economically or racially divided communities, the boundaries impact availability of food, public safety, and education. Spatial inequality exists regardless of segregation laws. In many rural and urban neighborhoods, school closure policies produce this same spatial injustice (Tieken and Auldridge-Reveles 2019). School closures are justified through cost efficiency, low academic performance, and to promote equity. Yet closures do not occur equally: closures affect poor students and poor communities at substantially higher rates (Bastress 2003). Most communities oppose school closures because students within the local boundaries are subsequently forced to attend more distant locations from home, often via busing.

Proponents of school closures argue that closing schools is cost-effective and provides possible opportunities for students attending those institutions to enroll at other schools with better academic records. The research suggests, however, that when students are forced to move to different schools as a result of closures, their short-term grades, test scores, attendance and afterschool participation all decline (Tieken and Auldridge-Reveles 2019). Communities are also affected by declining home values and greater income inequality (Lyson 2002). School closures are promoted as providing new and more equitable opportunities for students, but in reality, they often simply create greater inequity.

CONCLUSION

Educational reform in this country has seen many iterations, with most focused on the goal of equity. School funding is seen as the catalyst for promoting equity. The federal government, states, and localities all contribute to school funding, but all use different funding formulas. The ESSA requires states and localities to submit plans for increasing student achievement and access, especially for disadvantaged students, but requires accountability through reporting assessment data. Funding is not equal across geographical areas, nor among socioeconomic classes. All around the country, poor and disadvantaged students receive educations that are inferior to their peers from more affluent backgrounds and communities. The increase in school choice with the rise of charter schools and school vouchers has further complicated the issue by increased racial and economic segregation. While each decade brings new educational reforms seeking to level the playing field in terms of education quality, educational inequality remains a stubborn reality, in large part because it is directly related to wider and ongoing problems of social and economic inequality.

Christy Irish and Allison Ward Parsons

Further Reading

Archer, Jeff. 2000. "A Private Choice." In *Lessons of a Century: A Nation's Schools Come of Age*, edited by Virginia B. Edwards and staff of *Education Week*, 204–229. Bethesda, MD: Editorial Project in Education.

Bastress, Robert. M. 2003. "The Impact of Litigation on Rural Students: From Free Textbooks to School Consolidation." *Nebraska Law Review* 82:9–49.

Books, Sue. 1999. "School Funding: Justice v. Equity" *Equality and Excellence* 32 (3): 52–8. doi:10.1080/1066568990320306.

Brenan, Megan. 2020. "Over 8 in 10 Parents Now Say Child is Learning Remotely." Gallup. https://news.gallup.com/poll/307754/parents-say-child-learning-remotely.aspx.

Brookhart, Susan. M. 2013. "The Public Understanding of Assessment in Educational Reform in the United States." *Oxford Review of Education* 39 (1): 52–71. https://doi.org/10.1080/03054985.2013.764751.

Bustamante, Jaleesa. 2019. "K-12 School Enrollment & Student Population Statistics." https://educationdata.org/k12-enrollment-statistics.

Chen, Grace. 2018. "A Relevant History of Public Education in the United States." *Public School Review*. https://www.publicschoolreview.com/blog/a-relevant-history-of-public-education-in-the-united-states.

Children's Scholarship Fund. https://scholarshipfund.org.

Diner, Steven J. 1982. "Crisis of Confidence. The Reputation of Washington's Public Schools in the Twentieth Century." Studies in DC History and Public Policy Paper No. 1. ERIC Document 218 374. Washington, DC: University of the District of Columbia, Department of Urban Studies.

Edbuild. 2020. "Funded: National Policy Maps." http://funded.edbuild.org/national#formula-type.

EdChoice. 2019. "Fast Facts." Engage by EdChoice. https://www.edchoice.org/engage/fast-facts.

Educationdata.org. n.d. "K-12 School Enrollment and Student Population Statistics." https://educationdata.org/k12-enrollment-statistics.

Epple, Dennis, Richard E. Romano, and Miguel Urquiola. 2017. "School Vouchers: A Survey of the Economics Literature." *Journal of Economic Literature* 55 (2): 441–92. https://doi.org/10.1257/jel.20150679.

Frankenberg, Erica, Genevieve Siegel-Hawley, and Jia Wang. 2011. "Choice without Equity: Charter School Segregation." *Educational Policy Analysis Archives* 19 (1): 1–54.

Haertel, Edward H., and Joan L. Herman. 2005. "A Historical Perspective on Validity Arguments for Accountability Testing." In *Uses and Misuses of Data for Educational Accountability and Improvement*, edited by J. L. Herman and E. H. Haertel, 1–34. The 104th yearbook of the National Society for the Study of Education, part 2. Malden, MA: Blackwell.

IES (Institute of Education Sciences). 2010. "The Evaluation of Charter School Impacts: Final Report." National Center for Educational Evaluation and Regional Assistance Report 2010-4029. https://files.eric.ed.gov/fulltext/ED510573.pdf.

IES (Institute of Education Sciences), National Center for Education Statistics, U.S. Department of Education. 2016. "Table 206.30 Percentage Distribution of Students Enrolled in Grades 1 through 12, by Public School Type and Charter Status, Private School Orientation, and Selected Child and Household Characteristics: 2016." https://nces.ed.gov/programs/digest/d18/tables/dt18_206.30.asp?referer= schoolchoice.

Institute on Race and Poverty. 2008. *Failed Promises: Assessing Charter Schools in the Twin Cities*. Minneapolis: Institute on Race and Poverty at University of Minnesota Law School.

Lee, Jin, and Christopher Lubienski. 2016. "The Impact of School Closures on Equity of Access in Chicago." *Education and Urban Society* 49 (1): 53–80. https://doi.org/10 .1177/0013124516630601.

Lyson, Thomas A. 2002. "What Does a School Mean to a Community? Assessing the Social and Economic Benefits of Schools to Rural Villages in New York." *Journal of Research in Rural Education* 17:131–37.

Molnar, Alex, David Garcia, Margaret Bartlett, and Adrienne O'Neill. 2006. *Profiles of For-Profit Education Management Companies, 2005–2006*. Eighth annual report EPSL-0605-104-CERU. Tempe: Arizona State University.

Molnar, Alex, Gary Miron, Najat Elgeberi, Michael K. Barbour, Luis Huerta, Sheryl R. Shafer, Jennifer K. Rice. 2019. "Virtual Schools in the U.S. 2019." National Education Policy Center, Boulder. http://nepc.colorado.edu/publication/virtual-schools -annual-2019.

Monarrez, Tomas, Brian Kisida, and Matthew Chingos. 2019. "Do Charter Schools Increase Segregation?" *Education Next* 19 (4): 56–74.

NCES (National Center for Education Statistics), U.S. Department of Education. 2019a. "Public Charter School Enrollment." *The Condition of Education 2019*. https:// nces.ed.gov/programs/coe/pdf/Indicator_CGB/coe_cgb_2019_05.pdf.

NCES (National Center for Education Statistics), U.S. Department of Education. 2019b. "School Choice in the United States: 2019." https://nces.ed.gov/pubsearch/pub- sinfo.asp?pubid=2019106.

NCLB (No Child Left Behind) Act of 2001. 2002. Pub. L. No. 107-110, 115 Stat. 1425.

Prothero, Arianna. 2018. "What Are Charter Schools?" *Education Week*. https://www .edweek.org/ew/issues/charter-schools/index.html.

Saporito, Salvatore, and Deenesh Sohoni. 2006. "Mapping Educational Inequality: Concentrations of Poverty among Poor and Minority Students in Public Schools." *Social Forces* 85 (3): 1227–48.

Tieken, Mara, and Trevor Auldridge-Reveles. 2019. "Rethinking the School Closure Research: School Closure as Spatial Injustice." *Review of Educational research* 89 (6): 917–53.

U.S. Census Bureau. 2015. "Public Elementary-Secondary Education Finance Report, 2013 Data." https://www.cbpp.org/states-provide-nearly-half-of-school-funding.

U.S. Department of Education. 2009a. "Race to the Top." https://www2.ed.gov/programs /racetothetop/factsheet.html.

U.S. Department of Education. 2009b. "Race to the Top Initiative." https://www2.ed.gov/ programs/racetothetop/executive-summary.pdf.

U.S. Department of Education. 2010. "An Overview of the U.S. Department of Education." https://www2.ed.gov/about/overview/focus/what.html.

U.S. Department of Education. 2019. "Every Student Succeeds Act (ESSA)." https://www .ed.gov/essa?src=ft.

U.S. Department of Justice. "Title VI of the Civil Rights Act of 1964." https://www.justice
.gov/crt/fcs/TitleVI#1.

White, Kerry, and Robert Johnston. 1997. "Schools' Taxes Bartered Away to Garner
Jobs." *Education Week* 16, no. 24 (March 12): 26–29.

Whitman, David. 2015. "The Surprising Roots of the Common Core: How Conservatives
Gave Rise to 'Obamacore.'" Brown Center on Educational Policy, at Brookings.
https://www.brookings.edu/wp-content/uploads/2016/06/Surprising-Conservative
-Roots-of-the-Common-Core_FINAL.pdf.

Vergari, Sandra. 2007. "The Politics of Charter Schools." *Educational Policy* 21 (1):
15–39. https://doi.org/10.1177/0895904806296508.

Zimmer, Ron, and Richard Buddin. 2006. "Charter Schools' Performance in Two Large
Urban Districts." *Journal of Urban Economics* 60 (2): 307–26.

Food and Nutrition Programs

In 2016, the U.S. Department of Agriculture (USDA) reported that an estimated 12.3 percent of U.S. households were food insecure, meaning that 41 million Americans experienced limited or uncertain availability of food and lacked access to enough food for an active, healthy life. The implications of these high rates of hunger are wide reaching, given that food insecurity has been associated with several negative and lifelong impacts on health and on behavioral, social, and cognitive difficulties.

Food insecurity arises from a lack of income needed to purchase nutritious food and other resources. Income is the number-one predictor of food insecurity, with rates significantly higher than the national average for households with incomes near or below the federal poverty line. And although the U.S. economy, by many indicators, has been growing since the Great Recession, rates of food insecurity are still 2 percentage points higher than pre-2008 levels, causing continuing concern over the availability of food in low-income households.

SNAP

As a way to combat inequality in food security across households, the U.S. Department of Agriculture oversees four main in-kind transfer programs with the principal goal of improving access to nutritious food. One such program, the Supplemental Nutrition Assistance Program (SNAP), formerly known as the food stamp program, provides a monthly electronic food voucher to over forty million Americans each year with the goal of preventing hunger and reducing food insecurity among the nation's most economically vulnerable citizens.

In 1964, President Lyndon B. Johnson signed the Food Stamp Act as part of the Great Society program, an ambitious slate of federal initiatives to reduce poverty and improve quality of life across the country. The Act gave local areas the authority to introduce a federally funded food stamp program in their area to provide poor families with food purchasing assistance. Importantly, during this time, hunger and nutritional deficiencies in low-income U.S. households were relatively common. For example, a survey of low-income families in four states in the late 1960s found that over 15 percent of Americans had low hemoglobin levels as well as relatively high rates of deficiencies in vitamin C, riboflavin, and protein (Eisinger 1998).

At the time, some counties were already providing food aid to the poor via the Commodity Distribution Program (CDP), in which the federal government would purchase goods from farmers and distribute them directly to families. Critics argued that the program distributed food in inefficient and irregular ways, did not provide enough variety of resources, and advocated for agricultural interests over those of poor families. On the other hand, the Food Stamp Act allocated food vouchers, known at the time as food stamps, to participants who could use their in-kind benefits to purchase food at authorized groceries, giving families more flexibility and choice. The program's original intent was to strengthen the agricultural economy and improve nutrition levels in low-income households, thus reducing health problems associated with low birth weight, anemia, and osteoporosis.

Shortly after the initiation of the program, there were major additions to the existing law. In 1967, Congress amended it to allow for greater distribution of food and food stamps both to children and to retirees over the age of sixty-five. Over the next decade, the program grew dramatically, with all counties participating by 1975, increasing participation to over fifteen million individuals. Importantly, the program is credited with dramatic improvements in health, especially in rural areas; a 1977 report found that severe malnourishment had dropped dramatically since the initial program rollout.

Today's food voucher program maintains many of the same aims and objectives as the original pilot program. However, in recent years, nutritional assistance has evolved in a few major ways. First, from 1996 to 2004, states rolled out electronic benefits transfer, allowing agencies to issue benefits wirelessly, reducing the program's vulnerability to fraud and improving privacy for participants. Second, in an effort to further reduce stigma associated with food stamps, the 2008 Farm Bill changed the name of the food stamp program to its current one. Importantly, the bill also included $10 billion in additional funding over ten years and operationalized new initiatives of the Food and Nutrition Service (FNS), the USDA agency responsible for the SNAP program. These initiatives included fraud prevention, administration reform, and efforts to improve access.

Similar to the food stamp program, SNAP is a means-tested entitlement program, and benefits depend on household income and size. While SNAP is federally funded, benefits are issued by states, and states have the authority to tailor rules for eligibility and implementation. Each year, disbursed benefits total approximately $60.6 million, while monthly benefits average about $125 per person or $251 per household (USDA 2018). Given that SNAP is the only federal program with benefits available to nonworking, able-bodied individuals, food vouchers currently serve as the most fundamental safety net program in the United States, serving one in eight Americans. While other programs target mostly children, families with children, or the elderly, nearly all low-income households are eligible for food benefits, including poor families without children and single childless adults.

SNAP PARTICIPATION RATES

A number of categorical rules make recipients of other means-tested programs in many states automatically eligible for the program. However, enrollment is not automatic, and, as a result, SNAP take-up is well under 100 percent. Only about 75 percent of eligible individuals participate, implying that large information or stigma barriers still exist for many low-income Americans. Indeed, researchers found that informational mailings nearly doubled SNAP enrollment, while information paired with application assistance tripled SNAP enrollment (Finkelstein and Notowidigdo 2018).

Each month, benefits are loaded onto debit-like cards, to be redeemed for foods and nonalcoholic beverages at authorized groceries. Because SNAP benefits can only be redeemed for food, they should theoretically induce recipients to spend more money on groceries. But does this in-kind transfer actually incentivize individuals to spend more on food than they would otherwise? The role of SNAP on food choices largely depends on the function of benefits in the household budget. Economic theory predicts that if households view SNAP benefits as fungible, the only families made better off would be those that would have alternatively spent less than their SNAP allocation on qualifying foods. On the other hand, families who would have spent at least as much on qualifying foods as the SNAP allocation should have their choice of foods remain relatively unaffected.

The question remains: Based on the existing evidence, does SNAP make low-income households better off? Certainly, since food vouchers can only be used to buy a subset of goods that a household may need, these benefits should be worth less than cash. Nonetheless, if SNAP benefits do induce households to spend more on food, then there exists potential for food vouchers to increase total social welfare relative to other programs.

A large body of literature documents the empirical effects of SNAP receipt and finds that benefits reduce out-of-pocket food expenditures, which translates into reductions in food insecurity and hunger (Hoynes and Schanzenbach 2009; Ratcliffe, McKearnan, and Zhang 2011; Kreider et al. 2012; Schmidt, Shore-Sheppard, and Watson 2016; Hoynes, Schanzenbach, and Almond 2016). However, although the bulk of research suggests that SNAP effectively reduces food insecurity, there is no evidence that it has large and meaningful effect on diet quality.

The reported benefits of SNAP extend well beyond food insecurity. In particular, SNAP receipt has been documented to improve test scores, improve educational attainment, and lower student disciplinary infractions (Gassman-Pines and Bellows 2018; Gennetian et al. 2015, Bond et al. 2020). Moreover, nutritional assistance receipt can reduce incentives for individuals to commit financially motivated crimes aimed specifically at obtaining food, thereby improving the lives of low-income families and communities (Carr and Packham 2019).

Unlike the cash assistance program, Temporary Assistance for Needy Families, SNAP does not have work requirements. Therefore, one central issue that often arises is how nutritional assistance programs affect work behavior. Standard economic theory predicts that food vouchers would affect work incentives at lower household incomes and could reduce labor supply. Accordingly, there is some evidence of modest reductions in employment and hours after the introduction of food stamps, with effects concentrated among single-parent families (Hoynes and Schanzenbach 2009).

Although SNAP is the largest nutritional assistance program in the United States, three other nutritional assistance programs are of considerable note—WIC, NSLP, and SBP—and will be discussed in turn.

The first, Women, Infants and Children (WIC), is a federal assistance program and serves to help low-income pregnant, postpartum and breastfeeding women and their children under the age of five. WIC serves over half of eligible pregnant women and infants in the United States with the aim of ensuring the nutritional well-being of poor mothers and their young children. Eligible households include those earning less than 185 percent of the poverty line and whose members are deemed to be at "nutritional risk."

While the monthly WIC benefit averaged $41 per person in 2017, benefits depend on household size. Specifically, for a family that comprises a mother and infant, the monthly WIC benefit typically averages $150 to $165, comparable in size with a SNAP transfer for families with children.

WIC participants are issued monthly vouchers to exchange at participating retail groceries for a prespecified set of nutritious foods, including milk, cheese, and eggs. Unlike SNAP, which places no limitations on food purchases, WIC restricts foods by quantity, size, type, and, sometimes, brand. For example, while yogurt is an approved WIC purchase, only yogurts that are pasteurized and do not contain more than forty grams of total sugars per one cup of yogurt are allowed. Yogurts sold with mix-in ingredients and drinkable yogurts are not permitted.

Nonetheless, for many households, WIC helps reduce food insecurity by topping off nutritional assistance benefits for low-income families. Additionally, WIC provides health screenings, nutrition education, and referrals to other social services. As a result, WIC has been shown to result in large, positive effects on infant health, maternal health, and access to Medicaid, bridging gaps in both nutrition and health-care access for low-income mothers and children (Bitler and Currie 2005; Figlio, Hamersma, and Roth 2009; Hoynes, Page, and Stevens 2011; Rossin-Slater 2013).

SCHOOL-BASED PROGRAMS

In spite of the fact that nearly one in seven Americans participate in SNAP and/or WIC in any given year, over 25 percent of SNAP recipients report experiencing food insecurity (Mabli et al. 2013). Because SNAP and WIC do not fully eliminate hunger, lower-income children are also eligible for two school nutritional programs, including the National School Lunch Program (NSLP) and the School Breakfast Program (SBP).

The NSLP was implemented in 1946 in an effort to reduce malnutrition and childhood hunger. The SBP began as a pilot program in 1966 and was made permanent in 1975. Both programs are means-tested; children in families below 130 percent of the federal poverty level pay nothing for school meals, while children in families up to 185 percent of the poverty level pay a heavily subsidized rate. Higher-income children can purchase a school meal at the full "paid" rate.

Since their inception, there has been significant growth in the number of free and reduced-price (FRP) meals. About 15 percent of school lunches were FRP in 1969, while 74 percent were in 2017. Currently, the NSLP serves lunch to almost thirty million students or 60 percent of the total student population.

Empirical research suggests that the NSLP has been effective at inducing children to eat more during the school day. In particular, NSLP participants consume more vitamins and minerals at lunch than nonparticipants and consume more calories in a typical day (Gleason and Suitor 2001). However, there is little evidence that the program affects child weight, indicating that when food is provided at school, children may substitute away from higher-calorie foods at home (Millimet, Tchernis, and Husain 2010).

Moreover, given that the symptoms of hunger include fatigue, dizziness, and lack of concentration, one may expect that increasing food availability during the school day improves students' educational outcomes. However, the evidence on the extent to which both programs improve academic performance is mixed, although there is some evidence that the NSLP reduces academic suspensions (Gordon and Ruffini 2018). For example, Frisvold (2015) and Dotter (2013) both find that school breakfasts improve reading and math performance, but other studies report no effects (Imberman and Kugler 2014; Bartlett et al. 2014; Schanzenbach and Zaki 2014). Similarly, the existing literature tends to find SBP improves nutritional intake during breakfast and reduces food insecurity for young children, but it shows mixed results on overall nutritional intake (Bhattacharya, Currie, and Haider 2006; Fletcher and Frisvold 2017).

Overall, there is substantial evidence that nutritional assistance policies in the United States reduce hunger and food insecurity and impose lifelong benefits for women and children. Ellen Haas, undersecretary of the Department of Agriculture, summed up the importance of food and nutrition programs in a 1995 testimony, stating,

> [T]he three anchors of the Nation's nutrition security strategy [are] the Child Nutrition Programs, the Special Supplemental Nutrition Program for Women, Infants, and Children (WIC), and the Food Stamp Program. Together, these programs form a network of food and nutrition assistance that ensures that every low-income American—regardless of who they are or where they live—has access to a nutritious diet.

Yet, with a large proportion of low-income families still reporting food insecurity, it would seem that there may be some scope for such programs to play an even larger role. In light of recent proposed federal policies to cut SNAP and school meal programs, including the president's fiscal year (FY) 2018 budget and the House Budget Committee's FY 2018 budget resolution, these findings have important and far-reaching implications. Extrapolating from a large body of empirical findings, these proposed cuts could exacerbate food insecurity and widen gaps in educational and economic outcomes for low-income individuals.

Analisa Packham

Further Reading

Bartlett, Susan, Jacob Klerman, Parke Wilde, Lauren Olsho, Christopher Logan, Michelle Blocklin, Marianne Beauregard, and Ayesha Enver. 2014. *Evaluation of the Healthy Incentives Pilot (HIP): Final Report.* U.S. Food and Nutrition Service. Department of Agriculture. Cambridge, MA: Abt Associates.

Bhattacharya, Jayanta, Janet Currie, and Steven Haider. 2006. "Breakfast of Champions? The Effects of the School Breakfast Program on the Nutrition of Children and Their Families." *Journal of Human Resources* 41 (3): 445–66.

Bitler, Marianne, and Janet Currie. 2005. "Does WIC Work? The Effects of WIC on Pregnancy and Birth Outcomes." *Journal of Policy Analysis and Management* 24 (1): 73–91.

Bond, Timothy, Jillian Carr, Analisa Packham, and Jonathan Smith. 2020. "Hungry for Success? SNAP Timing, High-Stakes Exam Performance, and College Attendance." https://apackham.github.io/mywebsite/SNAP_SAT_v5.7.pdf.

Carr, Jillian, and Analisa Packham. 2019. "SNAP Benefits and Crime: Evidence from Changing Disbursement Schedules." *Review of Economics and Statistics,* 1–16.

Dotter, Dallas D. 2013. "Breakfast at the Desk: The Impact of Universal Breakfast Programs on Academic Achievement." http://www.appam.org/assets/1/7/Breakfast_ at_the_Desk_The_Impact_of_Universal_Breakfast_Programs_on_Academic _Performance.pdf.

Dunifon, Rachel, and Lori Kowaleski-Jones. 2003. "Associations between Participation in the National School Lunch Program, Food Insecurity, and Child Well-Being." *Social Service Review* 77 (1): 72–92.

Eisinger, Peter. 1998. *Toward an End to Hunger in America.* Washington, DC: Brookings Institution Press.

Figlio, David, Sarah Hamersma, and Jeffrey Roth. 2009. "Does Prenatal WIC Participation Improve Birth Outcomes? New Evidence from Florida." *Journal of Public Economics* 93 (1–2): 235–45.

Finkelstein, Amy, and Matthew J. Notowidigdo. 2018. *Take-Up and Targeting: Experiemental Evidence from SNAP.* NBER Working Paper 24652. National Bureau of Economic Research. http://www.nber.org/papers/w24652.

Fletcher, Jason, and David Frisvold. 2017. "The Relationship between the School Breakfast Program and Food Insecurity." *Journal of Consumer Affairs* 51 (3): 481–500.

Frisvold, David E. 2015. "Nutrition and Cognitive Achievement: An Evaluation of the School Breakfast Program." *Journal of Public Economics* 124:91–104.

Gassman-Pines, Anna, and Laura Bellows. 2018. "Food Instability and Academic Achievement: A Quasi-Experiment Using SNAP Benefit Timing." *American Educational Research Journal* 55 (5): 897–927.

Gennetian, Lisa A., Sharon Wolf, Heather D. Hill, and Pamela A. Morris. 2015. "Intrayear Household Income Dynamics and Adolescent School Behavior." *Demography* 52:455–83.

Gleason, Phillip, and Carol Suitor. 2001. *Children's Diets in the Mid-1990s: Dietary Intake and Its Relationship with School Meal Participation.* Special Nutrition Programs Report CN-01-CD1, U.S. Department of Agriculture, Food and Nutrition Service. Alexandria, VA: Office of Analysis, Nutrition and Evaluation. https://fns -prod.azureedge.net/sites/default/files/ChilDiet.pdf.

Gordon, Nora E., and Krista J. Ruffini. 2018. *School Nutrition and Student Discipline: Effects of Schoolwide Free Meals.* NBER Working Paper 24986. National Bureau of Economic Research. http://www.nber.org/papers/w24986.

Hinrichs, Peter 2010. "The Effects of the National School Lunch Program on Education and Health." *Journal of Policy Analysis and Management* 29 (3): 479–505.

Hoynes, Hilary, Marianne Page, and Ann Huff Stevens. 2011. "Can Targeted Transfers Improve Birth Outcomes? Evidence from the Introduction of the WIC Program." *Journal of Public Economics* 95 (7–8): 813–27.

Hoynes, Hilary W., and Diane W. Schanzenbach. 2009. "Consumption Responses to In-Kind Transfers: Evidence from the Introduction of the Food Stamp Program." *American Economic Journal: Applied Economics* 1 (4): 109–39.

Hoynes, Hilary W., Diane W. Schanzenbach, and Douglas Almond. 2016. "Long-Run Impacts of Childhood Access to the Safety Net." *American Economic Review* 106 (4): 903–34.

Imberman, Scott, and Adriana D. Kugler. 2014. "The Effect of Providing Breakfast in Class on Student Performance." *Journal of Policy Analysis and Management* 33 (3): 669–99.

Kreider, Brent, John V. Pepper, Craig Gundersen, and Dean Jolliffe. 2012. "Identifying the Effects of SNAP (Food Stamps) on Child Health Outcomes When Participation Is Endogenous and Misreported." *Journal of the American Statistical Association* 107 (499): 958–75.

Mabli, James, Jim Ohls, Lisa Dragoset, Laura Castner, and Betsy Santos. 2013. *Measuring the Effect of Supplemental Nutrition Assistance Program (SNAP) Participation on Food Security.* Nutrition Assistance Program Report, Food and Nutrition Service Office of Policy Support. Washington, DC: U.S. Department of Agriculture. https://fns-prod.azureedge.net/sites/default/files/Measuring2013.pdf.

Millimet, Daniel L., Rusty Tchernis, and Muna Husain. 2010. "School Nutrition Programs and the Incidence of Childhood Obesity." *Journal of Human Resources* 45 (3): 640–54.

Ratcliffe, Caroline, Signe-Mary McKearnan, and Sisi Zhang. 2011. "How Much Does the Supplemental Nutrition Assistance Program Reduce Food Insecurity?" *American Journal of Agricultural Economics* 93 (4): 1082–98.

Rossin-Slater, Maya. 2013. "WIC in Your Neighborhood: New Evidence on the Impacts of Geographic Access to Clinics." *Journal of Public Economics* 102:51–69.

Schanzenbach, Diane, and Mary Zaki. 2014. *Expanding the School Breakfast Program: Impacts on Children's Consumption, Nutrition, and Health.* NBER Working Paper Series 20308. National Bureau of Economic Research. http://www.nber/org/papers/w20308.

Schmidt, Lucie, Lara Shore-Sheppard, and Tara Watson. 2016. "The Effect of Safety-Net Programs on Food Insecurity." *Journal of Human Resources* 51:589–614.

USDA (U.S. Department of Agriculture). 2018. "Supplemental Nutrition Assistance Program (SNAP)." *National Level Annual Summary.* Washington DC: Food and Nutrition Service. https://fns-prod.azureedge.net/sites/default/files/pd/34SNAPmonthly.pdf.

Health Insurance

Health insurance is meant to facilitate access to health care services at "affordable" prices. Most Americans have private health insurance, typically through their employer. Others are covered through a variety of government-sponsored programs, such as Medicare and Medicaid. In 2018, 8.5 percent of Americans lacked health insurance at any point during the year, up from 7.9 percent in 2017. Private insurance is the primary type of coverage (67.3 percent of the population), with most such policies obtained through employers (55.1 percent of the population) (Berchick, Barnett, and Upton 2019). Additional details of 2018 health insurance coverage are shown in table 1.

Health insurance coverage is disparate across several groups and characteristics. Of Americans between nineteen and twenty-five years of age, 85.7 percent are insured, compared with 90.7 percent and 99.1 percent of those in the forty-five to sixty-four and sixty-five-plus age groups, respectively. Working-age adults with a disability are more likely to be insured than those without (90.4 percent and 88.5 percent, respectively) and those working full time and year-round are more likely to be insured (90.5 percent) than nonworkers (86.9 percent.) Finally, individuals in households with an annual income of less than $25,000 were less likely to be insured than those with over $150,000 in annual income (86.2 percent versus 96.8 percent, respectively) (Berchick, Barnett, and Upton 2019). The uninsured are a considerable policy and political focus. The U.S. health insurance market underwent considerable reform with the 2010 Patient Protection and Affordable Care Act (PPACA), also known as Obamacare. Since its implementation, the ACA has significantly reduced the number of Americans without health insurance, but millions more remain uncovered—and the future of the ACA is cloudy due to continued challenges to the law from liberals, who think the law does not go far enough, and from conservatives, who think the law has caused economic disruption and violated constitutional guarantees of freedom of action.

Table 1   Health Insurance Coverage, 2018

Uninsured (%)			8.5
With health insurance (%)			**91.5**
2018 Types of Coverage (%)			
Any Private Plan	67.3	**Any Public Plan**	34.4
Employment-based	55.1	Medicare	17.8
Direct-purchase[1]	10.8	Medicaid	17.9
TRICARE	2.6	VA and CHAMPVA	1.0

[1]Refers to coverage purchased directly from an insurance company or through a federal or state marketplace.

Source: Berchick, Barnett, and Upton (2019).

HOW HEALTH INSURANCE WORKS

Health care is expensive, and health insurance offers a way to reduce the risk of experiencing a large income outlay in the event of a serious health complication or illness. Health insurance policies are purchased by an individual directly or indirectly through an employer or the government. The duration of the policy, called the *term*, is typically twelve months. The price of a policy is the *premium*, often charged on a monthly basis. In exchange for the premium, the health insurance company shares the individual's health risk with other policyholders, or *enrollees*. All enrollees paying a similar premium for a similar service are in the same "pool," or *group*. Since only a fraction of all enrollees in the pool will get sick at one time, the financial arrangement is beneficial to both the insurance company and the individuals seeking to reduce their financial risk.

Each insurance policy covers all medical goods and services as stated in the policy. If a procedure, visit, or medication is *covered*, policyholders often pay less for it than if they did not have insurance. It is generally believed that consumers behave differently when they are insured compared with when they are uninsured. Specifically, the insured are more likely to engage in risky, health-diminishing activities (i.e., exercising less or speeding) since they are not bearing the full burden of the cost associated with a bad outcome. This tendency, called *moral hazard*, is mitigated by cost-sharing mechanisms built into insurance policies, such as deductibles, coinsurance, and copayments.

A *deductible* is a dollar amount that the enrollee pays before insurance begins to contribute funds toward payment for medical services. Out-of-pocket payments by the policyholder accumulate throughout the calendar year toward the deductible. For example, if a policyholder has a $500 deductible and receives a medical bill for $400, the individual must pay the entire $400. The same person, if billed $200 for another procedure in the same calendar year, is responsible for the first $100, thereby meeting the annual deductible. The rest of that bill ($100) and all other covered medical services are shared between the policyholder and the insurance company.

Once the deductible is met, the policyholder and the insurance company share the responsibility of payments through coinsurance and copayments. *Coinsurance* defines the percentage of a medical bill that the enrollee pays, while a *copayment* refers to a dollar amount. For example, with a coinsurance rate of 10 percent, the policyholder pays 10 percent of the bill, while the insurance company is responsible for the remainder. A copayment of twenty dollars means that the patient pays twenty dollars for a medical procedure. The service costs more than twenty dollars, but the insurance company is billed the remainder. Each of these cost-sharing mechanisms is intended to disincentivize overuse of medical care while keeping it affordable.

Health insurance is one of many goods and services consumers purchase each year, although the pricing is considerably more complicated than for other items. The IRS permits some individuals to purchase employer-provided health insurance with pretax dollars since they are not considered wages (Internal Revenue Service 2019). Others, including the self-employed, are not given this allowance. Therefore, a given health insurance policy is more expensive for the self-employed, and the price varies according to the individual's tax bracket.

Most Americans have access to a health insurance plan through their employers, and many take up that offer, using the pretax benefit. Self-employed individuals, those who earn income but have no employees, can also purchase private health insurance through the government-facilitated marketplace, which has income-based tax credits and other savings (U.S. Centers for Medicare and Medicaid Services, n.d.a). Federal and state governments sponsor several public health insurance programs for a variety of groups, including the elderly, pregnant mothers, and children (U.S. Centers for Medicare & Medicaid Services, n.d.b). The 2010 PPACA included Medicaid expansion to individuals living at 138 percent of the poverty level, although states, which jointly fund Medicaid programs with the federal government, were not required to follow the expansion. Some did not, for fear that they would not be able to support it during economic downturns and when federal subsidies for the expansion expired Additionally, some opposed it for political reasons. Unlike the federal government, many states are required to run a balanced budget, making the financial issues surrounding expansion a short-term concern for states. Those states that chose to expand their Medicaid program are often called *expansion states*.

Despite these options, in 2018, 8.5 percent of the U.S. population remained uninsured. The premium elasticity of demand for marketplace plans implies that a 1-percent increase in premium reduces plan-specific enrollment by 1.7 percent, likely in part due to the availability of substitutes (Abraham et al. 2017). The

Table 2   Uninsured Rates by Poverty Level, 2018

	Expansion States (%)	Nonexpansion States (%)
Below 100% of poverty level	16.9	35.6
100–399% of poverty level	12.7	21.2
At 400% or above of poverty level	3.5	6.2

Source: Berchick, Barnett, and Upton (2019, 13).

uninsured rate is higher in states without a Medicaid expansion and decreases with the percentage below the poverty level, as shown in table 2. Those further below the poverty level likely have access to a greater number of public programs and resources than do those at the margin. Individuals of greatest coverage concern are those in nonexpansion states who are living below 100 percent of the poverty level. These people are often too poor to afford health insurance on their own and make too much to qualify for government-sponsored support.

HEALTH INSURANCE CHANGES IN THE 2010S

The U.S. health insurance market underwent significant reform with the 2010 passage of the PPACA (Obamacare) in 2010. Over nine hundred pages long (excluding amendments), the bill covered many aspects pertaining to health care in the United States. Two of the major pieces of the legislation were the (1) individual mandate and (2) employer mandate, each aimed at expanding qualified health insurance coverage of Americans. *Qualified* health insurance is determined by the federal government and must include essential minimum benefits or coverage of specific services. The hope was that by giving individuals and employers a choice between health insurance coverage or a penalty, the number of uninsured would decline. Additionally, by adding younger and healthier individuals to the health insurance pools, the overall risk level of enrollees—and thus the cost—would fall. Arguments against the mandates included infringement of personal choice and liberty.

The individual mandate required that all U.S. citizens and legal residents have qualifying (public or private) health insurance coverage by 2014 or else pay a penalty enforced by the IRS. There were several exemptions to this requirement, however, including ones for low-income households. The law also provided for subsidies, or health insurance premium tax credits, to assist low-income households in the purchase of a plan. Individuals must provide evidence of health insurance coverage when filing income taxes or risk paying a penalty. The 2017 Tax Cuts and Jobs Act eliminated the penalty for noncompliance with the individual mandate, which went into effect in 2019. It is estimated that the elimination of the penalty reduced enrollment by 2.8 million, to a total of 13 million, and raised premiums by 3 percent, to 13 percent (Eibner and Nowak 2018). The employer mandate requires that all employers with fifty or more full-time-equivalent (FTE) employees offer affordable, minimum value, and qualified health insurance to full-time employees or else pay a penalty. *Affordability*, defined by PPACA, means employees pay no more than 9.56 percent of their family income for the health insurance coverage. *Minimum value* requires that the policy pay 60 percent of covered health-care expenses. As with the individual mandate, the policy must cover essential minimum benefits. To date, the employer mandate remains in effect despite some concerns about labor market effects due to the costs to employers (Kassens 2017). Concerns include the likelihood that employers close to fifty FTEs are incentivized to lay off those workers or cut hours to get under the threshold. A 2015 survey of Virginia CEOs found that over 60 percent of both small and large employers report health-care costs as being a considerable challenge, and at the time, over 65 percent supported repealing PPACA (Kassens 2016). Additionally, the mandate increases IRS information-reporting costs for employers (SHRM 2019).

DIAGNOSING AND FIXING AMERICA'S HEALTH COVERAGE INEQUITIES

During the Democratic presidential primary campaign in 2020, several proposals for further expanding health insurance coverage in the United States were touted by prominent candidates. Most of these proposals were variations of "Medicare-for-All," or a national health insurance program on a much greater scale than current programs are. Plans ranged from adding public features to private health insurance to nationalized health care (Commonwealth Fund 2019). For example, Senator Elizabeth Warren's Consumer Health Insurance Protection Act of 2018 (S. 2582) proposed to alter subsidies for marketplace plans for individuals not eligible for employer, Medicare, or Medicaid coverage. To assist in costs, the bill decreased the share of premiums that insurers either take in as profit or use toward administration expenses. Additionally, states and the federal government could bar premium increases in the individual health insurance market under her proposal (115th Congress 2018). In contrast, in 2017, Representative Keith Ellison sponsored the Expanded and Improved Medicare for All Act (H.R. 676), which proposed to create a national health insurance program that would replace most current government programs, including Medicare and Medicaid, and all private health insurance plans. The system required no premiums and would be funded from increased taxes on the top 5 percent of earners (115th Congress 2017). As of early 2020, the Congressional Budget Office (CBO) has not executed a cost analysis for either of these plans. All the proposals add more restrictions and further restrict the market process.

Market-based solutions are slowly taking hold to address health-care access and affordability issues. The health insurance and health-care markets are highly regulated, so any attempt at incorporating a market-based approach is unusual. Health insurance certainly provides potential for access to health care and for when it is received, typically at subsidized rates, but it is no guarantee, particularly for unplanned visits to doctors outside of the emergency room (ER). Even if one has health insurance when an acute health issue occurs, an immediate appointment may not be possible. Retail clinics are becoming an increasingly common option. They are typically housed within drugstores, big-box stores, and supermarkets and staffed by physician assists and nurse practitioners. The clinics offer a variety of services, including vaccinations, physicals, and treatment of minor illnesses such as the flu, are frequently open for twelve or more hours a day, and are relatively inexpensive, offering a fixed pricing schedule that is published online. One study found that retail clinics are 30–40 percent cheaper than a doctor's office visit and 80 percent cheaper than an ER visit and offer equal to superior quality of care (Godman 2016). In 2016, there were over two thousand retail clinics. Downsides to the retail clinics include concerns that records from the clinics will not make it to a patient's regular doctor's office and that the cause of the visit might be a symptom of a more serious illness that might be overlooked (God-man 2016). The latter is less of a concern, given that nurse practitioners' training goes beyond the basics, and the scope of practice laws that exist in many states are more for the purposes of physician rent seeking rather than patient protection. Physicians have market power over particular health services and rely on laws, such as scope of practice laws, to maintain it and the associated revenues (Kassens and Isaacs 2017).

CONCLUSION

Although most Americans (91.5 percent in 2018) have health insurance, there are disparities between the insured and uninsured. In 2018, the uninsured are typically young (nineteen to twenty-five years of age), work part time, have less than a high school diploma, and live at the margin of the poverty level. These individuals are most often in Medicaid expansion states, earn too little to afford health insurance, but do not qualify for government assistance. They face considerable financial constraints. Currently there are several proposals to reform the health insurance market, most a variation of Medicare expansion as compared to the PPACA Medicaid expansion. There is no strong evidence that these plans will, in fact, insure the remaining 8.5 percent of Americans who are uninsured nor are there reliable cost estimates of such plans. The PPACA, which came at a considerable expense, significantly reduced the number of Americans without health insurance, but millions of uninsured remain. Given that health insurance does not presently guarantee access to low-cost health care, some observers believe that market-based approaches such as retail clinics may be a more cost-effective method to provide health care to the uninsured.

Alice Louise Kassens

Further Reading

Abraham, Jean, Drake Coleman, Daniel Sacks, and Kosali Simon. 2017. "Demand for Health Insurance Marketplace Plans Was Highly Elastic in 2014–2015." *Economics Letters* 159: 69–73.

Aron-Dine, Aviva, Liran Einav, Amy Finkelstein, and Mark R. Cullen. 2015. "Moral Hazard in Health Insurance: Do Dynamic Incentives Matter?" *Review of Economics and Statistics* 97: 725–41.

Barringer, Melissa, and Olivia Mitchell. 1994. "Workers' Preferences among Company-Provided Health Insurance Plans." *Industrial and Labor Relations Review* 48: 141–52.

Berchick, Edward, Jessica Barnett, and Rachel Upton. 2019. *Health Insurance Coverage in the United States: 2018.* Washington, DC: U.S. Government Printing Office.

Commonwealth Fund. 2019. *Where Do U.S. Health Reform Proposals Fall on the Medicare-for-All Continuum?* https://www.commonwealthfund.org/many-varie ties-universal-coverage.

Eibner, Christine, and Sarah Nowak. 2018. *The Effect of Eliminating the Indivudal Mandate Penalty and the Role of Behavioral Factors.* New York: Commonwealth Fund. https://www.commonwealthfund.org/sites/default/files/2018-07/Eibner_individual_mandate_repeal.pdf.

Eillis, Randall, Bruno Martins, and Wenjia Zhu. 2017. "Health Care Demand Elasticities by Type of Service." *Journal of Health Economics* 55 (September): 232–43.

Godman, Heidi. 2016. "Retail Health Clinics: The Pros and Cons." *Harvard Medical School: Harvard Health Blog*, January 15, 2016. https://www.health.harvard.edu/blog/retail-health-clinics-the-pros-and-cons-201601158979.

Internal Revenue Service. 2019. *Tax Information for Businesses.* April 8, 2019. https://www.irs.gov/businesses" April 8, 2019. https://www.irs.gov/businesses.

Kassens, Alice. 2016. *Survey of Virginia Business Leaders.* Salem, VA: Roanoke College, Institute for Policy and Opinion Research.

Kassens, Alice Louise. 2017. "The Potential Economic Costs of the Affordable Healthcare Act." In *The American Middle Class: An Economic Encyclopedia of Progress and Poverty*, edited by Robert Rycroft, 63–6. Westport, CT: Greenwood Publishers.

Kassens, Alice Louise, and Justin Isaacs. 2017. "Impact of Standards of Practice Legislation on Advanced Practice Nurses and Health Care Outcomes." Working Paper (November): 1–21.

Liu, Su, and Deborah Chollet. 2006. "Price and Income Elasticity of Demand for Health Insurance and Health Care Services: A Review of the Literature." *Mathematica Policy Research Reference No. 6203-042*, 1–98.

"Obesity Rates by Country Population." 2019. November 6, 2019. http://worldpopulationreview.com/countries/obesity-rates-by-country.

111th Congress. 2010. "Patient Protection and Affordable Care Act, H.R. 3590." March 23, 2010, 1–906. https://www.govinfo.gov/content/pkg/PLAW-111publ148/pdf/PLAW-111publ148.pdf.

115th Congress. 2017. "Expanded and Improved Medicare for All Act, H.R. 676."

115th Congress. 2018. "Consumer Health Insurance Protection Act of 2018, S. 2582."

Phelps, Charles. 2018. *Health Economics.* New York: Routledge.

Ringel, Jeanne, Susan Hosek, Ben Vollaard, and Sergej Mahnovski. 2005. *The Elasticity of Demand for Health Care: A Review of the Literature and its Application to the Military Health System.* Washington, DC: RAND.

SHRM. 2019. "What Are the Employer Shared Responsibility Penalties under the Patient Protection and Affordable Care Act (PPACA)?" *ww.* December 19, 2019. https://www.shrm.org/resourcesandtools/tools-and-samples/hr-qa/pages/penaltiesforfailingtocomply.aspx" *HR Q&AS.* December 19, 2019. https://www.shrm.org/resourcesandtools/tools-and-samples/hr-qa/pages/penaltiesforfailingtocomply.aspx.

U.S. Centers for Medicare & Medicaid Services. n.d.a. *Health Coverage if You're Self-Employed.* https://www.healthcare.gov/self-employed/coverage.

U.S. Centers for Medicare & Medicaid Services. n.d.b. *Home.* https://www.cms.gov.

Housing Inequality

Housing is one of the largest consumer expenditures in the United States and is an important contributor to economic inequality.

Aggregate statistics regarding housing are impressive and emphasize the significance of the housing sector to the macroeconomy. Statistics from 1976 to 2012 show that residential housing investments and consumption spending on housing services have averaged a combined 17 to 18 percent of Gross Domestic Product (GDP). The housing industry generates an average of approximately 1.7 million new residential housing units each year. In the 1980s, single-family homes accounted for about 50 percent of the residential construction, while in the 2000s, the percentage went up to around 80 percent. Since 1973, the American Housing Survey has collected some basic housing characteristics, such as the size of the living area. Data show that median square footage of the living area has increased almost every year. In 1973, the average size of all homes was 1,660 square feet, while in 2015, the average size had increased to 2,687 square feet.

In the 1940s, a majority of the households were renters, but over the next twenty years, the homeownership rate rose considerably, to about 60 percent. This growth in homeownership rates was driven by the Federal Housing and Veterans Administrations' invention of the thirty-year amortizing, fixed-rate mortgage policy. The homeownership rate gradually climbed up and reached a peak of about 69 percent in 2004 before shifting down at the end of that decade, when the so-called Great Recession rocked the American economy. This grim economic downturn stemmed in considerable measure from a subprime mortgage crisis in the American housing market, as lenders made too many unsound mortgage loans to home buyers. It took several years for the American housing market—and the overall economy—to recover from this recession.

While the housing industry has steadily grown over time (albeit with upturns and downturns reflecting larger economic trends), housing inequality has always been a critical issue. Housing inequality usually is shown as an imbalance in the quality and quantity of housing in a society. It is often a result of poverty, discrimination, or segregation. Clearly defining and understanding housing inequality helps explain important subjects such as racial, social, consumption, and wealth inequality.

Housing inequality in the United States can be viewed from different angles. Housing inequality can be described through a distribution change of housing consumption across the entire population. Housing inequality can also be demonstrated through distribution changes of important factors, such as housing consumption and the homeownership rate, across groups differentiated by household incomes, race and ethnicity, age of householders, and many other characteristics.

HOUSING CONSUMPTION INEQUALITY

The level and distribution of *housing consumption* (expenditure on housing) by households is a fundamental aspect of a housing system. Some households live in palatial mansions, while others live in cramped and drafty apartments.

Urban economists David Albouy and Mike Zabek examined the distribution change in housing consumption across the entire population in the United States. They investigated housing inequality over eighty-five years, from the onset of the Great Depression in 1930 through the recovery from the 2008 financial crisis, up to 2012. They found a clear, U-shaped pattern in housing inequality over this eighty-five-year period. Housing inequality was high during the Great Depression, gradually declined afterward, hit bottom and started to climb up in the 1970s, and finally, in 2012, returned to the identical level of inequality as was present in the 1930s (Albouy and Zabek 2016).

The main driver of the rise in housing inequality may be the increase in *housing segregation*. As rich people become richer, they tend to invest more in high-quality neighborhoods. Housing inequality is thus strongly correlated with income inequality (Albouy and Zabek 2016). Research also shows that the increase in housing consumption inequality is less than the income inequality. Niku Määttänen and Marko Terviö (2014) estimated the impact of increased income inequality between 1998 and 2007 on the distribution of house prices in six U.S. metropolitan regions. They found that the increase in income inequality had a negative impact on the average house price.

In the meantime, housing consumption is unequal over the life cycle. Fang Yang (2009) found that the consumption profile for housing increases monotonically and then flattens out. At the beginning of the life cycle, households have minimal housing consumption. They then start accumulating housing. As households age, due to the high transaction costs for trading houses, households cannot decrease their housing stock quickly, and their housing consumption remains stable.

FACTORS IN HOMEOWNERSHIP INEQUALITY

The *homeownership rate* is the percentage of homes that are owned by their occupants. Homeownership rate is an important characteristic of the housing market. Homeownership in the United States has been a key driving force for upward mobility and wealth accumulation and is related to some vital social economic issues. Some researchers have argued that homeownership promotes civic and community involvement as well as stable neighborhoods and that homeowners invest more than renters in the improvement of housing.

Researchers have also found that homeowning has a cognitive and behavioral impact on children's outcomes (Haurin, Parcel, and Haurin 2002). Compared to renting, owning a home is associated with a 13- to 23-percent higher-quality home environment, higher levels of cognitive ability, and fewer child behavior problems. Broadly speaking, owning a home has been associated with greater stability and better home environments for children. These benefits can spill over into other areas of child development, including educational attainment. For example, children living in owned homes perform better in math and reading and have fewer behavioral problems. Stephen Whelan (2017) found that children in owner-occupied dwellings achieve better education outcomes, including high school completion and college attendance, than do children in rental households.

Of course, homeowners also have to learn how to do some maintenance jobs, how to solve their financial problems when they encounter unexpected home repair costs, and how to get along with their neighbors to maintain a healthy and stable neighborhood environment. All of these added responsibilities, however, are a potential driving force of learning and accomplishment.

Homeowning has been encouraged by policy makers since at least as far back as the 1920s, when President Herbert Hoover stated that "a family that owns its own home takes pride in it and has a more wholesome, healthful, and happy atmosphere in which to bring up children" (Green and White 1997).

In the past twenty years, the homeownership rate in the United States has been relatively stable, ranging from approximately 63 percent to 69 percent of all residences. However, homeownership rates vary considerable among different geographic regions across the country. Table 1 shows the homeownership rates for the United States as a whole and for four different regions in 2017. Homeownership rates for the midwestern and southern states were higher than the national average, while the northeastern and western states were lower than the national average. In particular, the midwestern states had the highest homeownership rate, with the western states having the lowest.

Homeownership is more common in rural and suburban areas. As shown in table 2, homeownership rates are the highest in rural areas, with approximately 72 percent of the households owning houses, while principal cities have the lowest rate, with only about 49 percent of the households owning houses. The higher

Table 1   Homeownership Rates for the United States and Different Regions in 2017

United States	63.9
Northeast	60.5
Midwest	68.4
South	65.6
West	59.2

Source: U.S. Census Bureau (2018).

Table 2   Homeownership Rates for Different Areas

	2015	2016	2017
United States	63.7	63.4	63.9
Inside Metropolitan Statistical Areas	62.2	61.9	62.3
In principal cities	48.9	48.4	49.2
Not in principal cities			
(Suburbs)	70.7	70.7	70.9
.Outside Metropolitan Statistical Areas	71.6	72.3	73.0

Source: U.S. Census Bureau (2018).

homeownership rate in rural and suburban areas may be caused by less expensive housing cost compared to that of urban/metropolitan areas.

Homeownership rates also vary depending on household characteristics such as income, race, and ethnicity, and age of householder. Homeownership tends to be more common for high-income households.

Homeownership Rates by Race and Ethnicity

Homeownership rates are unequal among different racial and ethnic groups in the United States. The homeownership rate of minorities in the United States has continued to lag behind that of white Americans. Table 3 presents summary statistics of homeownership rates from 1994 to 2017 by different categories. As shown in panel A, the homeownership rate is the highest for non-Hispanic white Americans and lowest for Black Americans. Between 1994 and 2017, the average homeownership rate for the non-Hispanic white sector is 73.5 percent, which is higher than the national average of 66.4 percent. During the same time period, the average homeownership rates for Blacks and Hispanics are only 45.3 percent and 46.3 percent, respectively.

Sanjaya DeSilva and Yuval Elmelech (2012) used data from the 2000 Integrated Public Use Microdata Series (IPUMS) and the 2006 American Community Survey (ACS) to study the homeownership inequality of different race and ethnicity groups, such as Black, Asian, white, and Latinx households. The paper investigates various socioeconomic and demographic characteristics as well as the distinct immigration experiences and spatial patterns that affect racial and ethnic inequality in homeownership. They found that despite the fact that recent arrivals have low homeownership rates, immigrants eventually catch up and surpass their native-born counterparts.

Racial residential segregation and discrimination in housing and mortgage markets might be partly responsible for the inequality. Many studies have found that Black and Hispanic households are discriminated against when seeking to

find a home or obtain a mortgage. Since the majority of house buyers need to purchase their homes with the help of mortgage loans, homeownership and mortgage
lending are highly correlated. Stephen Ross and John Yinger provided an in-depth
review of mortgage-lending discrimination in 1990s. They analyzed the loan-
approval and loan-performance data in the Boston area and found disparities in
the process of loan approval for minorities versus whites. The disparities in the
Boston data do represent discrimination (Ross and Yinger 2002). In a 2019 study,
Manthos D. Delis and Panagiotis Papadopoulos used data from 6.5 million loan
applications from 2004 through 2013 to examine mortgage-lending discrimination across the United States. They found that, compared with African Americans,
white applicants had approximately a 0.39-percent higher probability of being
granted a loan, and non-Hispanic applicants had a 0.25-percent higher probability
than Hispanic applicants did.

Homeownership Rate by Household Income

The homeownership rate is positively related to household income. Table 3,
panel B shows the homeownership rates for different income groups from 1994 to

Table 3　Summary Statistics of Homeownership Rates from 1994 to 2017

	Mean	Standard Deviation	Minimum	Maximum
United States	66.4	1.8	62.9	69.2
Panel A: By Race and Ethnicity Groups				
Non-Hispanic white alone	73.5	1.7	69.8	76.2
Black alone	45.3	2.4	41.2	49.7
All other races	54.8	3.3	46.3	60.6
Hispanic (of any race)	46.3	2.4	40.3	50.1
Panel B: By Household Income				
Households with family income greater than or equal to the median family income	81.2	2.0	77.8	84.6
Households with family income less than the median family income	50.8	1.4	48.0	53.1
Panel C: By Age of Householder				
Under 35 years	39.2	2.6	34.1	43.6
35 to 44 years	65.1	3.6	58.0	70.1
45 to 54 years	74.3	2.5	69.1	77.4
55 to 64 years	79.3	2.1	74.7	82.4
65 years and over	79.9	1.0	77.2	81.8

Source: U.S. Census Bureau (2018).

2017. Compared to the U.S. average, households with family income greater than or equal to the median family income have a much higher homeownership rate, with the highest, 84.6 percent, in 2006 and the lowest, 77.8 percent, in 2016, and an average of 81.2 percent during the period between 1994 and 2017. During the same time period, the homeownership rate of the households with family income less than the median family income ranged from 48 percent to 53.1 percent, with an average of 50.8 percent.

Homeownership Rate by Age of Householder

Homeownership rate varies by the age of the householder. Table 3, panel C shows the U.S. homeownership rate by age of the householder from 1994 to 2017. The general trend is that the older the householder, the higher the homeownership rate. Householders aged sixty-five years and older have the highest homeownership rate, averaging about 80 percent. Householders aged fifty-five to sixty-four years have a slightly lower homeownership rate, with an average of 79.3 percent. The next two groups are householders aged forty-five to fifty-four years and thirty-five to forty-four years, with an average of 74.3-percent and 65.1-percent homeownership rate, respectively. Compared to other age groups, householders under thirty-five years of age have significantly lower homeownership rate, only about 39 percent. The group sixty-five years and older also has the lowest standard deviation (the standard deviation is a measure of variation within a group; the lower the standard deviation, the less the variation) compared to the other four age groups.

The general trend of inequality by age of householders reflects a common norm of asset accumulation. As a consumer gets older, the possibility of purchasing a home tends to be higher. Several factors contribute to this trend, such as more wealth, better credit rating, and lifestyle changes.

Home Price-to-Income Ratio Inequality

The *home price-to-income ratio* is a key measurement of housing affordability. It is calculated by dividing the median home price by median household income in the area. Based on historical nationwide averages under healthy economic conditions, homeowners can afford a house if the price is roughly 2.6 times of their yearly household income. Across the nation, however, the home price-to-income ratio is extremely unequally distributed.

The Joint Center for Housing Studies at Harvard University published a home price-to-income ratio map in 2017. Coastal cities of California, such as Los Angeles and San Jose, have the highest home price-to-income ratios in the nation, while the most affordable metropolitan areas in the country are mainly in the Rust Belt, such as the Youngstown-Warren-Boardman region of Northeast Ohio. In Los Angeles it takes nearly ten years' income for the median household to buy the median-priced home. In contrast, in Youngstown, Ohio, the home buyer with median income only needs to spend two year's income to buy a median-priced home (Joint Center for Housing Studies at Harvard University 2017). The problem of housing affordability in areas with high home price-to-income ratio is mainly due to land use regulations and geographic constraints (i.e., bodies of water and mountainous terrain).

POLICIES TO REDUCE HOUSING INEQUALITY

As an important source of social and economic well-being, housing afford-ability and equality has always been promoted by policy makers. One of the important objectives of national housing policy is to provide an adequate supply of single-family-owned and rental housing that is affordable to people of all income levels, races, ages, and is suitable for their various needs (Katz et al. 2003). Sound housing policies also aim to promote racial and economic diversity (Katz et al. 2003) and reduce racial and economic segregation (Green and Malpezzi 2003, 85).

Since the 1930s, the U.S. government has used two approaches to promote affordability and equality in housing. The first approach targets the demand side of the housing market. The Federal Housing Administration (FHA) provides sup-port for the private housing industry by offering mortgage insurance to lenders who provide mortgages to single-family house buyers and developers of multi-family projects. The second approach aims at increasing the housing supply in the market through federal and local public housing authorities that build and manage apartment buildings for low-income households to rent. The public housing pro-gram subsidizes the construction, operation, and maintenance of publicly owned multifamily rental housing properties. The properties are rented to eligible low-income families, the elderly, and persons with disabilities at highly subsidized rates. Since the 1960s, the U.S. government has also allowed private enterprises to build and manage public housing.

The supply-side approach to housing had some success in providing affordable housing for low-income people. In 2013, approximately 1.15 million households lived in public housing units. Forty-eight percent of the tenants were Black, 23 percent are Hispanic, and the average annual household income was $13,724 (U.S. Department of Housing and Urban Development [HUD] 2013). However, poor management over time, combined with broader socioeconomic problems such as low-performing schools, led some of these projects to deteriorate badly. Crime ran rampant, and graffiti was common in the hallways. It was clear that many public housing tenants had a low quality of life. Some public housing projects were so bad they eventually had to be demolished, with the news media widely publicizing the implosion of the building into a heap of dust. Those demolitions have come to be symbolic of government ineptitude. In addition, research has shown that public housing depressed neighboring property values. Since the Nixon administration, the government has been focusing more on other programs. In 1993, Congress launched the HOPE VI program to demolish and redevelop distressed public housing.

Current housing policy takes a diversified approach. Tax and financial subsi-dies, the Low-Income Housing Tax Credit, and housing vouchers are some of the important programs in use.

Tax and Financial Subsidies

The federal government provides tax incentives for both home buyers and homeowners to promote homeownership. Homeowners can use mortgage interest and property tax as a deduction on their federal income taxes. More than fifty million homeowners received the benefit of the tax-free dollars in 2008 (Buckley and Schwartz 2012). First-time home buyers financed by tax-exempt bonds can obtain low-interest mortgages. Homeowners can also reduce taxes on the sale of residential properties. In addition, homeowners may not need to pay the capital gains tax when selling their properties. Specifically, based on the Taxpayer Relief Act of 1997, a homeowner who files the tax return as a single person pays no capital gains tax on the first $250,000 earned when selling a home. If homeowners file taxes as a married couple, they can have a $500,000 exemption.

The federal government also provides tax incentives for investing in particular types of housing, such as rental houses for low-income households, rehabilitation, and reuse of historic buildings.

Housing Vouchers

The housing voucher program, originally known as the Section 8 Existing Housing Program, is currently the largest housing allowance program. Unlike public housing that requires eligible families to live only in predetermined rental houses, families eligible for housing vouchers—low-income families, the elderly, and disabled tenants—may search for their own housing, including single-family homes, townhouses, and apartments. The participants are free to choose any housing that meets the requirements of the program and are not limited to units located in subsidized housing projects. In 2020, the housing voucher program allowed eligible families to pay 30 percent of their monthly adjusted gross income for rent and utilities, and the federal government paid the rest up to a payment standard for a given metropolitan area.

Low-Income Housing Tax Credit

The Low-Income Housing Tax Credit program provides tax incentives to encourage investing in low-income rental housing. It allows investors to reduce their federal income tax by one dollar for every dollar of tax credit received. Investors can claim tax credits on their federal income tax returns annually over a ten-year period, and the property must be occupied by low-income households for at least fifteen years. The Low-Income Housing Tax Credit program was viewed as the nation's most successful affordable rental housing production program. However, it has been criticized for its complexity, inefficiency, and affordability beyond the first fifteen years of its operation (Schwartz 2015, 149–53). In addition, the tax credit usually only targets households with incomes less than 50 percent of the area median. Thus it provides no incentive for developers to create mixed-income developments, since high income households do not receive tax credits.

Besides the federal housing policies, starting from the late 1970s, state and local governments also began implementing local housing programs. A wide variety of housing policies have been used by state and local governments, such as housing trust funds, inclusionary zoning, and Community Development Block Grants. With the more diverse housing policies, the government has more tools to work toward its policy objectives.

Lei Zhang

Further Reading

Albouy, David, and Mike Zabek. 2016. *Housing Inequality*, NBER Working Paper 21916. National Bureau of Economic Research. https://www.nber.org/papers/w21916.

Buckley, Robert M., and Alex F. Schwartz. 2012. "Housing Policy: The Evolving Subnational Role." In *The Oxford Handbook of State and Local Government Finance*, edited by Robert D. Ebel and John E. Petersen, 624–57. New York: Oxford University Press.

Delis, Manthos D., and Panagiotis Papadopoulos. 2019. "Mortgage Lending Discrimination Across the U.S.: New Methodology and New Evidence." *Journal of Financial Services Research* 56 (3): 341–68.

DeSilva, Sanjaya, and Yuval Elmelech. 2012. "Housing Inequality in the United States: Explaining the White-Minority Disparities in Homeownership." *Housing Studies* 27 (1): 1–26.

Green, Richard K., and Stephen Malpezzi. 2003. *A Primer on U.S. Housing Markets and Housing Policy*. Washington, DC: Urban Institute Press.

Green, Richard K., and Michelle J. White. 1997. "Measuring the Benefits of Owner-Occupied Housing: Effects on Children." *Journal of Urban Economics* 41 (3): 431–41.

Haurin, Donald R., Toby L. Parcel, and R. Jean Haurin. 2002. "Does Homeownership Affect Child Outcomes?" *Real Estate Economics* 30 (4): 635–66.

Joint Center for Housing Studies at Harvard University. 2017. https://www.jchs.harvard.edu/home-price-income-ratios.

Katz, Bruce, Margery A. Turner, Karen D. Brown, Mary Cunningham, and Noah Sawyer. 2003. *Rethinking Local Affordable Housing Strategies: Lessons from 70 Years of Policy and Practice*. Washington, DC: Brookings Institution.

Määttänen, Niku, and Marko Terviö. 2014. "Income Distribution and Housing Prices: An Assignment Model Approach." *Journal of Economic Theory* 151:381–410.

Ross, Stephen, and John Yinger. 2002. *The Color of Credit: Mortgage Discrimination, Research Methodology, and Fair-Lending Enforcement*. Cambridge, MA: MIT Press.

Schwartz, Alex F. 2015. *Housing Policy in the United States*. New York: Routledge.

U.S. Census Bureau. 2018. "Current Population Survey/Housing Vacancy Survey." https://factfinder.census.gov/faces/nav/jsf/pages/index.xhtml.

U.S. Department of Housing and Urban Development. 2013. "Picture of Subsidized Households." http://www.huduser.org/portal/datasets/picture/yearlydata.html.

Whelan, Stephen. 2017. "Does Homeownership Affect Education Outcomes?" IZA World of Labor. https://wol.iza.org/articles/does-homeownership-affect-education-outcomes.

Yang, Fang. 2009. "Consumption over the Life Cycle: How Different Is Housing?" *Review of Economic Dynamics* 12 (3): 423–43.

Regulation of Labor Markets

Throughout U.S. history, workers have attempted to claim greater control over their working lives, aspiring to dignity on the job, better pay, and better working conditions. From working life in colonial America to the textile mills of the 1800s, the coals mines of Appalachia in the 1900s, and the slaughterhouses of the twentieth century, there have been jobs in this country that are hazardous and fatiguing and that are insufficient to lift individuals and families out of poverty. There are few instances where improvement in workers' fortunes and the distribution of income have occurred without some degree of government regulation. However, not all labor market regulation has benefited workers and reduced income inequality.

HISTORY

As one historian noted, the capitalist labor system of America's colonial era offered unskilled workers little hope of "lifting themselves out of poverty" (Krawczynski 2013, 197). Local administrators felt they could "legislate prosperity and well-being for everyone, rich or poor" (Bureau of Labor Statistics 1934, 9), and government regulators of the day represented the interests of the well-to-do. The European practices of impressment of labor, wage ceilings, and price ceilings were employed afresh in America. Wage ceilings pushed laborers at the bottom of the socioeconomic strata into the ranks of the poor. Middle-strata craftspersons and laborers found the price caps on their goods and services—caps not imposed on the services of upper-class professionals—to be onerous. They accurately charged that these price caps had the effect of preventing their "rise up the economic ladder" (Krawczynski 2013, 199).

Labor chafed against undemocratic control and unequal outcomes. Unrest accelerated with the arrival of the Industrial Revolution in the late 1700s and its dramatic expansion across American cities and industries in the nineteenth century. Shoemakers of Lynn, Massachusetts, in 1844, through their newspaper, the

Awl, offered what was likely the first formal analysis of class antagonism in America:

> The division of society into the producing and the non-producing classes, and the fact of the unequal distribution of value between the two, introduces us at once to another distinction—that of capital and labor. . . labor now becomes a commodity. . . . Antagonism and opposition of interest is introduced in the community; capital and labor stand opposed. (quoted in Zinn 2003, 231)

The famous Pullman strike of 1894 offers a stark example of that opposition. In response to a 25-percent cut to their wages, railroad workers, many facing starvation, went out on strike. Fourteen thousand police, militia, and troops were called out to subdue five thousand striking workers. Violence erupted, resulting in thirteen deaths, fifty-three wounded, and seven hundred arrested. Such clashes, which also flared in other industries on a smaller scale, suggested to many workers that they needed to organize to protect themselves against ruthless employers.

Union organizing, however, was viewed by corporations as an affront to the rights of companies to manage affairs as they saw fit. Unions were resisted both before and after *Commonwealth of Massachusetts v. Hunt* (1842) legalized them. That ruling involved three critical points: (1) labor combinations had a right to exist as long as their means and ends were legal, (2) an entire union could not be held responsible for the actions of a few members, and (3) unions had the right to form a closed shop (where all workers must be members of the union). Employers resisted, and debate ensued as to what constituted legal means on the part of unions. Other courts were more hostile to labor and issued injunctions curtailing union activities, allowed the signing of yellow-dog contracts that prohibited workers from joining a union, disallowed the use of strikes or boycotts, and allowed the union-busting tactic of bringing in replacement workers (scabs).

National legal recognition of unions and the benefits and protections they offered came in fits and starts. In 1890, language was stripped from the final version of Sherman Antitrust Act that might otherwise have protected unions. Representative Madden (R-IL) stated that history had shown that "the victories won under [the Sherman Act] have been the suits against labor organizations, while great trusts and monopolies have grown and flourished" (Greenslade 1988, 160–61).

The Clayton Act (1914) attempted to correct what many saw as the vagueness of the Sherman Act regarding labor. The Clayton Act prohibited corporate price discrimination and exclusive dealing and allowed private lawsuits against corporations. Corporations could no longer prohibit unions nor could they use antitrust lawsuits to prevent labor strikes. Furthermore, wage bargains could not be construed as price fixing.

Expanded Labor Rights during the Great Depression

The unemployment and output shortages of the Great Depression caused reconsideration of the welfare of the labor force. The Norris-LaGuardia Act (1932) outlawed yellow-dog contracts and limited the use of court injunctions against striking workers (Society for Human Resource Management 2016). The National Industrial Recovery Act (NIRA) of 1933 was emergency legislation that moved the country closer toward today's labor laws. It provided for minimum wages and limited work hours, and it eliminated child labor in the textile industry. It stated that a potential employee did not have to join a union but reinforced the no-yellow-dog contracting of Norris-LaGuardia. President Franklin D. Roosevelt established an informal National Labor Board (NLB) to handle disputes. Although the NIRA was overturned in two years, during its span, union membership exploded, with membership in the United Mine Workers of America alone quadrupling to four hundred thousand in under a year (Social Welfare History Project, n.d.).

Labor unrest during the Great Depression turned from strikes to violence across many cities, motivating Senator Robert Wagner of New York to introduce a more lasting and constitutionally sound piece of legislation. The result was the National Labor Relations Act (NLRA) of 1935, which guaranteed a wide range of organized labor rights and provided for the creation of a National Labor Relations Board (NLRB) to enforce those rights. The law, which was a centerpiece of Roosevelt's "New Deal" program of sweeping economic and work reforms, acknowledged the "inequality of bargaining power between employees who do not possess full freedom of association . . . and employers who are organized in the corporate or other forms of ownership association" (Bernstein, n.d.). It guaranteed the rights of private-sector employees to form trade unions, engage in collective bargaining, and take collective action, including the right to strike. Employers were prevented from firing workers who might take complaints of unfair practices to the NLRB.

As the Great Depression continued, diminished savings eroded the base for future investment. The crash of 1929 and subsequent bank runs were equal-opportunity destroyers of wealth. In addition to financial reforms, the passage of the Social Security Act (1935), along with the 1939 amendments, offered relief from economic hardship for millions of Americans. The introduction of old-age insurance and unemployment compensation became a vital tool in combating economic downturns. Federal unemployment compensation guidelines are minimal, though, providing states with discretion to set their own laws. In general, state programs offer twenty-six weeks of unemployment compensation that replaces on average 38 percent of lost wages. Prolonged economic downturns can deplete state insurance systems if they are underfunded during stronger economic times; extending benefits is then only possible if the federal government makes loans to the states or provides additional funding (Boushey and Eizenga 2011).

Further gains to labor came in 1938 with the Fair Labor Standards Act (FLSA). It established a forty-four-hour workweek (now forty hours), overtime pay for additional hours worked, a minimum wage for covered workers, and a ban on most forms of child labor, and it set the general age of workforce entry at sixteen. Initially, the minimum wage applied to only 20 percent of the labor force (mostly white males). Extensions of the act have expanded coverage to more than 80 percent of the modern labor force. Ruby and Eisenbrey (2013, para. 4) point to a "special study conducted [at the time of the passage of the Act] by the Bureau of Labor Statistics [that] found that the Act would raise wages of almost 700,000 workers, reduce hours or prompt overtime pay for over one and a half million workers, and prohibit the continued employment of roughly 600,000 children aged 10 to 15."

The passage of these New Deal–era policies represented the culmination of centuries of labor organizing in an ever-maturing liberal democracy. Union membership grew from a low of less than three million in 1932 to more than eight million by 1939. This growth peaked in 1970 at seventeen million in terms of sheer numbers, although on the basis of a percentage of total workforce, it peaked much earlier (in 1953 at a 36-percent density rate). However, the NLRA, the Social Security Act, and the FSLA excluded agricultural and domestic workers, which impacted Blacks especially. An analysis in the *Ohio Law Journal* (2011) suggests that

> Congress accommodated and preserved . . . racism through the systematic, intentional exclusion of blacks from all the major enactments of the New Deal . . . Congress excluded blacks by proxy through occupational exclusions and by allowing southerners to discriminate against blacks through local, rather than federal, administration of benefits. By excluding agricultural and domestic workers, and therefore most southern black employees, from federal protections, southern representatives guaranteed that the New Deal posed little or no threat to the Jim Crow South. (Perea 2011, 104)

While those exclusions were ultimately eliminated from the Social Security Act and the FLSA, they still exist in the NLRA and now affect Latinx people, who constitute 83 percent of the U.S. agricultural labor force. Latinx agricultural workers today live in near destitution, with a median annual income of only about $7,500 (Perea 2011, 127).

American Politics and the NLRB

The work of the NLRB has been considerably challenged over the years. It has been resisted by corporate interests, and while it identifies as an independent federal agency, it is vulnerable to swings in interpretation of labor laws, because its members are appointed by the president and confirmed by the Senate to five-year terms (Domhoff 2013).

In 1946, Republicans gained control of Congress for the first time in eighteen years and promptly passed the Taft-Hartley Act (1947), which hampered labor's ability to organize in nonunionized sectors of the economy; added new rights for corporate executives relative to labor; downgraded the importance of the right to collective bargaining; outlawed mass picketing, secondary boycotts, and unauthorized "wildcat" strikes on the shop floor; gave the president the power to delay a strike by declaring a cooling-off period; and added independent contractors and low-level supervisors to the list of excluded covered work categories (Domhoff 2013; Human Rights Watch 2000).

The NLRB's realignment under the Nixon administration further impacted unions. In 1971, the NLRB "ruled that there was no duty for corporations to bargain on decisions that involved 'fundamental managerial issues,'" wrote scholar G. William Domhoff. "[This change] opened the way for outsourcing and plant removal without any notice or consultation. It thereby facilitated the unimpeded movement of production to low-wage American states and third-world countries. . . . [T]he outflow of jobs that is now viewed as one inevitable part of 'globalization' did not just naturally somehow happen due to the 'efficiency' of the market and technological changes, but due to a power struggle that the corporations won and the unions lost" (Domhoff 2013).

While the Nixon administration allowed corporations to reassert control over organized labor, bipartisan efforts to bolster workplace safety intensified in response to rising rates of occupational injuries and illness. As Representative William Steiger (R-WI) stated in 1970,

> In the last 25 years, more than 400,000 Americans were killed by work-related accidents and disease, and close to 50 million more suffered disabling injuries on the job. [S]uch injuries have cost billions of dollars in lost wages and production. (U.S. Department of Labor 2001)

The resulting Occupational Safety and Health Act of 1970 required employers to provide a safe and healthful workplace. It established the Occupational Safety and Health Administration (OSHA), which sets and enforces workplace safety standards and provides training, outreach, education, and assistance.

OSHA has maintained a relatively stable operating budget but, like the NLRB, has been subject to political fluctuations. It has averaged fewer than two thousand inspectors for more than six million workplaces subject to its oversight. OSHA is criticized by both the right and left:

> Critics on the political right have regarded it as . . . the promulgator and enforcer of expensive and ineffective standards . . . needlessly sending many small businesses to bankruptcy court. [C]ritics on the political left . . . argue that the agency is stymied by too few inspectors and too small a budget to carry the weight of its legislative mandate. (Weil 2003, para. 1)

Since OSHA's inception, however, there have been significant improvements in workplace safety compliance and reductions in injury rates.

For those injured on the job, there is a patchwork of state-level workers' compensation schemes. The United States provides national coverage only for government workers. The collection of individual state laws has been described as a "geographic lottery," with workers in different states encountering differing levels of compensation for identical injuries (Grabell and Berkes 2015).

While nearly 130 million workers are officially covered by workers' compensation programs, according to the American Public Health Association (2017), changes over the past two decades have resulted in exclusions that leave workers and their families having to bear 79 percent of the cost of most job-related injuries. This leaves "working people . . . at great risk of falling into poverty from work-related injuries" (Ibid.).

Family Leave Policies

Family leave policy emerged in the United States in 1993 with the passage (and signing by Democratic president Bill Clinton) of the Family Medical Leave Act

(FMLA). The FMLA provides certain categories of individuals (including both women and men) up to twelve weeks of *unpaid* job-protected leave for birth and care of a newborn, adoption or foster care, care for an immediate family member with a serious health condition, and an employee's own serious illness or injury. While as many as one hundred million families have benefited from the Act since its inception, coverage only applies to 60 percent of the workforce. Employees must have worked 1,250 hours over the course of 12 months for their current employer. Coverage is not required for companies of under 50 workers. Those excluded tend to face socioeconomic obstacles, particularly lower levels of education. Hispanics are disproportionately represented among those excluded. Many workers do not have access to leave because they are not aware coverage exists; others because their employers do not comply. In an age of increasingly diverse household arrangements, there are many who are excluded from coverage who are attempting to provide care for grandparents, grandchildren, unmarried domestic partners, same-sex partners, and others. (Center for Economic and Policy Research 2013; Diversitydatakids.org, n.d.).

Until just recently, the United States had been the only developed country without a nationwide program of *paid* family leave. However, in late 2019, the Federal Employee Paid Leave Act was signed into law, granting twelve weeks of *paid leave* to *most* federal employees for the birth or placement of a child. The hope is that Congress will enact some corrective legislation such that *all* federal employees will be eligible by the deadline of October 1, 2020. There is no similar legislation, however, pertaining to the private sector.

Studies of countries in Europe that provide several weeks or even months of *paid* leave reveal that "paid leave is associated with reduced infant mortality, improved child and maternal health . . . , higher labor force participation for women . . . , high family incomes, and [economic] growth" (Mason 2018). Studies of the three states with paid leave (California, New Jersey, and Rhode Island) suggest that in addition to providing newborns with the care that they need and mothers time to recover, maternity benefits resulted in women working more hours during the second year of their newborn's life and at higher wages. For poorer women taking maternity leave, there was a 40-percent reduction in the use of public assistance and food stamps. A number of California companies have expressed concern about the cost of such paid leave programs as well as government overreach, but studies indicate that most of those companies have not reported any problems in productivity or profits (Miller 2015).

The United States has no statutory-mandated rules for *paid* holidays or sick leave except for federal government employees; in the private sector, such benefits are available on a company-by-company basis, based on the compensation package negotiated at the time of employment. The actual benefits vary by industry, company size, wage category, and union coverage. Such benefits are available to nearly all workers in management, business, and financial occupations, for example, but only available to about half of service workers. As of the mid-2010s, there was slightly greater coverage of union versus nonunion workers with regard to paid holidays (79 vs. 75 percent) but substantially larger coverage as far as paid sick leave (85 vs. 65 percent) (Bureau of Labor Statistics 2016).

The coronavirus pandemic of 2020 has forced the issue of paid sick leave to the forefront of the political agenda. Legislation has been proposed that would allow workers to accrue seven days of paid sick leave. If there were another public health emergency such as the coronavirus outbreak, the legislation would allow for an additional fourteen days of paid sick leave.

Occupational Licensing and Other Regulations

Occupational licensing is another area where the government influences the well-being of the workforce. Prior to the 1900s, there were few licensed professionals in the United States. By 2015, nearly a quarter of the workforce required a license to practice their given occupation. Rather than a sweeping piece of governing federal legislation, licensure has become more prevalent over the years on a state-by-state basis, with state boards overseeing the process of license acquisition.

One perspective is that licensure essentially creates a monopoly over the service in question, raising wages of licensees. In this view, "the regulatory process has been captured by industry to erect entry restrictions for its own benefit" (Law and Kim 2004). The higher wages and restricted entry are examples of economic rents (benefits beyond the normal rate of return needed to keep the factor of production engaged in the market) (Nunn 2016). It has been suggested, however, that there may be a less self-serving idea at work. In the world of professional services, there is a problem of asymmetric information. In the absence of licensure, consumers, operating with less information than providers, might find themselves with a "lemon," a poor-quality good or service offered at a lower price than similar products of higher quality. Lemons can crowd out higher-priced, higher-quality products. Licensure and regulation help protect the welfare of consumers (Law and Kim 2004).

Those benefits in wages to license holders and better-quality services offered to consumers, though, come at a cost. Critics assert that some licensing is unnecessary and does not result in better service. Instead, consumers pay more than they should have to, and licensing requirements unduly restrict entry into various industries. According to some estimates, excessive licensing costs the American economy nearly two million jobs per year, as workers who may not be able to afford the education necessary to receive licensure are not allowed to work in their preferred occupations (Wimer 2018). A final economic cost is that, because of variations in states' licensing regulations—for example, a teacher license in one state may not be accepted in another state—licensure "acts as an impediment to worker mobility," a critical feature of a smoothly functioning labor market (Nunn 2016).

ANALYSIS

Government regulation of the labor market has played a critical role in improving the general well-being of workers; they spend fewer hours on the job and have less exposure to the elements and to dangerous conditions, to name a couple of improvements. Those benefits, however, have not been equally distributed. And it is not clear that the entirety of progress can be attributed to any particular set of changes in the labor market, such as OSHA laws, worker compensation laws, litigation, court rulings, enforcement, or union demands. Other factors are also at work, including improvements in workplace technologies, innovations in medical care, and diminished cultural tolerance of unhealthy practices in the workplace. Nevertheless, where workplaces are unionized, there is better adherence to OSHA laws, better health insurance, better safety equipment, and restrictions on excessive work shifts (Zoorob 2018). Other scholars have noted that unionized workers receive wages and benefits that are considerably higher than those of nonunionized workers, with a spillover effect that lifts the wages of nonunion workers (Walters and Mishel 2003).

Other analyses, however, suggest that unions come with a cost. Their emphasis on seniority makes it difficult to promote productive workers and dismiss underperforming workers. A unionized workplace requires dues that may be considered costly or unfair. For many unions, it is difficult for potential workers (especially women and Blacks) to break into the homogeneous workplace culture. High union wages result in a high cost of doing business that then gets passed along to consumers in the form of higher prices (or higher taxes in the case of government projects) (Josephson 2018).

The unionized workforce has been shrinking steadily since the 1970s, with fewer than fifteen million workers represented by unions in 2018, split almost equally between private and public sector unions. Private-sector unions have experienced the sharpest declines, falling from a density of nearly 25 percent in 1973 to less than 7 percent in 2018. Public-sector unions, though present since the late 1800s, grew in density with the passage of state and federal laws in the 1960s and 1970s that recognized the rights of public-sector workers to organize, with

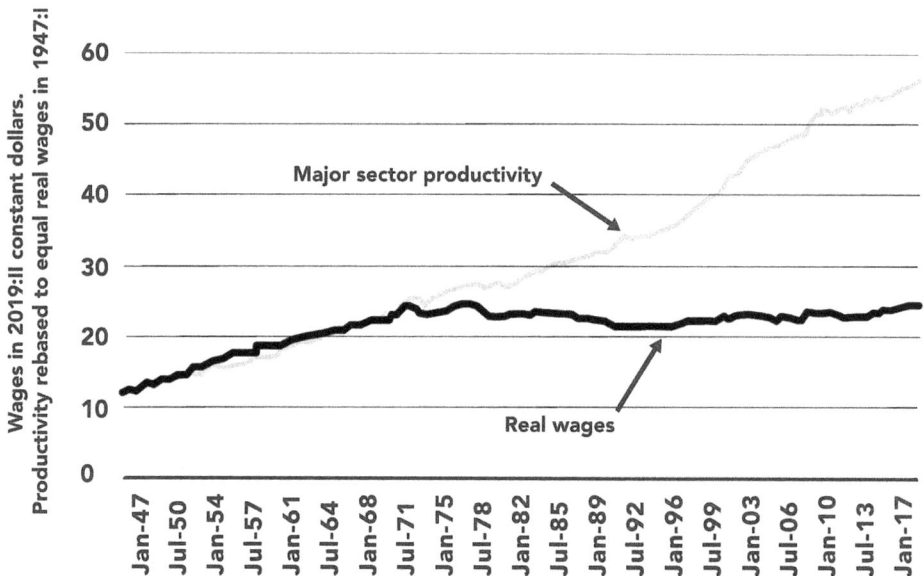

Figure 1 Major Sector Productivity versus Real Wages of Nonsupervisory and Production Workers (1947:1–2019:11) (BLA Tables CES0600000008, CWSR0000SA0, PRS85006093)

union membership holding fairly steady since 1973 at a density rate of one-third (Nunn, O'Donnell, and Shambaugh 2019).

Figure 1 shows the real wage of nonsupervisory and production workers and major sector productivity (output per hour) from 1947 to 2019. Immediately after World War II, labor occupied a position of relative strength resulting from New Deal–era legislation. As output in the economy grew (as measured by productivity gains) workers shared in those gains, at least initially.

However, after the early 1970s, as the economy continued to grow, workers' wages began to stagnate. Workers earned in 2019 just $0.33 per hour more than in 1973 (in 2019 constant dollars), even as productivity more than doubled. There is a growing body of research suggesting that the economic benefits of those productivity gains went mostly to Americans who were already wealthy. Emanuel Saez (2019) has estimated that the share of the nation's income going to the top 10 percent was over 50 percent in 2017. The top 10 percent held nearly 79 percent of the nation's wealth in 2016 (Inequality.org n.d.).

To a number of researchers, stagnating wages and widening inequality over time are linked to the declining role of unions in the U.S. workforce. Scholars have pointed out that from 1973 to 2007, private-sector union membership in the United States declined from 34 to 8 percent for men and from 16 to 6 percent for women. During this period, inequality in hourly wages increased by over 40 percent (Western and Rosenfeld 2011).

Such trends have prompted many observers to argue that the United States' middle class is vanishing. This disconnect of wages from economic growth was assessed by former senator John Edwards as such: "We shouldn't have two different economies in America: one for people who are set for life, they know their kids and grand-kids are going to be just fine; and then one for most Americans, people who live paycheck to paycheck" (quoted in Temin 2017, 3).

Worker Discontent amid Rising Inequality

If it were not for the evidence that wages have barely budged in comparable dollars for the past half-century even as inequality has grown, one might conclude that all is well with the labor force. Since June 2010, there has not been a single month of negative job growth. Since its Great Recession peak in October 2009 at 10 percent, the unemployment rate has fallen steadily, reaching 3.5 percent as of September 2019. That positive news from the Bureau of Labor Statistics (BLS), however, masks considerable worker discontent and unrest. As one analysis noted,

> ten percent of workers are burdened with irregular or on-call work shifts; almost four million workers are working part-time despite wanting to work full time; 7.8 percent of working-age labor force nonparticipants would like a job; over fifty percent of private sector, non-union workers are subject to mandatory arbitration; and nearly twenty percent of workers have a non-compete contract. (McIntosh, Nunn, and Shambaugh 2019)

Worker grievances exploded onto the national stage in 2018, with twenty major work stoppages spread over 485,000 workers. The sectors of education services, health care, and social services accounted for over 90 percent of idled workers (Bureau of Labor Statistics 2019). Demands from striking teachers that began in West Virginia for better pay, benefits, and dignity on the job dominated national headlines and then quickly spread to several other states.

Those strikes suggest to some a useful role for unions, despite their shrinking numbers. According to an analysis from the Hamilton Project (an economic policy initiative within the Brookings Institute), the economic costs associated with unions may be overstated. To the extent that communication and coordination problems exist between employers and workers, or that industries with a mobile workforce tend to underinvest in training, unions can play constructive roles. In a modern labor market, "market frictions, concentration (i.e., monopsony power), and employer-favoring institutions like non-compete contracts . . . give employers considerable leverage in setting wages" (Nunn, O'Donnell, and Shambaugh 2019, 13). In such cases, unions, "rather than distorting an otherwise competitive labor market," may simply "rebalance" a labor market that had tilted too far in the direction of corporate interests (Ibid., 13).

Potential Reforms

The Hamilton Project suggests approaches the labor market can pursue in the absence of a resurgence of private sector unions. All require some degree of assistance from the government, and most of have been tried with varying degrees of success in other countries. Sectoral bargaining is one option; it involves industry-wide instead of enterprise-level collective bargaining. Another approach involves wage boards, consisting of stakeholders (both workers and employers) from various industries or occupations who come together to negotiate minimum wage levels specific to different types of work. Another approach is the creation of works councils—common in Europe—consisting of employees elected by their peers to help coordinate with employers, thus giving workers a stronger voice (Nunn, O'Donnell, and Shambaugh 2019).

To the extent that workers perceive membership in a union desirable, NLRB rule changes could make it easier to form a union. A simple card-check system—currently used in Canada—could facilitate the process. Also, current NLRB policy, which does not grant independent contractors, domestic workers, and farmworkers the same collective bargaining rights as other employees could be amended to provide coverage to those excluded workers. In addition, NLRB rules need to be altered to allow workers to bring civil suits against employers who violate workplace rules (Nunn, O'Donnell, and Shambaugh 2019).

Regarding inequality, former Federal Reserve chair Ben Bernanke (2007) suggests that there is a role for policy makers to assist workers who experience "painful dislocations" in the face of technology or trade-related economic upheaval. He recommends policies that can assist with retraining and job search for dislocated workers and for the portability of health and pension benefits that might reduce job change costs. However, with 16.5 million people—a number far greater than the entire unionized labor force—at work in "contingent" or "alternative work arrangements" and receiving little more than a modest paycheck, there may simply not be any health or pension benefits for which portability matters (Gayle 2018).

The federal minimum wage, an administered rate, set by Congress, has been $7.25 per hour since 2009. As such, it has lost nearly 16 percent of its purchasing power. That loss of purchasing power is even more dramatic if one looks over a longer horizon. A sequence of five increases in the 1960s brought the minimum wage from $1.00 to $1.60 per hour ($11.96 in 2019 dollars). It has lost nearly 40 percent of its purchasing power since that peak. The minimum wage offers a textbook example of the difference between active and passive government regulation of the labor market. Raising the minimum wage five times in the 1960s is an example of the former. Leaving it unchanged since 2009 in the face of ongoing inflation is an example of the latter. In that case, even though the federal government took no action, workers at the bottom of the wage scale saw significant erosion of their purchasing power.

Economist Alan Krueger (who served as chair of President Obama's White House Council of Economic Advisers from November 2011 to August 2013) has recommended indexing the minimum wage either to inflation or to the wage rate of workers in the 25th percentile of the wage distribution (PBS 2013). In the absence of federal guidance, states and localities have finally begun to take steps to remedy the problem of minimum wages that have lost purchasing power. Economics professor Arindrajit Dube, writing for the Hamilton Project, offered a policy framework for states and localities wanting to establish a regional minimum wage; he recommended that such a wage be set on the basis of half the local-area median wage in conjunction with the local cost of living, with city and county cooperation at the regional level where possible (Dube 2014).

A cloud still hangs over union organizing, however, particularly in Republican and economically conservative circles. In 2018, the conservative-majority Supreme Court ruled in the case of *Janus v AFSCME* that public-sector unions may no longer collect fair-share fees from workers whom they represent but who choose not to become union members. "In functional terms, it is a national right-to-work law for state, county, city, and school district employees. Union membership will soon become solely voluntary" (Kamper 2018).

CONCLUSION

Looking back over four hundred years of labor history reveals a government that has often been torn in terms of its allegiances with labor and capital, sometimes actively (e.g., breaking strikes), sometimes passively (e.g., not raising the minimum wage), weighing in with decisions that affect the lives of millions. The distribution of value between labor and capital (which so often has tilted strongly in favor of capital), as the plot of productivity and wages above illustrates clearly, hangs in the balance of those government decisions.

John D. Abell and Elizabeth Perry-Sizemore

Further Reading

American Public Health Association. 2017. "The Critical Need to Reform Workers' Compensation." Policy Statement, Policy Number 20174, November 7. https://www

.apha.org/policies-and-advocacy/public-health-policy-statements/policy-database /2018/01/18/the-critical-need-to-reform-workers-compensation.

Bernanke, Ben. 2007. "The Level and Distribution of Economic Well-Being." Speech, Omaha, NE, February 6, 2007. https://www.federalreserve.gov/newsevents/ speech/bernanke20070206a.htm.

Bernstein, Irving. n.d. "Americans in Depression and War." U.S. Department of Labor. https://www.dol.gov/general/aboutdol/history/chapter5.

Boushey, Heather, and Jordan Eizenga. 2011. "Toward a Strong Unemployment Insurance System: The case for an Expanded Federal Role." Center for American Progress. https://www.americanprogress.org/issues/economy/reports/2011/02/08/9125/ toward-a-strong-unemployment-insurance-system.

Bureau of Labor Statistics. 1934. *History of Wages in the United States from Colonial Times to 1928. No. 604.* Washington, DC: U.S. Government Printing Office.

Bureau of Labor Statistics. 2016. "Employment Benefits Survey (March)." https://www .bls.gov/ncs/ebs/benefits/2016/ownership/civilian/table32a.htm.

Bureau of Labor Statistics. 2018. "Major Work Stoppages in 2018," *Bureau of Labor Statistics News Release*, February 8, 2019. https://www.bls.gov/news.release/archives /wkstp_02082019.pdf.

Center for Economic and Policy Research. 2013. "The Family and Medical Leave Act at 20: A Record of Success, But More Can Be Done." *CEPR Blog*, February 28, 2013. http://cepr.net/blogs/cepr-blog/the-family-and-medical-leave-act-at-20-a-record -of-success-but-more-can-be-done.

Diversitydatakids.org. "Family and Medical Leave Act." The Heller School, Brandeis University. http://www.diversitydatakids.org/data/policy/5/family-and-medical -leave-act.

Domhoff, G. William. 2013. "The Rise and Fall of Labor Unions in the U.S." Who Rules America?, February. https://whorulesamerica.ucsc.edu/power/history_of_labor_ unions.html.

Dube, Arindrajit. 2014. "Designing Thoughtful Minimum Wage Policy at the State and Local Levels." Hamilton Project, June 19, 2014. https://www.brookings.edu/re search/designing-thoughtful-minimum-wage-policy-at-the-state-and-local-levels.

Gayle, Caleb. 2018. "US Gig Economy: Data Shows 16m People in 'Contingent or Alternative' Work." *The Guardian*, June 7, 2018. https://www.theguardian.com/busi ness/2018/jun/07/america-gig-economy-work-bureau-labor-statistics.

Getman, Julius. 2015. "The NLRB: What Went Wrong and Should We Try to Fix It?" *Emory Law Journal* 64. http://law.emory.edu/elj/content/volume-64/issue-special/ panel-i/nlrb-what-went-wrong.html.

Grabell, M., and H. Berkes. 2015. "As Workers' Comp Varies from State to State, Workers Pay the Price." NPR, March 6, 2015. https://www.npr.org/2015/03/06/391149235/as -workers-comp-varies-from-state-to-state-workers-pay-the-price.

Greenslade, Joseph l. 1988. "Labor Unions and the Sherman Act: Rethinking Labor's Nonstatutory Exemption." *Loyola of Los Angeles Law Review*. http://digitalcom mons.lmu.edu/cgi/viewcontent.cgi?article=1587&context=llr.

Human Rights Watch. 2000. "Legal Obstacles to U.S. Workers' Exercise of Freedom of Association." In *Unfair Advantage: Workers' Freedom of Association in the United States under International Human Rights Standards.* https://www.hrw.org /reports/2000/uslabor/USLBR008-08.htm.

Inequality.org. n.d. "Wealth Inequality in the United States." https://inequality.org/facts/ wealth-inequality.

Josephson, Amelia. 2018. "The Pros and Cons of Unions." Smartasset, May 21, 2018. https://smartasset.com/career/the-pros-and-cons-of-unions.

Kamper, Dave. 2018. "How to Defeat the Post-Janus Union Attacks," *Jacobin*, June 27, 2018. https://www.jacobinmag.com/2018/06/janus-afscme-dues-opt-out-campaign.

Krawczynski, Keith T. 2013. *Daily Life in the Colonial City*. Santa Barbara, CA: Greenwood.

Law, Marc, and Sukkoo Kim. 2004. "Specialization and Regulation: The Rise of Professionals and the Emergence of Occupational Licensing Regulation." NBER Working Paper 10467. National Bureau of Economic Research. https://www.nber.org/papers/w10467.

Mason, Jessica. 2018. "The U.S. Is Decades behind the World on Paid Leave." *Slate*, February 6, 2018. https://slate.com/human-interest/2018/02/the-u-s-is-decades-behind-the-world-on-paid-leave-this-gives-us-an-advantage.html.

McIntosh, Kriston, Ryan Nunn, and Jay Shambaugh. 2019. "Who Watches Out for Workers?" Brookings, August 27, 2019. https://www.brookings.edu/opinions/who-watches-out-for-workers.

Miller, Claire Cain. 2015. "The Economic Benefits of Paid Parental Leave." *New York Times*, January 30, 2015. https://www.nytimes.com/2015/02/01/upshot/the-economic-benefits-of-paid-parental-leave.html.

Nunn, Ryan. 2016. "Occupational Licensing and American Workers." Brookings. https://www.brookings.edu/research/occupational-licensing-and-the-american-worker.

Nunn, Ryan, Jimmy O'Donnell, and Jay Shambaugh. 2019. "The Shift in Private Sector Union Participation: Explanation and Effects." Hamilton Project. https://www.hamiltonproject.org/papers/the_shift_in_private_sector_union_participation_explanations_and_effects.

PBS. 2013. "The Man and the Thinking behind the Minimum Wage Hike." February 14, 2013. https://www.pbs.org/newshour/economy/president-obama-is-pushing-a.

Perea, Juan F. 2011. "The Echoes of Slavery: Recognizing the Racist Origins of the Agricultural and Domestic Worker Exclusion from the National Labor Relations Act." *Ohio State Law Journal* 72 (1): 95–138. http://moritzlaw.osu.edu/students/groups/oslj/files/2012/04/72.1.perea_.pdf.

Ruby, Nathaniel, and Ross Eisenbrey. 2013. "Celebrating 75 Years of the Fair Labor Standards Act." *Working Economics Blog*, Economic Policy Institute. https://www.epi.org/blog/celebrating-75-years-fair-labor-standards.

Saez, Emmanuel. 2019. "Striking it Richer: The Evolution of Top Incomes in the United States (Updated with 2017 Final Estimates)." UC Berkeley, March 2, 2019. https://eml.berkeley.edu/~saez/saez-UStopincomes-2017.pdf.

Social Welfare History Project. n.d. "National Recovery Administration." Virginia Commonwealth University Libraries. https://socialwelfare.library.vcu.edu/eras/great-depression/u-s-national-recovery-administration.

Society for Human Resource Management. 2016. "Norris-LaGuardia Act." April 28, 2016. https://www.shrm.org/resourcesandtools/legal-and-compliance/employment-law/pages/norris-laguardia-act.aspx.

Temin, Peter. 2017. *The Vanishing Middle Class*. Cambridge, MA: MIT Press.

U.S. Department of Labor, Occupational Safety & Health Administration. 2001. "OSHA at 30: Three Decades of Progress in Occupational Safety and Health." https://www.osha.gov/as/opa/osha-at-30.html.

Walters, Matthew, and Lawrence Mishel. 2003. "How Unions Help All Workers." Economic Policy Institute. https://www.epi.org/publication/briefingpapers_bp143.

Weil, David. 2003. "OSHA: Beyond the Politics." *Frontline*, January 9, 2003. https://www
.pbs.org/wgbh/pages/frontline/shows/workplace/osha/weil.html.

Western, Bruce, and Jake Rosenfeld. 2011. "Unions, Norms, and the Rise in U.S. Wage
Inequality." *American Sociological Review* 76 (4): 513–37. https://www.asanet.org
/sites/default/files/savvy/images/journals/docs/pdf/asr/WesternandRosenfeld.pdf.

Wimer, Andrew. 2018. "Study Reveals the Billions of Dollars U.S. Consumers and the
Economy Lose to Occupational Licensing." *Forbes*, December 3, 2018. https://
www.forbes.com/sites/instituteforjustice/2018/12/03/study-reveals-the-billions-of
-dollars-u-s-consumers-and-the-economy-lose-to-occupational-licensing/
#275c466c39b6.

Zinn, Howard. 2003. *A People's History of the United States*. New York: Harper Collins.

Zoorob, Michael. 2018. "How Unions Help Prevent Workplace Deaths in the United
States." Scholars Strategy Network. https://scholars.org/contribution/how-unions
-help-prevent-workplace-deaths-united-states.

Taxes

In studying the increasing economic disparities between the rich and the poor in the United States (Saez and Zucman 2014, 2019; OECD 2008, 2019), many researchers devote attention to the federal income tax laws codified in the Internal Revenue Code of 1986, as amended ("I.R.C. §," followed by a section number in the following) to explore whether taxation in the United States currently magnifies, shrinks, or has no impact on those disparities. The language of the tax laws is neutral and applies identical rules to all. Yet the distribution of tax burdens among the members of the U.S. populace may not always be evenhanded, as some tax rules affect segments of the population disproportionately relative to other segments. This reality raises the question of whether taxation, either by design or inadvertently, contributes to the disparities between rich and poor (Troiano 2017).

Income taxation can increase disparities in wealth by the manner in which it distributes tax burdens and reallocates tax burdens when tax law changes. Even a 1 percent "across the board" rate reduction, for example, affects disparities. The rate reduction leaves the taxpayer who has $1 million of income with a wealth increase of $10,000. An identical percentage reduction for the taxpayer with $30,000 of income only increases that taxpayer's wealth by $300. The disparity between the two is thus increased by $9,700 even if lost revenue from a tax reduction is replaced with borrowing or reductions in government programs and not shifted to other taxpayers.

FUNCTION OF TAXATION

"Taxes are what we pay for civilized society," wrote Supreme Court justice Oliver Wendell Holmes in 1927. Revenue from taxes supports a broad range of governmental services, including police, fire, and military protection, public schools, roads, legislatures, judges and courts, regulatory agencies, and more. Most people agree that taxes are necessary, but there may be considerable disagreement concerning who, when, and how much each person should pay in taxes. Likely there are those who believe governmental services consume too much of total national resources and others who believe that governmental services provide too little. Some favor one type of tax, while others favor another. If tax structures were created to accommodate each different perspective, taxes might capture far more or far less of national resources, while the distribution of the tax burden among the populace would change with each accommodation.

The foundation of taxation is to collect sufficient revenue to support governmental functions and programs. Each governmental unit—whether federal, state, or local—prepares a budget that determines how much revenue is required to meet its spending needs. In proposing its budget, the governmental unit adjusts its taxes to produce the necessary revenue so that taxes are a function of spending needs, or the unit prepares its budget based on projected revenue from current taxes and allocates estimated revenue among governmental functions and programs so that spending is a function of taxes. The process is complex and may involve both adjustments in taxes and allocation of available but limited revenue.

DISTRIBUTION OF TAX BURDENS

Distribution of taxes among taxpayers is also complex. If some taxpayers pay less than they should, there is a revenue shortfall that other taxpayers must make up, just as the remaining members of a dinner party at a restaurant might do when a couple of them leave without paying their share of the check. The other members must pay more to meet the group's obligation to the restaurant. Even without a nonpaying member of the group, determining how to share the restaurant check can be complex. The agreement to share in the first place may mean that each member of the party pays an equal share or that the group will divide the check by the amount of each member's actual consumption or that each diner will pay according to the diner's individual wealth. Perhaps one group member wishes to have a more expensive wine and agrees to pay a higher proportion of the cost of the shared wine.

There is similarly an implicit agreement among all citizens and residents of the United States to share the cost of government through taxation. If some do not pay their share, all other taxpayers must pay more, although, unlike a restaurant check shared among the members of a small party, the additional amount of tax each other taxpayer must pay may be quite small when spread among millions of taxpayers. If many taxpayers do not pay, or pay less than their fair share of taxes, however, the additional burden for other taxpayers is not negligible. To the extent that the additional burden is shifted from wealthy taxpayers to those with low income, or from more affluent to less affluent taxpayers, the shift of tax burdens is likely to contribute to increasing disparities in wealth, because the wealthier taxpayer retains more wealth and the poorer taxpayer less. Ascertaining whether such a shift in burdens is occurring requires determining first the correct amount of the tax burden individual taxpayers should bear based upon their individual circumstances.

Splitting the restaurant check equally is simple, and diners in a small party tend to be similar in their economic circumstances, so any unfair shift of cost among the diners is small and has a negligible impact on their wealth. If diners frequent restaurants together regularly, the shift of the cost from one to another may balance in the long term. Would that same design work for tax distribution? Consider whether a capitation tax, also referred to as a head tax, would be fair to all. A capitation tax is a tax imposed in an equal amount on all individuals based on a criterion such as citizenship or residence. Assume such a capitation tax was imposed on all individuals residing in the United States. The federal budget is roughly $5 trillion annually. The U.S. population is three hundred million (rounded to the nearest hundred million), so each resident would pay about $17,000 tax annually to provide the revenue to support federal spending. A family of four consisting of two adults and two children would pay $68,000. Since children are less likely than adults to have resources from which to pay the tax, either the parents will pay the tax for their children, the tax exempts children and increases the burden on each adult, or the tax permits children to defer payment until they become adults—thereby saddling the children with a large deferred tax liability when they become adults.

Although the capitation tax treats everyone equally, the tax is unrealistic when applied to individuals whose resources are limited. Even with a minimum wage at $15 per hour, a family of four with both parents working full time—forty hours per week—at the minimum wage would give the family only $60,000 aggregate income and fall short of the family capitation tax burden. From this simple example, it is clear that equalization of tax burdens is impractical. With a population of three hundred million or more, some people will have to pay more than others to raise sufficient revenue for the federal budget. Cutting the budget would ameliorate but not eliminate the problem, because it simply is not possible to reduce spending enough to make a capitation tax practical.

TAXONOMY OF FAIR TAX DISTRIBUTION

Since some individuals will have to pay more than others to enable the government to meet its revenue needs, it is essential to establish principles to govern tax distribution lest distribution become unprincipled, arbitrary, and unacceptable to taxpayers. In establishing principles, the restaurant example suggests distributing taxes according to consumption of governmental services. As a tax principle, consumption of government services is a fee for services received. User fees also are not practical because so many services are so generalized—military protection, for example—that measurement of consumption would be so imprecise as to be unusable as a principle.

Alternatively, tax burdens might be distributed according to taxpayers' relative ability to pay. That principle is also imprecise and, as a measurement, requires assumptions that make generalized value judgments as to taxpayers' use of their resources. Yet generalization of ability to pay leads to the more customary assumption that the wealthier one is, the greater one's ability to pay. This assumption has been foundational in federal taxation for many years although its scope is controversial and it frequently has been subject to adjustment. Each adjustment in the ability-to-pay principle has led to redistribution of tax burdens. To the extent the burdens shift away from affluent taxpayers, they may increase on less affluent taxpayers. Even without an increased tax on the less affluent, the reduction permits the affluent to retain more income and increases wealth disparities.

Consider a small disparity and the effect of a tax change in the example of two families: one a married couple with two dependent children, the other a married couple with no children. Under the federal income tax, until 2018 taxpayers received an income tax deduction as a personal exemption for the taxpayer and each of the taxpayers' dependents (I.R.C. §151). In 2017, this personal exemption amount was $4,050. Family 1, filing a joint income tax return, would have a standard deduction of $12,700 (I.R.C. §63) plus four personal exemptions (two adults and two children), yielding a deduction of $16,200 for a total of $28,900 of deductions before any income becomes subject to income tax. Family 2, the couple filing jointly, would have become taxable at $20,800 using the standard deduction and only two personal exemptions.

In 2018, though, the personal exemption was no longer deductible, but the standard deduction increased to $12,000 per adult. The four-member family is taxable at $24,000 of income, as is the couple without children. The income tax begins to reduce the resources of the family with children at a smaller income than before the change and to increase the resources before becoming subject to tax of the family without children. The change in tax law applies uniformly and is neutral on its face, but it changes tax distribution based on family characteristics.

Some affluent individuals argue that their wealth does not increase their ability to pay taxes. They might assert, for example, that so much of their wealth is tied up in property that they might need to sell some or all of that property to generate the cash to pay the tax. Sale of the property may be inefficient and undesirable because the community at large benefits from the property owners' productive use of the property. Productive use of property might decline if its ownership becomes fragmented. As to income from the property, affluent taxpayers argue that they do not consume the income but deploy each additional dollar not paid in taxes productively. The argument continues that the affluent invest and produce jobs benefiting the community, while the less affluent consume and benefit only themselves. The less affluent, on the other hand, argue that their consumption is much more likely to focus on basic necessities such as food and shelter or inexpensive "quality of life" purchases, making the incremental dollar more important to them than to affluent taxpayers, who will thrive without the additional dollar. The less affluent argue further that without consumption, many businesses would fail for want of customers.

As difficult as it may be to ascertain who best uses money not paid in tax, it seems incontrovertible that the less affluent one is, the more likely the individual may lack sufficient resources to pay the tax. Even when individuals have the resources, additional taxes may prevent them from meeting their families' basic needs. The capitation tax example above illustrates that it is essential for affluent individuals to pay more than the less affluent and the poor do. Little if any controversy exists with respect to that proposition. Determining how *much* more is controversial and subject to intense debate, however.

TAXATION OF INCOME

The income tax applies a percentage to the taxpayer's taxable income to determine how much the taxpayer must pay. The rate of tax might increase as income increases—a rate structure commonly referred to as *progressive*. Or it might decline as income increases—a rate structure referred to as *regressive*. The rate of tax also might be flat so that each dollar of income is taxed at the same rate as each other dollar of income. In political discourse, this rate structure commonly is referred to as a "flat tax," which is a misnomer for a "proportional" tax. Progressive and regressive rate structures customarily apply their increases or decreases in rates only at the margin, meaning that the rate change applies only to the incremental dollar of income. One might imagine the structure as a set of steps ascending (progressive) or descending (regressive). All three rate structures usually collect a greater amount of tax from taxpayers with higher incomes than they do from taxpayers with lower incomes. It is also customary to exempt some taxpayers with very low incomes from the income tax, so a proportional tax is slightly progressive with a zero rate and a positive rate. The U.S. income tax uses a progressive rate structure and even applies a negative rate of tax to very low-income taxpayers as a welfare benefit in the form of the earned income credit, referred to as the Earned Income Tax Credit (EITC) (I.R.C. §32).

Alongside the tax principle that more affluent taxpayers must pay more than less affluent taxpayers must do is a second noncontroversial principle that like individuals should pay like taxes. This principle is referred to as *horizontal equity*. Under an income tax, for example, like individuals with equal incomes should pay equal taxes. While the principle seems straightforward, it is not. It raises a series of questions. Which taxpayers are alike? Are taxpayers living alone the same as single taxpayers who have minor children dependent on them for economic support? Is a taxpayer living in an expensive geographic area the same as a taxpayer who resides in an inexpensive area? Is each dollar of income the same as each other dollar of income, or should some income be treated more or less favorably than other income? Is income from wages the same as income from investment? Is income from theft the same as income from work? Are gifts income to their recipients as wages are income to employees? The answer our tax system provides to these difficult questions impacts the distribution of tax burdens among taxpayers. Whether intended or incidental, that distributional impact may contribute to the widening disparity between affluent and other members of the society.

During the middle decades of the twentieth century, economically advanced democracies such as the United States and the countries of Western Europe adopted income tax systems with progressive rate structures for the purpose of leveling and redistributing wealth among taxpayers. In the early 1950s, the maximum income tax rate imposed on high-income individuals reached 91 percent. Not all income was treated in the same way under that system, but the underlying principle was that as one's income increased, so did one's ability to pay tax. By taxing higher incomes more, the cost of government for lower-income taxpayers would be less burdensome and allow them to retain more of their income for consumption and savings.

The United States retreated from that redistribution principle gradually, beginning around 1970. From that point on, maximum rates of income tax steadily declined, reaching their lowest point in 1987 following the 1986 tax reform. The maximum rate in 1987 of 28 percent reduced the spread from lowest taxed income to the highest taxed income to 38 percent. The spread was 38 percent because as much as $8,000 of income from services was subject to a negative income tax of 10 percent under the earned income credit (Crandall-Hollick 2018).

If one assumes that high-income individuals actually paid income tax at the progressive marginal rates—a questionable assumption since high-income tax-payers have devoted considerable resources to avoiding taxes through both legal and illegal means (Ordower 2010)—that low-income individuals' incomes did not increase much more rapidly than that of high-income individuals did, and that high-income individuals' incomes did not plummet, the compression of the marginal rates of tax would redistribute some of the income tax burden from higher- to lower-income taxpayers. This observation ignores the effect of an increasing national debt, as federal government borrowing may have enabled the United States to satisfy its revenue needs with a smaller amount of tax collection. Absent substitution of debt for tax collection, the rate changes left lower-income taxpayers with less disposable income and wealth and higher-income individuals with more disposable income and wealth than before the changes. The rate changes contributed to the widening disparity between the rich and the poor in the United States even though each affluent taxpayer continued to shoulder more of the over-all income tax burden than each lower-income taxpayer did. This is consistent with the principle that the affluent pay more taxes than the poor, as the rates structure shifted from heavily progressive toward proportional.

IS ALL INCOME ALIKE?

Even within a progressive tax structure, differing treatment of taxpayers or types of income tends to distribute tax burdens in ways that might further contribute to aggregate disparities between rich and poor. Each dollar of income in the United States is not always treated the same under the income tax as each other dollar of income. Preferences for income from investments are significant under the federal tax law. Several significantly favored types of income are received more frequently and in greater amounts by affluent taxpayers.

Except for a brief period in the mid-1980s, the income tax has applied a lower rate to income from the sale or exchange of property (I.R.C. §1001; I.R.C. §1[h]). This income is referred to as *capital gain*. The tax law classification of that income is somewhat more complicated, but in general gains from the sale of investment property a taxpayer has owned for more than one year is taxed at a maximum rate 17 percentage points lower than the maximum rate applied to income from wages. The same rate benefit applies to dividends a corporation pays with respect to investment in its shares (I.R.C. §1[h][11]). There are many arguments for favoring capital gain, including the argument that capital gain is not economic real gain because it is inflation from the loss in value of the dollar as if that loss in value did not also affect wage income. Another argument is that capital gain encourages risk taking that assists economic development. Still another maintains that a favorable rate is appropriate because gain from the sale of long-held property is disproportionately large, since the sale concentrates gain that has accumulated over several years into the year of sale. Those arguments have been strongly refuted by Walter J. Blum and other prominent economists, however (Blum 1957).

Whether or not a compelling argument for favoring capital gain exists, it is clear that the capital-gain rate preference inures to the benefit of more affluent taxpayers who have disposable income to invest in property that will increase in value. Lower-income taxpayers tend to consume all their resources, so they are unlikely to have any significant amount of capital gain (Thornton and Hendricks 2019).

There is a further income tax benefit associated with investment property that wealthy individuals pass on to others when they die. The recipient of property from a decedent's estate does not have income on the receipt and takes a new tax basis in the property from which to measure future gain subject to the favorable capital gain rate (I.R.C. §1014; I.R.C. §1011; I.R.C. §1001). For example, if an individual buys investment property for $1,000 and sells it more than a year later for $10,000, the $9,000 of gain is subject to tax at a preferential capital gain rate (I.R.C. §1[h]). However, if that same individual leaves the property to a family member, and the new owner sells the property for the $10,000, the new owner will have no taxable income from the sale, because the owner will have a new basis in the property equal to the value of the property at the original owner's death and no income from receiving the gift. It is not the less affluent who take advantage of these tax rules, even though the rules apply to them as well as the wealthy. The rules about capital-gain preference and elimination of historical gain at death enable wealthier taxpayers who have resources to invest to retain additional amounts of gain income rather than paying them in tax.

Similarly, it is affluent rather than low-income individuals who are most likely to have the resources to invest in homeownership, whether by accumulating savings or borrowing from an institutional lender (Haneman 2019). Less-affluent individuals are far less likely to accumulate savings or be able to borrow to purchase a home. The income tax laws allow no deduction for rent one pays for use of one's residence (I.R.C. §262). Every dollar one earns is subject to the income tax even if one uses the dollar to pay rent and even if the landlord is using some of those rental dollars to pay deductible mortgage interest (I.R.C. §163) or deductible real estate taxes on the rented property (I.R.C. §164). An individual who uses previously invested money to buy a home no longer has taxable income from the invested money and no longer pays nondeductible rent. The value of the use of the owned home that substituted for the rented home is not taxable. This nontaxable use benefit increases as the value of the home increases and also as the marginal tax rate of the owner increases (Ordower 2015). If the owner borrowed to buy the home, the mortgage interest is deductible, as may be all or part of the real estate taxes. If the homeowner sells the home at a gain, the homeowner in most cases is only taxable on gain exceeding $250,000 ($500,000 in the case of a joint return) (I.R.C. §121), and additional gain is capital gain taxed at a preferential rate (Brown 2018). The tax benefits of homeownership are considerable and available more frequently and in greater amounts to affluent rather than less affluent taxpayers, a dynamic that almost certainly adds to the disparities between rich and poor.

Income from employment has become disfavored in the tax code relative to investment income and income from the conduct of a business. Although the performance of services as an employee is a trade or business, employees may not deduct business expenses they incur, while sole proprietors performing similar services and other businesses may deduct their business expenses (I.R.C. §62). Under a statute that became effective in 2018, owners of businesses also may deduct 20 percent of their qualified business income (I.R.C. §199A). Income derived from performance of services as an employee is not qualified business income, but income from most other trades or businesses does qualify for the 20-percent deduction (I.R.C. §199A[d]). Specified-service businesses, including the medical, legal, and accounting professions, only qualify for the deduction if the taxpayer's income from all sources remains less than a defined limit. All businesses in which capital is a material, income-producing factor generate qualified business income, may claim the 20-percent deduction, and may deduct their business expenses. Lower-income individuals work primarily as employees and do not qualify for this deduction, although independent contractors qualify because they are sole proprietors. Classification of workers as independent contractors often is incorrect. Often employers classify workers as independent contractors for tax reasons and to avoid the payment of employee expenses—health care, for example (U.S. Department of Labor, n.d.).

The Social Security tax offers another longstanding preference for investment income over income from work. Wages are subject to the Social Security tax of 6.2 percent (I.R.C. §3101). Employers are subject to an identical amount of tax on the wages they pay (I.R.C. §3301). Economists view the true incidence of the employers' share of the Social Security tax to fall on the workers through lower wages (Friedman 1965, 8; Brittain 1971, 110). Income from the performance of services as sole proprietor or co-owner of a business is subject to a complementary self-employment tax of 12.4 percent (twice the wage rate of the Social Security tax) (I.R.C. §1401). Income from capital is not taxed under either of these provisions, so wealthier individuals enjoy as much as a 12.4-percent rate preference over lower-income wage earners if their income is from investment rather than work. Even within the Social Security tax, higher-income individuals enjoy a preference. The Social Security tax has a two-bracket regressive rate structure. The tax applies only to income from services up to a cap that adjusts annually. The cap in 2020 is $137,700. There is the 12.4-percent combined employee/employer rate on income from services up to the cap and a zero rate on income from services in excess of the cap. The average tax rate for employees and the self-employed earning less than the cap is 12.4 percent. The average rate for those earning more declines as their wages increase; for example, the average tax is 6.2 percent for someone earning $275,000 and only 3.1 percent for someone earning $550,000, since only the first $137,700 is subject to tax at all. While the Social Security tax is a tax, payment of the tax is a condition for eligibility to receive Social Security benefits. So as regressive as the tax is, benefits do follow and diminish wealth disparities somewhat for retirement-age individuals who otherwise might not have been able to save for retirement.

OTHER REGRESSIVE TAXES

The Social Security tax is not alone in taxing only part (if any) of the income of high-income individuals while taxing a larger share or all the income of lower-income individuals. Most states impose a sales tax or a complementary use tax to purchased goods. Some states apply sales tax to services as well. Lower-income individuals tend to consume substantially all their income for basic necessities, leaving little to no income for investment. Meanwhile, higher-income individuals have the financial security to invest portions—sometimes quite large—of their income. Investments are not subject to sales tax. As a result, lower-income individuals pay sales tax on all their income except the amount they expend for rent, but higher-income individuals do not, since amounts they invest are free from tax. Sales taxes further reduce the resources of lower-income individuals but do not impact the investments of higher-income individuals.

Like sales taxes, a variety of other taxes on consumption disproportionately fall on nonaffluent individuals. Gasoline, alcohol, and tobacco taxes diminish the resources of those with lower incomes and less wealth, while their impact on wealthy individuals is small relative to their wealth, even though the amount of tax is identical. Lower-income individuals can also become subject to predatory policing regimes when local governments raise revenue by aggressively ticketing for traffic and other violations to make up for revenue shortfalls precipitated by limitations on increases in existing taxes. Such ticketing campaigns are taxes because their primary purpose is to raise revenue—a taxing function—rather than promote public safety—a policing function (Ordower, Sandoval, and Warren 2017, 136–44). Moreover, when higher-income individuals do become subject to the aggressive ticketing, fines are not adjusted to the income or wealth of the individual fined. The financial penalty, then, is a smaller relative burden for the individual with greater resources.

TAX ASSISTANCE TO LOW-INCOME FAMILIES: THE EARNED INCOME CREDIT

The EITC (I.R.C. §32), which has become a leading antipoverty program in the United States, provides an income tax–based supplement to the incomes of many low-income, working individuals. In doing so, the EITC is designed to narrow the disparity between rich and poor (Neumark and Wascher 2001; Burkhauser 2015). It operates as a negative income tax, and its amount is determined by both family size and income within certain low-income ranges. The mechanism the EITC uses to deliver the supplement is a refundable tax credit like the withholding tax (I.R.C. §31). It is a refundable credit, meaning it decreases the taxpayer's liability to pay income tax and provides a refund to the taxpayer to the extent the credit amount exceeds the taxpayer's tax payable.

Individuals or married couples who are either employees or self-employed service providers may claim a maximum EITC of between $529 and $6,557. Computation of the credit is a percentage of income from wages or other service income. The percentage increases from 7.65 percent of a maximum $6,920 of services income for individuals or couples with no qualifying children to 34 percent of a maximum $10,370 of services income with one qualifying child to 40 percent of a maximum of $14,570 with two qualifying children to 45 percent of a maximum $14,570 with three or more qualifying children. The services income maximums are adjusted annually for inflation, so the maximum credit usually increases from year to year. A qualifying child is a dependent child under age twenty-four if the child is the taxpayer's child, niece, or nephew living with the taxpayer.

As helpful to low-income workers as the EITC may be, it has been criticized for creating disincentives to upward mobility, demands for higher wages, and an increased minimum wage. Employers are likely to take the credit availability into account in determining workers' salaries, so the EITC may benefit employers in some instances and not the employees that the EITC is trying to help. Moreover, once the credit recipient's income from services reaches its applicable maximum, the credit increases no further. The credit decreases, however, as the recipient's income from all sources—including investments—climbs above certain levels. For each dollar of income in excess of the applicable level, the taxpayer must reduce the credit by 7.65 (no children), 15.98 (one child), and 21.06 (2 or more children) percent, respectively, of that additional dollar. The reduction begins in the case of a married couple with no qualifying children at $14,450 of income and at $24,820 with at least one qualifying child. For a single individual, that reduction begins at $8,650 and $19,030, respectively. Note that the credit does not increase family income above the poverty guideline, and the reduction in the credit begins below the poverty guideline (U.S. Department of Health and Human Services 2019). The EITC also disincentivizes recipients to save or invest. If the taxpayer has investment income, including both taxable and tax-exempt interest, dividends, rental income, and capital gains, in excess of $3,600, the taxpayer may not claim the EITC. This is the case even if the taxpayer's income from all sources is well below the level at which the credit otherwise would begin to be reduced by incremental income.

CONCLUSION

On average, a high-income individual certainly pays a larger overall share of the national tax burden under the income tax than does a low-income individual. Income from investments, however, often is treated more favorably than is wage income, causing the high-income individual's share to be smaller than it would be if all income were treated the same and progressive marginal income tax rates applied uniformly. If all income were treated uniformly and subjected to the income tax (including the Social Security tax), the tax on low-income taxpayers would decline and the tax on high-income taxpayers would increase to produce the same amount of revenue currently collected. That tax structure would allow low-income individuals to retain more of their income and high-income individuals to retain less of their income and contribute to closing or at least diminishing the inequality gap between rich and poor Americans that persists today. Whether such tax treatment would be fairer to all or might diminish productivity remain controversial questions of intense debate.

Henry Ordower

Further Reading

Blum, Walter J. 1957. "A Handy Summary of the Capital Gains Arguments." *Taxes* 35: 247–66.

Brittain, John A. 1971. "The Incidence of Social Security Payroll Taxes." *American Economic Review* 61:110–25.

Brown, Dorothy A. 2018. "Homeownership in Black and White: The Role of Tax Policy in Increasing Housing Inequity." *University of Memphis Law Review* 49: 205–27.

Burkhauser, Richard V. 2015. "The Minimum Wage versus the Earned Income Tax Credit for Reducing Poverty." IZA World of Labor, May 2015. https://wol.iza.org/uploads /articles/153/pdfs/minimum-wage-versus-earned-income-tax-credit-for-reducing -poverty.pdf.

Crandall-Hollick, Margot L. 2018. "The Earned Income Tax Credit (EITC): A Brief Legislative History." Congressional Research Service. https://fas.org/sgp/crs/misc/ R44825.pdf.

Friedman, Milton. 1965. "Transfer Payments and the Social Security System." *Conference Board Record* 11:7–10.

Haneman, Victoria J. 2019. "Contemplating Homeownership Tax Subsidies and Structural Racism." *Wake Forest Law Review* 363 (Spring). https://ssrn.com/abstract= 3311846.

Holmes, Oliver Wendell, Jr., Chief Justice. 1927. *Compañia General de Tabacos v. Collector*, U.S. 275: 87, 100 (dissenting opinion).

Internal Revenue Code of 1986, as amended (I.R.C.), *United States Code* Title 26.

Khimm, Suzy. 2012. "Why Does Mitt Romney Only Get Taxed at 15 Percent?" *Washington Post*, January 17, 2012. https://www.washingtonpost.com/blogs/ezra-klein/ post/why-does-mitt-romney-only-get-taxed-at-15-percent/2012/01/17/gIQA-7d8g5P_blog.html.

Neumark, David, and William Wascher. 2001. "Using the EITC to Help Poor Families: New Evidence and a Comparison with the Minimum Wage." *National Tax Journal* 54:281–317.

OECD. 2008. "Growing Unequal? Income Distribution and Poverty in OECD Countries." https://doi.org/10.1787/9789264044197-en.

OECD. 2019. "Income Inequality." https://data.oecd.org/inequality/income-inequality .htm#indicator-chart.

Office of Policy Development and Research. Evidence Matters. 2012. "Paths to Homeownership for Low-Income and Minority Households." https://www.huduser.gov/ portal/periodicals/em/fall12/highlight1.html.

Ordower, Henry. 2010. "The Culture of Tax Avoidance." *Saint Louis University Law Journal* 55: 47–128.

Ordower, Henry. 2015. "Income Imputation: Toward Equal Treatment of Renters and Owners." In *Controversies in Tax Law: A Matter of Perspective*, edited by Anthony C. Infanti, chapter 4, 47–64. Farnham, UK: Ashgate Press.

Ordower, Henry, J. S. Sandoval, and Kenneth Warren. 2017. "Out of Ferguson: Misdemeanors, Municipal Courts, Tax Distribution and Constitutional Limitations." *Howard Law Journal* 61: 113–47.

Saez, Emmanuel, and Gabriel Zucman. 2014. "Wealth Inequality in the United States since 1913: Evidence from Capitalized Income Tax Data." NBER Working Paper 20625. National Bureau of Economic Research. https://www.nber.org/papers/ w20625.

Saez, Emmanuel, and Gabriel Zucman. 2019. "Opinion: Alexandria Ocasio-Cortez's Tax Hike Idea Is Not about Soaking the Rich. It's about Curtailing Inequality and Saving Democracy." *New York Times*, January 22, 2019. https://www.nytimes.com/2019/01/22/opinion/ocasio-cortez-taxes.html.

Stigler, George J. 1946. "The Economics of Minimum Wage Legislation." *American Economic Review* 36 (3): 358–65.

Thornton, Alexandra, and Galen Hendricks. 2019. "Ending Special Tax Treatment for the Very Wealthy." Center for American Progress. https://www.americanprogress.org/issues/economy/reports/2019/06/04/470621/ending-special-tax-treatment-wealthy.

Troiano, Ugo. 2017. "Do Taxes Increase Economic Inequality? A Comparative Study Based on the State Personal Income Tax." NBER Working Paper 24175. National Bureau of Economic Research. http://www.nber.org/papers/w24175.

U.S. Department of Health and Human Services, ASPE Office of the Assistant Secretary for Planning and Evaluation. 2019. "2019 Poverty Guidelines." https://aspe.hhs.gov/2019-poverty-guidelines.

U.S. Department of Labor, Wage and Hour Division. n.d. "Misclassification of Employees as Independent Contractors." https://www.dol.gov/whd/workers/misclassification.

SECTION X

The Future of Inequality

Is Inequality a Threat to Democracy?

Inequality has been on the rise over the last three decades and has been a pervasive issue in elections throughout the 2010s. On one level, income inequality is a nonissue to observers who point out that in a market economy, there will always be winners and losers. In a market economy in which individuals are free to make choices and reap the rewards of the choices they made, it is a given that some will wind up with more than others. We cannot all be equal, because we do not all have the same natural endowments. Those with certain skills and abilities will often wind up with more than those without. And those who went to school to train for specific occupations that pay well will earn more than those who did not. In short, skilled workers will earn more than nonskilled workers. As a result, there is bound to be inequality. Moreover, as these trends continue, the gap between the top and the bottom is only likely to grow.

Others, however, see income inequality as a seminal issue because of what it really speaks to: the disappearance of the middle class. Inequality per se, however, is not the problem; rather it is the rate of increase in inequality. Unless we opt for an authoritarian state that will confiscate all private property and will then distribute to all so that each and everyone has exactly the same thing, it is not possible to have pure equality, at least in terms of outcomes. Still, when equality increases and the rate of inequality increases along with it, we can see the extremes getting larger. And this means that the middle class is shrinking.

This rate of increase in inequality, especially if it continues, represents a threat to democracy. First, it reflects the shrinking of the middle class, thereby resulting in two extremes. Second, it results in wealthy individuals and/or groups having an undue influence on public policy, which often results in the advancement of policies favorable specifically to them. More than policies that are unfavorable to those at the bottom of the distribution, it can effectively lead to them being dominated by those at the top. If one group is dominated by another, the one being dominated certainly does not enjoy equality of standing, which is a fundamental requirement of democracy. Although democracy does not require equality of outcomes, it does assume that wealth and income will be more evenly distributed.

Many econometric models of democracy suggest that the greater the level of inequality, the more susceptible a democracy is to revolution. And yet, the predicted revolution need not necessarily be along the lines of a Marxist one whereby the people will own the means of production. Rather it can be toward a more authoritarian/fascistic regime, in which the people put their faith in a autocrat who assures them that he/she has the answer to their problems. Democracy does require that individuals be responsible for their actions, but when people are prepared to submit to such a strongman, it means that they have lost faith in democratic institutions and processes.

RISING INEQUALITY

Inequality has always existed in that not all have had equal amounts of wealth and income, but it has only been a policy issue in recent years specifically because it has been increasing amid stagnant middle-class wages. Those at the top of the distribution have seen their incomes increase, while those at the bottom have seen their incomes decrease in real terms. Whereas prior to 1973, the incomes of families in the bottom fifth of the distribution rose more than those in the top fifth, low-income families in the United States afterward experienced a steady decline in real income from the late 1970s through the middle of the 1990s. Between 1979

Table 1   General Trends in Family Income Inequality

Year	90/10 Percent Ratio	90/50 Percent Ratio	50/10 Percent Ratio	Top-to-Bottom Quintile Ratio
2000	10.8	2.6	4.1	13.8
2001	9.7	2.5	3.9	13.8
2002	10.0	2.5	4.0	14.2
2003	10.2	2.5	4.0	14.3
2004	11.4	2.6	4.4	14.9
2005	11.5	2.6	4.4	15.2
2006	11.3	2.6	4.3	15.4
2007	11.5	2.7	4.3	15.4
2008	11.4	2.6	4.4	14.8
2009	12.0	2.6	4.5	15.7
2010	12.5	2.7	4.6	16.9
2011	13.2	2.7	4.8	16.9
2012	12.8	2.8	4.6	17.4
2013	13.0	2.8	4.7	17.6
2014	13.4	2.8	4.8	17.8
2015	13.9	2.8	4.9	18.4
2016	15.5	3.5	4.5	17.4
Change	**+43.5**	**+34.6**	**+9.8**	**+26.1**

Source: Ruggles et al. (2019).

and 2007, the top 1 percent of families had 60 percent of the income gains, while the bottom 90 percent only had about 9 percent of those income gains (Belman and Wolfson 2014). Inequality had reached its lowest ebb between 1950 and 1980, whereby the top decile of the income distribution claimed 30 to 35 percent of the nation's income. After 1980, however, income inequality exploded, with the top decile share of the national income rising to between 45 and 50 percent in the 2000s. This may, nonetheless, understate the problem, which in recent years has been couched as the very top pulling away from the rest because a subclass of "supermanagers" emerged who were earning extremely high compensation (Hacker and Pierson 2010; Piketty 2014).

Data from the Current Population Survey (CPS) in table 1 show increases in family income inequality between 2000 and 2016, on the basis of the 90/10, 90/50, 50/10, and top-to bottom quintile ratios. From table 1, it is evident that income inequality is rising. The rise in both the 90/10 and 90/50 percentiles appears to support the argument that the top has been pulling away from the rest. Certainly, the 90/50 measure suggests that the top has been pulling away from the middle. Even the increase in the 50/10 ratio suggests that incomes at the bottom, that is, below the median, have been falling.

THE THREAT TO DEMOCRACY

Democratic theory assumes a society of free, equal, and autonomous individuals. Although democracy may have different meanings to different people, an ideal of democracy is that all individuals are supposed to have equal standing. This means that each individual is equal before the law and has the same vote as other individuals, the same right to express oneself in the political sphere, and, perhaps most importantly, the same potential to influence what government does, even if the individual opts not to exercise that potential. All citizens, then, have the same access to governing institutions. Within this theoretical construct, which may also characterize American democracy, money is supposed to be irrelevant to one's standing. Both the rich and the poor are supposed to be equal in the eyes of their government (Hacker and Pierson 2010). Procedural equality is not usually concerned with how resources, wealth, and income are distributed but with how individuals stand in relation to one another. Individuals can have more than others so long as they are equal in terms of their legal and political standing. This conception of equality is especially critical to democratic society because it serves to secure another essential condition: personal freedom, which is also a necessary condition for individuals to function autonomously. The greater their autonomy, the more likely they are to participate in the democratic process. Individuals are free to pursue their goals and objectives, that is, self-interests, so long as their pursuit does not interfere with others' ability to pursue their own goals and objectives. In a very basic sense, and certainly within the context of classical political thought, this is what it means to talk about personal independence or autonomy.

Economist Bruce Kaufman (2005) suggests that democracy promotes self-development by giving people independence and autonomy as well as opportunities to have voice in the political process. That voice, however, is meaningless if their personal autonomy is undermined because those at the bottom find them-selves dependent on others and subject to exploitation. The personal autonomy that democracy requires means that there can be no domination. It is predicated on the idea that truly free individuals are not subject to domination. Dominating involves occupying a position where one can interfere on an arbitrary basis in another's life (Petit 2002). One who is dominated is unfree. To be free means that one is not in any way subject to the arbitrary whims of another (Petit 1997).

The greater the economic gap between the top and the bottom, the more power those at the top of the distribution have over—and the more potential to interfere with the lives of—those at the bottom. Therefore, freedom as nondomination requires that a person not be exposed to the possibility of interference on an arbi-trary basis. Nevertheless, the republican conception of liberty does allow the pos-sibility for interference that is not arbitrary if it is not necessarily restrictive of an agent's freedom. That is, agents are free only to the extent that they are not subject to the mastery of another (Maynor 2003).

A democratic polity operates on the premise that individuals will be politically autonomous, but it does not merely respect and ensure noninterference and nonco-ercion. On the contrary, it must also ensure that conditions for participation in that democracy are available to all individuals, for by doing so it guarantees a univer-sal application of citizenship. In fact, the state must guarantee conditions for full citizenship. Although economic equality is not essential to democracy, economic inequality could nonetheless pose serious problems in a procedural democracy (Gaffaney 2000). This has led to the notion that the maintenance of democracy requires the maintenance of a broad middle class.

On an individual level, unequal distribution of wealth and income may adversely affect individuals' ability to participate in the democratic process on an equal footing. It may result in procedural inequality to the extent that those lacking in wealth and income may not enjoy the same access to political and policy officials as rich or affluent Americans do. With a greater concentration of wealth at the top, those at the top are in a better position to use their wealth toward the attainment of their political and other ideological objectives (Bachrach and Botwinick 1992, 4–5). Those at the top of the distribution often enjoy inordinate power and are able to not only limit redistribution but also shape the rules of the game in favor of those with more resources (Stiglitz 2012). Various studies have found legislative bodies to be more responsive to affluent constituents than to nonaffluent constitu-ents (Bartels 2008; Gilens 2012; Volscho and Kelly 2012).

To talk about a broad middle class is to talk about a more evenly distributed income, or at least a bell-curve distribution, whereby few people occupy the extremes at the top and the bottom and the majority falls in the middle. Therefore, to the extent that democracy requires the maintenance of a broad middle class, the maintenance of democracy requires economic development (Lipset 1959). This theme has found expression in the literature on emerging democracies, particu-larly those in Eastern Europe that were for so long part of the eastern Communist Bloc (Mostov 1992; Maharaj and Ramballi 1998).

Economic development is important because it results in the generation of a broader middle class in which there is relative equality of condition among its members. Moreover, it establishes the foundation for individuals to function economically in a way that leads to their independence, or at least to function in a manner where they are less likely to be dominated. The more well-to-do the nation is, the greater are the chances that it will sustain democracy. A successful democracy requires a minimum level of aggregate wealth, a certain degree of industrialization and urbanization, and a certain level of education that will result in relatively few of its citizens living in poverty (Lipset 1959). But it also requires the maintenance of a middle class in order that the gap between the top and the bottom not be so wide that it leads to potential social unrest.

Law professor Ganeresh Sitaraman (2017) argues that the American constitution, and particularly the separation of powers delineated within, was predicated on the assumption of a strong and vibrant middle class. A fundamental form of oppression is when private actors are in a position to oppress and dominate others. When a society is deeply divided along lines of wealth and income, there is a concern that one social group might capture all the branches of government that are supposed to check each other and that this group will use government to oppress the other social groups.

Aristotle maintained that because the rich are unequal with respect to their wealth, they begin to think that they are unequal in all respects, that is, that they also possess superior moral worth, intelligence, and ability to govern. Over time, inequality leads to an erosion of trust as people become more dissimilar and interact with less frequency in meaningful ways. "Elites" soon begin to think that they are more capable of governing society, which is greatly at odds with republican government, which is rooted directly in the right of the people to govern themselves. When an ethos of inequality takes hold, economic elites increasingly aim to exercise power and influence. Power soon turns into the entrenchment of privileges, which ultimately reshapes the very structure of government and society. As economic inequality turns into political inequality, the rich may either oppress the poor or the poor may overthrow the rich.

The political and policy preferences of economic elites, who tend to participate in the political process to a greater extent than the rest of the population, also are more likely to diverge from those of the rest of the population. The wealthiest Americans tend to be far less supportive of policies that assist those at the bottom of the distribution. This even extends to policies designed to maintain Americans above the poverty line, such as the Earned Income Tax Credit (EITC) and the minimum wage. Although the wealthy give high importance to the problem of unemployment, they overwhelmingly reject government action to help with jobs (Page, Bartels, and Seawright 2013). This is an important reality, for more educated and economically affluent people—those who are more engaged with and connected to the political process—are the ones who get their policy preferences legislated into law more frequently than those who are less educated.

This dynamic is evident in the lax enforcement of antitrust laws in recent years. Law professor Tim Wu (2018) argues that when society allows for the unrestricted growth of concentrated power, it has managed to recreate the economics and politics of the late nineteenth and early twentieth centuries. During that era, extreme economic concentrations of wealth in the hands of a small percentage of the

American populace yielded gross inequality and material suffering, fueling an appetite for nationalistic and extremist leadership. That is, the road to fascism and dictatorship has historically been paved with the failure of economic policy to serve the needs of the general public. Essentially, political and social unrest is often a consequence of deep and enduring inequality (Acemoglu and Robinson 2006).

Antitrust law originally served as a kind of limit or check on private power by preventing the growth of monopoly corporations into something that might transcend the power of elected government to control. Private economic power came to be seen as the rival of elected governments, whereby firms might seek to control politics for their own purposes. It was during the post–World War II years, especially during the 1950s and 1960s, that strong antitrust laws became identified as part of a functional democracy. But during the 1960s and 1970s the opinion of some academics changed, turning away from an emphasis on the mere existence of monopoly power toward an emphasis on the impact on consumers. Their studies could not conclude that consumers were being harmed significantly by large firms (Wu 2018). Their recommendation that antitrust policy should be used sparingly was eagerly received by subsequent Republican administrations.

The more equal the society, the less likely are the masses to demand democratization. Democratization actually requires that society be sufficiently unequal so that the threat of revolution is credible. Under those circumstances, an elite may be willing to expand the political power of others (such as voting rights, for instance) because it perceives that it is in its interests to do so. Such flexibility effectively preserves the status quo by staving off a threat of revolution, which in the end may preserve the power base of the elite. The elite only democratizes to the degree necessary to stave off the threat of revolution, because the former effectively limits the power of the majority by diluting popular pressure and undermining the power of the majority.

Authoritarianism, on the other hand, tends to be more prevalent in those countries where there are higher levels of inequality. The redistributive demands of the worse-off citizens on the wealthy are particularly intense in highly unequal societies. Since in a democracy all individuals are able to vote, increasing levels of economic equality will bolster claims of democracy, as individuals will use their democratic right to vote to pressure the legislature into guaranteeing more equitable distributions of wealth and attention to other policy priorities. A more unequal distribution of wealth increases the redistributive demands of the population and the ultimate level of taxes in a democratic system. But what happens when the political system is unresponsive to a so-called democratic vote on the tax rate?

A truly democratic regime would not simply take away from the wealthy elite for the benefit of the masses—but it might set a higher tax rate on the wealthy elite for purposes of reducing economic inequality. In the extreme, if too much inequality results in increased redistributive pressure to the point that revolutionary action is taken by economically disenfranchised populations, the end result may well be a left-wing dictatorship whereby the poor now rule. In an authoritarian regime, a right-wing dictatorship readily represses the poor, excluding them from the decision-making process. In a communist or left-wing dictatorship, the poor rule after expropriating all the wealthy's capital. And in a democracy, everybody votes on the tax rate in accordance with what is known as the *median-voter theorem*. This holds that the more inequality there is, the greater will be the distance between the median income and society's average income. The greater the distance, the more calls there are for redistribution, and it is the distance itself that effectively determines the tax rate (Meltzer and Richard 1981). If members of Congress are becoming less responsive to nonaffluent constituents, however, then the median voter is no longer in a position to determine the size of government in terms of expenditures for programs and redistributive purposes. On the contrary, the median-voter theorem assumes responsiveness to the middle class.

Growing inequality in the United States may well be reflected in the increasing polarization of American politics. The United States is most likely not ripe for a revolution, for the reasons that Louis Hartz (1955) famously gave. Echoing Tocqueville that America was born free, Hartz argued that the absence of the feudalistic baggage characteristic of the Old World meant that there was little reason to rise up in rebellion. In the old order, where individuals were born into caste-like classes, the only way out was either through death or revolution. But in the United States, where there was no feudalistic tradition, individuals could get out of the class they were born into through upward socioeconomic mobility. Nevertheless, preliminary signs of tension have emerged over persistent and growing economic inequality in American society. These signs include greater calls for socialism, whereby there would be a more equitable distribution and equality of outcomes, which may be regarded as a substitute for redistribution.

IMPACT OF INEQUALITY ON CIVIC PARTICIPATION

Income inequality not only distorts democracy in terms of how institutions and political actors respond to different levels of income but may also have a profound effect on the development of social capital, which affects civic engagement. Democracy requires the active participation of citizens in the affairs of their communities, which extends beyond mere voting. Underlying social capital is the notion that civic virtue is most powerful when it is embedded in a dense network of social relations. American civil society has been defined by its associative life, in which Americans belong to voluntary organizations. And through these organizations, they participate in the affairs of their communities (Putnam 2000).

INEQUALITY AND COMMUNITY FRAGMENTATION AND ALIENATION

Income inequality, however, can also lead to *political anomie*—a breakdown of broadly shared moral and ethical standards. As family income inequality increases, those families below the median are further from the social norm than before. Similarly, those at the top of the distribution see a larger gap between themselves and the rest of the population. Many observers fear that the growth in income disparities among families has had a variety of adverse consequences for both families and communities. Families at the bottom of the distribution may end up drifting further from the mainstream and thus may also experience greater alienation as those with greater resources may come to see them as both more distinct and undeserving. This may also have consequences for how citizens, in turn, view the potential role and functions of government (Haveman et al. 2004). Poor people tend to experience greater social alienation because their tendency to participate less means that they may be out of touch with common interests. But participation is also less likely because the alienation that results from social isolation can increase the likelihood that some members will conclude that there are not benefits that accrue from community participation. Less inclination to participate, then, is not only a function of the absence of personal autonomy but of social alienation as well. Of course, these two may not be mutually exclusive, as one lacking in personal autonomy is likely to feel socially isolated because of the stigma attached. The alienation may also have something to do with trust, because trust rests on foundations of economic equality. When resources are unequally distributed, those at the top and the bottom are less likely to see themselves as sharing the same fate. Consequently, they have less reason to trust people of different backgrounds (Uslaner and Brown 2005).

One study on the relationship between income inequality and civic engagement in 2008 found that individuals in households with different levels of income had different levels of civic engagement. Six measures of civic engagement were looked at: daily discussions of politics; daily reading of newspapers, which was intended to speak to one's knowledge about and interest in politics; involvement in protests; attendance at political meetings; visiting public officials; and participating in civic organizations. Participation was found to be greater on all measures of engagement among those in households earning more than $100,000 a year than among those earning less than $30,000. Those at the highest end of the distribution were not necessarily more likely to be engaged than those between $30,000 and $99,999, but those in households between $30,000 to $59,999 were considerably more likely to be engaged than those in households below $30,000. Participation appeared to improve dramatically when one was in a household with income greater than $30,000. These differences alone would suggest that entry into the middle class might result in greater levels of civic participation. Moreover, logistical regressions found that those with higher incomes were more likely to be civically engaged and that those earning less than a minimum wage were least likely to be engaged (Levin-Waldman 2013).

This, of course, implies that as the middle class drops out, civic engagement from the masses will further decline. If only the affluent are engaged, it becomes a foregone conclusion that public officials and members of Congress will only represent *them*. After all, they are primarily representing those who vote. This is nothing new, because this was essentially economist Anthony Downs's (1957) argument, which rests on the assumption that all individuals, groups, and/or organizations, which would include governments, behave rationally. Each party seeks to maximize its advantage or utility, which means that each is motivated by self-interest. If individuals seek to maximize their utility, a political party will similarly seek to maximize its utility, which will often mean doing whatever is necessary to gain political support and win elections.

The Downsian model, then, is based on the assumption that every government seeks to maximize political support. It is further assumed that in a democratic society in which periodic elections are held, the primary goal of lawmakers is reelection. Citizens in this model are rational with regard to elections if their actions enable them to play their part in selecting a government efficiently. All political actors seek to maximize their utility. As elected officials seek to retain power, they are most likely to serve those interests that are most able to maximize their utility and get them reelected. Therefore, political actors seeking to retain power will support the interests of those who can contribute to their campaigns and are most likely to vote. It is true, however, that some politically marginalized, low-income citizens who tire of being discriminated against or ignored by law-makers and government officials form special-interest groups to advance their concerns. People who participate in these interest groups are less likely to feel that their vote and participation in American civic life are worthless. To the contrary, they are more likely to see their participation in the group as counting toward something of value and potentially even being decisive in improving public policy and American society.

Some public officials have been responsive to these groups by, for example, supporting programs that effectively increase the money utility of the poor. Because the principal goal of elected officials is to win election and then reelec-tion, many policies will only be supported to the extent that they garner votes from the electorate. Public officials are more likely to serve the interests of higher-income groups than lower-income groups because the former are more active in the political system and contribute money to campaigns. Public officials can effec-tively purchase their quiescence with programs or through redistribution that increases their effective money utility. In exchange for more programs that better serve their interests and make them better off, they are trading away their political voice. So by purchasing the quiescence of lower-income voters with policies that increase their money utility, public officials have the leisure to pursue policies that benefit those at the higher end of the distribution, because by doing so they will ensure that they continue to be reelected.

This state of affairs would imply that there will be more redistribution when there are higher levels of inequality and larger low-income populations. If policy makers are nonresponsive to those who are not affluent, however, it is not clear that the logic of the median-voter theorem holds any longer. On the contrary, the greater the level of inequality, the less likely the median middle-class voters decide anything, because there are simply fewer of them in existence.

POLARIZATION IN AMERICA

Although it cannot be predicted with certainty just how disruptive inequality will be to democracy if allowed to grow unchecked, observers point to many warning indicators. The United States is clearly seeing an erosion in democracy in that elected representatives no longer represent all people equally. Rather, there is greater responsiveness to those with the greatest financial resources, especially those contributing to political campaigns. Meanwhile, the politically marginalized poor find themselves frozen out. In more fragile democracies, the response is unrest. Even in the United States, historically regarded as a stable democracy, various social protest movements have become prominent. Although the results of the 2016 national election were not necessarily a response to rising income inequality, they were clearly a response to the larger economic conditions of which rising income inequality has been a symptom. Specifically, voters appeared to be rebelling against political elites who apparently were unable to deliver good job growth with rising wages. In that voters chose a candidate who, rhetorically at least, was opposed to open borders and free trade, they were effectively challenging the commitment of elites to globalism, which was the same globalism that resulted in the two-tier economy with highly skilled and paid workers at the top and poorly skilled and paid workers at the bottom. It might be a stretch to conclude that the election of Donald Trump represents a desire for authoritarianism. Arguably, however, a system that is not responsive to those in the middle or at the bottom, and in which many may feel that they are being dominated by those at the top, or at least their choices are being restrained by the wealthy and other elites, is a form of authoritarianism. Moreover, his critics view him as such, and if the voters were choosing what they might have thought were authoritarian solutions to economic conditions, they were clearly responding to the very economic conditions that have been the source of rising inequality in recent years.

It has been commonplace to divide the country into red states and blue states. The red states represent conservative areas and are primarily Republican, while the blue states are more liberal and are primarily Democratic. Based on the rhetoric of the 2016 presidential election, one might expect that those states that flipped from blue to red between the presidential election of 2008 and the presidential election of 2016 would have done so because the voters were gripped by anti-immigrant fervor, given that the Trump campaign made blunt rhetoric about the dangers posed by "illegal immigrants"—rhetoric that opponents decried as brazenly racist—a centerpiece of its election strategy. Data from the Current Population Survey (CPS), however, suggest something else was at work. CPS data indicate that states that flipped from blue to red in the 2016 election did so because of perceptions about changes in the economy. That is, the loss of manufacturing effectively left behind large numbers of workers who felt the global economy—and by extension decades of economic policy making—had left them and/or other Americans behind. There was little statistical support for the idea that voters were responding to an increase in undocumented workers. On the contrary, the presence of Mexican workers in red states appeared to have absolutely no significance. Rising inequality, of course, is not responsible for the changing base of the economy. Rather the changing base of the economy is reflected in rising income inequality. The two are very much interrelated. If the changing base of the economy can be said to be responsible for greater polarization, as data from the CPS suggest, then by extension we can conclude that increased polarization in the United States is also a function of rising income inequality.

CONCLUSION

Rising income inequality in the United States poses a serious threat to democracy. Because rising inequality signifies the disappearance of the middle class—and a broad middle class is essential to the maintenance of democracy—American society is increasingly stratifying into two extremes. At one extreme are those who are poorly paid and low-skilled, and at the other are well-paid and highly skilled individuals. These two extremes, without a middle of sufficient size to provide balance, is often a recipe for heightened tensions and unrest in a society. We already see that the more affluent are in a position to control government and obtain policies that are more favorable to them and may result in those at the bottom end of the distribution effectively being dominated by those at the top. This is especially so when those at the top can effectively secure policy that effectively subjugates those at the bottom. We already see that members of Congress are more responsive to more affluent constituents than they are to nonaffluent constituents. In fact, many elected representatives are decidedly nonresponsive to the nonaffluent. This in and of itself is a threat to democracy, because democracy requires free and autonomous individuals to have equal standing.

Rising inequality not only has the potential to result in a revolution because of the increased social strife but can also lead the masses to choose more authoritarian governing structures. Another possibility is that disaffected voters might choose candidates who portray themselves as autocrats capable of delivering the economic security and fairness they crave—and which other leaders have not had the talent or determination to provide. If one of the effects of inequality is the type of polarization that leads various groups to choose candidates at either extreme of the political spectrum, then that, too, represents a threat to democracy.

Oren M. Levin-Waldman

Note: This entry has been adapted with permission from Levin-Waldman, Oren M. 2020. "Globalism and Inequality Are the Real Threats to Our Democracy." *Challenge* 63 (2): 77–89. https://doi.org/10.1080/05775132.2019.1709725.

Further Reading

Acemoglu, Daron, and James A. Robinson. 2006. *Economic Origins of Dictatorship and Democracy.* Cambridge and New York: Cambridge University Press.

Bachrach, Peter, and Aryeh Botwinick. 1992. *Power and Empowerment: A Radical Theory of Participatory Democracy.* Philadelphia: Temple University Press.

Bartels, Larry M. 2008. *Unequal Democracy: The Political Economy of the New Gilded Age.* Princeton, NJ: Princeton University Press.

Belman, Dale, and Paul J. Wolfson. 2014. *What Does the Minimum Wage Do?* Kalamazoo, MI: W. E. Upjohn Institute for Employment Research.

Downs, Anthony. 1957. *An Economic Theory of Democracy.* Boston: Addison-Wesley.

Gaffaney, Timothy. 2000. *Freedom for the Poor: Welfare and the Foundations of Democratic Citizenship.* Boulder, CO: Westview Press.

Gilens, Martin. 2012. *Affluence & Influence: Economic Inequality and Political Power in America.* Princeton, NJ, and New York: Princeton University Press/Russell Sage Foundation.

Hartz, Louis. 1955. *The Liberal Tradition in America: An Interpretation of American Political Thought since the Revolution.* New York: Harcourt Brace Jovanovich.

Hacker, Jacob S., and Paul Pierson. 2010. *Winner-Take-All Politics: How Washington Made the Rich Richer—and Turned Its Back on the Middle Class.* New York: Simon & Schuster.

Haveman, Robert, Gary Sandefeur, Barbara Wolfe, and Andrea Voyer. 2004. "Trends in Children's Attainments and Their Determinants as Family Income Inequality Has Increased." In *Social Inequality*, edited by Kathryn Neckerman, 149–88. New York: Russell Sage Foundation.

Kaufman, Bruce E. 2005. "The Social Welfare Objectives and Ethical Principles of Industrial Relations." In *The Ethics of Human Resources and Industrial Relations*, edited by John W. Budd and James G. Scoville, 23–63. Champaign, IL: Labor and Employment Relations Association.

Levin-Waldman, Oren M. 2013. "Income, Civic Participation and Achieving Greater Democracy." *Journal of Socio-Economics* 43 (2): 83–92.

Lipset, Seymour Martin. 1959. "Some Social Requisites of Democracy: Economic Development and Political Legitimacy." *American Political Science Review* 53 (March): 69–105.

Maharaj, Brij, and Kem Ramballi. 1998. "Local Economic Development Strategies in Emerging Democracy: The Case of Durban in South Africa." *Urban Studies* 35, no. 1 (January): 131–48.

Maynor, John W. 2003. *Republicanism in the Modern World.* Cambridge and Malden, MA: Polity Press.

Meltzer, Alan H., and Scott F. Richard. 1981. "A Rational Theory of the Size of Government." *Journal of Political Economy* 89 (5): 914–27.

Mostov, Julie. 1992. *Power, Process and Popular Sovereignty.* Philadelphia: Temple University Press.

Page, Benjamin, Larry Bartels, and Jason Seawright. 2013. "Democracy and the Policy Preferences of Wealthy Americans." *Perspectives on Politics* 11 (1): 51–73.

Petit, Philip. 1997. *Republicanism: A Theory of Freedom and Government.* Oxford and New York: Oxford University Press.

Petit, Philip. 2002. "Keeping Republican Freedom Simple: On a Difference with Quintin Skinner." *Political Theory* 30 (3): 339–56.

Piketty, Thomas. 2014. *Capital in the Twenty-First Century.* Cambridge, MA, and London: Belknap Press of Harvard University Press.

Putnam, Robert. 2000. *Bowling Alone: The Collapse and Revival of American Community.* New York: Simon & Schuster.

Ruggles, Steven, Sarah Flood, Ronald Goeken, Josiah Grover, Erin Meyer, Jose Pacas, and Matthew Sobek. 2019. *IPUMS USA: Version 9.0 [dataset]. File years: 2000–2016.* Minneapolis, MN: IPUMS. https://doi.org/10.18128/D010.V9.0.

Sitaraman, Ganesh. 2017. *The Crisis of the Middle-Class Constitution: Why Economic Inequality Threatens Our Republic.* New York: Vintage Books.

Stiglitz, Joseph E. 2012. *The Price of Inequality.* New York: W. W. Norton.

Uslaner, Eric, and Mitchell Brown. 2005. "Inequality, Trust, and Civic Engagement." *American Politics Research* 33, no. 6 (November): 868–94.

Volscho, Thomas W., Jr., and Nathan J. Kelly. 2012. "The Rise of the Super-Rich: Power Resources, Taxes, Financial Markets, and the Dynamics of the Top 1 Percent, 1949–2008." *American Sociological Review* 77 (5): 679–99.

Wu, Tim. 2018. *The Curse of Bigness: Antitrust in the New Gilded Age.* New York: Columbia Global Reports.

The Future of Inequality in America

Inequality is a prevalent sociopolitical theme in the public sphere and within social scientific research. Particularly, the growing divide between affluent Americans and the rest of the U.S. population has been central to social discourse and political debate. By virtually all indicators of social class inequality, the divide between the rich and poor is getting worse. Three common measures of inequality—the wealth gap, income inequality, and rates of social mobility—all indicate that the wealth gap and income inequality are clearly increasing and social mobility is steadily decreasing (Leiserson, McGrew, and Kopparam 2019; Chetty et al. 2014; Shapiro, Meschede, and Osoro 2013).

Increases in wealth disparities have been pronounced. In 1989, the bottom 90 percent of the U.S. population held 33 percent of all the wealth, while the top 1 percent had 30 percent of the wealth. By 2016, the former number had decreased to 23 percent, while the latter number had increased to 40 percent (Leiserson, McGrew, and Kopparam 2019). Income growth has stagnated since the 1970s for all but the top earners in several categories—the top 20 percent (upper-middle class), top 5 percent, and top 1 percent (Gottschalk 1997; McCall and Percheski 2010; Reeves 2017). Income inequality via multiple measures—including individual wages and family income (adjusted and unadjusted for family size, including market and disposable income)—and indices, including Gini, Theil, and Robin Hood, all indicate growing rates of inequality compared to generations previous. Several measures that indicate contemporary levels of inequality are at their highest since the 1910s and 1920s (McCall and Percheski 2010). For families with children, income inequality has grown twice as fast compared to individuals, as labor market and household burdens are exacerbated (Western, Bloome, and Percheski 2008).

Relative social mobility is also diminishing compared to previous decades. Social mobility (both upward and downward) is already limited within the United States (Chetty et al. 2014), and compared to previous generations, mobility is stunted. This is attributable to the continued existence of an array of systemic advantages for children of the upper-middle and upper class. For example, one study found that forty-three of "modestly skilled" (as measured by score on the Armed Forces Qualifying Test and coding speed) adolescents from affluent households remain affluent in adulthood (Reeves and Howard 2013).

However, the majority of social science research is, and has been, focused on causes and consequences of inequality for the systematically disadvantaged rather than on the United States' economic "elite" (Kenworthy 2007; Khan 2012). Despite decades of research dedicated to unequal life course outcomes according to socioeconomic status—and the accompanying multitude of policy suggestions to address this inequality—little progress has been made to stymie growing inequality. We suggest the importance of moving research toward studying not just disadvantage but the reproduction of advantage. To understand the roots of social class inequality, its far-reaching consequences, and the continuing divergence of opportunity and outcomes according to socioeconomic status, it is imperative to critically examine *both* poverty and affluence—and the classes in between. In this way, scholars can seek new insights into mechanisms of inequality and make novel policy suggestions for curtailing and perhaps even reversing long-standing trends of growing inequality.

RAMPANT INEQUALITY AND ITS CONSEQUENCES

The effect of inequality on disadvantaged groups has been measured through individual outcomes as well as institutional frameworks. Income, wealth, and opportunity inequality have risen dramatically over the past several decades, disproportionately advantaging the affluent above and beyond their already advantaged position (Neckerman and Torche 2007). Institutions of higher education and employers favor the already advantaged (Friedman and Laurison 2019; Rivera 2015; Stevens 2009). Systems including education, health care, and labor work collaboratively to exacerbate inequality throughout the life course. This compounding of privilege illustrates the social theory of cumulative advantage—in which a favorable relative position tends to yield further positive gains (DiPrete and Eirich 2006).

Education

In early childhood, differences in the quantity and form of caregiver-child linguistic interactions are linked to long-term language skill outcomes. Specifically, children of middle-class parents are more likely to develop a more robust vocabulary compared to their working-class or poor counterparts. These gains exacerbate themselves once students enter the school system (Hart and Risley 1995), whereby children from low socioeconomic backgrounds score lower on cognitive testing than their high socioeconomic counterparts, and this gap increases year by year. This is unsurprising, considering that the most socioeconomically disadvantaged children often attend the lowest-resourced schools, compounding educational disadvantage (Lee and Burkham 2002). Incidence of high school dropping out is five times higher for low-income students than for their high-income counterparts (Chapman et al. 2011), followed by collateral consequences of low educational attainment compounding disadvantage over the life course, including high percentages of unemployment, low average wages, and poor health outcomes (Marmot and Smith 1997; Vilorio 2016).

Despite touting meritocracy, wealthy parents make educational decisions for their children that are only available because of their capacity to pay for them. These decisions include purchasing property in expensive townships boasting school districts with a track record of high academic performance, or paying for lucrative private school education. This educational advantage perpetuates children's socioeconomic privilege and frequently sets children of different class backgrounds on divergent trajectories (Johnson 2014; Kusserow 2004). Schools, among other institutions, also support this system of class privilege by responding preferentially to middle-class children. Compared to working-class kids, those from middle-class or wealthier families are more likely to possess the cultural repertoires necessary to successfully navigate relationships with authority and earn advantageous outcomes such as receiving help, good grades, and positive reinforcement from teachers (Calarco 2011; Lareau 2003). Rather than working to "level the playing field," classroom interactions exacerbate class privilege (Calarco 2011).

Higher education is represented as a gateway for upward social mobility, a break in the intergenerational cycle of inequality. However, in deciding who will be admitted to a prestigious university, admissions officers often favor applicants with considerable social and cultural capital as measured by family wealth, profession, and educational background (including ties such as alumnus status to the institution in question) (Astin and Oseguera 2004; Stevens 2009). As children of the affluent have capital and institutional support, they are more likely to become top-earners themselves, which further perpetuates inequality (Corak 2013).

Labor Market

While the perception is that systemic inequality may be mitigated by stepping-stones of mobility such as higher education, in reality these gatekeeping institutions are further supporting elite populations closing rank around themselves to preserve opportunity from one generation to the next (Friedman and Laurison 2019; Rivera 2015; Stevens 2009). Children from privileged backgrounds are groomed within their families, schools, and peer groups to desire elite jobs, and this goal is further supported through parents' capacity to purchase additional advantages for their already advantaged children (Binder, Davis, and Bloom 2016; Calarco 2011; Lareau 2003; Johnson 2014).

For example, high-powered, high-paying industries and businesses favor privileged applicants who come from higher socioeconomic brackets over their similarly qualified, potentially upwardly mobile counterparts (Rivera 2015). Even within elite workplaces, opportunities for advancement and mentorship are more likely to be bestowed upon those from elite socioeconomic backgrounds, as the latter candidates are more likely to be familiar with the cultural markers most valued by these employers (Friedman and Laurison 2019).

The Family

There has long existed a persistent gap in wealth by gender in the United States, whereby men on average have more wealth than women contemporaries (Ruel and Hauser 2013), though this gap is somewhat disrupted by marital status. Historically, the twentieth-century glass ceiling pushed women out of the labor force or relegated them to modestly compensated jobs, which severely limited their individual earning potential and subsequent upward mobility. Consequentially, this also worked to lessen familial wealth-building through higher rates of between-class marriages, as highly compensated men married moderately compensated or not-compensated women. Today, there is an increase in the number of highly compensated women within the workforce, and an increase in *homogamous* (within-class) marriages compared to the generations previous. This trend has the effect of further concentrating wealth and social capital within elite couples (Greenwood et al. 2014). Since the 1970s, rates of homogamous marriage have steadily increased, particularly concerning spouses' earnings (Schwartz and Mare 2005). Had the rate of homogamous marriage remained at its 1970s level, contemporary rates of earnings inequality might be up to 30 percent lower (Schwartz 2010).

Marriage itself is increasingly becoming an institution of privilege, reserved as a middle-class or affluent luxury (Cherlin 2010; Edin and Kefalas 2011), People from the middle and affluent classes are much more likely to get married than people from the poor and working classes and, consequently, are more able to take advantage of marital privileges such as tax incentives and medical benefits for that group. As rooted in policies that favor married couples, married individuals have higher average savings as compared to cohabitating individuals or never-married individuals, which feeds into patterns of wealth inequality (Lupton and Smith 2003).

Race

When examining class and wealth inequality through a critical race lens, a considerable gap in familial wealth is evident between white and Black Americans (Shapiro, Meschede, and Osoro 2013). For much of American history, laws and policies excluded Black families from opportunities to garner familial wealth, perpetuating intergenerational poverty. For example, the Homestead Act of 1862, which granted up to 240 acres of land to a family for as little as the deed-filing fee in exchange for five years of farming that land., excluded families of color. Up to forty-six million Americans today can trace all, or part, of their family wealth to the ownership and/or sale of this land (Lipsitz 2011).

Contemporary racialized practices privilege white people over their Black counterparts as well, stymieing opportunities to close the racial wealth gap. Financial institutions that have maintained policies favoring both white people and the already wealthy further contribute to the growing wealth gap. For example, Black families are twice as likely to be rejected for a mortgage as compared to white families, even controlling for income, credit score, and family structure (Charles and Hurst 2006). While polarizing labor markets, family advantage, and favorable public policies support wealth concentration between generations (Corak 2013), systemic racism affecting homeownership, income, employment, and educational attainment creates large discrepancies in rates of average wealth between white and Black families (Shapiro, Meschede, and Osoro 2013).

Health

Both longitudinal and cross-sectional studies have shown that children and adolescents from lower socioeconomic status households are at greater risk of developing an array of mental health and physical health issues as compared to their high socioeconomic status counterparts (Marmot and Smith 1997; Reiss 2013). Upward family mobility in childhood or adolescence is linked both to a reduction in the likelihood of mental health problems and to remission of currently existing problems (Reiss 2013). This dynamic is particularly troubling, as those at the greatest health risk are also those with the fewest health-care resources, and rates of social mobility are declining. Further supporting theories of cumulative disadvantage, studies have also found deepening linkages between socioeconomic status and rates of depression over the life course (Miech and Shanahan 2000).

Low socioeconomic status has negative effects on health throughout the life course, affecting dozens of health outcomes from birthweight and cancer to cardiovascular disease and mortality (Beck et al 2019; Kramer and Hogue 2009; Adler and Newman 2002). Environmental factors, lifestyle factors, health-care access, and health behaviors compound to create a persistent relationship between low socioeconomic status and high mortality rates (Adler and Newman 2002; Pappas et al. 1993). In a state-by-state comparison, higher rates of income inequality are linked to a poorer self-reported health status among residents, independent of individual and household income levels (Kennedy et al. 1996). Regional economic segregation corresponds to higher morbidity rates among those living in poverty, though it has protective health effects for elderly individuals who are affluent (Waitzman and Smith 2001).

Policy

Familial advantage, labor market systems, and public policies favoring the wealthy are drivers of increasing wealth and income inequality, labor market polarization, and lessening social mobility (Corak 2013). These drivers of disadvantage are likely to increase over time without significant policy changes mandating wealth redistribution or egalitarian offerings of opportunity (Chomsky 2017; Corak 2013). However, wealth redistribution—and its subsequent ameliorating effects on compounding systems of disadvantage—is unlikely at best in the current political environment. Economic policies within the United States have generally favored supporting the status quo, and those policies that *are* enacted for the purpose of change typically place heavy importance on the interests of the affluent (Gilens 2005). These trends are international, as reflected in the "Great

Gatsby Curve," which finds that countries with high levels of income inequality also have correspondingly low rates of social mobility (Corak 2013; Krueger 2012).

On a policy level, policing practices also perpetuate systems of inequality. Disproportionately focused policing of racial and ethnic minority neighborhoods and neighborhoods of lower-than-average socioeconomic status work to disrupt community and family stability, result in an overrepresentation of racial minorities and people of low socioeconomic status in prisons. These incarceration trends are linked to negative economic outcomes for individuals incarcerated, their families and dependents, and the wider communities in which they live (Clear 2009).

FUTURE OF INEQUALITY

Despite considerable research outlining opportunity and outcome differences between the systematically advantaged and their disadvantaged counterparts, the majority of social stratification research focuses on those living in poverty. The prolific contemporary literature on poverty stands in stark contrast to the comparatively little research on the affluent populations *driving* the mechanisms of inequality (Khan 2012), despite the half-century old call for social scientists to "study up" (Nader 1969). This paucity of critical research has contributed to an environment in which the structurally privileged remain ideally positioned to perpetuate socioeconomic systems that preserve their own advantage.

Without significant policy intervention, systems perpetuating inequality are at the very least going to maintain current levels of inequality, though both social theories of stratification and recent trends indicate the gap between the advantaged and disadvantaged will continue to grow. Even excluding the 1 percent, the wealth gap between the upper-middle sector of American society and the nation's middle- and working-class groups is growing—and the growth in income for the upper-middle class has been especially stark in the 2010s (Bradbury and Katz 2002; Neckerman and Torche 2007; Reeves 2017). This inequality occurs at the individual level, as a combination of deeply seeded ideologies and economic capital has established disparate educational pathways for children, resulting in divergent career opportunities for them (Johnson 2014). At the societal level, meanwhile, a host of factors shaped by public policies are continually lessening opportunity for social mobility (Corak 2013). Wealth disparities are further worsened when examining inequality through an intersectional lens, such as gendered wealth disparities (Ruel and Hauser 2013), racialized wealth disparities (Shapiro, Meschede, and Osoro 2013), wealth disparities by marital status (Lupton and Smith 2003), and disparities driven by policing priorities and incarceration rates (Clear 2009).

According to cumulative advantage theory, those in advantageous social positions are awarded further advantage, while disadvantage is compounded for those without systematic privilege (DiPrete and Eirich 2006). A person's social position bears concrete consequences over the life course—influencing health outcomes, educational trajectories, likelihood of incarceration, and labor market opportunities—in which those in disadvantaged positions have consistently poorer outcomes that worsen over time. Disadvantage and privilege are deeply entrenched in institutions and policies, as well as in individualized biases.

Current institutional and economic systems favor the wealthy in terms of both opportunity and outcome (Corak 2013). Additionally, these systems are becoming increasingly closed and *homophilous* (referring to the tendency of individuals to associate with others of the same kind), and wealth disparities—along with the consequences of these disparities across the life course—are growing (Neckerman and Torche 2007). Without policy and practice interventions, research suggests that inequality will worsen as more time passes, particularly as more advantage accumulates for the privileged (Corak 2013; Shapiro 2017).

Considering the growing rates of inequality and the inextricability of socioeconomic influence over almost every outcome, from education and health to family and the labor market, the future of opportunity looks bleak. Systems of inequality are increasingly complex, as they are interrelated to one another. This is particularly true in an American context. For example, within the system of education, family capital is *both* central to providing children early, lucrative opportunities to maintain their advantaged position *and* deemphasized in its understood importance to support meritocratic ideology and keep privilege invisible (Johnson 2014).

However, there is hope. If systems of disadvantage can be interrupted and reformed in multiple sectors of American culture and society over the life course, gains in one arena can most certainly translate into others.

For example, precise, concrete policy changes within the educational system to lift up disadvantaged students can drive reductions in inequality in other areas of American life. For example, reduced class sizes, higher teacher salaries, parent outreach programs, and nutritional programs in schools have all been shown to positively—and significantly—improve high school graduation rates (Levin and Belfield 2007). As educational attainment rises, so do average salaries (Vilorio 2016), which has positive effects on both physical and mental health (Marmot et al. 2008; Reiss 2013).

Similarly, increasing the minimum wage has paired positive gains for individuals, families, and health. An increase in the minimum wage centralizes immediate economic gains to modestly skilled (and most precariously employed) individuals and their families. Fringe benefits, including employer pension and employer-provided health care, do *not* experience proportional cutbacks as wage-related business expenses increase, and minimum-wage employees may instead have a minimally higher likelihood of receiving fringe benefits as wages increase (Simon and Kaestner 2004). While the connection between likelihood of receiving fringe benefits and increasing wages is framed as associated rather than causal, there is a causal relationship between increased minimum wage and unmet health needs. Specifically, higher minimum wages lead to a significant decrease in unmet health needs. Even accounting for insurance status, copays and out-of-pocket costs can be prohibitive to seeking necessary medical care—a barrier that is mitigated by increasing wages (McCarrier et al. 2011).

In order to effectively address the consequences of inequality, "structural drivers" of everyday realities must be addressed (Marmot et al. 2008). To do this, both basic public infrastructure and place-specific intervention are necessary (Blank 2005). For example, by weakening the direct relationship between individual resources and health care through providing universal health coverage, average health will improve—which has far-reaching, positive effects on stability, family income, labor market security, and education (Phelan, Link, and Tehranifar 2010). Investments in the public school system, housing, food, and transportation would have similar positive results (Blank 2005). Addressing socioeconomic inequality directly on both ends of the spectrum—through progressive welfare reforms and tax-based wealth redistribution policies—can support that social reinvestment. Region and context are also important considerations. For example, a region with a disproportionately high aging and poor population would more strongly benefit from assisted care investments as compared to investments in public schools, while the reverse would be true for high-poverty regions with high birth rates (Blank 2005).

The positive results of these investments come with three caveats. Though the absolute improvements in outcomes for the disadvantaged should not be overlooked, social investments will always disproportionately benefit those who are already better off (Phelan, Link, and Tehranifar 2010). Additionally, there has been widespread adoption of less visible but nonetheless significant policies and mechanisms favoring the advantaged. In higher education, stratification by socioeconomic status is worsening because of an increased reliance on markers of cultural capital to determine admission (Astin and Oseguera 2004; Stevens 2009). Similarly, within lucrative professions, mentors favor mentees who embody signals of a privileged social position compared to their upwardly mobile counterparts (Friedman and Laurison 2019). Finally, public infrastructure investments are conditional upon federal and state policy making, often reflective of public attitudes toward government-sponsored welfare. This last caveat is particularly worrisome, as average Americans increasingly believe that the rich-poor divide should be addressed (Neel 2020) and the government must help those in need (Debate.org n.d.; MacLeod, Montero, and Speer 1999), *but* they also believe that welfare expenditures are a nonessential and too expensive government endeavor and that those who receive support would be fine without it (Federal Safety Net n.d.; Gilens 2009; MacLeod et al. 1999). This second set of beliefs has led to contemporary policies supporting the conglomeration of wealth at the top percentiles and the slashing of public investment benefiting low-income populations.

These suggestions addressing rampant inequality are precise in nature—a small-scale change resulting in gains in one arena would in time result in paired gains in another arena. These gains would be incremental over generations, and as such these targeted interventions may be rightfully critiqued as not aggressive enough to address ballooning inequality, as they work *within* structures embedded with systematic bias. More drastically, removal of the structural drivers perpetuating inequality would have the greatest effect on systems of disadvantage and advantage. Reparations payment and wealth redistribution would swiftly address the racial wealth gap, just as dismantling legacy college admissions and the private school system, and overhauling the public school system to redistribute staff, resources, and students in an egalitarian manner would have far-reaching effects on systemic inequality in the family, overall health, individual wealth and fiscal security, and labor market participation. Yet these overhauls seem a far-fetched solution to an increasingly dire problem, particularly since it would take those in privileged positions to dismantle the systems by which they benefit; systems that are both valued by the privileged (Reeves 2017) and invisible to them in their everyday lives (Johnson 2014).

So, if inequality is growing and is supported by both private practices and public policy, negative life course outcomes associated with low socioeconomic status are exacerbated by that growing inequality, *and* policy intervention to effectively address inequality will take generations, what can be done?

Researchers have the potential to make significant discoveries and theoretical advancements by increasing study into privileged populations. In this way, we can expose—and hope to slow—the roots of growing inequality at the source. Race and ethnicity scholarship has accomplished this, making white privilege a visible structure in both historical and contemporary settings (Bonilla-Silva 2017). In studying how white children form racial ideologies, sociologist Margaret Hagerman (2018) explores the manner in which these children learn about and utilize privilege—and how in some cases they have learned to reject systems that perpetuate their structural advantage. Scholars of socioeconomic inequality can make similar inroads, not by studying the systematically disadvantaged and suggesting additional policies to support these populations but by studying the privileged in order to learn about the mechanisms that (re)produce structural advantage rather than outcomes associated with socioeconomic disadvantage. With this perspective, new insights and subsequent policy suggestions may offer creative and effective ways to address and even reverse worsening trends in socioeconomic inequality.

It is necessary, in the interest of knowledge, theory, and social justice, to shed light on the stories of the systematically disadvantaged—to make the invisible visible. However, the social realities of those occupying powerful positions are just as necessary to understand. It is their social patterns—both in interactions and institutions—that are actively working to reserve advantage for members of their socioeconomic group. This comes at the larger social expense of upward mobility, and perpetuates growing rates of inequality. More than five decades of policy suggestions rooted in research have supported public infrastructure investments as a solution to the consequences of inequality—though the pendulum has swung from high investment to low investment as generational attitudes and political ideologies change, with little consistent headway made to long-term gains. In that same time, the wealth gap and income inequality have grown consistently.

Through encouraging dynamic research into privileged populations, we can hope to gain a greater understanding of the important roots and drivers of inequality in American society. Without a new perspective—and the policy suggestions that would arise from studying affluence rather than poverty—evidence suggests that the wealth divide and resulting inequality impacting almost all outcomes across the life course will continue to grow.

Kristen Tzoc and Heather Beth Johnson

Further Reading

Adler, Nancy E., and Katherine Newman. 2002. "Socioeconomic Disparities in Health: Pathways and Policies." *Health Affairs* 21 (2): 60–76.

Astin, Alexander, and Leticia Oseguera. 2004. "The Declining 'Equity' of American Higher Education." *Review of Higher Education* 27 (3): 321–41.

Beck, Andrew F., Erika M. Edwards, Jeffrey D. Horbar, Elizabeth A. Howell, Marie C. McCormick, and DeWayne M. Pursley. 2019. "The Color of Health: How Racism, Segregation, and Inequality Affect the Health and Well-Being of Preterm Infants and Their Families." *Pediatric Research* 87: 227–34.

Binder, Amy, Daniel Davis, and Nick Bloom. 2016. "Career Funneling: How Elite Students Learn to Define and Desire 'Prestigious' Jobs." *Sociology of Education* 89 (1): 20–39.

Blank, Rebecca M. 2005. "Poverty, Policy, and Place: How Poverty and Policies to Alleviate Poverty Are Shaped by Local Characteristics." *International Regional Science Review* 28 (4): 441–64.

Bonilla-Silva, Eduardo. 2017. *Racism without Racists.* 5th edition. Lanham, MD: Rowman and Littlefield Publishers.

Calarco, Jessica McCrory. 2011. "'I Need Help!' Social Class and Student's Help Seeking in Elementary School." *American Sociological Review* 76 (6): 862–82.

Chapman, Chris, J. Laird, N. Ifill, and A. Kewal Ramani. 2011. "Trends in High School Dropout and Completion Rates in the United States: 1972–2009." Institute of Education Sciences annual report, October 2011. https://nces.ed.gov/pubs2012/2012006.pdf.

Charles, Kerwin Kofi, and Erik Hurst. 2006. "The Transition to Home Ownership and the Black-White Wealth Gap." *Review of Economics and Statistics* 84 (2): 281–97.

Cherlin, Andrew. 2010. *The Marriage-Go-Round: The State of Marriage and the Family in America Today.* New York: Vintage.

Chetty, Raj, Nathaniel Hendren, Patrick Kline, and Emmanuel Saez. 2014. "Where Is the Land of Opportunity? The Geography of Intergenerational Mobility in the United States." NBER Working Paper 19843. National Bureau of Economic Research. https://www.nber.org/papers/w19843.

Chomsky, Noam. 2017. *Requiem for the American Dream: The 10 Principles of Concentration of Wealth.* Cincinnati, OH: Seven Stories Press.

Clear, Todd. 2009. *Imprisoning Communities: How Mass Incarceration Makes Disadvantaged Neighborhoods Worse.* Oxford, UK: University of Oxford Press.

Corak, Miles. 2013. "Income Inequality, Equality of Opportunity, and Intergenerational Mobility." *Journal of Economic Perspectives* 27 (3): 79–102.

Debate.org. n.d. "Should the U.S. Government Increase Social Services for the Poor?" Debate.org. https://www.debate.org/opinions/should-the-us-government-increase-social-services-for-the-poor.

DiPrete, Thomas, and Gregory Eirich. 2006. "Cumulative Advantage as a Mechanism for Inequality: A Review of Theoretical and Empirical Developments." *Annual Review of Sociology* 32:271–97.

Edin, Kathryn, and Maria Kefalas. 2011. *Promises I Can Keep: Why Poor Women Put Motherhood before Marriage.* 2nd ed. Oakland: University of California Press.

Federal Safety Net. n.d. "Welfare Opinion: Public Opinion Polls on Welfare and Poverty." Federal Safety Net. http://federalsafetynet.com/welfare-opinion.html.

Friedman, Sam, and Daniel Laurison. 2019. *The Class Ceiling: Why It Pays to Be Privileged.* Bristol, UK: Policy Press.

Gilens, Martin. 2005. "Inequality and Democratic Responsiveness." *Public Opinion Quarterly* 69 (5): 778–96.

Gilens, Martin. 2009. *Why Americans Hate Welfare: Race, Media, and the Politics of Anti-Poverty Policy.* Chicago: University of Chicago Press.

Gottschalk, Peter. 1997. "Inequality, Income Growth, and Mobility: The Basic Facts." *Journal of Economic Perspectives* 11 (2): 21–40.

Greenwood, Jeremy, Nezih Guner, Georgi Kocharkov, and Cezar Santos. 2014. "Marry Your Like: Assortative Mating and Income Inequality." NBER Working Paper 19829. National Bureau of Economic Research. https://www.nber.org/papers/w19829.

Hagerman, Margaret. 2018. *White Kids: Growing Up with Privilege in a Racially Divided America.* New York: New York University Press.

Hart, Betty, and Todd Risley. 1995. *Meaningful Differences in the Everyday Experience of Young American Children.* Baltimore, MD: Brookes Publishing Co.

Johnson, Heather Beth. 2014. *The American Dream and the Power of Wealth.* 2nd edition. Abingdon-on-Thames, UK: Routledge.

Kennedy, Bruce, Ichiro Kawachi, and Deborah Prothrow-Smith. 1996. "Income Distribution and Mortality: Cross Sectional Ecological Study of the Robin Hood Index in the United States." *BMJ: British Medical Journal* 312 (7037): 1004–7.

Kenworthy, Lane. 2007. "Inequality and Sociology." *American Behavioral Scientist* 50: 584–602.

Khan, Shamus. 2012. "The Sociology of Elites." *Annual Review of Sociology* 38: 361–77.

Kramer, Michael R., and Carol R. Hogue. 2009. "Is Segregation Bad for Your Health?" *Epidemiologic Reviews* 31:178–94.

Krueger, Alan. 2012. "Rise and Consequences of Inequality." Speech, Center for American Progress, Washington, DC, January 12, 2012.

Kusserow, Adrie. 2004. *American Individualisms: Child Rearing and Social Class in Three Neighborhoods.* Basingstoke, UK: Palgrave MacMillan.

Lareau, Annette. 2003. *Unequal Childhoods: Class, Race, and Family Life with an Update a Decade Later.* Los Angeles: University of California Press.

Lee, Valerie E., and David T. Burkam. 2002. "Inequality at the Starting Gate: Social Background Differences in Achievement as Children Begin School." Economic Policy Institute. https://www.epi.org/publication/books_starting_gate.

Leiserson, Greg, Will McGrew, and Rakaha Kopparam. 2019. "The Distribution of Wealth in the United States and Implications for a Net Worth Tax." Washington Center for Equitable Growth. https://equitablegrowth.org/the-distribution-of-wealth-in-the-united-states-and-implications-for-a-net-worth-tax.

Levin, Henry, and C. R. Belfield. 2007. "Educational Interventions to Raise High School Graduation Rates." In *The Price We Pay: Economic and Social Consequences of Inadequate Education*, edited by Clive R. Belfield and Henry Levin, 177–99. Washington, DC: Brookings Institution Press.

Lipsitz, George. 2011. *How Racism Takes Place.* Philadelphia, PA: Temple University Press.

Lupton, Joseph, and James P. Smith. 2003. "Marriage, Assets, and Savings." In *Marriage and the Economy: Theory and Evidence from Advanced Industrial Societies*, edited by Shoshana Grossbard-Shechtman, 129–152. Cambridge: Cambridge University Press.

MacLeod, Laurie, Darrel Montero, and Alan Speer. 1999. "America's Changing Attitudes toward Welfare and Welfare Recipients, 1938–1995." *Journal of Sociology and Social Welfare* 26 (2): article 10.

Marmot, Michael, Sharon Friel, Ruth Bell, Tanja A. J. Houweling, and Sebastian Taylor. 2008. "Closing the Gap in a Generation: Health Equity through Action on the Social Determinants of Health." *The Lancet* 372 (9650): 1661–69.

Marmot, Michael, and George Davey Smith. 1997. "Socio-Economic Differentials in Health." *Journal of Health Psychology* 2 (3): 283–96.

McCall, Leslie, and Christine Percheski. 2010. "Income Inequality: New Trends and Future Directions." *Annual Review of Sociology* 36: 329–47.

McCarrier, Kelly P., Frederick J. Zimmerman, James D. Ralston, and Diane P. Martin. 2011. "Associations between Minimum Wage Policy and Access to Health Care: Evidence from the Behavioral Risk Factor Surveillance System, 1996–2007." *American Journal of Public Health* 101: 359–67.

Miech, Richard, and Michael Shanahan. 2000. "Socioeconomic Status and Depression over the Life Course." *Journal of Health and Social Behavior* 41 (2): 162–76.

Nader, Laura. 1969. "Up the Anthropologist: Perspectives Gained from Studying Up." In *Reinventing Anthropology*, edited by D. Hyms, 284–311. New York: Random House.

Neckerman, Kathryn, and Florencia Torche. 2007. "Inequality: Causes and Consequences." *Annual Review of Sociology* 33: 335–57.

Neel, Joe. 2020. "Is There Hope for the American Dream? What Americans Think about Income Inequality." NPR. https://www.npr.org/sections/health-shots/2020/01/09 /794884978/is-there-hope-for-the-american-dream-what-americans-think-about -income-inequalit.

Pappas, Gregory, Susan Queen, Wilbur Hadden, and Gail Fisher. 1993. "The Increasing Disparity in Mortality between Socioeconomic Groups in the United States, 1960 and 1986." *New England Journal of Medicine* 329: 103–9.

Phelan, Jo, Bruce G. Link, and Parisa Tehranifar. 2010. "Social Conditions as Fundamental Causes of Health Inequalities: Theory, Evidence, and Policy Implications." *Journal of Health and Social Behavior* 51 (1): S28–40.

Reeves, Richard. 2017. *Dream Hoarders: How the American Upper Middle Class is Leaving Everyone Else in the Dust, Why That Is a Problem, and What to Do about It.* Washington, DC: Brookings Institution Press.

Reeves, Richard, and Kimberley Howard. 2013. "The Glass Floor: Education, Downward Mobility, and Opportunity Hoarding." Report for Center on Children and Families at Brookings. https://www.brookings.edu/research/the-glass-floor-education -downward-mobility-and-opportunity-hoarding.

Reiss, Franziska. 2013. "Socioeconomic Inequalities and Mental Health Problems in Children and Adolescents: A Systematic Review." *Social Science and Medicine* 90: 24–31.

Rivera, Lauren. 2015. *Pedigree: How Elite Students get Elite Jobs.* Princeton, NJ: Princeton University Press.

Ruel, Erin, and Robert M. Hauser. 2013. "Explaining the Gender Wealth Gap." *Demography* 50 (4): 1155–76.

Schwartz, Christine. 2010. "Earnings Inequality and the Changing Association between Spouses' Earnings." *American Journal of Sociology* 115 (5): 1524–57.

Schwartz, Christine, and Robert Mare. 2005. "Trends in Educational Assortative Marriage from 1940 to 2003." *Demography* 42 (4): 621–46.

Shapiro, Thomas. 2017. *Toxic Inequality: How America's Wealth Gap Destroys Mobility, Deepens the Racial Divide, and Threatens Our Future.* New York: Basic Books.

Shapiro, Thomas, Tatjana Meschede, and Sam Osoro. 2013. "The Roots of the Widening Racial Wealth Gap: Explaining the Black-White Economic Divide." Research and Economic Policy Brief, February 2013, for the Institute on Assets and Social

Policy.   https://heller.brandeis.edu/iasp/pdfs/racial-wealth-equity/racial-wealth-gap/roots-widening-racial-wealth-gap.pdf.

Simon, Kosali Ilayperuma, and Robert Kaestner. 2004. "Do Minimum Wages Affect Non-Wage Job Attributes? Evidence on Fringe Benefits." *ILR Review* 58 (1): 52–70.

Stevens, Mitchell. 2009. *Creating a Class: College Admissions and the Education of Elites*. Boston: Harvard University Press.

Vilorio, Dennis. 2016. "Education Matters." U.S. Bureau of Labor Statistics. https://www.bls.gov/careeroutlook/2016/data-on-display/education-matters.htm.

Waitzman, Norman, and Ken Smith. 2001. "Separate but Lethal: The Effects of Economic Segregation on Mortality in Metropolitan America." *Milbank Quarterly* 76 (3): 341–73.

Western, Bruce, Deirdre Bloome, and Christine Percheski. 2008. "Inequality among American Families with Children, 1975 to 2005." *American Sociological Review* 73 (6): 903–20.

Editors and Contributors

EDITORS

Kimberley L. Kinsley, JD, MA, is senior lecturer of business law in the College of Business at the University of Mary Washington. She is the author of articles and chapters published on legal topics such as employment discrimination, privacy and data, 3D technology, and consumer safety. She is a member of the California and Colorado Bar Associations.

Robert S. Rycroft, PhD, is professor of economics at the University of Mary Washington. He is the author of *The Economics of Inequality, Discrimination, Poverty, and Mobility* and editor of *The American Middle Class: An Economic Encyclopedia of Progress and Poverty* and *The Economics of Inequality, Poverty, and Discrimination in the 21st Century.* He is a member of the American Economic Association and a Phi Beta Kappa.

CONTRIBUTORS

John D. Abell
Professor
Economics and Business Department
Randolph College, Lynchburg,
Virginia

Brady W. Conn
Research Assistant
Department of Economics
Indiana Wesleyan University, Marion,
Indiana

Patricia Crain de Galarce
Associate Dean
Graduate School of Education
Lesley University, Cambridge,
Massachusetts

Shannon N. Davis
Professor
Department of Sociology
George Mason University, Fairfax,
Virginia

Lauren DiRago-Duncan
PhD Candidate
Department of Economics
University of Kentucky, Lexington,
Kentucky

Garrett Lee Fiegenbaum
Undergraduate Student
Department of Economics
Truman State University, Kirksville,
Missouri

Katie Fitzpatrick
Associate Professor
Joseph R. Biden, Jr. School of Public
Policy & Administration
University of Delaware, Newark,
Delaware

Tamicah Gelting
Clinical Assistant Professor
Department of Occupational Science
& Technology
University of Wisconsin–Milwaukee,
Milwaukee, Wisconsin

Erin E. George
Assistant Professor
Department of Economics
Hood College, Frederick, Maryland

Robert J. Gitter
Professor
Economics and Business Department
Ohio Wesleyan, Delaware, Ohio

Myriam Halimi
Affiliate Faculty
Multidisciplinary Institute for Teacher
Education
Vrije Universiteit Brussel, Brussels,
Belgium

Madeline Hamiter
Undergraduate Student
Department of Finance, Banking and
Insurance
Appalachian State University, Boone,
North Carolina

Gesine K. Hearn
Associate Professor
Department of Sociology, Social
Work, and Criminology
Idaho State University, Pocatello, Idaho

Laura G. Hoffman
Assistant Director, Federal Affairs
American Medical Association
Washington, DC

Cameron Hub
Undergraduate Student
Department of Economics
Seattle University, Seattle,
Washington

Dana Hubbard
Associate Professor
Department of Criminology,
Anthropology, and Sociology
Cleveland State University, Cleveland,
Ohio

Christy Irish
Assistant Professor
College of Education
University of Mary Washington
Fredericksburg, Virginia

Justin Jarvis
Assistant Professor
Department of Economics
Truman State University, Kirksville,
Missouri

Heather Beth Johnson
Associate Professor
Department of Sociology and
Anthropology
Lehigh University, Bethlehem,
Pennsylvania

Jarrod Johnston
Associate Professor
Department of Finance, Banking and
Insurance
Appalachian State University, Boone,
North Carolina

Anna Maria Jones
Graduate Student
Graduate School of Education
Lesley University, Cambridge,
Massachusetts

Stacey Jones
Senior Instructor
Department of Economics
Seattle University, Seattle,
Washington

Alice Louise Kassens
Professor
Department of Business Administra-
tion and Economics
Roanoke College, Salem, Virginia

Jared A. Knowles
Undergraduate Student
Department of Economics
Hood College, Frederick, Maryland

Haydar Kurban
Professor
Department of Economics
Howard University, Washington, DC

Elizabeth M. Legerski
Associate Professor
Department of Sociology
University of North Dakota, Grand
Forks, North Dakota

Thomas E. Lehman
Professor
Department of Economics
Indiana Wesleyan University, Marion,
Indiana

Oren M. Levin-Waldman
Professor
Graduate School for Public Affairs
and Administration
Metropolitan College of New York,
New York

Angela G. Mertig
Professor
Department of Sociology and
Anthropology
Middle Tennessee State University,
Murfreesboro,
Tennessee

Henry Ordower
Professor
School of Law
Saint Louis University, St. Louis,
Missouri

Analisa Packham
Assistant Professor
Department of Economics
Vanderbilt University, Nashville,
Tennessee

Troy Paino
President
University of Mary Washington,
Fredericksburg,
Virginia

Allison Ward Parsons
Associate Professor
College of Education and Human
Development
George Mason University, Fairfax,
Virginia

Carolyn Cummings Perrucci
Professor
Department of Sociology and
Anthropology
Purdue University, West Lafayette,
Indiana

Robert Perrucci
Professor Emeritus
Department of Sociology and
Anthropology
Purdue University, West Lafayette,
Indiana

Elizabeth Perry-Sizemore
Professor and Division Head
Division of Social and Behavioral
Sciences
Randolph College, Lynchburg,
Virginia

Rhonda Phillips
Professor, Agricultural Economics
Department
Dean, Honors College
Purdue University, West Lafayette,
Indiana

Beth Redbird
Assistant Professor
Department of Sociology
Northwestern University, Evanston,
Illinois

Josipa Roksa
Professor
Department of Sociology and Curry
School of Education
Senior Advisor for Academic
Programs in the Office of the
Executive Vice President and Provost
University of Virginia, Charlottesville,
Virginia

Ivan C. Roten
Associate Professor
Department of Finance, Banking and
Insurance
Appalachian State University, Boone,
North Carolina

Blake R. Silver
Assistant Professor
Department of Sociology and
Anthropology
Director of Data Analytics and
Assessment in the Honors College
George Mason University, Fairfax,
Virginia

Joel B. Teitelbaum
Associate Professor
Milken Institute School of Public
Health
George Washington University,
Washington, DC

Kristen Tzoc
Doctoral Student
Department of Sociology
Boston University, Boston,
Massachusetts

Renee E. Walker
Associate Professor
Joseph J. Zilber School of Public
Health
University of Wisconsin–Milwaukee,
Milwaukee, Wisconsin

Thomas S. Weinberg
Professor
Department of Sociology
SUNY Buffalo State, Buffalo,
New York

Chris Wienke
Associate Professor
Department of Sociology
Southern Illinois University,
Carbondale,
Illinois

Devin Wiggs
PhD Candidate
Department of Sociology
Northwestern University,
Evanston,
Illinois

Lei Zhang
Associate Professor
Agribusiness and Applied Economics
North Dakota State University, Fargo,
North Dakota

Index

www.ingramcontent.com/pod-product-compliance
Lightning Source LLC
Chambersburg PA
CBHW080410270326
41929CB00018B/2969